A Companion to *Piers Plowman*

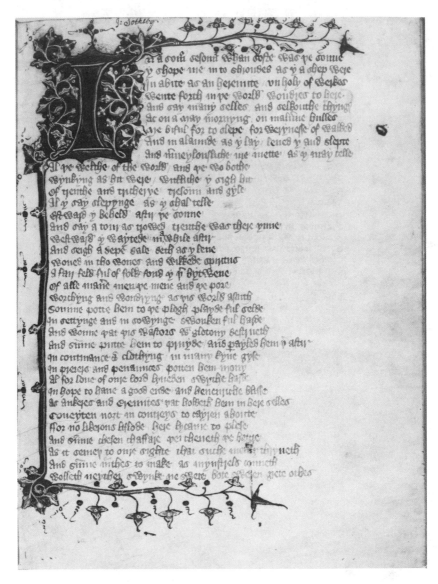

The opening lines of *Piers Plowman*, the C version (HM 143)
Reproduced by permission of The Huntington Library, San Marino, California

A Companion to
Piers Plowman

JOHN A. ALFORD,
EDITOR

UNIVERSITY OF CALIFORNIA PRESS
Berkeley   Los Angeles   London

University of California Press
Berkeley and Los Angeles, California

University of California Press, Ltd.
London, England

© 1988 by The Regents of the University of California

Library of Congress Cataloging-in-Publication Data

A Companion to Piers Plowman / John Alford, editor.
p.   cm.
Bibliography: p.
Includes index.
ISBN 0-520-06006-7 (alk. paper). ISBN 0-520-06007-5 (pbk.)
1. Langland, William, 1330?-1400? Piers the Plowman. I. Alford,
John A., 1938.
PR0215.C65 1988
821'. 1—dc19   87-24873
                                                              CIP

Printed in the United States of America

1   2   3   4   5   6   7   8   9

Contents

List of Abbreviations   vii

Preface   xi

INTRODUCTION: The Critical Heritage   1
Anne Middleton

I. *PIERS PLOWMAN* AND THE LATE MIDDLE AGES

  1. The Design of the Poem   29
    John A. Alford

  2. The Historical Context   67
    Anna P. Baldwin

  3. Langland's Theology   87
    Robert Adams

II. GENERIC INFLUENCES ON *PIERS PLOWMAN*

  4. Allegorical Visions   117
    Stephen A. Barney

  5. Satire   135
    John A. Yunck

  6. Medieval Sermons   155
    Siegfried Wenzel

III. THE TEXT AND LANGUAGE OF *PIERS PLOWMAN*

7. The Text   175
   George Kane

8. Dialect and Grammar   201
   M. L. Samuels

9. Alliterative Style   223
   David A. Lawton

EPILOGUE: The Legacy of *Piers Plowman*   251
   Anne Hudson

   Index   267

List of Abbreviations

AHDLMA	*Archives d'Histoire Doctrinale et Littéraire du Moyen Age*
AnM	*Annuale Mediaevale*
BIHR	*Bulletin of the Institute of Historical Research*
Blanch	Robert J. Blanch, ed. *Style and Symbolism in Piers Plowman.* Knoxville: University of Tennessee Press, 1969.
BJRL	*Bulletin of the John Rylands University Library of Manchester*
CCSL	*Corpus Christianorum, Series Latina*, Turnhout, Belgium
CHEL	*The Cambridge History of English Literature.* Ed. A. W. Ward and A. R. Waller. Vol. 2. Cambridge: Cambridge University Press, 1932.
CSEL	*Corpus Scriptorum Ecclesiasticorum Latinorum.* Vienna.
CT	*Canterbury Tales*
DA	*Dissertation Abstracts*
DAI	*Dissertation Abstracts International*
E&S	*Essays and Studies*
EETS	Early English Text Society
EIC	*Essays in Criticism*
ELH	*English Literary History*
es	extra series
ES	*English Studies*
EHR	*English Historical Review*

HLB	*Huntington Library Bulletin*
HLQ	*Huntington Library Quarterly*
Hussey	S. S. Hussey, ed. *Piers Plowman: Critical Approaches*. London: Methuen, 1969.
JEGP	*Journal of English and Germanic Philology*
JWCI	*Journal of the Warburg and Courtauld Institutes*
LSE	*Leeds Studies in English*
MÆ	*Medium Ævum*
MED	*Middle English Dictionary*
M&H	*Medievalia et Humanistica*
MLR	*Modern Language Review*
MP	*Modern Philology*
MS	*Mediaeval Studies*
N&Q	*Notes and Queries*
Neophil	*Neophilologus*
NM	*Neuphilologische Mitteilungen*
ns	new series
OED	*Oxford English Dictionary*
PBA	*Proceedings of the British Academy*
PG	J.-P. Migne. *Patrologiae Cursus Completus. Series Graeca*. 161 vols.
PL	J.-P. Migne. *Patrologiae Cursus Completus. Series Latina*. 221 vols.
PMLA	*Publications of the Modern Language Association of America*
PQ	*Philological Quarterly*
RES	*Review of English Studies*
SAC	*Studies in the Age of Chaucer*
SATF	*Société des anciens textes français*
SEL	*Studies in English Literature*

SP   *Studies in Philology*

STC   *A Short-Title Catalogue of Books Printed in England, Scotland and Ireland, and of English Books Printed Abroad, 1475–1640.* Compiled by A. W. Pollard and G. R. Redgrave. London: The Bibliographical Society, 1926; rev. ed. K. Pantzer et al., 1976–.

TRHS   *Transactions of the Royal Historical Society*

TLS   *Times Literary Supplement*

TSLL   *Texas Studies in Literature and Language*

Vasta   Edward Vasta, ed. *Interpretations of Piers Plowman.* Notre Dame: University of Notre Dame Press, 1968.

YES   *Yearbook of English Studies*

YLS   *Yearbook of Langland Studies*

Preface

A Companion to Piers Plowman has been designed to meet a need long felt by both beginning and advanced students of the poem. It brings together for the first time the essential information on every major aspect of the work — for example, the manuscripts, language, meter, historical milieu, literary and intellectual influences — and also provides an overview of modern critical approaches.

Though mainly a reference work, the book is arranged to facilitate a linear reading. Each chapter builds to some extent on its predecessors. The earlier parts are more general; the later, more specific and technical. Readers having little knowledge of the poem may wish to begin with chapter 1 before tackling the survey of scholarly trends in the Introduction.

Unless noted otherwise, all citations are to the Athlone editions (University of London) under the general editorship of George Kane: *Piers Plowman: The A Version*, ed. George Kane (1960); *Piers Plowman: The B Version*, ed. George Kane and E. Talbot Donaldson (1975); and *Piers Plowman: The C Version*, ed. George Russell (in press). Many readers may find it more convenient to use the classroom editions by A. V. C. Schmidt on B (London: Dent, 1978), and Derek Pearsall on C (London: Arnold, 1978; Berkeley: University of California Press, 1979), both of which have excellent notes. Happily, because these editions are based on the same manuscripts as Kane-Donaldson B and Russell C, variances in text and in line numbering are not often very great. However, readers who are still using the parallel text edition by W. W. Skeat (Oxford: Oxford University Press, 1886) face greater, though manageable, difficulties. The chief difference is in the C version: all passus numbers are off by one (Skeat counted the passus as I, II, III, etc.; Russell and Pearsall as Prologue, I, II, etc.). Unless noted otherwise, citations throughout the book are to the B version.

Internal documentation is keyed to the list of references at the end of each chapter. Citation is by author or, for multiple works, by author and date; where the list of references contains two works published by an author in the same year, the first of these is cited in the text as *a*, the second as *b* (e.g.,

Samuels 1972a). Biblical quotations in Latin are from the Vulgate (Clementine version); those in English are from the Douai translation of the Vulgate.

It is a pleasure to acknowledge the following persons for their help in this project: George Russell, for allowing quotation of his edition of the C version before publication; Robert Worth Frank, Jr., Hoyt N. Duggan, and M. Teresa Tavormina for many useful suggestions; Kathleen Blumreich Moore, for checking the citations and quotations for accuracy; and Dan Dixon of the University of California Press for his early interest and support. Several of the contributors themselves gave editorial assistance, but one in particular must be singled out here. Always ready to share his unparalleled knowledge of the text and his unfailing good sense, George Kane was extraordinarily generous with his time. To him the editor owes a special debt of gratitude.

J. A. A.

INTRODUCTION
THE CRITICAL HERITAGE

ANNE MIDDLETON

The critical history of *Piers Plowman* includes controversies that are, in kind and intensity, unlike those provoked by any other early English work, yet its reception over the course of six centuries also illustrates some of the main methods and motives in the study of medieval literature generally. Like Chaucer's work — and unlike that of the *Gawain* manuscript — *Piers Plowman* was widely copied and circulated, and never wholly lost to critical and scholarly view at any time since its composition. Until this century, however, its stature has been that of an English historical monument rather than a European literary masterpiece. Frequently cited in earlier periods as a mirror of fourteenth-century conditions, customs, and opinions, it reflected with equal clarity the spiritual and intellectual "home country" of each successive generation of readers, whose interpretations revealed the concerns and beliefs about their own societies they saw foreshadowed in Langland's Field of Folk.

It is, paradoxically, within literary studies that the poem has been a late arrival, and has largely remained "another country," slow to attract extensive formal and comparative study, and peripheral to the canon of literary masterpieces known to the general reader. (Such discussions of it as the one Jusserand reports having had with the President of the United States remain to this day a rare experience for those familiar with the poem.) The nature of its art, largely ignored for much of its history, has become a major focus of modern investigation. Only in the twentieth century have there been far-reaching efforts to recover and understand on its own terms the literary language and poetic procedures that define this alien terrain.

The following survey of six hundred years of reading *Piers Plowman* will attempt to define the main perspectives from which the poem has been approached, and to situate its critical fortunes within some of the broader inter-

pretive agendas in literary, social and intellectual history that have affected
its reception. As will become apparent, the labors of interpretation applied
to the poem over the centuries take on some of the most puzzling aspects
of the poem itself. Neither the poem nor its critical history can fairly be
described as a story of a steady progress toward clearly-defined goals. The
objectives and themes of *Piers Plowman* criticism, like those of the poem, seem
to vanish and recur, and undergo redefinition, refinement and recombina-
tion. As in the poem, some of the most dramatic and fruitful new directions
in its scholarship have issued from its most vigorous quarrels. And like those
of the poem, the effects of its scholarship have occasionally had far greater
general impact than its authors anticipated.

The large number of surviving manuscripts (see chapter 7), the frequent
appearance of the title in book bequests (Burrow 1957; Middleton 1982),
and the use of the name Piers Plowman in other writings for a type-figure
who gives voice to social complaint and ecclesiastical criticism, all attest to
its wide circulation in the two centuries following its composition (see Epilogue). Like Chaucer's critical reputation, that of *Piers Plowman* was established in its main outlines even before its author's death, but the reception
and influence of these two contemporaries contrasted strikingly from the
beginning. While Chaucer quickly became a pattern of the "rhetorical poet,"
a master of varied and edifying "sentence" and a model of graceful style and
the urbane use of language (Strohm 1982), Langland—probably because
alliterative verse was not widely used after 1400--was seen less as a poetic
exemplar than as a visionary spokesman for reform: he became the literary
father of English dissent. These early determinations of the "character" of
both were transmitted to later ages along with their work, influencing its
subsequent physical presentation and critical fortunes. They framed the questions that would, and would not, be put to it to the present day. What "every schoolboy knows" about *Piers Plowman*—if indeed he has heard anything
of it at all—will probably concern its ideological rather than its literary
character, and even now a college undergraduate is as likely to encounter
the work in an English history course as in an English literature survey.
Since many of the categories under which the poem has been considered
emerged in the course of interpreting it as a historical representation—as
a reflection of, and address to, its society—these will be examined in the
context in which they first appeared, and then in the form in which they
came to concern literary scholars.

HISTORICAL INTERPRETATIONS

The poem has always had intense "historical interest" in every sense of
the term (see chapter 2). Over the years it has been seen to represent great

historical issues and processes in three main ways: as illustration, as exhortation, and as vision or revelation.

I. THE POEM AS ILLUSTRATION

The most elementary historical use of the poem is as a record of the mental and material life of its time. As matter for the historian, its "data" — the customs to which it alludes and beliefs to which it attests — function somewhat as early texts do for the lexicographer: as a source of citations illustrating "usage" at particular dates and places. For generations of political, social, and ecclesiastical historians the poem has been a treasury of lively information about the daily habits, domestic life, agrarian and commercial practice, petty crime, popular pastimes, common sayings and beliefs, and political sentiments of its society (Chadwick); occasionally such studies also attempt to identify the writer's social position and opinions and to locate them within this picture (Owst, Jusserand). This method of social description also has the necessary and useful circularity of lexicography: every text illuminates the "usages" of every other. While historians such as Coulton illustrate fourteenth century social practices by citing the poem, the explanatory notes of Skeat's and Bennett's editions cite contemporary legal and political records to elucidate the poet's usage. Lexicons of material and social as well as verbal culture are indispensable tools for both historians and literary scholars, but chiefly for local illumination. More broadly applied — to explain whole episodes or speeches, for example, rather than terminology or specific allusions — they can be reductive, leveling the significance of a daring or unusual locution to the meaning most widely attested in contemporary usage, and thus equating the attributes of an individual writer's style and thought with the typical attitudes of his age.

Although the poem has been a source of illustration throughout its cultural career, this was its chief interest in the later nineteenth and early twentieth century, when social and intellectual history were gradually becoming differentiated from grand political history (Gilbert). For these "new histories" the poem — like the *Canterbury Tales*, particularly its *fabliaux*, and what would later be considered "bourgeois realism" generally — was valued for its descriptive richness and accuracy as a realistic canvas, depicting, in the virtually uncomposed plenitude also attributed to genre paintings, the "customs of our ancestors," and displaying them guilelessly to the historian's gaze (Bloch). The work of Jusserand shows a fairly enlightened application of this approach. He cited *Piers Plowman* liberally (as well as the writings of Rutebeuf, Chaucer, and Boccaccio), along with statutes and civic and ecclesiastical records, to illustrate *English Wayfaring Life in the Middle Ages* (1884;

English translation 1925; see especially pp. 420–22). His *Piers Plowman: A Contribution to the History of English Mysticism* (1893; English translation 1894), the first book-length study of the poem, was chiefly concerned — despite its title — to show the close parallels between the social criticisms expressed in the poem and the main interests of the commons in Parliament in the later fourteenth century. In general, those who cite the poem illustratively tend to equate its testimony with that of a contemporary chronicle or a parliamentary petition, neglecting the characteristic conventions of each kind of document. Historians and literary scholars are now more attentive to these conventions, noting that not only poems, but also chronicles and many other forms of contemporary "report" have fictive aspects and generic purposes that figure in their interpretation. The understanding of Froissart's work, for example, has been as ill-served as Langland's by its use simply as a "record" of Richard II's reign, rather than as a composition in which contemporary events are cast in relation to particular ends of the writer.

2. The Poem as Exhortation: The Rhetoric of Reform

A second main tradition in the historical study of the poem emphasizes the writer's persuasive designs on his society. It analyzes his work chiefly as an exhortation intended to influence the behavior and beliefs of its contemporaries rather than merely to illustrate them unwittingly for posterity. Several interpretive approaches share this broadly rhetorical conception of the poem. They differ, however, along a continuum, according to whether they read its moral address as chiefly literal, practical, and immediate, aimed at reforming contemporary mores, or as broadly figurative, speculative, and cosmic, and aimed at the salvation of man's soul. Toward one end of this spectrum lie the "satirical" readings of the poem, at the other the "prophetic" and "apocalyptic" views. Mediating between the two are those that emphasize the individual as well as collective focus of persuasion in the poem, and note that ultimate salvation and immediate moral reform were the twin objectives of the medieval penitential system for the cleansing of the conscience.

2a. Early Rhetorical Interpretations: The Poem as Public Address

The "letter of John Ball" — an exhortation purportedly addressed to the peasants of Essex during the 1381 revolt, invoking the name of Piers Plowman and urging its audience to "do welle and bettere" (see p. 251) — is possibly the earliest surviving testimony to the enduring notion that the poem

has a special capacity to represent, in the political as well as aesthetic sense
of the term, the collective voice of an ideal community. Though such readings vary in sophistication, their shared view of the poem as direct rhetorical discourse is marked by characteristic emphases and omissions. This
approach attends to the figurative language of the work only intermittent-
ly, as a local ornament of persuasion rather than as a part of sustained narrative or expository development. The interpretive summary of its "principall
poyntes" that Robert Crowley, the first printer of the poem (1550), prefixed
to the text as a guide to the reader illustrates this tendency. Traditional
metaphors, such as the castle of the soul, or the simile that "rych men be
like Pecockis" (B.12.236–69), are read as moral examples, with little regard
to their function in the longer speeches or scenes in which they occur. As
a consequence, what is said by the poem's several personifications is resolved
into the utterance of a single voice, loosely identified with that of the poet.
In this critical tradition, the writer and his creation Piers are frequently treated as interchangeable, and even those who show signs of having read the
poem with sustained attention sometimes (as Crowley does) give Piers's name
to the authorial presence they find throughout the work.

This treatment of the poetic voice of the work shares with the illustrative
treatment of its content a largely naive understanding of both. Derived from
such early responses as that of John Ball, these readings were subsequently
assimilated to Reformation polemics: the reformist Crowley considered the
work a "crye . . agaynste the workes of darckenes" by one of those elected
by God to "se hys truth" and foretell to the age of Edward III the coming
English reformation. The perception of the author as an outspoken reformist, and of Piers as a metonymic wise layman or working-class hero, was
given fresh impetus in the later nineteenth century by efforts — energetically
exemplified by Furnivall — to construct from early English texts an educa-
tional syllabus of vernacular classics (Benzie). Skeat's slightly bowdlerized
school edition of the B *Visio*, apparently made at Furnivall's suggestion, attained immediate success and remarkable staying power in this kind: it was
until quite recently the most widely-used school text of the poem. Because
many readers' knowledge of the poem often began (and ended) with this
edition, it was widely assumed that the contemporary public concerns and
social perspective of its early passus — features which had attracted early im-
itators and established the early perception of it as a satire — were the fundamental emphasis of the whole poem. The early "dissenting" view of the
poem was thus assimilated into the broadly progressive or Whig interpretation of English history; Trevelyan's discussion of it (1926) is broadly representative.

As Anne Hudson and Pamela Gradon have shown, not all of those who
appropriated Piers's name in their own cause necessarily grasped the com-

plexities of Langland's work. The immediate response to it by some of its contemporaries as reformist rhetoric, however, may have had a reciprocal impact on its revision. Several critics (Donaldson, Russell, Baldwin) believe that the C text shows the poet's effort specifically to discourage association of his work with either Lollard views or the actions of the 1381 rebels. The C version alters the preceding B text most minutely in those places where B could have been read as placing "poor preachers" (as both Lollards and their opponents called the proselytizing adherents of their sect) above the traditional instructive authority of the church, or as suggesting that laymen had apostolic authority. The C version also adds more unequivocal con-demnation of vagrants and of those workers who spurn the traditional terms of "leel" service, both of which groups had been seen as the cause of the 1381 revolt.

2b. Authorship: The Identity of the Reformer

Because the opinions and advocacies of the poem were so deeply a part of its early reputation, the identity of the author was necessarily an object of curiosity, particularly to those who saw him as of their brotherhood. The Protestant antiquary John Bale and the circle around him, including Nich-olas Brigham and Crowley, were the chief sources of information about the author in the mid-sixteenth century, though not all of it was sound. Spenser probably owed his knowledge of the poem to Crowley's printing, and perhaps to Bale's circle his uncertainty about the author's name: he refers to him in the *Shepheardes Calender* only as "the Pilgrim that the Ploughman playde a whyle." Bale provides the earliest surviving, and probably the original, attribution of the poem to "*Robert* Langland or Longland." This name ap-parently arose from a misreading of the first line of B.8, "Thus yrobed in russet I romed aboute," which appears in two surviving manuscripts as " . . y robert. . . . "

The name William Langland as the author of *Piers Plowman* is attested externally by a very full Latin note of about 1400 in a manuscript of the C version; he is said to be the son of Stacy (or Eustace) de Rokayle of Shipton-under-Wychwood, who held land of the Despensers (for the full text of this note, and other evidence about authorship, see Kane, *Evidence*). The name is also recorded internally in several places: "Will" is identified both as dream-er and writer of the visions that make up the poem, and he engages in dia-logue with allegorical personages who address him by name. On two occasions (B.12.16–24, C.5.11–34) they invite him to account for his ap-parently idle life, which seems to them to be preoccupied with "making" at the expense of both productive labor for the community and prayerful reflection and penance for the good of his soul. On another occasion, the dreamer provides what has generally been regarded as an anagram of the full name:

> I haue lyued in londe . . . my name is longe wille.
>
> (B.15.152)

Early in the B continuation, when Scripture "scorns" Will with the charge that he is one of those who "know not themselves" (*seipsos nesciunt*), his discouragement plunges him into a "lond of longynge" (B.11.8). The name of this place, where he meets worldly temptations and is forced to recognize his own mortality, may be another such "signature." Signatures, in which the poet names himself as an actor within the fictive world of the poem or inscribes his name and characteristics in the form of acrostics, punning anagrams, or place-names, are common in late-medieval vernacular literature. They are used by Rutebeuf, Deschamps, Villon, and Antoine de la Salle, as well as Chaucer, Gower, Hoccleve, and Usk (see Chambers 1939b; Kane 1965a, b); often, as here, their effect is to emphasize the poet's ethically representative role as sinful and striving Everyman (Burrow 1981; Allen 1982, 260–83; Minnis 160–217).

The question of authorship, as distinct from interest in the author, is indissolubly bound to the textual fact of the poem's survival in three versions. These and their chronology were not fully distinguished until the midnineteenth century by Skeat. Wright, in his edition of the B text (1842, 1856; see chapter 7), which he believed to be both earlier than C and superior to it, conjectured that C's revisions were made by "some other person" than the B author, and were motivated by the desire to "soften down" the strong political sentiments of B. Though this tentative suggestion is both undeveloped and isolated in the critical history of the poem before the twentieth century, it is characteristic of all subsequent speculation about the participation of more than one author in the composition of the poem: it begins in a critical judgment about the relative poetic quality, the dominant genre, and the structural coherence of the versions, and rests most heavily upon a perception of a marked difference between them in political attitudes.

These were also the chief arguments of J. M. Manly, whose hypothesis of multiple authorship became a major talking point of *Piers Plowman* scholarship and criticism early in the twentieth century. Having first proposed it in an article in 1906, Manly developed his view (that as many as five authors were responsible for the three versions of the poem) in a place that assured it the widest possible scholarly attention: the *Cambridge History of English Literature* (1908). (For a bibliography of the dispute, see Middleton [1986], "Authorship Controversy" and Commentary.) As a central issue of debate, this proposition virtually vanished from scholarly interest within a generation, almost as suddenly as it had arrived. The question was laid to rest not by new evidence but by a general eclipse of the kinds of textual and critical reasoning, characteristic of turn-of-the-century literary studies, that had raised it in the first place. For this reason, and because this episode in the intellectual history of the poem affected many of the argumentative forms and emphases of subsequent *Piers Plowman* studies, the shadow cast by the "authorship controversy" — visible well into the 1940s — is now more instructive than its substance.

Manly intended his hypothesis to account for what he considered major gaps in literary structure and discrepancies of sense, both within and between versions. In his view these could only point to a succession of revisers, each misconstruing and patching a predecessor's work. While he posited a "lost leaf" to explain what he described as omissions in A's second vision, and incoherences in the B version of the episode, his claims neither began in, nor referred to, close study of the textual evidence — though they prompted more detailed collation of the A manuscripts by Manly's student Thomas Knott and perhaps hastened the application to the poem of modern methods of textual analysis. Manly believed that better texts would resolve the question he had raised; however, later textual scholars have pointed out that a determination of authorship is implicit in the processes of establishing the text and does not simply derive from them (Patterson 1985 and Kane, below). Manly's critical axioms were also characteristic of the period. In fragmenting authorship to explain an additive or reiterative literary structure, his interpretive strategy followed a late-nineteenth century pattern in accounting for the form of long poems of early societies. *Beowulf* and the *chansons de geste*, for example, were analyzed as layered assemblages of the work of several hands. His perception of flaws of sense and structure was based on a firm conviction that the A *Visio* defined the genre and merits of the entire work: it was a satire, its author a man of "unerring hand," and thus B and C represent a decline from the original inspiration and form of the first two visions, not the expansion of a poetic plan. Since disputing Manly's critical views required scholars to define more carefully both the generic conventions of the poem and its distinctive usages, his challenge had the ironic and unintended effect of hastening the advent of its modern comparative literary study.

2c. The Poem as Satire

Of the literary modes to which medieval and early modern criticism attributed an explicitly and predominantly reforming moral purpose, satire was the one most widely specified as the genre of *Piers Plowman*; "allegory," a term rarely applied to the poem as a whole before the twentieth century, was reserved for local figurative devices. One reader of Crowley's printed text who recorded his reading in its margins, for example, appreciates as "a goodly allegorie" figures like (cloth)-"fullyng" as baptism (B.15.453), and Noah as a type of "curatoures" (B.10.415). Considering the poem as a whole, however, Crowley's contemporary Puttenham labeled it a satire (1589), identifying "that nameless" who wrote it as "a malcontent of that time" and placing him in the tradition of the Latin satirists "Lucilius, Iuuenall and Persius" as one who "intended to taxe the common abuses and vice of the people in rough and bitter speaches." This remark reveals a notion of a poetic voice and an implied authorial character which for some time colored inferences about the writer's life, temperament, style, and motives for writing. For example, Manly (1908) presumed that the poet concealed his identity because his indictments of contemporary society were so devastating, and his ecclesiastical opinions so heterodox, as to incur the risk of punishment for their author. Since this sharply critical tone and purpose seemed to some more prominent in A than in B or C, the idea that the three versions are the work of more than a single writer has always depended largely on this perceived difference in temper and motive between the versions (Fowler 1961).

Against this general view of medieval satire as a potent and destructive attack on the social fabric (e.g., Tucker, Robbins) there was in the mid-twentieth century a thoroughgoing reaction. It was claimed that satire as a distinct literary mode was unknown in the Middle Ages (Bestul 1974), and that medieval writings of social censure or correction were so discontinuous with both Roman and Renaissance practice and theory as to constitute a wholly different literary genre called *complaint* (Peter). According to Peter, what placed *Piers Plowman* and most other Middle English poems "on contemporary conditions" (as the Wells *Manual* classified them) in this category was their universalizing perspective, meliorative purpose, and censure of classes or groups rather than individuals. Only Chaucer, he believed, practiced true satire in this period. Neither Peter's view of medieval genre definitions, nor the earlier notion that medieval satiric writings expressed radical opposition to the culture's currently received ideas of social order, has been supported by subsequent study. Scholarship on the poem has amply shown the poet's familiarity with several major topics and conventions of satire (see Yunck below), and recent work on the sources of medieval literary terms has confirmed that satire was a mode of writing known and quite clearly defined in the Middle Ages. All of the characteristics of what Peter called complaint have since been shown to be fundamental to the medieval theory and practice of satire, founded upon a consensus of the early glossators of Horace, Persius, and Juvenal, and transmitted in the teaching of these *auctores* in medieval schools. According to these teachings, the purpose of complaint was to excite pity for the speaker, not to effect reform in the reader, a fundamental objective of medieval satire (Miller).

As the earliest, and among the fullest, assays of its literary genre, the satiric readings of *Piers Plowman* may be taken as the starting point for its specifically *literary*-historical scholarship. Generic interpretation presupposes that a writer's purpose and methods are shaped not only by his social and intellectual circumstances and perceptions, but most profoundly by his own and his audience's prior experience of other texts (cf. Mann 2). Literary conventions and only secondarily the writer's opinions and direct observation supply the vocabularies of his depictions—of corrupt friars, for example—and allow him to establish a fictive identity and attitude appropriate to his purpose: the historical William Langland need not have been a "malcontent," as some earlier readings assumed, or an itinerant cleric, as Will is described in the poem. Yet while more is generally known now than a century ago about medieval literary terminology and values, critics are more reluctant to ascribe any single definite genre or dominant form to the poem. Morton Bloomfield's survey (1962, 3–43) of several of the medieval literary modes that contribute to its complex tone and procedures illustrates the extreme resistance of the poem to easy classification, and also suggests why genre itself, one of the most elusive and difficult of literary terms, is nevertheless an indispensable concept of historical criticism.

3. The Poem as Historical Vision: Satire, Prophecy, Apocalypse

Several of the genres, forms, and modes that have been proposed as informing *Piers Plowman* contain an implicit sense of the imaginative and didactic uses of history, a way of seeing present phenomena as imprinted by both past and future. The rhetoric of the medieval satirist shares with that of the medieval preacher a conviction of the permanently exemplary value of the past. These moralists' scathing depiction of contemporary vice derives its "redeeming social value" as an art of correction from its pervasive, if largely implicit, reference to an original and divinely-ordained order of things; it is explicitly invoked in estates satire (see Yunck below). Respected human institutions are presumed to have been founded in a distant and hallowed antiquity ("dauid, in hise dayes, dubbide kni3tes," A.1.96, B.1.98, C.1.101), and these posited early forms of human relations are assigned the status of ethical models or ideals. A claim to knowledge of the beginnings of current practices is therefore in such discourse no mere antiquarian curiosity. Just as legal and political authority is conceived by medieval writers to derive from both legitimate succession to office or estate and knowledge of precedcnt and root principles, so personal and social rectitude is defined by its conformity to a model of correct conduct preserved in the historical record and sanctioned by long usage. According to an analogy frequently invoked by medieval moralists between human virtue and grammatical and semantic propriety, modern corruption is a kind of solecism, a debased formation, unsuccessful at transmitting any true and proper meaning, and unauthorized by etymology and sound usage (see below pp. 18, 38).

Early views of the poem as a record of a time of exceptional gloom and anxiety, cultural decline, and perpetual crisis take on a different look in the light of these standard literary assumptions of the moralist. The frequent reference by Will and his instructors to ideal originals, as well as the development of debate in the poem as a dialogue of cited authorities, declare a fundamental tenet of medieval ethical thought and writing: that truth and well-doing are defined by manifestly lawful and regular ("leel" and "rect") relations to first principles.

When the chief reference point for understanding the present becomes the promised ultimate destiny of human society rather than an exemplary past, the hortatory posture of the public moralist yields to that of the prophet. From this perspective, the pervasive corruption of the present signifies not merely its deplorable ethical distance from its roots, but the terrifying nearness of its impending end in tribulation and judgment.

Although many of the early reformists were, like Crowley, attracted by the poem's overtones of urgent warning (King 1976), the prophetic and apocalyptic perspective on contemporary life as the threshold of the world's last days was not fully explored as an organizing principle in the poem until the mid-twentieth century. Morton Bloomfield (1962) first situated the work within the traditions of medieval prophetic historiography and apocalyptic pessimism. He showed that in the later fourteenth century there was especially high interest throughout Europe in millennial schematizations of history, particularly in the writings of Joachim of Flora, and that while on the continent such writings found their warmest reception among mendicant scholars, in England they were assimilated to monastic historical thought. According to many of these sources the mid-1360s were to be times of particular dread and expectation, when a Western Antichrist would appear; Bloomfield considered these forebodings to be the immediate stimulus for the writing of the poem, dating the A version 1362–65.

Although Bloomfield's study illuminates many unexplored aspects of the intellectual climate of the poem and the historical context for some of its chief thematic concerns, his work was not intended primarily as a study of cultural influences or of the sources and analogues of the poet's thought. (For subsequent studies of the eschatology of the poem, and the debate about its apocalyptic designs, see Adams below.) In Bloomfield's view, prophetic and apocalyptic discourses embody a single distinctive way of perceiving in history a comprehensive pattern, a teleological ordering toward salvation. Through several echoing and foreshadowing relations to other events, each event in human time becomes saturated with multiple complementary meanings. In its largely symbolic reading of temporal phenomena, this prophetic view of historical events complements that of the moralist: the present becomes most significant in pointing to a promised future rather than a defaced past, and the instructive intelligibility of the whole resides not in its foundations but in its fulfillment or completion. History is not simply a written record: it is an act of writing still in progress, fully comprehensible only in its ending.

This prophetic vision of history thus furnishes a model of an ideally coherent and meaningful narrative. It suggested to Bloomfield (and to several critics who applied this notion to more detailed analysis of the poem than his book provided, e.g., Salter 1968; Ames 1970; Carruthers 1970; Aers 1975; Adams 1985b) an approach to *how* events mean in the poem, how they are not only conceived symbolically, but also imagined as connected allusively and figuratively to each other within a literary structure that had hitherto been read as loosely episodic. It thus defined a sense in which the poem as a whole, rather than as an assemblage of topical polemics, could be said to be "about" history, and to represent contemporary life. Despite the expository emphases of his book, it was neither as a literary genre (see Emmerson 1981, 1984) nor as an element of doctrine that Bloomfield's notion of prophetic and apocalyptic vision proved to be a seminal idea for understanding the art and meaning of the poem, but as a fertile suggestion about the generative principles of its form and method.

LITERARY CRITICISM AND THE HISTORY OF IDEAS: THE PROBLEM OF FORM

The emphases in Bloomfield's presentation — which tended to absorb a reader in its immense learning and wealth of critical suggestion rather than in sustained arguments, and to avert immediate attention from what proved to be some of its most provocative points — are in part explained by the state of formal criticism of medieval literature at the time his book appeared. Substantial scholarship and learning had been applied to details of the poem well before its structure and poetic methods received extensive critical analysis. The generation preceding Bloomfield's work on prophecy and medieval symbolism had seen the first sustained efforts to characterize the general tenor of the poet's thought and outlook as more than a collection of trenchant observations in vigorous figurative language; it also offered the first few tentative attempts to discern the organizing principles of the poem. In this era these two quests for coherence were equated: the plan or unifying principle of the work, which critics of this period tended to call its "theme" rather than design or form, would be revealed as a superordinating authorial "philosophy" (Wells 1938). From the 1920s through the 1950s several scholars, hoping to improve upon the rather piecemeal topical readings that had thus far constituted interpretation (e.g. Owst), sought the materials of its unifying outlook both externally, in devotional and mystical as well as moralistic writings (Hort 1938), and internally, in its often-repeated terms. For several interpreters these came together in the three "Lives" Dowel, Dobet, and Dobest, which were considered formal divisions of the poem, and were accorded the status of a unifying doctrine. These were identified with various other threefold hierarchies: of objective social orders or estates (Coghill 1933), modes of spiritual life (Wells 1929; Dunning 1956), or stages in the soul's ascent toward divinity (Meroney 1950; Hussey 1956; for appraisal of these notions, see chapter 1; also Chambers 1939a, 102–05; Donaldson 1949, 156–61; Frank 1957).

The rise and fall of critical interest in the "false and mischievous analogy" (Meroney 1950) of the three lives illustrates how scholars in this period approached poetic form as a critical problem, and conceived of the relation of this inquiry to the historical study of contemporary thought. If these triads were unconvincing as keys to poetic form or meaning, it is not only because the scholars who proposed them were not sufficiently versed in the theological and philosophical ideas they invoked (Dunning, for example, was very learned). Nor is it only because they were misguided about the status of these terms in the poem: as passus rubrics they were probably scribal in origin (Adams 1985a), and as three degrees of the same term they appear to be a "rhetorical scheme for amplification" (see below, p. 46). They fail as critical analysis because they tend to equate Langland's form and meaning with those of a body of thought parallel and external to the poem, irrespective of its form of expression, and do not sufficiently consider the writer's procedures and style in selecting, combining, and representing these intellectual and spiritual concerns (see Aers 1975, 100). As John Lawlor, surveying these efforts, observes, "A unity of theme, or 'doctrine,' and hence a mutual relationship of the major parts of the work will not . . . of themselves . . . counter these objections [i.e. such as that of C. S. Lewis (161) that Langland 'hardly makes his poetry into a poem']" (Lawlor 115).

In the first half of this century the figure of Piers was subjected to the same kinds of interpretation as the Three Lives. His symbolic meaning was sought in a variety of "ideas" current in fourteenth-century culture and writing (Troyer; Burdach; for a survey of these efforts see Frank 1957, 13–15; Aers 1975, 71–92). The critical problem of form was, however, only intensified by the plenitude of possible meanings such inquiries proposed. What was required was not simply a way of choosing among competing possibilities but rather ways of accounting for their multiplicity, and of describing in historically plausible terms how and why the poet deployed this wealth of suggestion within the poem. Increasingly from the late 1950s on, critics began to consider the poet's ways of developing and connecting his figures, not as shortcomings in organizational power and control, as Lewis implied, but as his chief means of achieving the sublimity that readers (including Lewis) found and continued to find in the poem, despite their claims that its structure was chaotic or unintelligible.

It was here that Bloomfield's accounts of medieval symbolism (1958) and personification (1963) complemented the suggestions of his book. Taken together these critical projects illustrate some of the central new developments in medieval literary studies in this period, and how they changed the critical agendas of *Piers Plowman* scholarship. Whether critics called the poet's methods typological (Ames) or figural (Salter), the enterprise of several *Piers* scholars was now to expound how medieval figurative ways of reading and writing informed the construction as well as the symbolism of the poem. Most of these notions tended in one way or another to invoke the "commonplace" — fundamental to the critical ambitions of Bloomfield's work — that "Christian allegory is an allegory of events" (Aers 1975, 3–16). Critics began to examine how the poet's methods enabled his readers to experience the meaning of his figures "as it were in doing" (Bloomfield 1963, 171).

Not long after art historians in England and America began to assimilate continental iconographical studies in their interpretations of medieval visual art, scholars of medieval vernacular literature attempted to ground historically-based critical accounts of literary meaning upon the interpretive principles and practices that had guided the exposition of scriptural meaning in the Middle Ages. Although by this time critics had developed the habit of characterizing the poem in its entirety as an allegory (e.g. Owen), without the overtones of distaste that had attached to the term and the literary mode through much of the nineteenth century, it was only in the middle of the twentieth that they began to reflect in large numbers on what they meant by it, and to examine allegory generally both as a rhetorical device and as an interpretive method used in the philosophical, mythical, and political writings of antiquity, as well as in biblical interpretation (see chapter 4). It was also in this period that the work of the great philologists Auerbach (1946, 1958) and Curtius (1948) began to be reflected in critical scholarship on English literature. Encompassing in its Olympian perspective the literary cultures of all of western Europe since antiquity, their scholarship examined these literary devices and procedures as the common intellectual heritage and poetic vocabulary that had joined readers to writers for over a thousand years. Langland's art, while still far from immediately accessible to description, was no longer inaccessible to reasoned and systematic inquiry. If it remained "another country" to its modern readers, they could nevertheless begin to learn its language and customs.

THE HISTORICAL STUDY OF FORM:
RECENT DEVELOPMENTS

From the two traditional critical conceptions, outlined above, of what might be called the poet's sense of history and its uses — as hortatory or as revelatory — derive two late twentieth-century critical traditions. Because they descend from two different notions of the poet's chief mode of representing historical phenomena, and two opposed reference points for historical explanation (origins and ends), each has on occasion identified itself in contrast to the other as "historical" criticism. Both are entitled to the name, however, and in practice they are complementary in framing the major interpretive questions and scholarly methods in recent *Piers Plowman* studies.

On the one hand, the "revelatory" or visionary critical tradition examines a work of literature as a comprehensive and cosmic (Fletcher) structure, oriented to a single end, and emphasizes those principles of poetic meaning which harmonize its parts. The poem is assumed to effect moral or spiritual cognition through symbolic forms. In practice, therefore, this approach tends to favor figurative over literal interpretation. The Fable of the Rats inserted in the B version of the first dream, for example, is according to this approach not about an episode in the delicate relations between commons, council and king in 1376, nor even a satire on civil injustice and cowardice, but an exemplary illustration of the excessive concern for temporal goods, amplifying the unitary theme of the work (Robertson and Huppé 30–32).

On the other hand, the view that the poem is essentially hortatory leads to exploration of the immediate and topical relations between the poet and his contemporary milieu; it seeks the immediate referential origins of the text. Work in this tradition neither presupposes nor greatly emphasizes a unitary plan in the work. It tends rather to see Langland's art in the mastery of a great variety of complex smaller-scale effects, whose reiteration or aggregation provides the poem's only discernible form. Critical analyses in this tradition more often begin with the part than the whole — a difficult passage, a puzzling figure — and its scholarship tends to investigate the ways in which various expository or persuasive discourses (sermons and commentaries, for example) may have served as the poet's models or sources in particular instances. The "hortatory" notion of the poem also leads to studies of the presumed immediate social and intellectual context of the writer, and on the reception of his work.

In the last twenty years scholarly and critical projects in both traditions have been both more sharply-focused and more confined in reach than those at midcentury. While they often develop suggestions latent in the work of their predecessors, they offer much more than refinement on the scholarship of two energetic decades. The two traditions have also tended to converge; and it is with the understanding that they are now at most contrasting emphases or starting points for inquiry that one may identify a few major recent critical projects with one or the other origin and basic premise.

I. UNITARY INTERPRETATION: EXEGETICAL CRITICISM

In principle, and in their own practice, the "exegetical" criticism of Robertson and Huppé belongs squarely within the former tradition in its uncompromising application of scriptural interpretation in its most schematic form. Their approach was widely and vigorously debated in medieval literary studies, and *Piers Plowman* was the charter text upon which they demonstrated their method. It proceeds from the Augustinian axiom that the fundamental *sententia* or unitary theme of Scripture is charity, and that the purpose of all Christian interpretation (of Scripture or of any other text that a Christian wishes to take seriously as useful rather than harmful to read) is to disclose and promote this theme. Those portions of the text whose literal sense does not perform this function must be read figuratively. In addition to the *literal* or historical sense, three figurative levels of reference disclosing the spiritual meanings of Scripture became canonical in patristic exegesis: the *allegorical*, pertaining to the life of the Church throughout human time as the medium of faith; the moral or *tropological*, concerning the ordering of the individual's life toward salvation; and the *anagogical*, referring to eternal life and the ultimate destiny of souls. A well-known distich served as a mnemonic:

> Littera gesta docet, quid credas allegoria,
> Moralis quid agas, quo tendas anagogia.

The letter exhibits deeds (events); allegory, what you should believe; the moral level, what you should do; the anagogical, where you should be going.

Conceived as an interpretive procedure for yielding maximal spiritual benefit to the reader of Scripture, the "exegetical method" could be applied to any text so as to produce for its Christian user a construction of its "permanent symbolic value" (Robertson and Huppé 234), irrespective of the specific ends of its writer; by this process alone could classical literature be rendered fit spiritual food for medieval Christians, though it was not always applied exhaustively (Green 121). Only by applying this method to medieval literary texts, Robertson and Huppé argued, could modern readers understand them "historically" (rather than "subjectively") — by which they meant as these texts were designed to be read, though in itself this design was a method for stripping away historical specificity of meaning (see Minnis 72). From a reconstructive procedure for "saving the appearances" of complex writings at least partly non-Christian in provenance, systematic figurative construction became the fundamental method and motive of all Christian composition, as Robertson argues at greater length in his *Preface to Chaucer* (1962).

It is on this last point that many who endorse Robertson and Huppé's argument for the fundamental importance of the scriptural quotations in the poem, and of scriptural interpretation for the study of medieval literature generally, qualify their support for these interpreters' specific axioms and procedures. As R. E. Kaske — much of whose work subsequently offered more detailed accounts of the poet's handling of Scripture and exegetical tradition — puts it: "[Their] work . . . is like a pinnacle without a sufficiently wide base. . . . [Its] most significant weakness . . .is its tendency to proceed from general assumptions to the explanation of particulars, instead of vice versa; the resulting paradox is that it does not make intensive enough use of the exegetical tradition which is its distinctive tool" (Kaske 1960, 32). (For a brief survey of the debate provoked initially by exegetical criticism, and a retrospective longer view of its significance, see Bethurum [ed.] 1960; Bloomfield 1952, 1958; Aers 1975; Patterson 1987.)

2. Applied Exegetics and Poetic Method

In the past thirty years, scholars have done much to provide a base for understanding the specific ways in which the poet received and used the traditions of scriptural exposition. Proceeding by close analysis of especially puzzling or intricate passages — an activity which some have called "crux-busting" — Kaske and others have shown how the methods of exegetical exposition became in Langland's hands the instruments of poetic invention and development. The work of John Alford and Judson Allen has demonstrated the poet's familiarity with such late-medieval aids to biblical study as *distinctiones* and concordances of passages on common themes. These compendia, as well as aids to the composition of sermons (see chapter 6) and handbooks instructing confessors in the probing of a penitent's conscience (Braswell), are characteristic forms for the orderly dissemination of sacred doctrine and moral knowledge mandated by the Fourth Lateran Council of 1215 (see pages 141 ff.). This array of post-Lateran tools of Christian teaching and interpretation is now seen as the primary mediating form of the poet's acquaintance with exegetical tradition.

By tracing in more detail the paths of exegetical tradition Langland is most likely to have followed, these scholars have tended to avoid Robertson and Huppé's more sweeping claims, and have diverged sharply from their "method" in critical purpose as well as procedure. Robertson and Huppé explicitly and systematically eschewed citations of both homiletic and scholastic expository sources in favor of pre-thirteenth century texts and those of the anti-mendicant seculars (6–16), whom they believe the poet considered the true heirs of apostolic succession and patristic interpretive traditions (Bloomfield 1952). Their pursuit of the presumed deep or "original" rather than proximate intellectual underpinnings of the poem declares their broader critical aim of displaying the essential mentality, rather than the specific expository resources, of exegetical tradition. By citing solely the four great Latin fathers Ambrose, Augustine, Jerome, and Gregory as sources for a dominant metaphor, Margaret Goldsmith's recent study of the poem (1981) declares its allegiance to their original methods and objectives.

Study of medieval biblical interpretation has also drawn several scholars' attention to the theories of language and literary form that devolved from it. Late scholastic scriptural expositors (whose general literary importance and possible influence on vernacular writers were dismissed by Robertson and Huppé) classified the diverse literary purposes, genres and authorial "voices" of the books of the Bible in terms that were also used by fourteenth-century English writers for their own work (Minnis), and may provide a vocabulary for reconstructing aspects of their "poetics."

The momentous project of interpreting and expounding God's word in man's words, with precise respect for its several spiritual significations, also drew patristic and scholastic thinkers to systematic reflection on the nature and modes of verbal meaning. Highly complex accounts of grammatical structure, reference, and modes of signifying had by the later Middle Ages infused the university study of language. The poet's familiarity with the sophisticated terminology of these disciplines is shown in his use of elaborate grammatical metaphors and analogies (e.g., B.13.128–55; C.3.332–405). Explications of several of these passages, formerly considered "barely intelligible and very dull" (Skeat), have also explored the medieval intellectual rationale for using them (Kaske 1963; Middleton 1972; Alford 1982). Some recent general interpretations of the poem have proposed that it encompasses a critical reflection on the epistemological as well as moral problems of effective knowledge and understanding, and explores the practical implications of these questions for its own poetic method (Carruthers 1973; Martin 1979).

3. SOCIAL CONTEXTS OF LITERARY PRACTICES

The complementary (and older) tradition of *Piers Plowman* criticism, which reads the poem primarily as an address to contemporaries and emphasizes its practical rather than speculative designs, continues to foster a strong interest in both the audience and the author of the poem. In the absence of the sort of records of his life and career that survive for Chaucer, for example, scholars are constrained to reconstruct the author's social and intellectual circumstances almost entirely by inference from general historical knowledge, from the poem itself, and from the material records of its survival, the physical form and distribution of its manuscripts (see Kane below). Modern scholars tend to be more cautious than their distant predecessors in inferring from poetic statement the author's position on specific political, religious, and theological issues of his age (see chapter 3 on the complexity of this task) and take into account the conventional aspects of his pronouncements on many topics (anti-mendicant polemic, for example). They are more likely to try to reconstruct his thought through his literary procedures than vice versa. David Aers (1980) thus substantially reframes in late twentieth-century terms the familiar nineteenth-century assumption that poets "represent" the typical views and common perceptual equipment of their societies.

Many richly detailed topical studies published in the last twenty years have situated *Piers Plowman* in a late fourteenth-century intellectual climate and social landscape which differs markedly from the version current a century or even fifty years ago. Among these are Janet Coleman's study of the moral theology of the late medieval nominalist philosophers as it bears on the concerns of the poem (1981), and some valuable analyses of the detailed knowledge of legal practice and theory shown by the poem (Birnes 1975; Alford 1977a, 1988; Baldwin 1981; Stokes 1984). Substantial revisions in the broader picture of later fourteenth-century English life have been provided by recent historical work in two related areas: the thought and influence of Wyclif and the Lollard movement, and the social forms of literacy and learning (McFarlane; Hudson). These studies have altered significantly the terms within which questions of the writer's religious heterodoxy, social and political attitudes, and reception by readers have been posed.

The literary form, as well as the social context, of the poem has also been illuminated by recent studies of its late medieval literary and intellectual milieu. Unlike the works of Chaucer, which readily acknowledged their many debts to several "maistres" in the classical and medieval literary tradition, *Piers Plowman* yields to "sources and analogues" study little trace of its immediate literary antecedents and possible models: it appears that what Chaucer called "alle poesie" played little part in Langland's conception of his "making." The latter's use of Latin quotations is distinctive, however, and those from Scripture and patristic writings were the earliest to be identified. More recently, a substantial number have been traced to various kinds of collections and compendia: homiletic and encyclopedic material, *sententiae*, proverbs and legal maxims, and in general those digests, anthologies, and compilations which were the distinctive form for transmission of much learning in the later Middle Ages (Smalley 1960; Allen 1971).

Recent studies of Langland's sources, however, have moved from identification of quotations to consider the working methods and notions of literary organization implied by the way the poet uses these texts. John Alford (1977b), following the suggestion of Robertson and Huppé, regards the Latin quotations as the seed-crystals of the poet's invention. Langland expands his themes by linking one quotation to another through the methods of word-association or "concordance" used by biblical expositors; this, Alford argues, constitutes the poet's basic compositional method. Recently Allen (1984) has analyzed the Pardon episode as an example of how this technique aided the poet in the development of episodes. As criticism has moved from seeking analogues to understanding how anterior texts inform a poet's thought-processes and his modes of address, contextual scholarship has drawn closer to formal interests.

The two complementary traditions in recent critical scholarship thus converge upon questions that invite both literary and historical interpretation. What and how the poem means, its status and position among the modes of writing current in the poet's culture, and what the enterprise of writing such a work meant to a particular fourteenth-century author and his society, are questions that occupy what is still a common field of inquiry for historians and literary scholars. Both the intellectual form and experience of the poem itself, which seems to cast such questions into the foreground, and its controversial critical history continue to exact from contemporary readers exceptional care and self-awareness about the assumptions they bring with them to the "other country" of the past, and to one of its most moving and perplexing masterpieces.

REFERENCES

Adams, Robert. "The Reliability of the Rubrics in the B-Text of *Piers Plowman*." *MÆ* 54 (1985): 208–31.
———. "Some Versions of Apocalypse: Learned and Popular Eschatology in *Piers Plowman*." *The Popular Literature of Medieval England*. Ed. Thomas J. Heffernan. Knoxville: University of Tennessee Press, 1985. 194–236.
Aers, David. *Piers Plowman and Christian Allegory*. London: Arnold, 1975.

————. *Chaucer, Langland and the Creative Imagination*. London and Boston: Routledge and Kegan Paul, 1980.

Alford, John. "Literature and Law in Medieval England." *PMLA* 92 (1977): 941–51.

————. "The Role of the Quotations in *Piers Plowman*." *Speculum* 52 (1977): 80–99.

————. "The Grammatical Metaphor: A Survey of Its Use in the Middle Ages." *Speculum* 57 (1982): 728–60.

————. *Piers Plowman: A Glossary of Legal Diction*. Cambridge: Brewer, 1988.

Allen, Judson Boyce. *The Friar as Critic: Literary Attitudes in the Later Middle Ages*. Nashville: Vanderbilt University Press, 1971.

————. *The Ethical Poetic of the Later Middle Ages*. Toronto: University of Toronto Press, 1982.

————. "Langland's Reading and Writing: *Detractor* and the Pardon Passus." *Speculum* 59 (1984): 342–62.

Ames, Ruth M. *The Fulfillment of the Scriptures: Abraham, Moses, and Piers*. Evanston: Northwestern University Press, 1970.

Auerbach, Erich. *Mimesis*. Bern: A. Francke, 1946. Trans. Willard Trask. Princeton: Princeton University Press, 1953.

————. *Literatursprache und Publikum in der lateinischen Spätantike und im Mittelalter*. Bern: A. Francke, 1958. Trans. Ralph Manheim. *Literary Language and Its Public*. Bollingen Series 74. New York: Pantheon, 1965.

Baldwin, Anna P. *The Theme of Government in Piers Plowman*. Cambridge: Brewer, 1981.

Bennett, J. A. W., ed. *Piers Plowman: The Prologue and Passus I-VII of the B Text*. Oxford: Clarendon, 1972.

Benzie, William. *Dr. F. J. Furnivall: Victorian Scholar Adventurer*. Norman, Oklahoma: Pilgrim Books, 1983.

Bestul, Thomas. *Satire and Allegory in Wynnere and Wastoure*. Lincoln: University of Nebraska Press, 1974.

Bethurum, Dorothy, ed. *Critical Approaches to Medieval Literature: Selected Papers from the English Institute, 1958–1959*. New York and London: Columbia University Press, 1960.

Birnes, William J. "Christ as Advocate: The Legal Metaphor in *Piers Plowman*." *AnM* 16 (1975): 71–93.

Bloch, Howard. "Naturalism, Nationalism, Medievalism." *Romanic Review* 76 (1986): 341–60.

Bloomfield, Morton W. Review of Robertson and Huppé 1951. *Speculum* 27 (1952): 245–49; rpt. in Bloomfield 1970, 289–95.

————. "Symbolism in Medieval Literature." *MP* 61 (1958): 73–81; rpt. in Bloomfield 1970, 82–95.

————. *Piers Plowman as a Fourteenth-Century Apocalypse*. New Brunswick, NJ: Rutgers University Press, 1962.

————. "A Grammatical Approach to Personification Allegory." *MP* 60 (1963): 161–71; rpt. in Bloomfield 1970, 243–60.

————. *Essays and Explorations: Studies in Ideas, Language, and Literature*. Cambridge, MA: Harvard University Press, 1970.

Braswell, Mary Flowers. *The Medieval Sinner: Characterization and Confession in the Literature of the English Middle Ages*. Rutherford, NJ: Fairleigh Dickinson University Press; London and Toronto: Associated University Presses, 1983.

Burdach, Konrad. *Der Dichter des Ackermann aus Böhmen und seine Zeit*. Berlin: Weidmann, 1926–32.

Burrow, John A. "The Audience of *Piers Plowman*." *Anglia* 75 (1957): 373–84.

————. "Langland Nel Mezzo del Cammin." *Medieval Studies for J. A. W. Bennett.* Ed. P. L. Heyworth. Oxford: Clarendon, 1981. 21–41.

Carruthers [Schroeder], Mary. "*Piers Plowman*: The Tearing of the Pardon." *PQ* 49 (1970): 8–18.

Carruthers, Mary. *The Search for St. Truth: A Study of Meaning in Piers Plowman.* Evanston: Northwestern University Press, 1973.

Chadwick, Dorothy. *Social Life in the Days of Piers Plowman.* Cambridge: Cambridge University Press, 1922; rpt. New York: Russell and Russell, 1969.

Chambers, R. W. *Man's Unconquerable Mind.* London and Toronto: Jonathan Cape, 1939.

————. "Robert or William Longland?" *London Medieval Studies* 1 (1948 for 1939): 430–62.

Coghill, Nevill K. "The Character of Piers Plowman Considered from the B Text." *MÆ* 2 (1933): 108–35; rpt. Vasta 54–86.

Coleman, Janet. *Piers Plowman and the Moderni.* Rome: Edizioni di Storia e Letteratura, 1981.

Coulton, G. G. *Medieval Panorama.* Cambridge: Cambridge University Press, 1938; rpt. New York: Meridian, 1955.

Crowley, Robert, ed. *The Vision of Pierce Plowman.* London, 1550 (STC 19906, 19907, 19907a).

Curtius, Ernst Robert. *Europäische Literatur und lateinisches Mittelalter.* Bern: A. Francke, 1948. Trans. Willard R. Trask as *European Literature in the Latin Middle Ages.* Bollingen Series 36. New York: Pantheon, 1953.

Donaldson, E. Talbot. *Piers Plowman: The C-Text and Its Poet.* Yale Studies in English 113. New Haven: Yale University Press, 1949; rpt. Hamden, CT: Archon, 1966.

Dunning, T. P. *Piers Plowman: An Interpretation of the A Text.* Dublin: Talbot, 1937. 2nd. ed. rev. and ed. T. P. Dolan. Oxford: Clarendon, 1980.

————. "The Structure of the B-Text of *Piers Plowman*." *RES* 7 (1956): 225–37.

————. "Action and Contemplation in *Piers Plowman*." Hussey 213–25.

Emmerson, Richard K. *Antichrist in the Middle Ages: A Study of Medieval Apocalypticism, Art, and Literature.* Seattle: University of Washington Press, 1981.

————. "The Prophetic, the Apocalyptic, and the Study of Medieval Literature." *Poetic Prophecy in Western Literature.* Ed. Jan Wojcik and Raymond-Jean Frontain. Rutherford, NJ: Fairleigh Dickinson University Press; London and Toronto: Associated University Presses, 1984. 40–54.

Fletcher, Angus. *Allegory: The Theory of a Symbolic Mode.* Ithaca: Cornell University Press, 1964.

Fowler, David C. *Piers the Plowman: Literary Relations of the A and B Texts.* Seattle: University of Washington Press, 1961.

Frank, Robert Worth, Jr. *Piers Plowman and the Scheme of Salvation.* Yale Studies in English 136. New Haven: Yale University Press, 1957; rpt. Hamden, CT: Archon, 1969.

Gilbert, Felix. "Intellectual History: Its Aims and Methods." *Daedalus.* Proceedings of the American Academy of Arts and Sciences. 100:1 (1971): 80–97.

Goldsmith, Margaret. *The Figure of Piers Plowman.* Cambridge: Brewer, 1981.

Gradon, Pamela. "Langland and the Ideology of Dissent." *PBA* 66 (1980): 179–205.

Green, Richard Hamilton. "Classical Fable and English Poetry in the Fourteenth Century." Bethurum 110–33.

Hort, Greta. *Piers Plowman and Contemporary Religious Thought.* London: Society for Promoting Christian Knowledge; New York: Macmillan, 1938.

Hudson, Anne, ed. *Selections from English Wycliffite Writings*. Cambridge: Cambridge University Press, 1978.

Hussey, S. S. "Langland, Hilton, and the Three Lives." *RES* ns 7 (1956): 132–50.

Jusserand, J. J. *English Wayfaring Life in the Middle Ages*. Trans. Lucy Toulmin Smith. New York: G. P. Putnam's Sons, 1925. (Originally published in French in 1884.)

——. *Piers Plowman: A Contribution to the History of English Mysticism*. Trans. M. E. R. London: T. Fisher Unwin; New York: G. P. Putnam's Sons, 1894 (trans. of *L'épopé mystique de William Langland*. Paris: Libraire Hachette, 1893); rpt. New York: Russell and Russell, 1965.

Kane, George. *Piers Plowman: The Evidence for Authorship*. London: Athlone, 1965.

——. *The Autobiographical Fallacy in Chaucer and Langland Studies*. Chambers Memorial Lecture. London: H. K. Lewis, 1965.

Kaske, R. E. "Patristic Exegesis in the Criticism of Medieval Literature: The Defense." Bethurum 27–60.

——. " 'Ex vi transicionis' and Its Passage in *Piers Plowman*." *JEGP* 62 (1963): 32–60.

King, John N. "Robert Crowley's Editions of *Piers Plowman*: A Tudor Apocalypse." *MP* 73 (1976): 342–52.

Knight, S. T. "Satire in *Piers Plowman*." Hussey 279–309.

Lawlor, John. "The Imaginative Unity of *Piers Plowman*." *RES* ns 8 (1957): 113–26; rpt. Blanch 101–16.

Lewis, C. S. *The Allegory of Love*. Oxford: Oxford University Press, 1936.

Manly, J. M. "The Lost Leaf of 'Piers the Plowman.' " *MP* 3 (1906): 359–66.

——. " 'Piers the Plowman' and Its Sequence." *The Cambridge History of English Literature*. Vol. 2. *The End of the Middle Ages*. Ed. A. W. Ward and A. R. Waller. Cambridge: Cambridge University Press; New York: G. P. Putnam's Sons, 1908. 1–42.

Mann, Jill. *Chaucer and Medieval Estates Satire*. Cambridge: Cambridge University Press, 1973.

Martin, Jay. "Will as Fool and Wanderer in *Piers Plowman*." *TSLL* 3 (1962): 535–48.

Martin, Priscilla. *Piers Plowman: The Field and the Tower*. London and Basingstoke: Macmillan; New York: Harper and Row, Barnes and Noble, 1979.

McFarlane, K. B. *John Wycliffe and the Beginnings of English Nonconformity*. London: English Universities Press, 1952.

——. *Lancastrian Kings and Lollard Knights*. Oxford: Clarendon, 1972.

Mcroney, Howard. "The Life and Death of Longe Wille." *ELH* 17 (1950): 1–35.

Middleton, Anne. "Two Infinites: Grammatical Metaphor in *Piers Plowman*." *ELH* 39 (1972): 169–88.

——. "The Audience and Public of *Piers Plowman*." *Middle English Alliterative Poetry and Its Literary Background*. Ed. David Lawton. Cambridge: D. S. Brewer, 1982. 101–23.

Miller, Paul Scott. "The Medieval Literary Theory of Satire and Its Relevance to the Works of Gower, Langland, and Chaucer." Unpub. Ph.D. dissertation, The Queen's University, Belfast, 1982.

Minnis, A. J. *Medieval Theory of Authorship: Scholastic Literary Attitudes in the Later Middle Ages*. London: Scolar Press, 1984.

Muscatine, Charles. "Locus of Action in Medieval Narrative." *Romance Philology* 17 (1963): 115–22.

Owen, Dorothy. *Piers Plowman, A Comparison with Some Earlier and Contemporary French Allegories*. M. A. thesis, University of London, 1912; rpt. Folcroft, PA: Folcroft Library, 1971.

Owst, G. R. *Literature and Pulpit in Medieval England.* 2nd. rev. ed. Oxford: Blackwell, 1961 (orig. pub. 1933).

Patterson, Lee. "The Logic of Textual Criticism and the Way of Genius: The Kane-Donaldson *Piers Plowman* in Historical Perspective." *Textual Criticism and Literary Interpretation.* Ed. Jerome J. McGann. Chicago: University of Chicago Press, 1985. 55–91; rpt. in Patterson 1987.

———. *Negotiating the Past: The Historical Understanding of Medieval Literature.* Madison: University of Wisconsin Press, 1987.

Peter, John. *Complaint and Satire in Early English Literature.* Oxford: Clarendon, 1956.

Puttenham, George [?]. *The Arte of English Poesie.* London: Richard Field, 1589 (STC 20519).

Robbins, Rossell Hope. "Middle English Poems of Protest." *Anglia* 78 (1960): 193–203.

Robertson, D. W., Jr. *A Preface to Chaucer.* Princeton: Princeton University Press, 1962.

———, and Bernard F. Huppé. *Piers Plowman and Scriptural Tradition.* Princeton Studies in English 31. Princeton: Princeton University Press, 1951; rpt. New York: Octagon Books, 1969.

Russell, G. H. "Some Aspects of the Process of Revision in *Piers Plowman.*" Hussey 27–49.

Salter, Elizabeth. "Medieval Poetry and the Figural View of Reality." *PBA* 44 (1968): 73–92.

Smalley, Beryl. *The Study of the Bible in the Middle Ages.* Oxford: Blackwell, 1952; rpt. Notre Dame, IN: University of Notre Dame Press, 1964.

———. *English Friars and Antiquity in the Early Fourteenth Century.* Oxford: Blackwell, 1960.

Stokes, Myra. *Justice and Mercy in Piers Plowman: A Reading of the B Text Visio.* London and Canberra: Croom Helm, 1984.

Strohm, Paul. "Chaucer's Fifteenth-Century Audience and the Narrowing of the 'Chaucer Tradition.'" *SAC* 4 (1982): 3–32.

Szittya, Penn R. "The Antifraternal Tradition in Middle English Literature." *Speculum* 52 (1977): 287–313.

———. *The Antifraternal Tradition in Medieval Literature.* Princeton: Princeton University Press, 1986.

Trevelyan, G. M. *History of England.* Vol. 1. *From the Earliest Times to the Reformation.* 3rd ed. London: Longmans, Green, 1926; rpt. Garden City, NY: Doubleday, 1953.

Troyer, Howard William. "Who is Piers Plowman?" *PMLA* 47 (1932): 368–84; rpt. Blanch 156–73.

Tucker, Samuel M. *Verse Satire in England before the Renaissance.* Columbia University Studies in English, ser. 2, vol. 3:2. New York: Columbia University Press, 1908.

Wells, Henry W. "The Construction of *Piers Plowman.*" *PMLA* 44 (1929): 123–40; rpt. Vasta 1–21.

———. "The Philosophy of *Piers Plowman.*" *PMLA* 53 (1938): 339–49; rpt. Vasta 115–29.

Wesling, Donald. "Eschatology and the Language of Satire in *Piers Plowman.*" *Criticism* 10 (1968): 277–89.

Yunck, John A. *The Lineage of Lady Meed: The Development of Medieval Venality Satire.* Notre Dame, IN: University of Notre Dame Press, 1963.

GUIDE TO FURTHER STUDY

Bloomfield, Morton W. "The Present State of *Piers Plowman* Studies." *Speculum* 14 (1939): 215–32; rpt. Blanch 3–25.

Colaianne, A. J. *Piers Plowman: An Annotated Bibliography of Editions and Criticism, 1550–1977.* New York: Garland, 1978.

DiMarco, Vincent. *Piers Plowman: A Reference Guide.* Boston: G. K. Hall, 1982. (Covers publications through 1979.)

Fowler, D. C. *"Piers Plowman." Recent Middle English Scholarship and Criticism: Survey and Desiderata.* Ed. J. Burke Severs. Pittsburgh: Duquesne University Press; Louvain: E. Nauwelaerts, 1971. 9–28.

Hussey, S. S. "Eighty Years of *Piers Plowman* Scholarship: A Study of Critical Methods." Unpublished London University M.A. thesis, 1952.

Middleton, Anne. *"Piers Plowman."* Chap. 18 of *A Manual of Writings in Middle English.* Ed. Albert Hartung. New Haven: Connecticut Academy of Arts and Sciences, 1986. 7:2211–34 (Commentary), 2419–48 (Bibliography). (Covers publications through 1985.)

Wells, John Edwin. *A Manual of Writings in Middle English 1050–1400.* New Haven: Connecticut Academy of Arts and Sciences, 1916. 9 supplements, 1919–1952.

The Yearbook of Langland Studies. East Lansing, MI: Colleagues Press, 1987– . (Includes annotated bibliography of preceding year's publications, beginning with 1985.)

I

PIERS PLOWMAN
AND THE LATE MIDDLE AGES

1

THE DESIGN OF THE POEM

JOHN A. ALFORD

PRELIMINARY PROBLEMS

What is *Piers Plowman* about? Does it have a central argument to which each part of the poem contributes? Almost unanimously critics agree that it is one of the most difficult poems ever written: few "are certain of its meaning" (Frank 1); it "constantly challenges but evades interpretation" (Woolf 50); it "gives rise to more questioning and doubts than any other Middle English poem" (Hort 2).

Many of the difficulties can be traced to two problems, both of which are peculiar to *Piers Plowman*.

The first problem can be described, for lack of a better word, as ontological. Before trying to explain *Piers Plowman*, we are forced to ask: "What is it?" The question hardly arises with other Middle English works. We know, for example, what *Sir Gawain and the Green Knight* is. It is British Library MS Cotton Nero A.x, folios 91ª to 124ᵇ. We even presume that we know, despite its complicated textual history, what *The Canterbury Tales* is. *Piers Plowman*, however, presents a unique problem. It exists in three distinct versions, known as the A, B, and C texts, generally considered to be the successive revisions of a single author (see chapter 7 below). Critics have dealt with this problem in different ways. Some have attempted to treat all three versions simultaneously (Kirk, Martin). Others have focused their attention on a particular version (Dunning 1937 on A, Robertson and Huppé on B, Donaldson on C). But nearly all have shown a tendency in the case of obscure passages to move across versions in search of help, a practice encouraged by Skeat's parallel-text edition (1886). The implications of this have not always been appreciated. To use one version as a touchstone for the interpretation of another suggests that *Piers Plowman* exists, intertextually, in all three versions at once. In fact, nothing could be more revealing than our ability to speak of "the B text" and "the poem" together and to mean different things by each (Donaldson 181; Martin 1). What does "the poem," as this phrase is actually used, signify? Is it an imaginary construct based on all three versions, an inferred entelechy, an authorial intention more clearly revealed with each revision? Some definition of boundaries must precede any attempt to explain the design of the poem.

The second problem confronting us in this chapter is formal. "One of the things that make *Piers Plowman* an unusually difficult poem," R. E. Kaske observes, "is the fact that it seems organized in so many different ways at once" (1974, 320). Most obviously, each version is divided into *passus* (the word is both singular and plural and means, literally, "steps" in the progress of the narrative). The A text has a prologue and eleven or twelve passus (see pp. 188–89 below); the B text, a prologue and twenty passus; the C text, a prologue and twenty-two passus. These do not always correspond. For example, the material treated by B in passus 5 is divided by A into passus 5 and 6, by C into passus 5, 6, and 7. Neither do the passus always correspond with narrative logic; at times they break off unaccountably in the middle of episodes, dreams, speeches (see Donaldson 32–37).

A number of manuscripts also show a larger, two-fold division into the *Visio* (A Prol.–passus 8, B Prol.–passus 7, C Prol.–passus 9) and the *Vita* (A passus 9–12; B passus 8–20; C passus 10–22). Despite a long tradition of use by *Piers Plowman* scholars, the value of these titles (called "colophons") is questionable. They are descriptively inaccurate (the whole poem, after all, is a *visio*); they have led readers to magnify the discontinuity of the text; and there is no evidence that they are anything more than scribal afterthoughts. The Athlone editions cited throughout this book omit them altogether.

If the division into *Visio* and *Vita* is probably scribal, the subdivision of the latter into the *vita de do-wel, do-bet, & do-best* is almost certainly so. Earlier studies that took these headings to indicate an important formal principle (e.g., Wells 1929, 1938; Coghill 1933; Robertson and Huppé; Frank; Bloomfield 116) must be approached with caution. As Donaldson points out, "Although according to the colophons of B and C the *Vita* purports to take up the three kinds of life one at a time, the lines of demarcation between them . . . are far from clear" (157). Precisely which passus are devoted, respectively, to Dowel, Dobet, and Dobest? The manuscripts do not agree. In fact, Adams identifies "five different schemes for segmenting the [B version] narrative" and concludes that the rubrics are "not only useless for interpretation but also inauthentic, the wrong-headed offspring of some mediaeval editor rather than of the author himself" (1985, 209).

In short, the impression that *Piers Plowman* "seems organized in so many different ways at once" is based partly on the rubrics. To give much weight to these external markers — unstable, often competing, and some of doubtful authority — is to create problems. The most trustworthy principles of organization are those embedded firmly in the text itself, such as the three dreams that make up the A version and the eight that make up the B and C versions. The following table shows their disposition (the parentheses indicate dreams-within-dreams):

A	B	C
(1) Prol.11 to 5.3	(1) Prol.11 to 5.3	(1) Prol.8 to 4.196
(2) 5.8 to 8.127	(2) 5.8 to 7.145	(2) 5.109 to 9.294
(3) 9.58 to 12.99-105 [106-17 John But]	(3) ⎡ 8.67 to 11.4 / (11.5 to 11.406) / 11.406 to 12.297 ⎦	(3) ⎡ 10.66 to 11.165 / (11.165 to 13.214) / 13.214 to 14.217 ⎦
	(4) 13.21 to 14.335	(4) 15.24 to 18.178)
	(5) ⎡ 15.11 to 16.20 / (16.20 to 16.166) / 16.167 to 17.356 ⎦	(5) 18.181 to 19.336
	(6) 18.4 to 18.431	(6) 20.6 to 20.475
	(7) 19.5 to 19.481	(7) 21.5 to 21.481
	(8) 20.51 to 20.386	(8) 22.51 to 22.386

The dreams function most clearly as thematic units in B, that is, they each take up new subject matter or define a new stage in the argument (see Frank 3; Burrow 1965, 247; Hussey 1969, 3; Kirk 15 ff.; and on the importance of the narrator's *waking* moments, Bowers 129–64). Their function is illustrated less clearly in the other versions. The A text was not finished (only two dreams are complete); neither was the revision of the C text (for example, as shown in the table above, the dreamer awakes at 18.178 from an inner dream that has no beginning). Except for the fourth and fifth dreams, however, the correspondences between B and C are fairly close.

With respect to these preliminary problems, the positions taken in this book are, of necessity, practical ones. We cannot dispense with the structural markers that have become traditional in *Piers* scholarship; but with one exception, the dreams, we will use them as little more than convenient points of reference. Neither can we limit ourselves to one version. A companion to *Piers Plowman* must include discussion of all three. It is possible, however, to think of "the poem" provisionally in terms of the questions raised. The poet's answers may vary considerably from version to version — as one might expect them to over the course of a lifetime — but the questions remain constant. So although the B text explores the notion of Dowel further than A, and although the C text has more to say about the nature of *meed* than either A or B, the concerns themselves do not change substantially. Neither does the language in which they are couched. *Truth, loyalty, law, love, will* — regardless of the version these are part of the indispensable vocabulary of *Piers Plowman* criticism.

The following discussion takes the form of an interpretative summary. Although it might have been more efficient to deal with the major questions in the order of their importance rather than in the order of their appearance, such an approach not only would have presumed a familiarity with the text that many readers of the *Companion* do not have, but it also would have ignored an essential feature of the poem's design. The sequence in which things happen is crucial. One critic stresses the importance "of apprehending the whole work serially, experiencing its crises as they occur and not as they may be extracted from their setting for the purpose of cross-reference and detailed comparison" (Lawlor 125; cf. Martin 58); another insists that certain elements of the poem "constitute a pattern . . . only if the order in which they appear is taken seriously" (Kirk 10); others point to the dialectical progress of the argument (Hort 28–43; Bloomfield 16 and passim; Adams 1978, 292; Murtaugh 5–30). In short, *what* a particular passage means often depends on *where* it occurs. "The key to almost every enigma of *Piers Plowman*," as Kirk says, "is a sense of its sequence" (11).

"TRUTH IS BEST"

The first question in all three versions — the question to which the poem will recur again and again — is put emblematically. The narrator reports that in a dream on the Malvern hills (Worcestershire) he saw "a fair feeld ful of folk," placed between a "tour" on a hill and a "dongeon" in a valley, that is, in Middle English, between two *castles*. (To translate the words into Modern English as "tower" and "dungeon," as is often done in explications of the scene, is to obscure their significance.) In the fourteenth century a castle meant something. It was still viewed as a stronghold of feudal authority, not simply as a private residence (still less as a tourist attraction!), and thus the scene provokes us to ask: To which castle or lord do these folk owe their faith, their loyalty or (to use the feudal term) their *truth*?

The entire Prologue develops logically out of the imagery of these opening lines. In the simplest version (the A text), it is little more than a catalogue of the folk on the field, distinguished according to whether they observe the duties of their estate. Many do: "Summe putte hem to plou3" and "In preyours & penaunce putten hem manye, / Al for loue of oure lord lyuede wel streite." But many do not: parsons abandon their flocks for London "To synge for symonye" and "bisshopis bolde & bacheleris of deuyn / Become clerkis of acountis." (On the medieval view of society as an organization of "estates," see chapter 2; for a comparison of Langland's and Chaucer's handling of estates satire, see Cooper.)

The insertion of two episodes in B and C adds a political dimension. The first, a coronation (inspired perhaps by the recent accession of Richard II [1377]), concerns the truth of kings and their obligation to rule with justice; the second, the famous belling of the cat fable, concerns the truth of subjects and their obligation to obey. Although much speculation has centered on the historical significance of these two episodes (see below pp. 78–79), we should not lose sight of their broader purpose in the Prologue. Their addition "transforms the Prologue from a descriptive complaint to a thesis" (Stokes 75). In the first episode, as Bloomfield describes it, "The good king, the *rex justus*, supported by the nobility and the clergy, and counseled by practical reason, sets up the ideal commonwealth in which each class will have its proper role to play" (109; see also Bowers 104–20). The second episode, focusing on the commons, enforces a similar point of view. After much discussion concerning the oppression of rats by "a cat of a court," a wise mouse finally says, "Forþi I counseille al þe commune to late þe cat worþe . . . / For hadde ye rattes youre raik [way] ye kouþe noȝt rule yowselue . . . / Forþi ech a wis wiȝt I warne, wite wel his owene" (B.Prol. 187–208), that is, "each man, and therefore each class, should know and keep his own place" (Donaldson 110; cf. Kean 243).

Thus the Prologue announces the entrance of the poem into one of the liveliest and most important discussions of the day. Truth as a social ideal is the dominant, one might almost say the characterizing, concern of late fourteenth-century poetry. Though typically truth finds its highest expression in the order of knighthood (e.g., *Sir Gawain and the Green Knight*, Chaucer's *Franklin's Tale*, the Middle English *Yvain*), it is a virtue to be observed by all orders of society (see, for example, Chaucer's short poems "Truth" and "Lak of Stedfastnesse," the Vernon lyric "Truth is Best" [ed. Brown 168–70], or several of the Digby poems [ed. Kail]). Again and again writers of the period extol truth as the political virtue *par excellence*. And again and again they lament its decline, citing as the two main causes "meed" (money, the acquisitive instinct) and "will" (wilfulness, "singularity," personal ambition) — see "Lak of Stedfastnesse"; Brown 169; Kail 23, 57, 69–71.

Clearly the word *truth* carries with it a specific world-view, at the center of which is that social system known to us as feudalism. Truth is not simply an abstract loyalty, such as any society in any age could embrace, but a loyalty manifested concretely in the obligations of status, in the duties of knighthood, in the subordination of one individual to another. By the late fourteenth century the breakup of this system had become obvious (see chapter 2). Thus truth emerged as a battle-cry at the very moment when the passing of the old order was felt most keenly. What Yunck has to say about meed is no less applicable to truth itself: "The theme becomes . . . a vehicle of protest against a new world of nationalism, money, taxes, and collectors, in favor of a world long past and idealized, of feudal obligations and privileges, of settled class-distinctions, of personal mutual devotion between lord and vassal (such was the idealization) as the basis of social order" (219).

Like so much literature of the period, *Piers Plowman* is partly an argument for turning back the clock (even, paradoxically, as it describes society's headlong rush toward a fated, apocalyptic end). But Langland's is by far the most complex analysis of the problem. He was not content simply to repeat the current clichés; he was driven to find the causes behind them. Why is "treuþe the best"? What exactly is "meed"? How does one distinguish between will as "wilfulnesse" and will as the positive and necessary exercise of moral choice? His incessant questioning resulted in a poetic *summa* on truth.

Passus 1 represents Langland's basic attempt to broaden the conceptual framework of truth. (On fourteenth-century usage of the word see Kane 1980.) A "lovely lady" descends from the castle on the hill to tell the dreamer "What þe mounteyne bemeniþ, & ek þe merke dale, / And ek þe feld ful of folk" (A.1.1–2). Although her exposition is steeped in the language of feudalism, her concern is spiritual as well as social. She observes that most of the folk on the field — clearly reminiscent of the "cockle" of Matt. 13:18–43 (Dunning 1980, 14) — take no account of "oþer heuene þanne here." She identifies the lord of the hill castle as Truth, "fader of feiþ"; the other lord as Wrong, "fader of falshede" (cf. John 8:44). Truth has the right to our service, called *latria* by medieval theologians (q.v. *The Catholic Encyclopedia*), because from him we derive both life and the means to sustain it. Wrong has no claims: he himself is utterly faithless, he has counseled many (Adam, Eve, Cain, Judas) to treachery, and those who "trusten on his tresour bitrayed are sonnest." Ultimately, the description implies, our choice of liege is between God and the Devil, the respective sources of all truth and all treachery.

The choice should be an easy one. It is complicated, however, by cupidity. Although God has given us the necessities of life "in mesurable maner," most of us want more. In fact, Dunning argued, the subject of the entire A version is the right use of temporal goods, "*Temporalia — sub specie aeternitatis*" (1980, 6–7). However, Langland will insist later that *mesure* is to be observed in all things — not only in *temporalia* but also in sex, in work and recreation, in the quest for knowledge, in poetic activity itself. Anything whatsoever that interferes with the service we are bound to render God is to be avoided. The Lady's repeated use of the word *tresour* recalls the biblical injunction: "Lay not up to yourselves treasures on earth . . . but lay up to yourselves treasures in heaven . . . for where thy treasure is, there is thy heart also" (Matt. 6:19–21).

Indeed, as soon as the dreamer realizes that his guide is Holy Church herself, he falls to his knees and exclaims:

> "Teche me to no tresour but tel me þis ilke,
> How I may sauen my soul, þat seint art yholden."
> "Whanne alle tresours arn triȝed treuþe is þe beste;
> I do it on *Deus caritas* to deme þe soþe."
>
> (A.1.81–84)

Here in a nutshell is the poem. "How may I save my soul?" — this is the central question. "Truth is best" — this is the answer, and virtually all of *Piers Plowman* is an inquiry into its ramifications.

The impact of these lines on contemporary readers can only be imagined. For many, answering a spiritual question with a political proverb must have driven home in a strikingly new way the assumed relation between the two realms (see Simpson). Holy Church goes on to develop that relation explicitly. Kings should enforce truth through their knights, "For dauid, in his dayes, / Dubbide kniȝtes, / Dide hem swere on here swerd to serue treuþe euere," and Christ himself knighted ten orders of angels, "Tauȝte hem þoruȝ þe trinite þe trouþe to knowe: / To be buxum at his bidding; he bad hem nouȝt ellis" (A.1.92–108). The Trinity, the model of perfect harmony, is the source of all truth; the rebellious Lucifer, who "brak buxumnesse" (John 8:44, Isa. 14:14), is the source of all untruth. Hence, those who "werche well . . . shal wende to heuene / Ther Treuþe is in Trinitee"; those who "werchen with wrong" shall follow their lord to hell (1.128–33).

Nothing, it seems, could be plainer. But with Langland every answer generates a round of new questions. Where, the dreamer asks, does our knowledge of this precious truth originate? Holy Church replies:

> It is a kynde knowyng þat kenneþ in þin herte
> For to loue þi lord leuere þanne þiselue;
> No dedly synne to do, diȝe þeiȝ þou shuldist.
> þis I trowe be treuþe. . . .
>
> (A.1.130–33)

How we construe the first word may significantly affect our whole perception of Langland's theme. Goodridge's translation is undoubtedly correct: "*There* is a natural knowledge in your heart, which prompts you to love your Lord better than yourself and to die rather than commit mortal sin. That, surely, is Truth." That truth in this sense can be apprehended by "kynde knowyng" is a fundamental tenet of natural law. The *locus classicus*, which seems to lie behind the present passage, is Rom. 2:14–15: Paul observes that even the Gentiles, "who have not the law, do by nature those things that are of the law [and] shew the work of the law written in their hearts, their conscience bearing witness to them" (cf. C.7.205–12, C.17.153).

How love fits into this scheme is the final question taken up by Lady Holy Church. She has already "confirmed" her text "treuþe is þe beste" by *Deus caritas*, that is, 1 John 4:8: "He that loveth not, knoweth not God; for God is charity." And she has said, making the connection even more explicit, "To love your Lord better than yourself . . . That, surely, is Truth." However, to reduce such statements to the simple equation "truth is love" (Robertson and Huppé 45; Salter 97) is to obscure the complexity of their relationship. Truth is more comprehensive, as genus to species, though it expresses itself most fully in love (both a disposition of the will and an outward pattern of behavior). Just as "faith without works is dead" (James 2:26), Holy Church explains, so "chastity without charity" (that is, without *works* of charity) is useless, like a lamp without light. Such half-way devotion, in fact, is "no truth of the trinity but treachery of hell." Real truth or devotion will express itself in charitable behavior toward the Lord's other creatures. That, Holy Church, concludes, is "the key of love that unlocks grace" and "the narrow way that leads into heaven." (On the relation between works and grace in Langland's soteriology, see Adams 1983 and chapter 3, pp. 95–98).

The structure of Holy Church's speech resembles that of a medieval sermon (pp. 165–67 below) and is replicated to some extent in the poem as a whole (Dunning 1980, 47; Bloomfield 153; Salter 95; Kaske 1974; Murtaugh 5): her insistence that one must choose between serving *temporalia* or truth is played out dramatically in the *Visio*, and her teaching that one knows truth through "kynde knowynge" and perfects it through charity is further developed in the *Vita*. Beyond this pattern of emphases, her speech also bequeaths to the rest of the poem a broader than usual context in which to explore the meaning of truth and the problems conventionally associated with it, such as "meed" and "will." The validity of truth as a standard of social conduct derives from the fact that it is the principle upon which heavenly order itself rests. God, in the aspect of a great feudal lord, commanded truth of his angels. One participates in this order through obedience to God's vicars on earth, that is, the king and his justices, the church, parents, husband—in short, any authority that does not require one to act against the divine commandments.

THE TRIAL OF MEED

The next section of the poem (passus 2–4) elaborates on the first part of Holy Church's speech. It dramatizes the protasis of her theme ("Whanne alle tresours arn trized") by personifying "tresor" and then putting it, literally, on trial. The result is one of Langland's most complex satirical portraits: Lady Meed (see Mitchell; Benson; Griffiths 26–40). As John Yunck has demonstrated, she is the culmination of a centuries-long tradition of venality satire and incorporates most of its ambivalences. On the one hand, meed in such forms as bribery, extortion, and excessive profit undermines truth and "makes right relationships between classes impossible" (Bloomfield 111); on the other hand, meed is also the just reward of truth ("The trewe servant is worthy hys mede" [Kail 7]; cf. A.2.87).

Langland tries to clarify the issue of meed's ambiguous nature by means of the figure of marriage. When the dreamer first sees Lady Meed in the midst of Wrong's followers — "Hire array me rauysshed; swich richesse sauz I neuere" — she is about to wed Fals. Theology denounces the match. "God graunted to gyue Mede," he says, "to truþe" (B.2.120). The principals agree to settle the question at law, and the whole rout heads for London, Lady Meed seated "on a shirreue shod al newe" and Fals "on a sisour [juror] þat softeliche trottide" (A.2.128–29). The king rebukes Meed ("Ac wers wrouztest þou neuere þan þo þou fals toke," A.3.96) and proposes that she marry instead one of his knights, Conscience. The match would seem, on the face of it, to solve the problem. But Conscience will have nothing to do with her. On the contrary, assuming his natural role as accuser (cf. 15.31–32, Rom. 2:15), he reels off a list of charges against her, a virtual summary of satirical commonplaces. Despite the fact that Meed may be used for good or ill, in herself "almost morally neutral" (Mitchell 191), Conscience is wary of her irresistible power to corrupt. He perceives, more deeply than the king, "the subtle entanglements of the soul which may arise from even the most honorable of gifts in the highest of causes" (Yunck 291).

Part of the problem inherited by Langland was semantic — the use of one word to describe a number of things having contradictory values. Meed counters the charges against her by citing all the positive meanings of her name (wages, gifts, alms, mass pence, reward, compensation, benefice, payment for merchandise, and so forth). Conscience attempts to resolve the confusion, in typical scholastic fashion, by means of division: "Ther are two manere of Medes, my lord" (3.231). What distinguishes them is the presence or absence of *mesure*, a word already used by Holy Church to mean "moderation" and now by Conscience to invoke the idea of "exact equivalence." There is a "Mede mesurelees" (for example, a bribe) that has no correlation to merit or accomplishment; however, the wages taken in exchange for honest labor "is no manere Mede but a mesurable hire," and "In marchaundise is no Mede . . . [but] a permutacion apertly, a penyworþ for anoþer" (3.255–58). The concept is clear enough, but *meed* remains an equivocal and confusing term. In the C text Langland coins a new term, *mercede*, to signify "mesurable" meed, and then adds an elaborate (and notoriously difficult) grammatical analogy in which mercede and meed are distinguished "as two maner relacions, / Rect and indirect." (See Amassian and Sadowsky; Murtaugh 44–50; Coleman 90–99; Griffiths 35–40.)

The problem is only partly semantic, however. Behind Langland's effort to unravel the many strands of meaning in the word *meed*, there lies the complex casuistry of moral economics, developed over the course of centuries by the church fathers, the scholastic theologians, and above all the canon lawyers. Nobody doubted that "Worþi is þe werkman his mede to haue" (A.2.87, B.2.123, quoting Luke 10:7), but at what point precisely does "mesurable hire" become "mesurelees" gain? Or how is "permutacion apertly" to be distinguished from "derne usurie"? In the shady area between patent right and wrong, many of Meed's followers have learned to prosper. They require payment for services beforehand, *pre manibus* (C.3.299, C.9.45), withhold wages until the next day (C.3.306–07; cf. Levit. 19:3), chaffer in "eschaunges and cheuysaunces" (5.246), lend on condition of a "present" (13.375–76) or with the hope of default in order to seize the collateral (5.241–43), and so forth.

There is also a pressing theological question involved in the definition of meed. Theology has said, "God graunted to gyue Mede to truþe," and Conscience reiterates that God "of his grace gyueþ [meed] / To hem þat werchen wel whiles þei ben here" (A.3.219–20). Is the meed of salvation "mesurelees," that is, disproportionate to merit (Mitchell 183–84; Murtaugh 43–48), or is it "mesurable," that is, conditional and in some way commensurate with works performed (Coleman 79–99; Adams 1983, 398–401)? This question will concern Langland in later passus (see below pp. 43, 51, 95–98).

The morally ambiguous nature of meed highlights the crucial role of the conscience in the drama of salvation, for its function is to judge whether a specific act in a given situation is or is not consistent with truth. Alone, however, it cannot fulfill its office. Thus when Conscience is ordered to be reconciled with Meed (" 'Kisse hire,' quaþ þe king"), he refuses to act without the counsel of Reason (A.4.1–5). A great deal of scholarly interest has focused on Conscience (e.g., Carruthers 1970a; Martin 122–29), much less on Reason (see Alford 1988a). But the two are a pair. Their relation reflects the Scholastics' understanding of Rom. 2:14–15, the same passage alluded to earlier by Holy Church. Reason, "the law written upon the heart," furnishes the self-evident precepts of natural law (such as "truth is to be kept") which Conscience, "bearing witness," effectuates under the more particular circumstances of positive law (Baldwin 21–23; Potts 700–04). Because it deals in first principles, Reason is said to be infallible; because it must apply those principles in doubtful cases, Conscience is always liable to err. It is Conscience's vulnerability, especially to guile and hypocrisy, that makes it the chief target of the enemies of truth (e.g., 3.19, 3.42, 19.344-50, 20.294-386).

Summoned by the king to rule on the dispute between Conscience and Meed, Reason arrives at court just in time to deal with a separate though related matter (4.47-103). Wrong has been arrested for violating Peace, that is, "the king's peace" (Baldwin 43), and Meed has offered "a present" to satisfy justice. Friends of the defendant ask Reason "to haue ruþe on þat shrewe." Reason's answer is swift and unequivocal: before mercy there must be truth in every estate, for *Nullum malum inpunitum et nullum bonum irremuneratum*, "No evil shall go unpunished and no good unrewarded" (4.113-48). Clearly Reason personifies both a function and a principle. He embraces not only the moral faculty of natural reason (often called *synderesis* by the Scholastics [Schmidt 1969, 142-43], "kynde wit" by Langland [Prol. 121, 4.158]) but also the idea, contained in the Latin word *ratio*, of "a reckoning or account" and by extension "rule, order, justice." (Hence, the numerous puns on his name: Reason will "acounte" with Conscience [4.11] and "rekene" with Meed [4.177].) There is, then, a certain tautology in Reason's judgment of Wrong and Meed: that which signifies order (including *mesure*) must, by definition, be opposed to that which is without order and *mesurelees*.

Persuaded finally that Meed "muche truþe letteþ," the king turns her over to Reason for sentencing. Then he proposes that the three of them — Reason as his Chancellor and Conscience as his Justice (C.4.183-86) — rule his kingdom together. (On reason and conscience as key concepts in the history of English jurisprudence, see Baldwin 40-42; Alford 1977a, 942-43.) Here the first vision ends.

THE PILGRIMAGE TO TRUTH

If the previous three passus dramatized the protasis of Holy Church's theme ("When all treasures are tried"), then the next three passus will dramatize its apodosis ("truth is best"). Again the setting is the "fair field full of folk" and again the emphasis is on truth as a class virtue. In what is often described as a *sermo ad status* (p. 162), Reason (Conscience in the A version) admonishes the folk to observe the obligations of their estate: the commons to work and "wynne here sustinaunce / Thorw som trewe trauail . . ." (C.5.126-27); the clergy to practice what they preach; and those who rule and maintain the law, to "lat truþe be [their] coueitise / More þan gold ouþer giftes." As earlier, in the same message before the court, Reason personifies the concept of *ratio* or order, here manifested in the principle of social hierarchy (see Barney 285; Murtaugh 89-90). After addressing the different classes in turn, Reason summarizes his advice in a general exhortation to all. In stead of relying on pilgrimages to "Seynt Iames and Seyntes at Rome," he concludes, "Sekeþ Seynt Truþe, for he may saue yow alle" (5.57).

Reason's sermon stirs the folk to repentance (5.60 ff.). Their offenses against truth are particularized in the confessions of the seven deadly sins (see pp. 144–45 below on Langland's satirical handling of the episode, and Griffiths 47–63). In several respects the scene is a replay of the trial just concluded. The theme of mensurative justice stressed by Reason and Conscience in the king's court is here repeated in the "tribunal of penance" (see *The Catholic Encyclopedia*, "Penance," 11:619). There can be no pardon without "satisfaction." To Coveitise, Repentance says, "*Non dimittitur peccatum donec restituatur ablatum*," (5.273a), that is, "The sin is not forgiven until the thing taken is restored," and to Robert the Robber, "*Reddite*" (5.461), that is, "Pay what you owe" (Luke 7:42, Rom. 13:7). In God's court, no less than in the ideal king's, justice is an inviolable principle.

Having repented that they ever angered God "in word, þouȝt or dedes," a thousand persons undertake to lead reformed lives or, as the allegory of pilgrimage expresses the idea, "to go to truþe" (5.512). But without any sense of direction they "[bluster] forþ as beestes." They need guidance. They get it not from a palmer — who with his many souvenirs ("signes") from Sinai, Bethlehem, and other holy places represents the superficial and, one infers, usual understanding of pilgrimage — but from a lowly plowman named Piers. He is the very incarnation of the virtue they seek. "I do," he says, "what truþe hoteþ." (On the symbolism of plowmen and plowing, see Barney; Aers 1975, 109–25; Bowers 121–28.) From Piers the folk learn that the chief landmarks on the highway to Truth are the Ten Commandments. He directs them to wade the ford of "Honor thy father and mother," to pass by the enclosed field of "Thou shalt not covet," and so forth, until they come to Truth's castle. There, he says, recalling Holy Church's own words, "Thow shalt see in þiselue truþe sitte in þyn herte / In a cheyne of charite" (5.606–07). Put quite simply, the way to Truth consists of truth itself. Virtue is not something external. Just as one acquires kindness by being kind, or patience by being patient, so one comes to truth by being true.

This is a difficult way indeed! "[F]or drede of mysturnynge" the folk are hesitant to proceed without a guide. Piers offers to lead them if they will help him plow his half-acre, which lies "by þe heiȝe weye," the "alta via ad *fidelitatem*" (C rubrics; cf. B.12.37). Soon we see "alle manere of men" laboring according to their estate under the direction of Piers — laborers plow; women sew and make cloth; a knight helps to keep order. Obviously the scene corrects the opening vision of the field full of folk and plays out the definition of truth implicit in Reason's sermon. "To go to truþe" is to serve God through obedience. For years, however, it was generally assumed that the work on Piers's half-acre *interrupted* the pilgrimage to Truth (e.g., Dunning 1980, 112; Donaldson 164–68; Bloomfield 113). John Burrow opened up a new direction in *Piers* criticism by arguing that the plowing on the half-acre is "substituted" for the pilgrimage to Truth (1965). For example, Piers calls himself "a pilgrim at plow," apparels himself "in pilgrimes wyse" by putting on "his clothes of alle kyn craftes" and hangs "his hopur on his hales in stede of a scryppe" (C.8.56–60). Burrow concludes: "I hold, then, that Piers and his faithful followers — 'alkyn crafty men that konne lyven in treuthe' — are on the highway to Truth, 'non pedibus, sed moribus' [not with their feet but with their conduct (Augustine)], when they stay at home labouring in their vocations and helping their neighbours, since this is the way of truth which Truth himself taught" (219).

The ideal cannot be maintained for long. However sincere the folk's resolve to live in truth following their confession, the scene on the half-acre begins more and more to resemble that of the Prologue. Some of the workers malinger. Others help to plow with a mere "how trolly lolly!" When Piers sees that neither his threats nor those of the knight has any effect, he calls in Hunger: " 'Awreke me of wastours,' quod he, 'þat þis world shendeþ!' " (6.173). (On hunger as a recurring theme, see Mann; Spearing.) Several critics have interpreted Piers's inability to enforce truth in others as a sign of his own inadequacy (e.g., Kirk 74–75; Carruthers 1973, 73–77). Yet it is possible to read the episode as a comment not on the ideal of perfect obedience but on the nature of those who fail, for a variety of reasons, to live up to it. At any rate the efforts of the folk have not been totally without merit. As Burrow points out, "Truth's pardon is the object of the pilgrimage to Truth; so the granting of it can only mean that the object of the pilgrimage has been attained" (1965, 257; but see the demurrer by Aers 1975, 121).

"Treuþe herde telle" of the activity on the half-acre and granted a "pardon" to "alle þat holpen to erye [plow] or to sowe, / Or any maner mestier [occupation] þat myȝte Piers helpe" (7.1–8). The pardon presumes a feudal division of labor. How faithfully each person has observed the duties of his estate determines the length of time spent in purgatory. A priest, who is a self-proclaimed expert in such matters, asks to see the pardon. Piers unfolds it, and looking over their shoulders the dreamer reads:

Et qui bona egerunt ibunt in vitam eternam;
Qui vero mala in ignem eternum.

(7.113–14)

The lines come from the Athanasian Creed ("And those who do well will go into eternal life; those who do evil, into eternal fire"). This has been the insistent theme of the poem so far, emblemized by the two castles of the Prologue, stated explicitly by Holy Church, reiterated by Reason, and now confirmed by Truth himself. The action has reached its logical conclusion —

only to give way to a very puzzling incident. "Peter!" the priest exclaims, "I can find no pardon here!" He has seen pardons before, and none of them looked like this. "For pure tene" [anger], Piers rips the document in half and vows to leave off sowing in favor of Christ's injunction that we be "no3t bisy aboute þe bely ioye; / *Ne soliciti sitis*" (7.119 ff.). A bitter exchange between Piers and the priest wakes up the dreamer, who ponders the meaning of their words and the trustworthiness of dreams. Here the *Visio* ends.

The pardon scene represents the most notorious crux in the entire poem. (For a quick survey of the major critical responses, see Coghill 1944; Frank; Burrow 1965; Woolf; Carruthers 1970; Adams 1983; Allen). Scholarship has focused primarily on three questions. Is the pardon valid? Does its preoccupation with works deny the importance of grace in salvation? What is the significance of Piers's tearing of the pardon?

Is the pardon valid? The question was first raised in this form by Nevill Coghill (1944, 51). Behind it lies another, more critical question: What exactly is being pardoned? Coghill assumed that its object was the forgiveness of sin. It represented "of course" the pardon purchased on Calvary (1933, 64; 1944, 52; thus also Robertson and Huppé 93; Woolf 69). As Dunning pointed out in 1937, however, the form of the pardon as described by Langland is that of an indulgence, the normal object of pilgrimages in the Middle Ages. Indulgences do not offer but rather *presuppose* the forgiveness of sin. As *The Catholic Encyclopedia* explains:

> In the Sacrament of Penance the guilt of sin is removed, and with it the eternal punishment due to mortal sin; but there still remains the temporal punishment required by Divine justice, and this requirement must be fulfilled either in the present life or in the world to come, i.e., in Purgatory. An indulgence offers the penitent sinner the means of discharging this debt during his life on earth. ("Indulgence," 7:783)

The gist of the paragraph above was conveyed in medieval indulgences (and in Truth's pardon) by the often misunderstood formula *a culpa et a poena*, "from the guilt and from the punishment." What an indulgence offered was consequent upon the forgiveness of sin already obtained in the sacrament of confession. Langland's view was entirely orthodox. "In the first place, the folk have already been to confession; and in the second place, the pardon purchased by Truth is explicitly mentioned as referring to *Purgatory* and *not* Hell" (Dunning 1980, 120). Dunning's analysis is surely correct. Failure to respect the literal meaning of Truth's "pardon" can only result in a misinterpretation of the scene. Carefully surrounding the pardon with all the attributes of a medieval indulgence, Langland steadily directs the action toward its shocking climax, the unfolding of the document itself. What appears — "two lynes" from the Athanasian Creed — is not at all what the pilgrims or the priest who offers to "construe ech clause" or the readers of the poem were led to expect. And that is the whole point. Do well *instead of* seeking indulgences (Burrow 1965), for "the only real pardon is Dowel" (McLeod 23). If the question about the pardon's validity is understood in these terms, then Langland offers an explicit answer:

> Now haþ þe pope power pardon to graunte . . .
> Ac to truste on þise triennals, trewely, me þynkeþ
> It is noȝt so siker for þe soule, certes, as is dowel.
> (7.179–86)

The pardon's emphasis on "doing well" leads to the next question, the role of works in the scheme of salvation. According to Coleman, "The pardon is not an acceptance to salvation but a sign that good works have released Piers and his heirs from worldly penance as preparation to receive God's grace" (102). The relation between works and grace is further explored by Adams (1983), who characterizes Langland's position on the matter, thoroughly orthodox for the period, as "semi-Pelagian" (see also pp. 96 ff. below) Justification from sin requires not only sanctifying grace but also the observance of the moral law. "In reality, the latter requirement precedes and, humanly speaking, causes the former since God has covenanted to reward with grace those who do their very best" (375). The doctrine expresses itself again and again as a regular pattern in the poem. Holy Church instructs the dreamer that truth "is þe lok of loue þat leteþ out my grace" (1.202); Reason insists that not until all classes observe truth will he show mercy (4.113 ff.); and even the pagan emperor Trajan is said to have obtained, by means of his "pure truþe," the gift of grace and salvation (11.140 ff.).

An understanding of the questions treated above provides the necessary basis for attempting an answer to the third, "What is the significance of Piers's tearing of the pardon?" (A.8.101, B.7.119, C omitted). Most emphatically he does not tear a version of the pardon purchased on Calvary, and he does not repudiate the need to "do well" (which, after all, is the main argument of the poem). Most recent explanations of this puzzling incident descend from Robert Frank's analysis (23–33). He sees the problem as a "clash between form and content":

> [F]or this pardon contains a message which is by implication an attack on pardons. . . . In accepting its message, Piers is rejecting bulls with seals. In tearing the parchment, Piers is symbolically tearing paper pardons from Rome. . . . The act, then, because of the special character of the pardon, was intended as a sign that Piers had rejected indulgences and accepted the command to do well. Unfortunately, it was a very confusing sign. (28)

Although Burrow adopts Frank's solution, he moderates the view that "Piers had rejected indulgences": "It cannot be said of pardons, as of pilgrimages, that Langland simply did not believe in them. . . . Langland's fear, as so often, is that the external form or institution — even though it is acceptable in itself — may come to usurp the place of the inner spiritual reality" (1965, 260). In tearing the pardon, Burrow suggests, Piers "demonstrates against" the form.

A number of critics have expressed the distinction between "the external form" and "the inner spiritual reality" in terms of the Old and the New Law. For example, Murtaugh says: "So the pardon scene presents to us the Old Testament 'figure' and its fulfillment, the decalogue of Moses and the Redemption, superimposed one upon the other" (101). The key word is *ful-fillment*. The tearing must not be construed as a criticism of the Old Law. Christ himself insisted, "I am not come to destroy [the law], but to fulfil" (Matt. 5:17). To the common misconception that the Old Law was invalidated by the New, Ruth Ames's book is a useful corrective (esp. pp. 186–92). As she notes, "The law has been fulfilled by Christ . . ., [but] the road to heaven is still through the commandments, through the faith and morality of Abraham and Moses" (192; cf. Carruthers 1982, 180). According to medieval exegetes, the transition from the Old Law to the New Law was prefigured in Moses's breaking of the tablets in Exodus 32. Several scholars (e.g., Coghill 1944; Meroney; Carruthers 1970b) have argued that the patriarch's action lies behind Piers's tearing of the pardon. In both cases the impetus is righteous anger, and in both cases the form of a written document is destroyed without its content's being rejected.

The "real crux" of the pardon scene, Burrow suggests in a second article (1969), is not the tearing at all (cf. McLeod) but rather Piers's resolve to substitute the life of *ne soliciti sitis* for that of plowing: "Of preieres and of penaunce my plouȝ shal ben herafter" (7.124). "A real change has occurred," he says, "not in Piers's attitude to his occupation, but in Langland's attitude to his image" (120). The poet became dissatisfied with the attempt to explain the good life dramatically and decided to address the issue more directly. At the same time, this final substitution in the *Visio*, though not a rejection of the hard labor idealized on the half-acre, implies at least the possibility of a deeper, more inward expression of truth. From the emphasis on truth in the first two dreams as a social obligation, manifested primarily in obedience and good works, Langland descends in the next to an examination of its source in the heart. No longer is the dreamer a spectator who looks over the shoulders of others; "Will" is now the center of the action.

THE INWARD JOURNEY

The dreamer's next vision, the third, marks the beginning of what is traditionally called the *Vita*. Society's pilgrimage to Truth is recast as the individual soul's quest for Dowel. This substitution, like the earlier ones, represents an attempt to delve more deeply into the meaning of truth. But in addition it changes the method. Langland's earlier treatment was "dramatic and pictorial"; now it becomes "abstract and ratiocinative" (Burrow 1969, 118)—a quality that largely explains the diminished appeal of these passus for many readers. Yet this development is faithful to the plan laid out, more or less, in Holy Church's speech. After defining truth, she teaches that it can be apprehended through "kynde knowyng." This unmediated knowledge, achieved simply by consulting one's own faculties, is now Langland's subject (see Frank 65 ff.; Burrow 1969, 121). The vision reflects "the movement of the mind into itself" (Bloomfield 64) or, to quote from the most elaborate study of its psychology, "the inward journey" (Wittig). Over the next several passus, "Will" (as the dreamer is called for the first time at 8.129) will meet a succession of figures intended to personify different aspects of the mental process.

The vision begins as if it were a reprise of the Prologue (and in fact the passus has been referred to often as the "Prologue to the Life of Do Well"): "Thus, yrobed in russet, I romed aboute / Al a somer seson for to seke dowel . . ." (on the image of the poet as a wandering hermit, see Godden; Bowers 97–104). The narrator's encounter with two learned friars offers a preview of things to come in showing Will's "wilfulness" (11.373–441, 12.97–98, 155 ff., 13.65–89, 106–11), his penchant for scholastic modes of argument (8.20–25, 10.349–50, 12.280–82; see Bloomfield 161–69; Schmidt 1969), and his slow-wittedness (8.57–58 [cf. 1.138– 39], 10.5–8, 10.377–78). When he leaves the friars, he still believes that he lacks "kynde knowing" and dedicates himself to "go lerne bettre."

The first step in the learning process is represented by Thought. His place in the narrative is parallel with that of Holy Church. Both are guide-figures (one external, the other internal) standing at the head of a sequence; both engage in very similar dialogues with the dreamer (cf. 1.71–78, 8.70–75); both provide the conceptual framework for what follows (Holy Church furnishes the general analysis of truth, and Thought divides it into the lives of Dowel, Dobet, and Dobest). The three lives will be a recurring motif in vision three (9.1–16, 97 ff., 199–210; 10.132–39, 192–93, 236–76, 335–40; 11.46–51, 408–16; 12.25–37) and even beyond (13.103–71, 14.16–22, 19.102–98).

Trying to define these "þre faire vertues" was once the preoccupation of *Piers* scholarship (see Introduction). However, earlier attempts to equate the three, respectively, with the active, contemplative, and mixed lives (Wells 1929; Coghill 1933; cf. Dunning 1956) or with the purgative, illuminative, and unitive ways of mysticism (Mcroney; cf. Donaldson 158, 196) are now generally regarded as reductive. Frank's criticism marked a turning point (34–44). He argued that Langland did not give any of the terms a fixed meaning but treated them instead as divisions of the generic term Dowel: "By Dowel, Dobet, and Dobest the third he meant . . . do well, do better, do best — nothing more" (44). About the same time Hussey reached a similar conclusion: "Once the idea of Dowel is clear, Dobet and Dobest follow naturally, not as different 'lives' or 'states' but as degrees of the same thing" (1956, 256; cf. Middleton 1972, 171). In short, Langland seems to have used the triad primarily as a rhetorical scheme for amplification. Such schemes are commonplace in medieval literature (see p. 160 below for the practice of dividing the theme of a sermon). We have not found an exact precedent for dividing truth in this way, but the author of the penitential treatise *The Book of Vices and Virtues* divides *untruth* into evil, worse, and worst (EETS 217 [1942], 13).

Will's desire to obtain "more kynde knowynge" of Dowel (8.113) takes him from Thought to other, more specialized personifications of the intellectual life. The sequence represents that of the learning process: Wit (native intelligence) joined with Study (*studium*, application) leads to Clergy (learning) which resides with Scripture (books, writing), and all of these together contribute to Imaginatif (prudential judgment).

The further Will proceeds, however, the more confused he becomes. The promise of *qui bona egerunt*, "do well and be saved," is not so simple as it looked at first. Thinking more deeply on it leads to hard questions about predestination, the salvation of the righteous heathen, and so forth. Eventually lost in the mind's labyrinth, Will seems to give up the quest. Neither learning nor Dowel appears to be crucial to salvation. For who "wrouȝte" [wrote] better than Solomon and Aristotle? And yet "al holy chirche holden hem in helle!" (A.11.271). Or who did worse than Mary Magadalen (a whore), or David (who killed Uriah), or Paul (who persecuted the early Christians)? Yet despite their wickedness they are in heaven! Feeling betrayed by his own intellect, the dreamer retreats into simple piety (A.11.302–13). Shortly after this, the A text ends abruptly (see pp. 189–89 below).

Most scholars agree that the first version of *Piers Plowman* remained unfinished. The poet had reached an impasse. He could not, Donaldson suggests, "solve the riddles posed by predestinarianism and the dogma concerning the damnation of the righteous heathen" (172; cf. Chambers 130–31; Kirk 114–20). The B continuation, Frank notes (58), offers an "ingenious and satisfying" solution, the dream-within-a-dream. It suspends the main action (see Wittig 231–48), allowing the dreamer (and the poet) to step back and analyze what has gone wrong. It anticipates a similar device seen frequently in Renaissance drama, the play-within-a-play. In both *Piers Plowman* and *Hamlet* (to cite only the most familiar example), the internal fiction forces a character to confront his own moral imperfection and by this means activates his sense of guilt; the end in the case of Claudius is "to catch the conscience of a king," in the case of the dreamer to *shame* the will into reform. The dreamer's failure to admit his own condition is the heart of the problem. Up to this point he has conducted the search for Dowel as if it could be known without being lived. The inward journey has been marked repeatedly by conflict between the intellect and the will, by the dreamer's refusal to accept what his reason was telling him. In the mirror of the inner dream, Will sees with terrifying clarity his own perversity, beginning with his fall into concupiscence and ending with his absurd rebuke of Reason itself. The inner dream dissolves in embarrassment: "Tho cauȝte I colour anoon and comsed to ben ashamed / And awaked þerwiþ" (11.405–6). There follows a brief lecture by Imaginatif on shame as the last remedy of a sinful soul; like a drunk in the ditch, the wayward will is not moved by the advice of learning or the chiding of reason but only by necessity ("lest he sterue") and shame. The chastened dreamer agrees: "Ther smyt no þyng so smerte, ne smelleþ so foule / As shame" (11.436–37).

The inner dream, beginning in fear (11.115) and ending in shame, strikes the affective half of the soul, an essential partner in the intellect's search for Dowel. As Wittig has shown in great detail, the entire inward journey is a progress toward the right ordering of both *intellectus* and *affectus* in relation to God. True knowledge can come only when the will is properly disposed. Once the dreamer confronts his own condition—his concupiscence, his wilfulness, his mortality and possible damnation—he is better prepared, through humility, to know the meaning of Dowel. The answers that eluded him earlier are now revealed (at least to the satisfaction of fictional, if not theological, requirements). A few of the problems, most notably the salvation of the heathen (see Adams 1983; Whatley; and pp. 99–100 below), are resolved in the inner dream itself, but most are left for the speech by Imaginatif in the next passus.

Imaginatif is the most important of Will's intellectual guides. He explains the place of learning in the life of Dowel, analyzes the dreamer's progress thus far, and brings to a close the action of the third vision. Exactly what this figure represents, therefore, is a major concern. Why did Langland assign to this relatively unimportant faculty in scholastic psychology, the *vis imaginativa* (Bloomfield 172), such a crucial role in the dreamer's education? As Wittig points out, "The figure who argues, reasons, preaches, and quotes Scripture scarcely operates as if he were a mere combiner of sense impressions" (265).

The meaning of Imaginatif lies partly in the external evidence (see Bloom-field 170–74; Harwood; Minnis; Kaulbach) and partly in Langland's text. First, if the dreamer's main problem has been his failure to commit both *intellectus* and *affectus* to the pursuit of Dowel, as Wittig argues, then Imaginatif as the mediator between the rational and sensitive aspects of the soul must be essential to the solution. Arguing from the adjectival ending of the name (though see Kaulbach 20–21), Wittig prefers to describe Imaginatif as an *activity*, the activity of "representing vividly to oneself" that brings the dreamer at last to self-recognition (270–73). But Imaginatif permits Will to "imagine" in another way as well, to extrapolate from his memory of past experience what consequences his present course of behavior will have for the future. In this capacity Imaginatif represents the exercise of prudence (a virtue to which medieval iconography gave three eyes, one in the back of the head and two in the front, to signify the union of memory and foresight). Thus Imaginatif introduces himself to Will: "I haue folwed þee, in feiþ, þise fyue and fourty wynter, / And manye tymes have meued þee to mynne on þyn ende" (12.3–4); and this operation is associated explicitly with prudence in B.19.276–78:

> *Spiritus prudencie* þe firste seed highte [was called],
> And whoso ete þat ymagynen he sholde,
> Er he dide any dede deuyse wel þe ende.

In short, Imaginatif provides the larger perspective in which all the functions of Will's earlier advisers may be coordinated toward the proper, anticipated end. Finally, it should be stressed that Imaginatif is the faculty that makes possible Langland's whole enterprise. Bloomfield notes that "'imaginatif' in any medieval psychological system would be responsible for dreams" (172) — and, it might be added, not only dreams, which are the stuff of *Piers Plowman*, but the creation of all similitudes (Harwood) and thus of poetry in general. At the conclusion of the inward journey, then, the poet comes face to face, as it were, with his own genius. And the question raised by Imaginatif about his poetry (12.16–28) would haunt Langland, apparently, for the rest of his life: was it a help or a hindrance in his own *itinerarium* to truth? (Donaldson 136–55; Burrow 1969, 117–18; Middleton 1982b, 110–19; Bowers 191–218).

THE SEARCH FOR CHARITY

Shaken by his self-image in the inner vision, the dreamer commits himself affectively to the search for truth, and this movement from intellect to will "parallels Lady Holy Church's extension of 'kynde knowyng' into lov-

ing" (Murtaugh 29). The dreamer now understands, as he says to Imaginatif, "To se muche and suffre moore, certes, is dowel" (11.412). "To suffre,"
the context makes clear (11.376–424), means to endure patiently (cf. Latin
patior, "to suffer, experience, submit to"). This virtue he has now acquired.
His progress is expressed allegorically by the company he keeps: his guides
in the search for charity are Conscience and Patience.

Will's resolve "to se muche and suffre more" is severely tested when he
and Patience attend a dinner given by Conscience — the whole account a
masterful blending of allegory and social realism (Kirk 145–53). Their meal
consists of a sour loaf of "do penance," a drink of "long-endure," a dish of
"have mercy on me, O God," and other such fare. In contrast the learned
friar sitting at the high dais, who only a few days earlier at St. Paul's ex-
tolled the virtues of penance, is now gorging himself on "sondry metes, mor-
trews and puddynges, / Wombe cloutes and wilde brawen and egges yfryed
wiþ grece." (On Langland's food imagery see Spearing, Mann.) The dreamer
cannot contain his indignation. "What is Dowel?" he asks the glutton. "Is
it penance?" Conscience signals Patience to restrain Will and then, more
politely, puts the same question himself.

This richly ironic scene points up the difficulties of those persons who,
like Will, have undertaken to live the life of Dowel. They must do so
in a world whose hypocrisy constantly challenges their resolve and patience. The learned doctor, modeled after the scribes and pharisees who "love
the first places at feasts" (Matt. 23:1–7; cf. Luke 14:8–11), echoes the empty
formalism of the palmer who has never heard of Truth, and of the priest
who cannot recognize Truth's pardon, but worse than either he *knows* the
meaning of Truth and yet refuses to live it. In short his example confirms what the dreamer, "disputyng" with his own mental faculties in the
earlier vision, has already concluded: learning is no guarantee of a virtuous
life.

The point is not merely repeated, however; it serves as the basis for the
next step in Langland's argument. Asked the same question as the friar —
"What is Dowel?" — Clergy responds that Piers the Plowman has "set alle
sciences at a sop" except love only. Patience then takes up the theme (though
part of his speech is given in C to Piers himself, who suddenly materializes
for ten lines [C.15.138–48]). What love means to Patience is not only "love
God and neighbor" (13.127) but also, "Love thine enemies" (13.136–47),
a commandment that fits both his own name and, quite pointedly, the present
situation. Despite Langland's brilliant satire of the friar, the true focus of
the banquet scene is Will. He must learn charity through patience. The way
to love God is to love one's own soul "with words, works and will" (a recurring triad in the poem [Burrow 1969]); the way to love one's enemy is to
"cast coals on his head with kind speech and beat him with love" (13.142–47).

Love is a talisman against all harm. "Carry it with you," Patience says, paraphrasing Rom. 8:38–39, "and neither fire nor flood nor fear of thine enemy shall ever trouble you . . . for *pacientes vincunt* [the patient conquer]."

Although numerous aspects of patience are scattered throughout the first three visions, it is only here in the fourth that suddenly all come together in a single personification. Patience emerges as the chief guide to Dowel. He consolidates humility, long-suffering, penance, willing poverty, faith or "recklessness" (*ne soliciti sitis*), and imperturbable love. (For varying emphases on these aspects of Patience, see Donaldson 169–80; Frank, 70–76; Kaske 1963; Orsten; Godden). Coming on the heels of the intellectual search for Dowel (by means of Wit, Study, Clergy, Scripture, Imaginatif), Patience incorporates the elements of the affective search. There are two forms of knowledge — "to se muche and suffre more," that is, to know through reading and observation (12.64–135) and to know through direct experience. The relation between these two forms is allegorized as a rivalry between Clergy and Patience. Clergy offers to teach Conscience from any book of the old law "þe leeste point to knowe / That Pacience þe pilgrym parfitly knew neuere" (13.185–87). Conscience replies, "Me were leuere . . . / Haue pacience parfitliche þan half þi pak of bokes" (13.200–01).

The dinner party breaks up as Conscience takes leave of Clergy in order to accompany Patience, "to be tried and made perfect" (cf. James 1:3–4). His parting does not signal a rejection of learning, whose counsel remains necessary (13.202–05), but rather a new stage in the dreamer's moral awareness.

This stage is objectified in the next episode. On the road to Dowel, the three pilgrims Patience, Conscience, and Will encounter one of the poet's most colorful and moving creations, Haukyn the Active Man. (On his name and occupations — "minstrel" and "waferer" — see Godden 138–42). Unlike the hypocritical friar he seems "true" in both words and works. Indeed, at first sight, he seems to be the perfect embodiment of the ideal sought but not attained on Piers's half-acre (a connection explored by numerous critics, most notably Maguire, Spearing 1960). He hates "all idleness" and works hard to provide food for beggars, friars, the pope and "alle trewe trauaillours and tiliers of þe erþe." "Haukyn takes the reader right back to *Passus* 6," as Wittig observes, "[b]ut this time the active everyman is seen from the inside" (64). Upon closer inspection Will and Conscience notice that Haukyn's "cote of cristendom" is stained with all the deadly sins (see Alford 1974). Haukyn is "inobedient," "singuler by hymself," and "yhabited as an heremyte, an ordre by hymselue" — in many ways the alter ego of the dreamer himself (see Robertson and Huppé 168; Bloomfield 27; Carruthers 1973, 122). He has tried to do well. Yet within an hour after leaving confession he habitually soils his coat again "þoruȝ werk or þoruȝ word or wille of myn herte" (14.14). "What Haukyn with his spotted garment illustrates," Frank explains, "is the fact that active life, living in this world with its many demands, especially those of the body, inevitably involves man in sin" (76). Thus Haukyn represents Langland's definitive answer to one of the central questions raised by the *Visio*: "Can it, after all, be argued that this form of life, with its patient performance of hard work, and its faithful fulfilment of obligations, is sufficient for salvation?" (Maguire 102).

It cannot. But this is not to say that this form of life is unnecessary or without merit. On the contrary, this facsimile of truth lacks only the right *will* that would make it truth indeed. The parallels with the pardon scene are suggestive. Godden observes, "The two contrasting roles played by Piers in the Pardon scene [that is, before and after the tearing] are here manifested in Haukyn and Patience, worker and pilgrim-hermit . . ." (149-50). In both cases, a preoccupation with hard work gives way to *ne soliciti sitis* (7.121-35, 14.29-46). The shift signifies not a repudiation but a qualification. Against the earlier view that Langland was rejecting the active for the contemplative life (e.g., Chambers 154; Donaldson 176), Frank sees the formula *ne soliciti sitis* as a call to patient poverty, a phrase actually associated during the Middle Ages with the *idealization* of labor (75-77). To work without solicitude is to transform a mundane activity into a constant and perpetual testimony of one's faith in God. Physical labor feeds the body; "leel bileve," the soul (14.29-33). Quoting Matt. 4:4, "Not in bread alone doth man live" (which repeats the "message of the Pardon" [Dunning 1969, 213]), Patience offers Haukyn spiritual food. As in the pardon, so here Langland tries to concentrate all the meaning of a central truth in one quotation; and as before, the dreamer looks intently to catch a glimpse of what it is:

> But I listnede and lokede what liflode it was
> That pacience so preisede, and of his poke hente
> A pece of þe Paternoster and profrede vs alle;
> And þanne was it *fiat voluntas tua* sholde fynde [sustain] vs alle.
> (14.47-50)

Fiat voluntas tua, "thy will be done." To cast oneself wholly on the will of God is the essence of patience, the ground of charity, the way to truth. Patience links all of these explicitly (14.98-101). The vision concludes with a long encomium on patient poverty, Haukyn sobs for his "unworthiness" (a conventional sign of true contrition [cf. 19.377, 20.369]), and "þerwiþ I awakede."

Assuming the authenticity of the colophons Dowel, Dobet, and Dobest (see p. 30 above), many critics have been led to declare the search for Dowel concluded at this point. However, the greater part of Langland's teaching on the proper disposition of the will, without which it is impossible to do

well, yet lies ahead. Having learned patience — "the ground in which charity grows" (Donaldson 179) — the dreamer is now prepared for Love's epiphany
in the next vision. His guide is Anima (Soul) or, as the C text renames him
(maybe in order to stress even more the affective component of Dowel),
Liberum-arbitrium, that is, free will (see Donaldson 180–96; Schmidt 1969).
In the dreamer's exchanges with this figure the progressive definition of
Dowel in terms of "words, works, and will" is re-enacted. First, Anima rebukes him for his prideful desire to know "alle þe sciences vnder sonne"
(15.50–79, C.16.211–37), then stresses the importance of turning knowledge
into deeds (15.80–148, C.16.238–83), and concludes with a discourse on
the *sine qua non* of Dowel, a charitable will (15.149–613, C.16.284–17.322).

Scholarly attention has centered less on Anima's long discursive treatment
of love, however, than on the emblematic tree of charity (16.1–89,
C.18.1–123). Anima's pictorial rendering is like countless other tree-diagrams
of the period. The name of the tree is patience, the root is mercy, the trunk
is pity, the leaves are "lele wordes," the blossoms are obedient speech and
kind "lokynge," and the fruit is charity. Will is not satisfied. He wants to
see the tree, to *taste* its fruit: "I wolde trauaille . . . þis tree to se twenty hundred
myle, / And to haue my fulle of þat fruyt forsake al oþer saulee" [food]. Anima explains that the tree of charity grows in his own heart, tended by *liberum arbitrium*, who holds the land "to ferme" (that is, in lease) from Piers
the Plowman.

At the mention of Piers's name, the dreamer "al for pure Ioye" swoons
into a deeper "louedreem," in which Piers himself shows Will the actual tree.
The "idiom" has changed (Salter 74). The second dream-within-a-dream
functions to some extent as an answer or alternative to the first. It replaces
the earlier image of cupidity and the dreamer's old self with one of charity
and the self he can become. Its complexity, however, seems deliberately to
resist analysis. The tree has three props, that is, the three persons of the
Trinity, and bears three fruits — marriage, widowhood, and virginity (see
Tavormina). These schemes are not only correlated ("The sone . . .
resembleþ wel þe widewe," etc.) but have outside referents as well; the Holy
Ghost is related to *liberum arbitrium*, to the virgins at the top of the tree, to
"monkes and monyals," to the contemplative life, and so forth (C.18.53–100).
The allegory is charged with such a multitude of overlapping schemes, "a
pluralizing of the tree image" (Donaldson 188), that many readers have com-
plained of being unable to see the tree for the forest. (There is a convenient
summary of critical responses in Aers 1975, 79–109; see also Griffiths 82–91.)
Did Langland, in his attempt to convey something of the mystery and in-
finite interaffiliations of love, lose control of his material? Peter Dronke puts
the question in a historical context. After surveying the theme of *arbor caritatis* in medieval literature — typically characterized by the interplay of al-

legory and symbol, concept and image, the abstract and the dramatic—
Dronke concludes that its "disordered scenery" is an essential part of its purpose: "What we have in Langland . . . is less a toleration of inconsistencies
than a number of instinctive contraventions of the norms of allegoresis, in
order to achieve a richness not fully explicable, a whole that is greater than
the sum of its parts" (213). The image's unpredictable, sometimes bizarre
transformations yield some of the poet's "most profound" effects.

Certainly the abrupt transition from Piers's "gardyn" to the Virgin's
"chambre" surprises us—as if the two events were not mere cause and effect
but somehow part of the same moment, mysteriously shared, one contained
in the other. Poetically the metamorphosis is of a kind with Langland's earlier
substitutions, and its catalyst, like the tearing of the pardon, is an act of
violence. Chasing the devil, who has just stolen the "apples" Adam, Abraham and John the Baptist, Piers strikes at him "for pure tene" with one of
the props of the Trinity (the Son) in order to recover the fruit, and with
this angry gesture the whole agitated scene suddenly collapses into the sereni-
ty of the Annunciation. The allegorical explanation of the Redemption thus
gives way to the literal story in the gospels. The inner dream concludes with
a swift-paced account of Christ's passion and crucifixion ("On cros vpon Calu-
arie crist took þe bataille / Ayeins deeþ and þe deuel") and Will wakes up
into the outer framing vision.

Like the first dream-within-a-dream, Will's *louedreem* suspends the action
of the main narrative. Before swooning, his last words are "Piers þe Plowman!" and upon recovering they are his first thought. The intervening action does not really "happen." He still has not *seen* or *tasted* the fruit of the
tree for which he would travel, as he told Anima, "twenty hundred myle."
He has not witnessed as actual events the Crucifixion or the defeat of the
devil. He has not come face to face with his ideal, Piers. All this lies ahead—
as if Will's second inner dream, like the first, were a prophecy, a mirror
of himself *in potentia*, a privileged foretaste of the outcome of his present
course.

After further instruction by Faith (Abraham), Hope (Moses), and the standard exemplar of charity, the Good Samaritan—instruction that centers on
the tree of charity's enigmatic synthesizing of love and the Trinity (Frank
88–92)—the dreamer is ready for his sixth vision, the perfection of Dowel
in Christ. It is, by general agreement, the finest expression of Langland's art.

THE PERFECTION OF DOWEL

Because the next vision describes a literal reality, it is easy to lose sight
of the allegorical matrix. However, the vision is an integral part—the

culmination — of Will's search for truth. Langland presents Christ's passion not only as a historical but also as a psychological event. The dreamer, who learned long ago "to se muche and suffre moore," participates in the action. He is one of the crowd at Christ's triumphal entry into Jerusalem, he recoils in fear at the sight of the Crucifixion, he descends into limbo to await Christ's coming there. Only now, after his long peregrination from pride through shame and penance to the desire for charity, is the dreamer prepared for this experience. In a sense his vision of the Redemption arises out of and partly reflects his own spiritual state.

The narrator falls asleep during Lent and then, his waking time projected into his dream, finds himself in Jerusalem on Palm Sunday. (For a commentary on the view that such references to the liturgical year constitute a structural principle in the poem, see Adams 1976). There he witnesses the triumphal entry. Jesus is depicted as a knight on his way to joust with the devil for "Piers fruyt." He looks a bit like the Good Samaritan, traditionally a type of the Savior (Ames 180–84), and "somdeel" like Piers himself. As Faith explains, "This Iesus of his gentries wol Iuste in Piers armes, / In his helm and in his haubergeon, *humana natura* (18.22–23). When the dreamer sees the knight again, "peynted al blody" after the battle of the cross, Jesus and Piers seem to have merged completely: "Is þis Iesus þe Iustere . . . Or it is Piers þe Plowman?" (19.4–14).

Here the image of the Christ Knight, conventional in Middle English (Gaffney; Waldron), is charged with the accumulated meaning and mystery of Langland's own creation, Piers. All the previous references to Piers may be seen in retrospect as leading steadily toward the dreamer's vision of the Incarnation. They are listed below. (The A version is omitted, since Piers is mentioned only once, at 12.102, after the pilgrimage to Truth; in the bracketed references to the C version, Piers has been replaced by *Liberum Arbitrium*).

Context	*B*	*C*
THE PILGRIMAGE TO TRUTH	5.537–7.206	7.182–9.353
Patience appears "Ilyk Peres"		15.34
Clergie on Piers and love	13.124–33	15.129–37
PIERS ON PATIENCE AND LOVE		15.138–48
Activa Vita as Piers's apprentice		15.195
Paternoster said for Piers	13.237	15.213
Piers perceives the will	15.196–212	16.337
PIERS AND THE TREE OF CHARITY	16.18–89	[18.1–123]
Jesus to recover "Piers fruyt"	16.90–96	
Piers teaches Jesus "lechecraft"	16.103–10	[18.138–45]
Will searches for Piers	16.167–71	[18.179–81]
Christ looks "somdeel" like Piers	18.10	20.8

Christ in "Piers armes"	18.18–26	20.17–25
Christ to fetch "Piers fruyt"	18.33	20.32
Piers/Christ "peynted al blody"	19.4–14	21.4–14
PIERS AS VICAR OF CHRIST	19.182–481	21.182–481
Conscience prays in name of Piers	20.77	22.77
Piers's pardon "ypayed"	20.304–21	22.304–21
Conscience to seek Piers	20.380–85	20.380–85

That the figure of Piers steadily grows in significance is plain. Critics have interpreted in various ways the correlation between his development and the poem's unfolding drama of truth. (For several major approaches see Troyer; Coghill 1933; Raw; Aers 1975; Jennings.)

However, it is generally agreed that the evolving figure of Piers corresponds in some way to the dreamer's own progress. As Bloomfield says, "Just as Piers begins as a plowman and ends as the Christ-man, man may become through imitation of him like God" (149; cf. Mills 211 and passim). Behind this process, Bloomfield and others (e.g., Raw, Murtaugh, Goldsmith) see the doctrine of the *imago dei*, the image of God in man, first set forth by Holy Church (1.88–91) and invoked explicitly in the tree of charity episode (C.18.7). Raw explains the basic assumption as follows: "Man's perfection consists in his likeness to God. The more closely he resembles God, the more faithful he is to his own nature, for he was created in the image and likeness of God (*Genesis* i, 26)" (150). The pursuit of truth or Dowel can be described, then, as an attempt to realize the *imago dei* in ever purer form.

Because he embodies truth, as that virtue is deepened and elaborated over the course of the poem, Piers can be identified with both Christ on the one hand and the aspirations of the dreamer on the other. He symbolizes the perfect conformity of wills that unites God and man. As Anima advises the dreamer concerning charity:

> Therfore by colour ne by clergie knowe shaltow hym neuere,
> Neiþer þoruȝ wordes ne werkes, but þoruȝ wil oone,
> And þat knoweþ no clerk ne creature on erþe
> But Piers þe Plowman, *Petrus id est christus*.
>
> (15.209–12)

Although many critics have followed Skeat in assuming that "Here *Piers the Plowman* is completely identified with *Jesus Christ*" (see Donaldson 183), certain qualifications need to be made. Medieval exegetes used the formula *id est* to express all sorts of relation, including "is a figure of," and not equality only (Aers 1975, 86–88). Anima's words echo Holy Church's teaching on the *imago dei*, that truth in words, works, and will makes one "a god by þe gospel"—a god, as Aquinas explained, "by similitude, not by equality"

(Raw 167). To be *like* Piers is to be *like* Christ (Mills). Coghill's judgment remains sound: "Let us for the moment be cautious of any hasty identification of Christ with Piers. That they are in an important sense identified cannot be denied, but it would be truer to say of them that Jesus *lives* Piers (for Piers is a way of Life), than that Jesus *is* Piers or that Piers *is* Jesus" (1933, 67). Thus, Anima's advice that "wiþouten help of Piers Plowman" (15.196) the dreamer will never find charity is simply another way of saying that charity is the product of a certain "way of life"; it is, as the tree of charity episode makes even more explicit, the "fruit" of patience, humility, goodness (16.4–9); it is "Piers fruyt" (16.94, 18.33). Similarly, Anima's statement that Piers taught Jesus, "lered hym lechecraft his lif for to saue" (16.104), may be taken to mean not only that Jesus learned "from a creaturely perspective" (Aers 1975, 109; Murtaugh 117–22) but also that *what* he learned, a way of life, was allopathic medicine against sin and the onslaughts of the devil.

These associations are all gathered up in the image of Christ "in Piers armes." Christ's panoply symbolizes at once his vulnerable *humana natura* and his invincible truth—the truth of *fiat voluntas*, expressed in his prayer before the battle of the cross, "Nevertheless not as I will, but as thou wilt" (Matt. 26:39), and proclaimed after his victory by Paul, "Being made in the likeness of men and in habit found as a man, He humbled himself, becoming obedient unto death, even to the death of the cross" (Phil. 2:7–8).

Langland's account of the battle itself is relatively short (18.36–91). He is far more interested in the theological implications. How can God's mercy, so lavishly poured forth in the Crucifixion, be reconciled with his exacting justice? In many respects, it is the same question raised by the pardon scene, which promised an indulgence but delivered a judgment. Langland is now ready to confront the issue head-on. First he defines it explicitly in the debate among the four daughters of God, a conventional allegorization of Ps. 84:11, "Mercy and truth have met each other: justice and peace have kissed" (see below p. 129). The debate occurs both before and after the Harrowing of Hell. On the one hand Truth and Righteousness argue that to forgive mankind for the sin of Adam and Eve would go against law and against the word of God, who "gaf þe doom hymselue." On the other hand Peace (speaking for Mercy also) argues that "god hath forgyue and graunted to alle mankynde, / Mercy, my suster, and me to maynprisen [provide bail for] hem alle" (C.20.187–88). The debate rages. But the daughters can find no way to reconcile the principles they each represent.

In the middle of their argument, Christ arrives to claim his own—the fruit of the tree of charity stolen by the devil. The wily fiend tries to turn the tables by accusing Christ himself of robbery! Had God not said, "If Adam ete þe Appul alle sholde deye / And dwelle wiþ vs deueles"? (18.281–82).

The appeal is to law. In fact, the scene as a whole belongs to a popular literary type known as "the trial of Satan" and shows a scrupulous regard for the niceties of English legal procedure (see Birnes; Alford 1977a). Christ and the devil are portrayed as crafty lawyers locked in dispute over the question of "rights." Christ makes no attempt to overrule the law on which the devil bases his claim; instead he appeals to the principle of equity. Although the devil has enjoyed "seisin" for "seuene þousand wynter," his possession has not been "in good faith." That is, he acquired it through deceit.

> So leue it noȝt, lucifer, ayein þe lawe I fecche hem,
> But by right and by reson raunsone here my liges:
> *Non veni soluere legem set adimplere.*
> [I am not come to destroy but to fulfill the law.]
> Thow fettest myne in my place maugree alle resoun,
> Falsliche and felonliche; good feiþ me it tauȝte
> To recouere hem þoruȝ raunsoun and by no reson ellis,
> So þat þoruȝ gile þow gete þoruȝ grace it is ywonne.
>   (18.348–53)

The riddle of Truth's pardon is answered, and answered definitively. God's mercy is not incompatible with his justice. On the contrary, as Christ emphasizes several times, "I may do mercy *þoruȝ my rightwisnesse.*" For divine pardon is linked inextricably to a penitential system through which sinners can pay what they owe. Those "þat diden ille," Christ says, "shul be clensed clerliche and keuered of hir synnes / In my prisone Purgatorie til *parce* it hote" (18.390–92), that is, until mercy cries "Enough!"

> "Thus by lawe," quod oure lord, "lede I wole fro hennes
> Tho ledes þat I loue, and leued in my comynge."
>   (18.400–01)

With this conclusion, the four daughters are reconciled ("Clippe we in couenaunt, and ech of vs kisse ooþer"); Truth trumpets the joyful hymn *Te Deum laudamus*; the dreamer awakes to the sound of Easter bells and says to his family, "Ariseþ and reuerenceþ goddes resurexion, / And crepeþ to þe cros on knees and kisseþ it for a Iuwel" (18.427–28). Finally, it seems, the truth of Will's dream life has penetrated his waking life: "he is filled with the zeal of sudden understanding" (Bowers 154).

This is the climactic moment toward which the action of the poem has been moving steadily — "the ecstatic finale" (Frank 94), "in a profound sense . . . the true end of the poem" (Bloomfield 125). It is the moment where many readers have wished that Langland had simply stopped. But he was too realistic for that. The world did not end with the Resurrection. As Schmidt explains, "Langland's subject is God's action in history, and . . . it should come as no surprise that the spiritual climax and the conclusion

of *Piers Plowman* do not coincide. The divine action remains unfinished . . ."
(1983, 139).

THE VISIO REVISITED

The last two passus have been called "The Visio Revisited" (Kirk 179).
As many critics have observed (Barney 292; Murtaugh 54–62; Martin 122),
the parallels with the scene on Piers's half-acre are numerous. Again the
context is social, again Piers oversees the work of plowing and harvesting,
again the focus is on pardon. Yet everything looks strangely different. If
society has not changed since the first two visions, the dreamer certainly
has. He sees with new eyes. For one thing he perceives the half-acre in more
allegorical terms — the literal grains sown by Piers are now the cardinal virtues, the harvest is "the crop of truth," and so on — "and this to the Christian
Middle Ages means that it has been reconstituted in terms of its deepest
reality" (Murtaugh 54). For another thing the dreamer, like Piers, "parceyueþ
moore depper / What is þe wille" (15.199–201). Through the now transpar-
ent words and works of numerous folk on the field, he sees the fractured
image of his worst self—a thousand "wills." It is a dark picture. Many of
the apocalyptical elements latent in the poem's imagery, including the field
itself (cf. Matt. 13:38–43), come together at last. Bloomfield made a thorough
study of these elements, and if few critics have adopted his characterization
of the poem generically as "a fourteenth-century apocalypse," a great many
have adopted his perspective (see p. 12 above). "To put it bluntly," Adams
says, "Langland seems to have believed that he was seeing the end of the
world in his lifetime" (1978, 293; but contrast Aers 1980, 77–79).

The opening of the penultimate vision gives little indication of what is
to follow. It focuses on the early days of the age of grace. After a retrospective look at Christ's ministry, the poet moves in rapid succession from his
post-resurrection epiphanies to his conferring of the power of the keys, the
Ascension and Pentecost. The treatment of these events is multi-layered and
displays one of the most remarkable features of the dream-vision genre, its
palimpsestic quality. The dreamer's experience of the biblical account is
penetrated on one side by the church service in progress (see lines 1–8 and
the quotations from the liturgy in 74a, 80a, 152, 160, 169, 210) and on the
other by the elements of his previous visions (Christ's ministry exemplifies
the three degrees of Dowel, the keys are given to *Piers*, and so on). The
action is represented historically, reenacted liturgically, signed allegorically.

Most important is the fusion of the historical Peter and his allegorical
namesake. Christ's last act on earth was to institutionalize the work of pardon:

> [He] yaf Piers pardon, and power he grauntede hym,
> Myght men to assoille of alle manere synnes,
> To alle maner men mercy and for3ifnesse
> In couenaunt þat þei come and kneweliche to paie
> To Piers pardon þe Plowman *redde quod debes.*
>
> (19.183-87)

Again, as in the formula *Petrus id est Christus*, what is asserted here is not the literal identity of two figures (which, after all, have entirely different modes of being) but rather the union of a person and a principle. The pope is the caretaker of truth (see Matt. 16:19 and *The Catholic Encyclopedia*, "Keys, power of the," 8:631-33). He has been delegated the authority to pardon the sins of everybody who *reddit quod debit*, who "pays what he owes." "As pure truþe wolde," those who pay what they owe will be rewarded, and those who do not will be punished (19.191-98). But what does it mean "to pay what one owes"? With the help of this allusion to Christ's parable of the ungrateful servant (Matt. 18:23-35), Langland develops the penitential doctrine (stated earlier at 5.273a) of *Nunquam dimittitur peccatum, nisi restituatur ablatum* ("The sin is not forgiven unless the thing taken is restored"). In keeping with the *Vita*'s location of truth primarily in the will, however, what one owes is not simply the outward act (for example, the restitution of stolen property or usurious gain) but also the inward obligation of love. "The debt referred to in *redde quod debes*, Frank explains at length, "is man's debt of love to God and his neighbor" (108 ff.). The parable from which the phrase is taken ends with the warning that just as the lord punished the ungrateful servant, "so also shall my heavenly Father do to you, if you forgive not every one his brother *from your hearts*" (Matt. 18:35). Love is the enabling mechanism of pardon. It is, as Holy Church said in the beginning, the key that "vnloseth grace" (C.1.197).

The action takes a sinister turn, however, after the singing of *Veni creator Spiritus*:

> Thanne song I þat song; so dide manye hundred,
> And cride wiþ Conscience, "help vs, crist, of grace!"
> Thanne bigan grace to go wiþ Piers Plowman
> And counseillede hym and Conscience þe comune to sompne:
> "For I wole dele today and dyuyde grace
> To alle kynne creatures þat kan hise fyue wittes,
> Tresour to lyue by to hir lyues ende,
> And wepne to fighte wiþ þat wole neuere faille.
> For Antecrist and hise al þe world shul greue
> And acombre þee, Conscience, but if crist þee helpe.
>
> (19.211-20)

The "weapons" distributed by Grace, intended to ward off pride and envy, are the familiar vocations of the *Visio*: "Some wyes he yaf wit . . . And some he kennede craft . . . And some he lered to laboure . . . And some to deuyne and diuide . . . And some to se and to seye what sholde bifalle [the dream-er's own gift?] . . . And alle he lered to be lele, and ech a craft loue ooþer" (lines 229–50; cf. 1 Cor. 12, Ephes. 4:1–3). Grace then gives Piers "foure grete Oxen" (the gospels) with which "to tilie truþe"; and for seed, he gives him the cardinal virtues, prudence, temperance, fortitude and — "the chief seed þat Piers sew" — justice, which includes equity and the concept of good faith (19.274–308). After sowing these seeds, Piers harrows them with the "olde lawe and newe lawe þat loue myȝte wexe" (19.310). To store the har-vest he builds a barn, Unity, "holy chirche on englissh" (19.328).

The action is an obvious reprise of the pilgrimage to truth, but the threat is far more insidious. The wasters of the *Visio* are small fry by comparison. The forces of Antichrist occupy the highest offices of church and state, and having the appearance of truth they undermine the system from within. It was easy to identify the troublemakers on the half-acre: a Breton tells Piers to "go pissen with his plowȝ"; a waster who has never worked declares "now wol I noȝt bigynne!" (6.154–70). The new enemies of truth are more subtle. Their sins appear in the guise of the cardinal virtues themselves. A curate observes that "*Spiritus prudencie* among þe peple is gyle" (19.455). A lord declares that he is entitled by "right and reason" to take from his reeve all that his auditor advises "And wiþ *Spiritus fortitudinis* [to] fecche it, wole he, nel he" (19.464). A king proposes that since he is the head of law, and his subjects "but membres," "what I take of yow two, I take it at þe techynge / Of *Spiritus Iusticie* for I Iugge yow alle" (19.473–74). Even after waking up, the dreamer, "heuy chered" and hungry, is tempted by Need to steal his food and excuse the act "by techynge and by tellynge of *Spiritus temperancie*" (20.1–50; see Adams 1978; Szittya 267–79). In the "*Visio* revisited," the chief weapon of the ene-mies of truth is guile. Their chief target is the conscience.

The last vision is dark indeed. Antichrist overturns the "crop of truþe" and in its place causes guile to grow, disguised as goodness (20.51–57). Soon he has "hundredes at his baner." Conscience and the faithful retreat into the bastion of holy church, but instead of protection they find more guile, more pride and sloth and envy. "Proude preestes . . . / In paltokes and pyked shoes, purses and longe knyues, / Coomen ayein Conscience; wiþ Coueitise þei helden" (20.218–20). The friars are the worst of all. One "sire *Penetrans domos*" (cf. 2 Tim. 3:6, and Szittya 3–10, 247–87), acting as spiritual physi-cian to those in the house of unity, lets sinners get by with token penance ("a litel siluer"). The justice of *redde quod debes*, upon which the entire peniten-tial system rests, is severely compromised. Contrition, "þe souerayne salue for alle synnes of kynde," is itself sick (on the medical imagery, see Adams 1978, 296; Schmidt 1983; Yunck pp. 143–44 below). Equally alarming is the helplessness of Conscience; taken in by the guile and flattery of the friars, by the kind words of Hende Speche, even by the desire for Pees, the moral faculty has lost its bearings. Only Piers can help. The poem ends as Conscience, betrayed by the institution itself in which he placed his trust (Aers 1980, 78–79), sets out to "seken Piers þe Plowman." The cycle established earlier—the pilgrimage to Truth, the search for Dowel—must be repeated yet again, this time by the very guide who had once so confidently led Will. In such treacherous times and circumstances, the will's hard-earned desire to "do well" is, tragically, not enough.

The inconclusive ending has given rise to many theories. One holds that *Piers Plowman* is essentially unfinished: "to the end, the poem was still evolving" (Russell 46). Another holds that the ending reflects the poet's emphasis on process: "Langland's last and most individual stroke is in deepest conformity with his whole design" (Lawlor 126). Still another explains the poem as the record of one man's perplexities in the face of social, religious, and intellectual problems which the available forms of thought were inadequate to explain: "Its ultimate expression of helplessness, the real feeling of its end, must derive from Langland's perception of the impossibility of resolution" (Kane 73–74). Finally it must be said that any conclusion contrived merely in order to satisfy the canons of narrative art would have destroyed the integrity of the poem itself. Langland conveys the impression that he wanted only to tell the truth, and in the end he refused to palliate real problems with "fictional satisfactions" (Martin 51). Indeed, he seems deliberately to have eschewed many of the conventions associated with the making of fiction and to have adopted a literary mode whose "affective force depends on . . . the deflection of systematic explanation" (Middleton 1982a, 115; see also Lawton). Possibly his refusal "to tie everything up into a consonant whole" was determined by his eschatological point of view: "[T]he eschatological plot is no fiction, and it has no imaginable end, because congruence and consonance are not its ultimate values. Its conclusion lies beyond the capabilities of plot and form" (Carruthers 1982, 187).

That *Piers Plowman* displays an overall design, a pattern or sequence of related patterns, is clear. Yet the demonstration of that design, however well-supported by the text, inevitably misrepresents the experience of reading it, "the real feeling of its end." This paradox is part of the poem's greatness. What Langland communicates is not only a poetic synthesis of the major questions concerning "truth"—the most ambitious of his age—but also the anxiety, frustration, and fierce desire to *understand* that drove him to attempt it.

REFERENCES

Adams, Robert. "Langland and the Liturgy Revisited." *SP* 73 (1976): 266–84.

———. "The Nature of Need in 'Piers Plowman' XX." *Traditio* 34 (1978): 273–301.

———. "Piers's Pardon and Langland's Semi-Pelagianism." *Traditio* 39 (1983): 367–418.

———. "The Reliability of the Rubrics in the B-Text of *Piers Plowman*." *MÆ* 54 (1985): 208–31.

———. "Some Versions of Apocalypse: Learned and Popular Eschatology in *Piers Plowman*." *The Popular Literature of Medieval England*. Ed. Thomas J. Heffernan. Knoxville: University of Tennessee Press, 1985. 194–236.

Aers, David. *Piers Plowman and Christian Allegory*. London: Arnold, 1975.

———. *Chaucer, Langland and the Creative Imagination*. London: Routledge & Kegan Paul, 1980.

Alford, John A. "Haukyn's Coat: Some Observations on *Piers Plowman* B.XIV.22-7." *MÆ* 43 (1974): 133–38.

———. "Literature and Law in Medieval England." *PMLA* 92 (1977): 941–51.

———. "The Role of the Quotations in *Piers Plowman*." *Speculum* 52 (1977): 80–99.

———. "The Idea of Reason in *Piers Plowman*, " *Medieval English Studies Presented to George Kane*, ed. by Donald Kennedy, R. A. Waldron, and Joseph Wittig. Cambridge: Brewer, 1988. 199–215.

———. *Piers Plowman: A Glossary of Legal Diction*. Cambridge: Brewer, 1988.

Allen, Judson B. "Langland's Reading and Writing: *Detractor* and the Pardon Passus." *Speculum* 59 (1984): 342–62.

Amassian, Margaret, and James Sadowsky. "Mede and Mercede: A Study of the Grammatical Metaphor in *Piers Plowman*, C: IV: 335–409." *NM* 72 (1971): 457–76.

Ames, Ruth M. *The Fulfillment of the Scriptures: Abraham, Moses, and Piers*. Evanston: Northwestern University Press, 1970.

Baldwin, Anna P. *The Theme of Government in Piers Plowman*. Cambridge: Brewer, 1981.

Barney, Stephen A. "The Plowshare of the Tongue: The Progress of a Symbol from the Bible to *Piers Plowman*." *MS* 35 (1973): 261–93.

Benson, C. David. "The Function of Lady Meed in *Piers Plowman*." *ES* 6 (1980): 193– 301.

Birnes. William J. "Christ as Advocate: The Legal Metaphor of *Piers Plowman*." *AnM* 16 (1975): 71–93.

Bloomfield, Morton W. *Piers Plowman as a Fourteenth-Century Apocalypse*. New Brunswick, NJ: Rutgers University Press, 1962.

Bowers, John. *The Crisis of Will in Piers Plowman*. Washington, DC: Catholic University of America Press, 1986.

Brown, Carleton. *Religious Lyrics of the XIVth Century*. 2nd ed. Oxford: Clarendon Press, 1952.

Burrow, John A. "The Action of Langland's Second Vision." *EIC* 15 (1965): 247–68; rpt. in Blanch 209–27.

———. "Words, Works and Will: Theme and Structure in *Piers Plowman*." Hussey 111–24.

Carruthers [Schroeder], Mary. "The Character of Conscience in *Piers Plowman*." *SP* 67 (1970): 13–30.

———. "*Piers Plowman*: The Tearing of the Pardon." *PQ* 49 (1970): 8–18.

———. *The Search for St. Truth: A Study of Meaning in Piers Plowman*. Evanston: Northwestern University Press, 1973.

. "Time, Apocalypse, and the Plot of *Piers Plowman.*" *Acts of Interpretation: The Text and Its Contents, 700–1600.* Essays on Medieval and Renaissance Literature in Honor of E. Talbot Donaldson. Ed. Mary J. Carruthers and Elizabeth D. Kirk. Norman, OK: Pilgrim Books, 1982. 175–88.

The Catholic Encyclopedia. 15 vols. New York: The Encyclopedia Press, 1913.

Chambers, R. W. *Man's Unconquerable Mind.* London: Cape, 1939.

Coghill, Nevill K. "The Character of Piers Plowman Considered from the B-Text." *MÆ* 2 (1933): 108–35; rpt. Vasta 54–86.

. "The Pardon of Piers Plowman." Gollancz Memorial Lecture. *PBA* 30 (1944): 303–57; rpt. Blanch 40–86 (abridged).

Coleman, Janet. *Piers Plowman and the Moderni.* Rome: Edizioni di Storia e Letteratura, 1981.

Cooper, Helen. "Langland's and Chaucer's Prologues." *YLS* 1 (1987): 71–81.

Donaldson, E. Talbot. *Piers Plowman: The C-Text and Its Poet.* Yale Studies in English 113. New Haven: Yale University Press, 1949.

Dronke, Peter. "Arbor Caritatis." *Medieval Studies for J. A. W. Bennett.* Ed. P. L. Heyworth. Oxford: Clarendon Press, 1981. 207–53.

Dunning, T. P. *Piers Plowman: An Interpretation of the A Text.* 1937; 2nd ed. rev. and edited by T. P. Dolan. Oxford: Clarendon Press, 1980.

. "The Structure of the B-Text of *Piers Plowman.*" *RES* ns 7 (1956): 225–37; rpt. Blanch 87–100.

. "Action and Contemplation in *Piers Plowman.*" Hussey 213–25.

Frank, Robert Worth, Jr. *Piers Plowman and the Scheme of Salvation.* Yale Studies in English 136. New Haven: Yale University Press, 1957.

Gaffney, Wilbur. "The Allegory of the Christ Knight in *Piers Plowman.*" *PMLA* 46 (1931): 155–68.

Godden, Malcolm. "Plowmen and Hermits in Langland's *Piers Plowman.*" *RES* ns 35 (1984): 129–63.

Goldsmith, Margaret. *The Figure of Piers Plowman: The Image on the Coin.* Cambridge: Brewer, 1981.

Goodridge, J. F., trans. *Piers the Plowman.* Rev. ed. Hardmondsworth: Penguin, 1966.

Griffiths, Lavinia. *Personification in Piers Plowman.* Cambridge: Brewer, 1985.

Harwood, Britton J. "Imaginative in *Piers Plowman.*" *MÆ* 44 (1975): 249–63.

Hort, Greta. *Piers Plowman and Contemporary Religious Thought.* New York: Macmillan, 1938.

Hussey, S. S. "Langland, Hilton, and the Three Lives." *RES* ns 7 (1956): 132–50; rpt. Vasta 232–58.

Jennings, Margaret. "*Piers Plowman* and Holychurch." *Viator* 9 (1978): 367–74.

Kail, J., ed. *Twenty-Six Political and Other Poems.* EETS 124. London: Kegan Paul, Trench, Trübner, 1904.

Kane, George. *The Liberating Truth: The Concept of Integrity in Chaucer's Writings.* John Coffin Memorial Lecture. London: Athlone, 1980.

. "The Perplexities of William Langland." *The Wisdom of Poetry: Essays in Early English Literature in Honor of Morton W. Bloomfield.* Ed. Larry D. Benson and Siegfried Wenzel. Kalamazoo, MI: Medieval Institute, 1982. 73–91.

Kaske, R. E. " 'Ex vi transicionis' and Its Passage in *Piers Plowman.*" *JEGP* 62 (1963): 32–60.

. "Holy Church's Speech and the Structure of *Piers Plowman.*" *Chaucer and Middle English Studies in Honour of Rossell Hope Robbins.* Ed. Beryl Bowland. London: Allen and Unwin, 1974. 320–27.

Kaulbach, Ernest. "The 'Vis Imaginatif' and the Reasoning Powers of Ymaginatif in the B-Text of *Piers Plowman*." *JEGP* 84 (1985): 16– 29.

Kean, P. M. "Love, Law and *Lewte* in *Piers Plowman*." *RES* ns 15 (1964): 241–61; rpt. Blanch 132–55.

Kirk, Elizabeth D. *The Dream Thought of Piers Plowman*. New Haven: Yale University Press, 1972.

Lawlor, John. "The Imaginative Unity of *Piers Plowman*." *RES* ns 8 (1957): 113–26; rpt. Vasta 278–97.

Lawton, David. "The Subject of *Piers Plowman*." *YLS* 1 (1987): 1–30.

Maguire, Stella. "The Significance of Haukyn, *Activa Vita*, in *Piers Plowman*." *RES* 25 (1949): 97–108; rpt. Blanch 194–208.

Mann, Jill. "Eating and Drinking in *Piers Plowman*." *E&S* 32 (1979): 26–42.

Martin, Priscilla. *Piers Plowman: The Field and the Tower*. London: Macmillan, 1979.

McLeod, Susan H. "The Tearing of the Pardon in *Piers Plowman*." *PQ* 56 (1977): 14–26.

Meroney, Howard. "The Life and Death of Longe Wille." *ELH* 17 (1950): 1–35.

Middleton, Anne. "Two Infinites: Grammatical Metaphor in *Piers Plowman*." *ELH* 39 (1972): 169– 88.

———. "The Audience and Public of *Piers Plowman*." *Middle English Alliterative Poetry and Its Literary Background*. Ed. David Lawton. Cambridge: D. S. Brewer, 1982. 101–54.

———. "Narration and the Invention of Experience: Episodic Form in *Piers Plowman*." *The Wisdom of Poetry: Essays in Early English Literature in Honor of Morton W. Bloomfield*. Ed. Larry D. Benson and Siegfried Wenzel. Kalamazoo, MI: Medieval Institute, 1982. 91–122.

Mills, David. "The Role of the Dreamer in *Piers Plowman*." Hussey 180–212.

Minnis, A. J. "Langland's Ymaginatif and Late-Medieval Theories of Imagination." *Comparative Criticism* 3 (1981): 71–103.

Mitchell, A. G. *Lady Meed and the Art of Piers Plowman*. Chambers Memorial Lecture. London: Lewis, 1956; rpt. Blanch 174–93.

Murtaugh, Daniel. *Piers Plowman and the Image of God*. Gainesville: The University Presses of Florida, 1978.

Orsten, Elizabeth. "Patientia in the B-Text of *Piers Plowman*." *MS* 31 (1969): 317–33.

Potts, Timothy C. "Conscience." *The Cambridge History of Later Medieval Philosophy*. Ed. Norman Kretzmann et al. Cambridge: Cambridge University Press, 1982. 687–704.

Raw, Barbara. "Piers and the Image of God in Man." Hussey 143–79.

Robertson, D. W., Jr., and Bernard F. Huppé. *Piers Plowman and Scriptural Tradition*. Princeton: Princeton University Press, 1951.

Russell, George. "Some Aspects of the Process of Revision in *Piers Plowman*." Hussey 27–49.

Salter, Elizabeth. *Piers Plowman: An Introduction*. Oxford: Blackwell, 1969.

Schmidt, A. V. C. "Langland and Scholastic Philosophy." *MÆ* 38 (1969): 134–56.

———. "*Lele Wordes* and *Bele Paroles*: Some Aspects of Langland's Word-Play." *RES* ns 34 (1983): 137–50.

Simpson, James. "Spiritual and Earthly Nobility in *Piers Plowman*." *NM* 86 (1985): 467–81.

Spearing, A. C. "The Development of a Theme in *Piers Plowman*." *RES* ns 11 (1960): 241– 53.

Stokes, Myra. *Justice and Mercy in Piers Plowman: A Reading of the B Text Visio*. London and Canberra: Croom Helm, 1984.

Szittya, Penn. *The Antifraternal Tradition in Medieval Literature*. Princeton: Princeton University Press, 1986.

Tavormina, M. Teresa. " 'Bothe Two Ben Gode': Marriage and Virginity in *Piers Plowman* C.18.68–100." *JEGP* 81 (1982): 320–30.

Troyer, Howard W. "Who is Piers Plowman?" *PMLA* 47 (1932): 368–84.

Waldron, R. A. "Langland's Originality: The Christ-Knight and the Harrowing of Hell." *Medieval English Religious and Ethical Literature. Essays in Honour of G. H. Russell.* Ed. G. Kratzmann and J. Simpson. Cambridge: Brewer, 1986. 66–81.

Wells, Henry W. "The Construction of *Piers Plowman*." *PMLA* 44 (1929): 123–40; rpt. Vasta 1–21.

———. "The Philosophy of *Piers Plowman*." *PMLA* 53 (1938): 339–49; rpt. Vasta 115–29.

Whatley, Gordon. "The Uses of Hagiography: The Legend of Pope Gregory and the Emperor Trajan in the Middle Ages." *Viator* 15 (1984): 25–63.

Wittig, Joseph. "*Piers Plowman* B, Passus IX–XII: Elements in the Design of the Inward Journey." *Traditio* 28 (1972): 211–80.

———. "The Dramatic and Rhetorical Development of Long Will's Pilgrimage." *NM* 76 (1975): 52–76.

Woolf, Rosemary. "The Tearing of the Pardon." Hussey 50–75.

Yunck, John A. *The Lineage of Lady Meed: The Development of Mediaeval Venality Satire*. Notre Dame: University of Notre Dame Press, 1963.

2

THE HISTORICAL CONTEXT

ANNA P. BALDWIN

THE HISTORICAL APPROACH

Historical criticism is based on the assumption that the author's separation from us in time crucially affects our understanding of his work. He may be linked to his past by literary traditions, he may anticipate the future through his own genius, but for all that, he cannot extricate himself from his historical context. It affects not only his vocabulary and the way he sees the world, but what he sees. This is particularly true of an author like Langland who constantly describes and comments on his society and searches for ways of saving it.

The importance of discovering the precise historical context for the three texts has encouraged critics to use apparent topical allusions to date them. The work done by Jusserand (37–38), Huppé (1939), Bennett (1943a) and Cargill on the A text is consistent with Kane's conclusion (p. 184 below) that its manuscript tradition originated within the years 1368–1374, though there are probable allusions to earlier events in A.3.176–95 (the Normandy Campaign of October 1359–May 1360) and A.5.13–14 (the "pestilences" and "southwestryne wynd" of 1362). The additional work done on the B text by Huppé (1941), Gwynn (1943), Bennett (1943b), Donaldson (1949) and Baldwin (1982), and on the C text by Devlin (1928) is also consistent with the view (pp. 184–86 below) that their manuscript traditions originated in 1377–81 and 1381–85 respectively. Langland actually dates a drought to 1370 in B.13.268–70. Probable allusions to the events of the period 1360–86 will be discussed in the course of this chapter; such allusions sharpen the tone of Langland's social and political comment and help us to focus it more precisely.

When however we come to consider the wider social context of the poem, historical facts begin to lose their hardness, although historians such as Trevelyan, Homans and Chadwick have used *Piers Plowman* to discover the conditions of the time. This use of a literary work depersonalises and defictionalises it. Thus Jusserand's historical study of the poem provided invaluable parallels between Langland's complaint and the petitions of the Commons in Parliament, but one should resist his conclusion that Langland therefore speaks for the whole community of England. Coleman is more aware of the religious standpoint from which Langland surveys his society, and she interprets him as a poet who has "read back into [his] frequently spiritual themes the worldly and realistic context of [his] times" (274). Literary scholars who use a knowledge of history to elucidate but not to depersonalise Langland's themes include Donaldson (1949) who, like the present writer (Baldwin 1981), has tried to define Langland's political attitudes, and Bloomfield (1962), for whom Langland's picture of a corrupted world provides the poet with "the main evidence that a new or reformed age is about to dawn" (113). More recently, Aers has interpreted Langland's apocalypticism as his way of resolving the "tension between an imaginatively grasped historical present and a cherished frame of ideas received from the past" (64). That Langland was a chronicler of social change is clear, but that he resisted such change is questionable. He seems rather to define how the individual should respond to it. Accordingly this chapter will use the traditional analysis of society in terms of the three estates in order to demonstrate both Langland's historically accurate perception of how each was developing, and his interpretation of the individual's role within them.

THE PEASANTRY: PIERS AS PLOWMAN

In the traditional model of society the peasants who "work for all" are placed at the bottom, below the clergy who "pray for all" and the knights who "fight for all" (and, we might add, rule all). By centring his poem on a plowman Langland is, in effect, reversing the model. At the beginning of the *Visio* plowmen head the list of estates (A and B.Prol.20, C.Prol.22; cp. Chaucer's *General Prologue*), and theirs is the chief craft established by Kynde Wit to profit the community (B.Prol.119; C.Prol.145). At the end of the *Visio* they are the first to be granted the pardon of Truth (A and B.7.1–8; C.9.1–8). In the *Vita* it is the plowman whom Christ most resembles (e.g., B.18.10; B.19.6) and who founds the Church as Peter, the first pope (B.19.182–273). The terms of Piers's pardon encourage us to include among "plowmen" not only the relatively privileged class of professional plowmen (described by Hilton 1975, 20–36) but also "Alle libbynge laborers þat lyuen by hir hondes" (B.7.62). But even if Piers is a peasant of some standing, he is still a representative of the working community, and he even appears in B.19.258 as a reeve, who was almost inevitably a bondsman (see

H. S. Bennett 166). Does Langland want to turn his social world upside-down?

The Feudal System

A first impression of the poem would suggest that he does not, for it is full of approving references to the old feudal system. As Bloch has shown (1:278-79, 2:441-52), this system was characterized by stability, control, and a low emphasis on monetary relations. The lord gave the use of land — whether a baronry or a few half-acre strips; his "man" responded with customary services which, if he was a bondsman, were often agricultural work on his lord's demesne (though they could include many other sorts of service, for example the messenger service described in C.13.33-64; see Neilson 61-62, 66). Each side was bound in mutual contract, the "faithkeeping" which is the basic meaning of the Middle English word "truth" (see *Truth* and *Troth* in *OED*; cf. above, pp. 33-34). Faithkeeping depends on the honesty and justice of both parties, and honesty and justice are further meanings of "truth." Piers uses the word in both senses when he tells the king not to oppress his serfs:

> Loke þow tene no tenaunt but truþe wole assente. . .
> For þow shalt yelde it ayein at one yeres ende
> In a wel perilous place þat Purgatorie hatte.
> (B.6.38-44)

The knight's lapses in faith-keeping and honesty towards his tenants will be justly remembered in the prison of purgatory.

It should not surprise us therefore that the feudal relationship is often used in the poem as a paradigm for the relationship between man and God, in spite of the fact that Langland also insists that the baptized are "free men þoruȝ fullynge" (B.19.39). Scripture accurately describes the legal incapacity of a bondsman to own possessions or to live where he chose (H. S. Bennett 277-317; Pollock and Maitland 1:416, 368) as an analogy of the Christian's dependence upon God — and this time it is the bondsman who is threatened with the prison of purgatory if he tries to escape his feudal obligations:

> Ac he may renne in arerage and rome fro home. . .
> Ac reson shal rekene wiþ hym and rebuken hym at þe laste . . .
> And putten hym after in prison in purgatorie to brenne.
> (B.11.129-33)

Similarly, Adam's disobedience to God, in engendering Cain during a period of penance, is compared to a bondsman's disobedience to his lord:

As an hewe þat erieth nat auntreth hym to sowe
On a leye land aȝeynes his lordes wille.

(C.10.216-17)

Having failed to plow his land properly, the peasant dares to sow seed on
land that should be lying fallow for pasture—a quibbling play with the
familiar sexual associations of the plow. Such breaches of the agreed rota-
tion of crops in the village fields were punishable in the lord's manor court.
This court enforced truth between neighbours as well as truth between a
lord and his man (see H. S. Bennett 45, 47-48; Ault 24, 52-54), and in
the C text the just regulation of boundary marks between strips is seen as
being no different from the justice enforced by a king on his whole community:

So comune claymeth of a kyng thre kyne thynges,
Lawe, loue and lewete and hym lord antecedent,
Bothe heued and here kyng, haldyng with no parteyȝe
Bote standynge as a stake þat stikede in a mere
Bytwene two londes for a trewe marke.

(C.3.378-82)

The king, the lord, the peasant must all observe the same truth, and in using feudal metaphors to express it Langland is not necessarily trying to rein-
state the feudal system. Truth is a Christian virtue not restricted to one social
pattern.

THE BLACK DEATH AND SOCIAL CHANGES

Indeed when Piers first sets out to direct the sinners to Truth, he specifically avoids the feudal model, in which he would inevitably have been the
directed, not the director. Instead it is he who tells both knight and peasants
what to do; he pays his labourers in money, not in the use of land; and
he has no manor court to enforce their justice and faithkeeping. This allegory of Christian freedom reflects a change in rural organization which
had begun before the Black Death of 1348, and was associated with the increased replacement of bond services by money rents, itself an important
part of the development of a money economy (Bolton 207-21). The epi-
demics of the plague in the second half of the fourteenth century accelerat-
ed the change by reducing the population by between a third and a half.
This increased the supply of land and decreased the supply of labour, so
that wages rose, and "high farming" by lords with bondsmen on big estates
was more expensive, though it flourished still in some places. Peasants who
had "no land to lyue on but hire handes" (B.6.307) began to leave their

manors legally or illegally and to roam the country in search of higher wages. The Statutes of Labourers, enacted between 1349 (the year following the first devastating outbreak of plague) and the end of the century, attempted to control wages and prices, to enforce the keeping of contracts, and to make the idle work (Putnam 1–6, 71–97; Holdsworth 2:460–64; Hilton 1969, 32–43). They attempted, in short, to transfer the feudal principles of "truth" into a wage-economy, but they achieved only partial success. In the circumstances it became easier for the lords to rent their demesnes to peasants than to cultivate them themselves (examples of such "peasant-units" are given by Maitland; Davenport; Lomas). The social estates were putting themselves into a new relation with each other, a relation governed not by custom but by money.

There was no reason why such relationships should not also have been governed by truth. In the C text Langland adds a long section to Conscience's attack on Meed to prove that monetary "mercede" can be given according to Truth (C.3.286–406)

> That bothe the lord and the laborer be leely yserued.
> (C.3.310)

Piers is the servant of Truth (B.5.540) and tries to enforce his master's principles on the peasant-unit of his half-acre strip by paying only for honest work and requiring his labourers to stay a full year (B.6.65–66, 114). These are the very principles backed by the Statutes of Labourers, and Piers is obeying the law when he refuses alms to the able-bodied (forbidden 1349), as is the knight when he threatens idlers with the stocks (C.8,163; cf. *Rot. Parl.* 2:340–41). But Piers is too kindly, and the knight too courteous, to enforce these penalties. Their self-restraint seems to be a response to the new, more independent status of the labourers, and it is only Hunger, a natural sanction which affects all men equally, who drives the idlers back to work. As soon as Hunger has been satisfied, some peasants specifically defy the Statutes, demanding better food and higher wages:

> And þo nolde Wastour noȝt werche, but wandred aboute. . .
> Laborers þat haue no land to lyue on but hire handes
> Deyneþ noȝt to dyne a day nyȝt olde wortes . . .
> But he be heiȝliche hyred ellis wole he chide. . .
> And þanne corseþ þe kyng and al þe counseil after
> Swiche lawes to loke laborers to chaste.
> (B.6.302–18)

It was true that standards of living had risen. The Black Death, by reducing the population, achieved "a more efficient balance between labour, land and capital" (Hatcher 33). Langland's tone is condemnatory because he realises the dangers in the labourers' new position of strength. But he does not threaten them with more social controls. It is now up to them to choose whether they will work in accordance with Truth and so defend all society from Hunger (B.6.321-31) or whether they will allow their new self-determination to become mere self-interest. Langland turns society inside-out rather than upside-down. Its success as a whole will depend on the decisions of individual plowmen.

THE PEASANTS' REVOLT

When Langland was first writing the half-acre scene in the A text, he would have been unaware of the full dangers to society of the peasants' new feeling about their changing position, but the events of 1381 may (as Donaldson suggests, 108-09) have provoked some changes in different parts of the C text. In that year peasants, mainly from the Home Counties and East Anglia, rebelled against oppressions which must no longer have seemed inevitable, particularly the unprecedented taxation of the previous decade, which culminated in three "poll" or head-taxes (1377, 1379 and 1380). The last of these demanded a shilling — three days' wages for a labourer — from every adult in the kingdom. The rebels occupied and terrorized London for several days, demanding (among other things) an end to these taxes, to the Statutes of Labourers, and to villeinage itself. They killed not only the Chancellor, Archbishop Sudbury (see Fowler for a speculative reference in B.15.528) and the Treasurer, but also all the lawyers and judges they could find, holding these responsible for enforcing these hated laws (Hilton 1975, 137-236; Maddicott 61-64).

The rebels' violence must have appalled Langland, yet it is a dramatic indication of the way *Piers Plowman* could be read that some of their leaders seem to have quoted the poem in their letters to one another (see below pp. 251-52). Even if the rebels were wrong to use Langland's hero as a type of chiliastic avenger (if this is what they were doing), they were right to believe him the champion of the poor. Unlike so many of his contemporaries, Langland seems to write from a personal experience of poverty (e.g., C.9.70-97), and to respect rather than to patronize the honest peasant. He even suggests more than once that poverty in itself should count as a penance for sin and so help a man into heaven (see B.7.100-5; C.12.194-209; C.13.79-92). It is the poor who are the true inheritors of Langland's kingdom.

THE CLERGY

THE WYCLIFFITE MOVEMENT

Langland's genuine and yet triumphant plowman seems to have been taken over by religious as well as political rebels. Piers's "progeny" includes the plowmen-priests of late fourteenth-century Wycliffite tracts (see Epilogue), and this fact raises the question of Langland's relation to Wyclif, which is connected to the question of Langland's relation to the Peasants' Revolt, because Wyclif's followers were suspected of having fomented the Revolt by their preaching (see Aston 273–79). Most of them were driven from Oxford in 1382. It is from about this time that we can date the beginnings of a Wycliffite sect, which gradually lost its academic pretensions and became genuinely popular, moral and reformist, attacking the institutionalised Church and proposing instead a community of Bible-reading individuals led by "poor priests," themselves often laymen (see Leff 2:559-605; McFarlane 1952, 76–130; Hudson 1-29). However, their characteristic beliefs, except on political issues, cannot be detected in Wyclif's own writings until after 1377, by which time the A text and much of the B text of *Piers Plowman* must already have been written.

The C text, however, coincides with the great outcry against the Wycliffites in the early 1380s, and it may be because of this that Langland adds passages to it in which he dissociates himself from "lollares" (C.5.1–5; C.9.139–61, 188–254). This word had meant "idlers" for some time, but Langland could just conceivably be using it in a specific heretical sense (it is used in this way in 1382 in *Fasc. Ziz.* [312]), though the Wycliffites were not commonly called "lollards" till the 1390s. In any event, Langland failed to prevent his poem from being used by the later Lollards in their propaganda (see pp. 252 ff. below).

Indeed, there are striking similarities between some of Langland's criticisms of the clergy and those made by the Wycliffites (see Gradon; Lawton). Langland's plowman-hero is closer to God than the clergy described in the poem (see Burdach 210), leading sinners on an inner pilgrimage to no known shrine (cf. Hudson 23), and obtaining there no papal indulgence because, as one Wycliffite tract puts it, "þer comeþ no pardon but of god for good lyuynge & endynge in charite" (*English Works of Wyclif* 238). The B text contrasts this plowman with the actual pope waging war on his fellow-Christians (B.19.442–46; cf. Hudson 150), and the C text reinforces this point (C.17.233–35) and adds a condemnation of "ydolatrie" (C.Prol.95-102). Although such criticisms were made by others besides Wycliffites (Gower, for example, criticises the papal wars in *Vox Clamantis* 3.9; cf. Gradon), these similarities do demonstrate again that Langland tends more toward individual than hierarchical methods of reform. For him, as for Wyclif, it is the individual's personal qualities which determine his true status, and not the status which empowers the individual.

SECULAR RIGHTS OVER CHURCH PROPERTY

It is really only on the political issue of "dominion" (the right to own temporal property), which Wyclif was discussing from about 1373, that there is any possibility of direct influence by him on Langland (see Gradon 186–88). Yet although Langland sometimes seems to echo Wyclif's very words, their attitudes may be more typical of the period than we imagine, accustomed as we are to interpreting Wyclif in the light of his later heresies (see Wilks 1972). It was a period of general and even official anticlericism (see Tout 3:270–82; Barnie 52–55; Wilks 1972) directed most fiercely against the pope, who throughout the first phase of the Hundred Years' Wars was French and lived at Avignon. (The papacy returned to Rome in January 1377 only to fall into an even more discreditable schism in September 1378, an event almost certainly alluded to in B.Prol.107–11, C. Prol.134–38.) Suspicions of the French and Flemish monks who lived in "alien priories" in England was extreme, and they were virtually disendowed in 1363; this provided a precedent for later threats of general disendowment (see Knowles 157–66). By the Statutes of Provisors and Praemunire (1351 and 1353) Edward III also curtailed the pope's rights to "provide" his own nominees to certain benefices, and after a personal quarrel, Pope Urban V was effectively stopped from receiving any English dues or taxes from 1364 until 1372 (see Holmes 7–20). (There was to be renewed resentment, described by Palmer and Wells, when the new pope, Gregory XI, then began a policy of aggressive tax-collection, and even received royal approval for a grant of £10,000 from the English clergy at a conference where Wyclif was one of the delegates.)

These measures are symptoms not only of war-time xenophobia, but also of the growing feeling that the English king had final authority over all the lands in his kingdom, and that the clergy were unpatriotic and even treacherous in sending money (and perhaps secrets?) overseas, particularly as the export of sterling bearing the king's sign had been illegal since 1299 (*Stat. Realm* 1:131–35, 273, 299, 383; 2:17). Such feelings lie behind Reason's comparatively mild desire, expressed in the Parliament Scene, that

> . . .alle Rome renneres, for Robberes of biyonde,
> Bere no siluer ouer see þat signe of kyng sheweþ.
> (B.4.128–29; see Bennett 1943a, 567–68)

A related though less widely held resentment concerned the clergy's claim to be exempt from the taxation agreed to by Parliament, though they did make "voluntary contributions" to the war effort. When war was resumed in 1369 after a nine-year truce, and England began to suffer defeats, the Parliament of 1371 not only demanded the replacement of clerical ministers by secular ones before it would vote any taxes, but also demanded that the clergy should be obliged to pay them too. Two friars came before this Parliament to argue that "the law of God and of nature wishes expressly that all possessions, including those of the clergy as of others, should be in common in all cases of necessity" (Galbraith 580). Whatever his opinion of clerical taxation, Langland seems to suspect the motives of those who argue in this way. In his description of the disintegration of society he implies that friars who prove by Plato and Seneca "That alle þynges vnder heuene ouȝte to ben in comune" (B.20.276) do so out of envy. Similarly, when a king in this corrupted world demands dues from both clerical and lay parts of "his body" the kingdom, the implication is that he does so out of avarice rather than *Spiritus Iusticie* (B.19.465–76). Yet Conscience seems to allow his claim if it is made for the defence rather than the exploitation of the kingdom:

> "In condicion," quod Conscience, "þat þow þe comune defende . . .
> *Omnia tua sunt ad defendendum set non ad deprehendendum.*"
> [It is all yours to defend, not to despoil]
>
> (B.19.477–79)

The passage seems once again to echo the government's own policy, this time as it was expressed by Wyclif himself in 1377: "Since therefore the realm of England ought . . . to be one body, and the clerks, lords, and community its members, . . . it follows that our realm can lawfully keep its treasure for its defence, in any case in which necessity requires it" (*Fasc. Ziz.* 258; trans. Myers 656–57). Wyclif had been an occasional spokesman for the royal policy on papal dues (as here) and on clerical taxation since at least 1371, and in *De Civili Dominio* (1377) he developed these arguments more fully, distinguishing, as Langland does in the previous quotation, between a force which acts "*ad depredandum*" and one used "*ad evitandum invasionem defensione*" (*De. Civ. Dom.* 2:7; see Gwynn 1940, 213–14).

This kind of argument is but a short though significant step from Wyclif's fully developed belief expressed both in *De Civili Dominio* and in *De Officio Regis* (1378) that the clergy should be disendowed at once by the laity. It is not clear that Langland ever advocated this, although Anima does say that temporal possessions have poisoned the Church (B.15.561), and like Wyclif he gives the laity the task of purging out the poison: "Takeþ hire landes, ye lordes, and leteþ hem lyue by dymes" (B.15.564). The same point is probably being made by Clergy (B.10.322–35; said by Reason in C.5.168–79) when he prophesies that one day a king will come who will make the monks perform a genuine penance "*ad pristinum statum*" (back to their original state). The phrase is used by Wyclif in *De Officio Regis* (p. 213; see Baldwin 1981, 93–94) when speaking of the king's duty to disendow the Church. (Gradon [188–89] and Alford [280–81] have indicated a much more orthodox context for the same phrase.) Moreover, Wyclif's theory of dominion, on the basis of which he advocated disendowment, was largely derived from the *De Pauperis Salvatori* (1356) of Richard Fitzralph, who never used it to urge such a course (see Walsh 377–406). At the time when Langland was writing the A and B texts, the questioning of papal rights over English property and of the terms on which the Church held property at all had not yet become contaminated by heresy. Indeed, it was an important strand of public opinion, and even (as Wilks suggested in 1972) of official policy.

THE KING AND THE NOBILITY

The later fourteenth century was a period of weakness at the apex of government. Between 1357 and 1380, when England was rapidly losing her position overseas, the king was either a dotard or a child. The aristocracy were gaining power both in the localities and at court long before this, and the responsibilities of government seemed increasingly to be submerged in self-interest. In the *Visio* Langland shows how aristocratic self-interest had dominated military policy, corrupted the loyalty of royal counsellors, and undermined the administration of justice throughout the realm. Langland represents this social crisis as a conflict between Meed and Conscience. For although these characters primarily represent moral attitudes, they also have a political dimension, in that Meed uses the power and unscrupulous methods increasingly associated with the nobility, and Conscience defends the principle of "truth" (justice, loyalty) in government at all levels.

THE KING AS MILITARY LEADER

The verbal debate between Meed and Conscience in passus 3 is centred on the conflict between their different attitudes to the Hundred Years' War with France (A.3.176–208; B.3.189–207; C.3.234–64). The A text was probably written in the early 1370s, and in it Meed looks back with some complacency to the first successful phase (1343–60) of the war when the king and the aristocracy had enriched themselves with plunder and lands (see Hewitt 106–07; McKisack 1960). Conscience, however, is associated with a "cowardly" peace policy. Langland makes few changes when writing this part of the B text, but his extensive revisions in the C text indicate a growing hostility to the war.

In the A and B texts Meed refers with distaste to the Treaty of Bretigny (March 1360), by which Edward III was granted nearly half of France and a ransom for the captured French king of three million gold écus:

> Cowardly þou consience conceiledest him þennes
> To leuen his lordsshipe for a litel siluer
> (A.3.193–94)

Many of the English nobility objected, as Meed does here, to Edward's obligation under the treaty to renounce his hereditary right to the French throne, and urged him to press for total victory (Barnie 12–14, 36–37). But Edward thought (wisely) that he had done as much as he could, particularly as the hardships of the previous winter's campaigning in Normandy (see A.3.176–81) had convinced him that God wished him to end the war. According to Froissart he had "devoutly vowed and promised . . . that he would agree to peace" (*Chronicles*, chap. cdlvi; trans. Jusserand 37). When the French began to recover their conquered lands in 1369, criticism of the supposed waste of Edward's earlier advantage, and of the ransom itself, gathered strength. The new lands in Aquitaine and Brittany had already begun to revert to French hands when, in 1372, the Castillian navy (newly allied with France) destroyed the English fleet off La Rochelle. The English army could not then get to France in time to save what was left of their newly conquered territories. By 1374 only Bordeaux, Calais, and a handful of strongholds in Normandy and Brittany remained in English hands (see Holmes 21–32; Bayley).

While most of his contemporaries were criticising those supposedly responsible for these military failures (see *Rot. Parl.* 2:304; Barnie 146; Coleman 71–76), Langland was criticising the war itself, whether successful or not. For him (cf. Wyclif's *De Ecclesia*, 427) the aim of this war was to satisfy Meed, in defiance of Conscience.

In the C text Langland replaced the now long-outdated reference to the Normandy Campaign of 1359–60 by twenty-five new lines, which express still more strongly his abhorrence of the war. Throughout the 1370s and most of the 1380s the English armies were much larger and fought more constantly than in the earlier period. Yet they achieved little of strategic importance, largely because the new and wiser French king allowed the English to plunder and burn their way through the very heart of France, on one devastating chevauchée after another, rather than let the French army engage in the big battles they had always lost in the past (see Barnie 28–31; Hewitt 99–104, 110–18; Holmes 37–45; Myers 103). Meed describes how the Conscience of the English armies was beginning to sicken at the damage they were doing:

> Ac thow thysulue sothly, hoso hit segge durste,
> Hast arwed many hardy man þat hadde wille to fyhte,
> To berne and to bruttene, to bete adoun strenghtes.
> In contrees there the kyng cam, consience hym lette.
>
> (C.3.236–39)

So expensive was such campaigning that soon only the threat of actual invasion could induce the Commons to vote any more taxes, and their unprecedented refusal to vote any at all between 1381 and 1383 (following the disastrous experiment of the poll taxes) effectively brought England to negotiate peace with France. It is clear that by then public opinion had turned against continuing the war (see Barnie 24, 41–45, 127–38; Coleman 76–78, 84–92), and it was perhaps the imminence of the peace which caused Langland to remove the last of the following despairing lines from the B text (cf. Bennett 1943b, 61):

> Al þe wit of þis world and wiȝt mennes strengþe
> Kan noȝt parfournen a pees bitwene þe pope and hise enemys,
> Ne bitwene two cristene kynges. . . .
>
> (B.13.173–75)

INTERNAL GOVERNMENT: THE PROBLEM OF COUNSEL

In discussing the king's internal rule of his kingdom, Langland once again takes an original line, but here he is writing more in accordance with a definite literary tradition: the *Mirror for Princes* genre (see Gilbert 3–15; Coleman 99–102). Like most authors of such texts he concentrates on what Ferguson calls "the problem of counsel": who should advise the king and hold the great offices of state? The literature mirrors a historical truth, for by the fourteenth century political crisis always resulted when the king allowed himself to be guided by a court circle of personal friends, rather than by the great landowners who dominated Parliament (see Tuck 1971). In 1327 and 1399 such crises even led to the deposition of the king. For Langland, as for other writers within this genre, the counsellor who acts and speaks with truth (loyalty and honesty) is the one whom the king should trust (see for example *Secreta Secretorum* [Steele 161] and *Mum and the Sothsegger* 1171–79).

In the coronation scene added to the A text (B.Prol.112–45; C.Prol. 139–57), the king is offered different kinds of counsel. The passage has been discussed elsewhere in detail (e.g., Donaldson 85–120; Baldwin 1981, 12–16). The point to be stressed here is that only in the B text, probably written shortly after Richard II's actual coronation, is the "comune" (community) given any political role. Its counsel helps to "shopen lawe and leaute" (B.Prol. 122), without which, claims the "Goliardeis," no king should be permitted to reign (139–42). By contrast, the C text throws the king entirely on his internal advisors "Kynde Witt" and "Consience" (147, 151), which, as will be seen, is more consistent with the political model suggested in passus 3 and 4.

In the "Rat Fable," which follows in both B and C texts (B.Prol.146–208; C.Prol.165–216), the "comune" of rats and mice do try not merely to counsel the cat, but to prevent him from hindering their activities in any way. Langland hints strongly that their activities would be destructive (B.Prol.196–201; C.Prol.213–16) and that the cat is exercising a legitimate authority (see Donaldson 94). On one level he clearly suggests a king (e.g., B.Prol. 196; C.Prol.206), who should not be so "belled" or bound by loyalty to self-seeking nobles that he can no longer enforce justice upon them.

However, as neither Edward III nor the "kitoun" (B.Prol.194) Richard II had much authority in the later 1370s when the B text was probably being written, Huppé (1941) and Bennett (1943b) have plausibly suggested that the cat can be identified more specifically with John of Gaunt, the king's eldest surviving son and—after himself—the greatest landowner in the kingdom. It was clear that John disapproved of any attempt by the House of Commons to shackle royal authority, for in February 1377 he had imprisoned its Speaker, that courageous "mouse" Peter de la Mare, for leading the Commons in their most daring interference with government. In the "Good Parliament" of the previous year they had "impeached" (publicly condemned) six of Edward's worst counsellors, and banished from the court his notorious mistress Alice Perrers (see Holmes 100–26). The same fable of "belling the cat" had been used in a sermon preached during this Parliament by Bishop Brinton, who, unlike Langland, used it to urge the Commons to action (see Brinton *Sermons* 2:317; Owst 1925; Kellogg; Huppé 1941; Bennett 1943b). The Bad Parliament of February 1377, dominated if not packed by John of Gaunt, reinstated all those who had been impeached, allowed Alice to return to Edward's side, and so proved the Commons to be politically ineffective (see Tout 3:312–21; Armitage-Smith 145–59, 194–95). These acts aroused so much hostility against John of Gaunt that when his father died a few months later he judged it expedient to take no part in the Councils which governed during Richard's minority. Any identification of him with Langland's cat would therefore probably imply the wielding of an unjustifiable authority. It was perhaps to dispel this implication and legitimise the cat that Langland in the C text sets the fable in a law-court (C.Prol.158–64), where the cat can suggest the judge as well as the king. A judge (as the ensuing vision of Meed will indicate) clearly acts more effectively if no one has bought private protection from his claws.

For the vision of Meed, we must go back a little in time to find a political context, for the structure of the allegory in passus 2–4 remained essentially the same after the A text was completed. Meed begins to represent a factor in political (as well as moral) life when she is brought to court as a valuable bride whose marriage the king has in his gift (as his ward would be; see Mitchell; Baldwin 1981, 32–38). In this scene she stands for the wealth and patronage which a medieval king could use to reward honesty and loyalty— the "true" services of Conscience (see Tuck 1971; Wolffe 34–65). Conscience, however, soon exposes her as a corruptor of truth (B.3.120-69; C.3.157-215). The political implication of his refusal to marry her is that true counsel is not to be had by a king who offers lavish patronage, which is likely to attract only greedy courtiers to his side.

The reign of Edward II (referred to in A.3.116; B.3.127) offered a striking example of the misuse of royal patronage, for Edward aroused widespread hostility by his generosity to a few courtiers whose counsel seemed to offer him little guidance (see Tout 2:188-223). Unlike his father, Edward III avoided creating a court party for most of his long life, taking instead the advice of his great magnates of Parliament (see McKisack 1960). But in the 1360s and 1370s he lost much of the respect which this policy had gained for him, by allowing two courtiers who were not great magnates too many rewards and too much of his confidence — William of Wyckham and Alice Perrers. Wyckham's lavish spending of the country's wealth on royal building and display (cf. A.3.199) was matched only by the position he made for himself (see Tout 3:235-75). The lords ousted him from power in 1371, but his influence was replaced by that of Alice Perrers, the king's mistress since the death of the queen in 1369 (cf. A.3.185). He gave her immense gifts, both through the Exchequer, where she had her own bag (see Hall 57), and directly, particularly in jewels, of which, like Meed, she was very fond. Worse still, he allowed her to interfere with the government and the administration of justice, pursuing, it was claimed, "diverse Businesses and Quarrels in the King's courts by way of maintenance" (i.e. legal corruption: *Rot Parl.* 2:329; see Tout 3:287-301; Holmes 68-89, 103, 136-39). In fact, she brings to mind both the effect and the personality of Meed so clearly that several scholars (Cargill; Huppé 1939; Bennett 1943a) have preferred to date this part of the A text to the early 1370s when her influence was already apparent, rather than to the late 1360s when Langland would be fortuitously anticipating later events.

In the C text Langland makes two additions which seem to allude not to Edward's court but to Richard II's, and which provide the principal evidence for dating this text to the early 1380s. They also correspond to a similar addition which Gower made at about the same time to *Vox Clamantis*, 3.7 (see Coleman 152-54). In the first addition Conscience warns the king against harbouring Meed:

> Ther ne is Cite vnder sonne ne noon so ryche reume
> Ther he is alowed and ylet by þat laste shal eny while
> Withouten werre oþer wo oþer wickede lawe
> And custumes of coueytise þe comune to destruye.
> Vnsittyng soffraunce, here suster, and heresulue
> Han almest mad, but marye the helpe,
> That no lond ne loueth the and ʒut leeste thyn owene.
>   (C.3.204-10)

In the second (C.4.187-94) Reason reinforces the warning against "unsittynge soffraunce."

These lines may be accusations against the inefficient Councils which ruled the country during Richard's minority (he was only ten when crowned). These did continue the war, and they did subject the country to the "wickede lawe" of the poll taxes. But the lines seem to be more specifically directed against the king himself, who must therefore have been old enough to carry some responsibility. Richard's generosity to his courtiers had been under attack since 1378 (see *Rot. Parl.* 3:16, 73-74, 100-01, 115, 139), but his "soffraunce" (tolerance) of their greed lost all official restraints when he took over the government in 1382 and appointed Michael de la Pole as Chancellor. By any standards the counsels he was offered by these courtiers violated "truth." They raised money by all possible means — the Crown itself was pawned — and two of Richard's closest friends went so far as to appropriate lands which Edward III had set aside in his will for religious bequests (see Steele; Given-Wilson). By using the Privy Seal and Signet (Secret) Seal to override the law (see C.4.189-90), Richard could protect his courtiers from rival claimants to such lands (cf. *Rot. Parl.* 3:162b-63a, 212a, 222b-23a). Complaints against the government reached such a pitch in Parliament that in 1386 Richard was threatened with deposition, and once more placed under the control of a Council (see Tout 3:385-418; Tuck 1973, 42-47, 58-107; McKisack 1959, 424-47). The king's friends' choice of Meed rather than Truth had already lost him much of his kingdom's love.

INTERNAL GOVERNMENT: THE KING AS FOUNTAIN OF JUSTICE

In passus 4, with his characteristic stress on the individual, Langland presents the king's own Conscience and Reason as his true counsellors. These insist that he will not be loved by his subjects until he once again becomes the agent of justice in his kingdom (see for example their "predictions" of a reign of Reason at B.3.284-330; and B.4.137-48). It was in fact a maxim of the *Mirror for Princes* literature that the king's principal function was the dispensing of justice, often called Truth, as it is in *Piers Plowman* (see e.g. Kail 9-14, 50-55; Steele 54-55, 143; *Richard Redeless* passus 1). Conscience's indictment of Meed in passus 3 indicates that Meed has undermined justice in the local courts and administration, the borough courts, and the high courts at Westminster. (Winfield 131-60, and Harding 97-98, 113-14, give some indication of the widespread legal corruption in fourteenth-century England.) Meed has bribed and influenced her way through the entire mechanism responsible for preserving the king's peace in his kingdom. In passus 4 we see that very Peace come to complain of injustice to the ultimate court of appeal (B.4.47-60), and we see Meed, even there, seeking to pervert justice.

As shown elsewhere (Baldwin 1981, 39–50) there are many records of petitions like Peace's, particularly in the later fourteenth century when the
"retinues" of great lords (remarkably like Lady Meed's) included local and
even central legal and administrative officials, who could protect the lords
themselves and their servants from the rigours of justice (see McFarlane
1973, 102–21; Bellamy 1–36, 199–200; Maddicott 40–88). This left the lords
and their retainers free to bully their neighbours and act "as Kings in the
country, so that right and law are almost set at nothing" (*Rot. Parl.* 3:100b).
Some of the nobility even supported and were supported by criminal bands;
Langland himself mentions the Folville gang in B.19.247 (see Bellamy
69–88).

The oppressed commoners had no recourse but to appeal directly to the
king or the chancellor (in what became known in the early fifteenth century
as his "Court of Conscience" in Chancery) for *ad hoc* justice or "equity." Such
petitioners complain, for example, that their oppressors are "so great in their
country in kinsmen, alliances and friends" that they cannot be prosecuted;
or that they will never be brought to justice "unless our lord the King be-
takes himself against them seriously" (Baildon xxx, 6, 48). So also in *Piers
Plowman* Peace should have been able to obtain redress at common law for
any of Wrong's crimes; his desperate presence at Westminster is proof positive
that the king's truth or justice has been incapacitated by Meed (see Avery).

The king's council and chancery developed their own equitable methods
for cases where "one party [was] so great and rich and the other so poor"
that justice could not otherwise be obtained (*Rot. Parl.* 3:446). Yet in too
many cases the court of King's Council failed to impose even the mild punishment of a fine on the "great party," who was generally of the same class
as the councillors themselves and engaged in practices in which they themselves participated (see Baldwin and Leadam xlv–xlvi). In the *Visio* the king's
Parliament is also inclined to support Meed when she intervenes directly
in the case of her protegé Wrong:

> Somme radde Reson to haue ruþe on þat shrewe;
> And to counseille þe kyng and Conscience boþe
> That Mede moste be maynpernour Reson þei bisouȝte.
>   (B.4.110–12)

With injustice triumphant from the lowest to the highest courts in the
land, it is not surprising that Langland seems to reject the institutional so-
lutions to the misgovernment of the realm — that is, the right counsellors
or the right use of Parliament — offered by other *Mirror for Princes* texts. We
do not read in *Piers Plowman* that

> Wanne alle a kyngdom gadrid ysse
> In goddis lawe, by on assent,

> For to amende þat was mysse,
> Þerfore is ordayned a parlement.
> Trouþe wiþ glad chere þeder went,
> And falsed stondis ay in drede. . . .
>
> (Kail 55)

In Langland's poem it is the king acting as an individual and listening only to his internal Conscience and Reason, who decides to punish Wrong and Meed and to attack the lawyers who have sided with them against Truth (B.4.171-81). One can see this as an absolutist solution to the problems of government (Baldwin 1981, 50–54), but it is perhaps truer to see it as an apolitical solution. Langland has again turned his world inside-out, for in a sense the king's Conscience and Reason are no different from those of his meanest subject.

Even in its social commentary, then, the poem is more about moral than political reform. Yet it should not be read as a traditionalist's indictment on the changes taking place within his society. The Truth which Langland sees as being missing from that society will not be found by reimposing an outdated hierarchy, but by training the new individualism to share the responsibilities of freedom. From this point of view, the king, the priest, the plowman, and Langland's reader are equal in their search to find "treuthe . . . in thy sulue herte" (C.7.255).

REFERENCES

Aers, David. *Chaucer, Langland and the Creative Imagination.* London: Routledge and Kegan Paul, 1980.

Alford, John A. "More Unidentified Quotations in *Piers Plowman.*" *MP* 81 (1984): 278–85.

Armitage-Smith, Sydney. *John of Gaunt.* London: Constable, 1904; rpt. 1964.

Aston, M. "Lollardy and Sedition 1381–1431." *Peasants, Knights and Heretics.* Ed. R. H. Hilton. Cambridge: Cambridge University Press, 1960; rpt. 1976. 273–318.

Ault, W. O. *Open-Field Farming in Medieval England.* London: Allen and Unwin, 1972.

Avery, M. E. "The History of the Equitable Jurisdiction of Chancery before 1460." *BIHR* 42 (1969): 129–44.

Baldwin, Anna P. *The Theme of Government in Piers Plowman.* Cambridge: Brewer, 1981.

———. "A Reference in *Piers Plowman* to the Westminster Sanctuary." *N&Q* 29 (1982): 106–08.

Baldwin, J. F., and I. S. Leadam, eds. *Select Cases before the King's Council 1243-1482.* Selden Society 35. Cambridge, MA: Harvard University Press, 1918.

Baildon, W. P., ed. *Select Cases in Chancery 1364-1471.* Selden Society 10. London: Quaritch, 1896.

Barnie, J. *War in Medieval Society.* London: Weidenfeld and Nicolson, 1974.

Bayley, C. C. "The Campaign of 1375 and the Good Parliament." *EHR* 55 (1940): 370–83.

Bellamy, J. *Crime and Public Order in England in the Later Middle Ages.* London: Routledge & Kegan Paul, 1973.

Bennett, H. S. *Life on the English Manor.* Cambridge: Cambridge University Press, 1937.

Bennett, J. A. W. "The Date of the A-text of *Piers Plowman.*" *PMLA* 58 (1943): 566–72.

———. "The Date of the B-text of *Piers Plowman.*" *MÆ* 12 (1943): 55–64.

Bloch, M. *Feudal Society.* Trans. L. A. Manyon. 1940; rpt. London: Routledge and Kegan Paul, 1962.

Bloomfield, Morton W. *Piers Plowman as a Fourteenth-Century Apocalypse.* New Brunswick, NJ: Rutgers University Press, 1962.

Bolton, J. L. *The Medieval English Economy 1150–1500.* London: Dent, 1980.

Brinton, Thomas. *The Sermons of Thomas Brinton, Bishop of Rochester (1373–1389).* Ed. Mary Aquinas Devlin. Camden Society Third Series. Vols. 85–86. London: Royal Historical Society, 1954.

Burdach, K. *Der Dichter des Ackermann aus Böhmen und Seine Zeit.* Berlin: Weidmann, 1926–32.

Cargill, O. "The Date of the A-text of *Piers Ploughman.*" *PMLA* 47 (1932): 354–62.

Chadwick, Dorothy. *Social Life in the Days of Piers Plowman.* Cambridge: Cambridge University Press, 1922.

Coleman, Janet. *Medieval Readers and Writers.* London: Hutchinson, 1981.

Davenport, F. G. *The Economic Development of a Norfolk Manor 1086–1565.* London: Cass, 1960.

Devlin, Sister Mary A. "The Date of the C-Version of *Piers Plowman.*" *Abstracts of Theses*, Humanistic Series 4. Chicago: University of Chicago Press, 1928.

Donaldson, E. Talbot. *Piers Plowman: The C-text and Its Poet.* Yale Studies in English 113. New Haven: Yale University Press, 1949.

Ferguson, A. B. "The Problem of Counsel in *Mum and the Sothsegger.*" *Studies in the Renaissance* 2 (1955): 67–83.

Fowler, D. C. "A Pointed Personal Allusion in *Piers the Plowman.*" *MP* 77 (1979): 158–59.

Froissart, Jean. *Les Chroniques.* Ed. J. A. C. Buchon. Paris: Desrez, 1835.

Galbraith, F. "Articles Laid before the Parliament of 1371." *EHR* 34 (1919): 579–82.

Gilbert, A. H. *Machiavelli's Prince and Its Forerunners.* Durham, NC: Duke University Press, 1938.

Given-Wilson, C. "Richard II and His Grandfather's Will." *EHR* 93 (1978): 320–37.

Gower, John. *The Major Latin Works of John Gower.* Trans. E. W. Stockton. Seattle: University of Washington Press, 1962.

Gradon, Pamela. "Langland and the Ideology of Dissent." *PBA* 66 (1980): 179–205.

Gwynn, A. *The English Austin Friars in the Time of Wyclif.* Oxford: Oxford University Press, 1940.

———. "The Date of the B-text of *Piers Plowman.*" *RES* 19 (1943): 1–24.

Hatcher, J. *Plague, Population and the English Economy: 1348–1530.* London: Macmillan, 1977.

Hall, H. *The Antiquities and Curiosities of the Exchequer.* London: Stock, 1898.

Harding, A. *The Law Courts of Medieval England.* London: Allen and Unwin, 1973.

Hewitt, H. J. *The Organization of War under Edward III, 1338–62.* Manchester: Manchester University Press, 1966.

Hilton, Rodney H. *The Decline of Serfdom in Medieval England*. London: Macmillan, 1969.

———. *Bond Men Made Free: Medieval Peasant Movements and the English Rising of 1381*. London: Temple Smith, 1973.

———. *The English Peasantry in the Later Middle Ages*. Oxford: Oxford University Press, 1975.

Holdsworth, W. *A History of English Law*. Vol. 2. 4th ed. London: Methuen, 1936.

Holmes, George. *The Good Parliament*. Oxford: Clarendon, 1975.

Homans, G. C. *English Villagers of the Thirteenth Century*. Cambridge, MA: Harvard University Press, 1941.

Hudson, Anne. *Selections from English Wycliffite Writings*. Cambridge: Cambridge University Press, 1978.

Huppé, Bernard F. "The A-text of *Piers Plowman* and the Norman Wars." *PMLA* 54 (1939): 37–64.

———. "The Date of the B-text of *Piers Plowman*." *SP* 38 (1941): 34–44.

Jusserand, J. J. *Piers Plowman: a Contribution to the History of English Mysticism*. Trans. M. E. R. London: Unwin, 1894.

Kail, J., ed. *Twenty-six Political and Other Poems*. EETS 124. London: Kegan Paul, Trench, Trübner, 1904.

Kellogg, Eleanor H. "Bishop Brunton and the Fable of the Rats. " *PMLA* 50 (1935): 57–68.

Knowles, David. *The Religious Orders in England*. Vol. 2: *The End of the Middle Ages*. Cambridge: Cambridge University Press, 1955.

Lawton, D. A. "Lollardy and the *Piers Plowman* Tradition." *MLR* 76 (1981): 780–93.

Leff, G. *Heresy in the Later Middle Ages*. 2 vols. Manchester: Manchester University Press. 1967.

Lomas, R. A. "The Priory of Durham and its Demesnes in the Fourteenth and Fifteenth Centuries." *Econ. History Rev.* 31 (1978): 339–53.

McFarlane, K. B. *John Wycliffe and the Beginnings of English Nonconformity*. 1952; rpt. London: Pelican, 1972.

———. *The Nobility of Later Medieval England*. Oxford: Clarendon, 1973.

McKisack, May. *The Fourteenth Century 1307–1399*. Vol. 5 of *The Oxford History of England*. Oxford: Clarendon, 1959.

———. "Edward III and the Historians." *History* 45 (1960): 1–15.

Maddicott, J. R. "Law and Lordship: Royal Justices as Retainers in Thirteenth- and Fourteenth-Century England." *Past and Present*, Supplement 4 (1978).

Maitland, F. W. "The History of a Cambridgeshire Manor." *EHR* 9 (1894): 417–39.

Mitchell, A. G. "Lady Meed and the Art of *Piers Plowman*." *Chambers Memorial Lecture*, University College. London: Lewis, 1956.

Mum and the Sothsegger. Ed. Mabel Day and Richard Steele. EETS 199. London: Humphrey Guilford, 1936.

Myers, A. R. *English Historical Documents*. Vol. 6 (1327–1485). London: Eyre & Spottiswoode, 1969.

Neilson, N. *Customary Rents*. Oxford Studies in Social and Legal History 2. Oxford: Clarendon, 1910.

Owst, G. R. "The *Angel* and the *Goliardeys* of Langland's Prologue." *MLR* 20 (1925): 270–79.

———. *Literature and Pulpit in Medieval England*. Oxford: Blackwell, 1933; rpt. 1966.

Palmer, J. N., and A. P. Wells. "Ecclesiastical Reform and the Politics of the Hundred Years Wars during the Pontificate of Urban V (1362–70)." *War, Literature and*

Politics in the Late Middle Ages. Ed. C. T. Allmand. Liverpool: Liverpool University Press, 1976. 169–89.

Pollock, F., and F. W. Maitland. *The History of English Law before the Time of Edward I*. 2 vols. Cambridge: Cambridge University Press, 1895; rpt. 1968.

Putnam, Bertha. *The Enforcement of the Statutes of Labourers during the First Decade after the Black Death, 1349–1359*. New York: Columbia University Press, 1908.

Rotuli Parliamentorum II and III. Ed. J. Strachey. London, 1767, 1777.

Statutes of the Realm. Vols. I and II. London: Dawson's, 1810, 1816.

Steel, A. "English Government Finance, 1377–1413." *EHR* 51 (1936): 29–51, 577–97.

Steele, Richard, ed. *Three Prose Versions of the Secreta Secretorum*. EETS es 74. London: Kegan Paul, Trench, Trübner, 1898.

Thomson, John A. *The Later Lollards: 1414–1520*. Oxford: Oxford University Press, 1965.

———. *The Transformation of Medieval England, 1370–1529*. London: Longman, 1983.

Tout, T. F. *Chapters in the Administrative History of Mediaeval England*. Vols. 2 and 3. Manchester: Manchester University Press, 1920–28.

Trevelyan, G. H. *England in the Age of Wycliffe*. 1899; rpt. London: Longmans, 1920.

Tuck, J. A. "Richard II's System of Patronage." *The Reign of Richard II: Essays in Honour of May McKisack*. Ed. F. R. H. Du Boulay and C. M. Barron. London: Athlone, 1971. 1–20.

———. *Richard II and the English Nobility*. London: Arnold, 1973.

Walsh, K. *A Fourteenth-century Scholar and Primate: Richard Fitzralph, in Oxford, Avignon and Armagh*. Oxford: Clarendon, 1981.

Wilks, M. "*Reformatio Regni*: Wyclif and Hus as Leaders of Religious Protest Movements." *Studies in Church History* 9. Ed. D. Baker. Cambridge: Cambridge University Press, 1972. 109–30.

———. "Royal Priesthood: The Origins of Lollardy." *The Church in a Changing Society*. Uppsala: Proceedings of the Commission Internationale d'Histoire Ecclésiastique Comparée Conference [1977], 1978. 63–70.

Winfield, P. H. *The History of Conspiracy and Abuse of Legal Procedure*. Cambridge: Cambridge University Press, 1921.

Wolffe, B. P. *The Royal Demesne in English History*. London: Allen and Unwin, 1971.

Wyclif, John. *De Civili Dominio Liber Secundus*. Ed. Iohann Loserth. London: Wyclif Society, 1900.

———. *The English Works of Wycliffe*. Ed. F. D. Matthew. EETS 74. London: Kegan Paul, Trench, Trübner, 1902.

———. *Fasciculi Zizaniorum Magistri Johannis Wyclif*. Ed. W. W. Shirley. Rolls Series 5. London: Longman, Brown, Green, 1858.

———. *Tractatus de Civili Dominio Liber Primus*. Ed. R. L. Poole. London: Wyclif Society, 1885.

———. *Tractatus de Ecclesia*. Ed. Iohann Loserth. London: Wyclif Society, 1886.

———. *Tractatus de Officio Regis*. Ed. A. W. Pollard and C. Sayle. London: Wyclif Society, 1887.

Yunck, John A. *The Lineage of Lady Meed: The Development of Mediaeval Venality Satire*. Notre Dame: University of Notre Dame Press, 1963.

3

LANGLAND'S THEOLOGY
ROBERT ADAMS

Reflecting well-known trends in academic research and publishing, modern scholarship on the theology of *Piers Plowman* may be roughly divided into two periods and, to some extent, almost two genres. The earlier period comprises the work of scholars who were primarily philologists (e.g., Dunning, Donaldson, Robertson and Huppé, Bloomfield, and Lawlor) and who usually presented their conclusions as broad sketches of the entire poem's oulook in book-length studies. The strength of such studies was their comprehensive scope, and the common weakness was their spotty and sometimes superficial acquaintance with the history and technicalities of medieval theology. By contrast, the recent period has belonged to scholars with somewhat stronger backgrounds in philosophy, theology, and intellectual history. Their work has typically appeared in specialized journals, oftentimes those restricted to *medievalia* (e.g., Wittig, Harwood, Middleton, Baker, Gradon, and Whatley). Contributions from these scholars have usually been narrowly topical and well grounded in primary sources but lacking the breadth of earlier work. In discussing Langland's theology, therefore, this chapter will seek to do justice to both phases, first by describing some of the general tendencies of Langland's thought that have been of perennial concern, and later by taking up some of the specific topics that have attracted more recent investigators or that invite future research; it will conclude with a brief evaluative survey of sources and parallels that have commonly been adduced for Langland's theology.

GENERAL TENDENCIES OF LANGLAND'S THEOLOGY

Many of the earlier controversies about Langland's theological outlook arose from the divergent answers given to such questions as these three: Is Langland mainly concerned with the redemption of society or with that of the individual? Is *Piers Plowman* a poem about the way to perfection or simply the way to salvation? Is Langland's approach to ultimate reality mainly vertical or horizontal (cf. Rowland 1-3; Bischoff 1976a, 13-14) — the mystic's ascent, *beyond time*, to an instant of illumination or the prophet's pilgrimage, *through time*, toward a kingdom that is not yet? Thus, although Robert Frank and Morton Bloomfield would concur in their answers to the third of these questions (both see the poem as mainly horizontal — committed to redemption through the gradual unfolding of sacred history), the major disagreements between their important studies of *Piers* often result from their disparate answers to the first two. Where Bloomfield emphasizes the poem's social dimension and sees the poet as offering an eschatological vision of the corporate perfection of Christendom, Frank is convinced that the poem's center of gravity may be found in the humble Dreamer's slow progress toward personal salvation. On the other hand, the polarities suggested by the aforementioned questions sometimes highlight unexpected common assumptions among critics as well as differences. Hence Robertson and Huppé, whose book bears so little apparent resemblance to Bloomfield's, share with him a basic agreement that the poem is socially oriented and concerned with various levels of perfection. Similarly, although Robertson and Huppé do not endorse Edward Vasta's view that *Piers Plowman* is a poem about the inner spiritual life and the mystic's ascent to God, they are much closer to Vasta than to Bloomfield or Frank on this third issue; for while acknowledging the presence of temporality (e.g., some apocalyptic elements), their reading of *Piers* as a static, four-level allegory causes them to see the poem as a kind of encomium to the Great Chain: the key to happiness is to find your level and perform its duties loyally.

Social or Individual?

Readers today must still decide for themselves whether the poem's center of focus is social or individual. The poem's development makes clear that progress is possible on both levels. However, certain individuals (e.g., Will and Haukyn) are depicted as attaining irreversible spiritual growth, whereas social achievements are shown to follow a circular course of unfulfilled promise and frustrating decay (for a contrasting opinion, see Bloomfield 1962, 99-154; also Arn). In Langland's view, societies as well as individuals stand in need of regeneration, but only a remnant of any society will consent to more than a temporary reformation of manners.

To point this out is not in any sense to deny the reality, the prominence, or the intensity of social criticism in *Piers*. It is merely to assert that the poet is concerned with something else as well, something more fundamental. For

Langland, the characteristic faults of the three estates—the hypocrisy and worldliness of the clergy, the selfishness of the commons, and the arrogance of the nobility—derive their importance from their destructive impact on the lives of countless individual souls wandering between the "tour" of Truth and the "dongeon" of Care. And in this poem, those edifices are not only the first realities. They are the final ones—the destinations of souls, not of societies.

Yet this seemingly pessimistic social outlook does not cause Langland to withdraw into a self-centered quietism. Undeniably the poet's apocalyptic perspective sometimes involves a certain degree of fatalism (e.g., the relapse of the laborers in passus 6 after their deliverance from Hunger); but the rhetoric of such a posture necessarily encourages repentance, even while it insists that too little time remains. While winding ever higher towards more perfect love of God and obedience to his will, the path to beatitude in *Piers Plowman* always revolves around its starting place, the other half of the New Law: love of neighbors. Unlike a modern sociologist, Langland never assumes that relief of social ills is, of itself, a worthy end. Instead, all situations requiring love of neighbors, or loyalty (= *truþe*), present tests of our love of God and of our accord with Truth. We are vividly reminded, by the disappointing frequency of our neighbors' recalcitrance and ingratitude (e.g., the cutpurse and apeward who refuse Piers's guidance in passus 5 or the Bretoner who curses the Plowman in passus 6), that serving them is a means and not an end. The goal is not something like Sweden: the goal is deification (cf. Vasta 68–83).

> For who is trewe of his tonge, telleþ noon ooþer,
> Dooþ þe werkes þerwiþ and wilneþ no man ille,
> He is a god by þe gospel, a grounde and o lofte,
> And ek ylik to oure lord by Seint Lukes wordes.
> (1.88–91)

In sum, Langland's sociology seems moderately Augustinian (cf. *City of God* XV.1). The city of man is doomed. Of course that fact does not relieve us of the more mundane obligations to demonstrate fidelity and love in flawed human society, but neither should we expect our efforts to alter its ultimate destiny. Hence, though the social virtues may often seem fruitless in their immediate context, they are the necessary means by which individual pilgrims advance on their way to the Heavenly City. At the end of the poem an older, wiser, and less virile Will has ceased to indulge in idle questions and has entered Unity (a rather quixotic gesture in the light of its precarious condition) and is learning to love. But at no point does the poet ever retract Holy Church's sweeping generalization from passus 1:

> The mooste partie of þis peple þat passeþ on þis erþe,
> Haue þei worship in þis world þei kepe no bettre;

Of ooþer heuene þan here holde þei no tale.
(1.7–9)

SALVATION OR PERFECTION?

The well-known dilemma of the second question — salvation or perfection? — is one that we have probably created for ourselves. Langland urges upon his reader one goal only: beatitude. To achieve that final happiness, the poem repeatedly implies, one must always make one's best effort — fighting against the temptation to despair that afflicts Haukyn when he wishes that he had died immediately after baptism (14.323–24). At certain points in the narrative, a precise, guaranteed method for achieving perfection is described. One may sell all one owns, give to the poor, work only for one's daily bread, and trust Providence for survival (e.g., 11.255–82). Such a course of action has its roots in well-known New Testament injunctions (e.g., Matt. 19:12, 16–24); indeed, the familiar monastic vows of poverty, chastity, and obedience represent merely a particular historical attempt to formalize those injunctions. For Langland, however, these venerable means to holiness never acquire the legalistic status that they had for the religious orders. The human vocations in which religious perfection is attainable are too rich and varied for so practical a poet to be tempted to legislate artificial restrictions. The mode of one's life is not the issue — the degree of effort is. Even merchants' lives offer opportunities for authentic holiness (7.24–33). But whatever a person's circumstances or social position may require, everywhere echoes the confession of Clergy at the banquet, reminding us that nothing less than Dobest will finally save one's soul:

> For oon Piers þe Plowman haþ impugned vs alle,
> And set alle sciences at a sop saue loue one;
> And no text ne takeþ to mayntene his cause
> But *Dilige deum* and *Domine quis habitabit*;
> And demeþ þat dowel and dobet arn two Infinites,
> Whiche Infinites wiþ a feiþ fynden out *dobest*,
> *Which shal saue mannes soule*; þus seiþ Piers þe Plowman.
> (13.124–30)

As Anne Middleton has noted, the term "Infinites" in this riddle derives from grammatical terminology and signifies *imperfection* or *incompleteness:* "Dowel and Dobet are in this sense of the term 'imperfect': positive and comparative degrees of something intelligible only in its completed form, the superlative degree, Dobest" (173). Likewise, the first proof-text cited by the Plowman — Matt. 22:37 — stipulates that fulfilling the Law requires a *total* commitment, loving God "with thy whole heart, and with thy whole soul, and with thy whole mind." Thus all of the long-winded discussions of the Three Lives (i.e., Dowel, Dobet, and Dobest) that precede the banquet are redefined by the force of Piers's perception that there is only one Christian life, a continuously renewed pilgrimage toward the perfect love of God and neighbor (cf. Mensendieck 416; Frank 7–8, 34–39; and Middleton 175–76, on Langland's rejection of the Three Lives; for a contrasting opinion, see Bloomfield 1958, 245–53).

Has Langland's moral stringency increased unexpectedly between passus 7, where we are told that Dowel will suffice to confer eternal life, and passus 13, where Dobest is demanded? Probably not. Rather, a central premise of Langland's ethics (see p. 97 on *facienti quod in se est*) is that sins of omission or sloth are fully as important as the more colorfully active human failings and that one is not, in fact, doing well if one is not seeking to do the best one can (e.g., cf. 8.100–06; 9.14–15; 10.357–64; 14.192–96; and 15.60–61).

If, therefore, Langland may be termed a "perfectionist," his perfectionism is dynamic and pastoral and resists formulaic definition. Clearly, a considerable distance separates him from many acknowledged masters of the traditional perfectionist devotion (Riehle 22). No one could seem further removed from the ascetical elitism of *The Cloud of Unknowing* or the emotional hyperbole of Dame Julian's *Revelations* (but cf. Schmidt on Julian). Furthermore, Langland seems rather ambivalent — even cautiously unsympathetic — toward the conventional, graded scale of religious obligations sometimes expressed in the metaphor of marriage/chastity/virginity (= layfolk/clerics/monastics). This scale and its metaphoric counterpart were taken for granted by authors with whom he might seem more at home than with Julian, such as Walter Hilton (Hussey 1956) or Bernard of Clairvaux (Donaldson 189–98). Of course Langland does employ the aforementioned metaphor prominently in the Tree of Charity episode, designating the fruit by the conventional terms for the three states of religious life (16.67–71); and this has led some (e.g., Bloomfield 1958) to believe that the poet is endorsing strongly the customary, scaled increments of devotional and ethical duty. A more balanced evaluation, which emphasizes Langland's insistence in C that "bothe two [marriage and virginity] ben gode," is offered by Tavormina. But the hierarchy of the fruit is probably less significant than the fact that *it all falls* — a kind of democracy of original sin.

In Langland's universe, there seems to be no convenient distinction between the optional divine counsels and the obligatory commandments. The very concept of supererogatory works, so basic to most perfectionist schemes, seems incompatible with his thinking. Supererogation — that is, doing more than God requires and thus accumulating a surplus of merit — lies at the heart of the doctrine of the treasury of merit, which in turn is the source of the pardon-mongering that Langland so hated. Nowhere do we find in *Piers* a character who threatens to do more than God requires, although many insist on doing much less. Langland accepts the notion that people will merit heavenly rewards in different degrees (12.192–213), but he never seems interested in adding extra stars to his own crown or to his reader's. What one senses throughout *Piers Plowman* is not the desire for any special seat at the Lamb's table but simply the anxious thirst for heaven itself.

One of the clearest indications of Langland's preoccupation with mere salvation is his concern throughout *Piers* to define the scope and efficacy of baptism and penance. Technically, these two rites are known as "sacraments of the dead." Those who lack them are, until they receive the appropriate sacrament, in a condition of spiritual death, either from the effects of original sin or from actual sin unrepented. Ordinarily, these two are the only doors whereby one may enter, or re-enter, spiritual life. They impart saving grace, rendering one acceptable to God, while the Eucharist and other sacraments offer additional grace to one already in a state of acceptation. Rarely does one find a perfectionist scheme oriented toward the sacraments. Even adoration of the Host is considered, by some of Langland's great mystic contemporaries, a relatively carnal form of devotion. Yet it would seem logical that a perfectionist, if he paid much heed to the sacraments at all, would focus on those whose purpose is to increase one's measure of holiness. In reality, except for the short but notable Easter Mass episode at the beginning of passus 18, there is no such emphasis in *Piers Plowman*. Thus, however one assesses the orthodoxy of Langland's views on baptism and penance, the fact that he discusses these "sacraments of the dead" at such length reveals the modesty of his theme—salvation.

We are faced, then, with somehow accepting simultaneously two positions that the older scholarship (e.g., Frank versus Vasta or Bloomfield) made to seem incompatible: Langland's pilgrimage seeks no more exalted shrine than salvation, but reaching that goal costs the kind of total effort customarily reserved for the few—the spiritual athletes. Fortunately, recent historical work on late medieval theology has shown that this "democratic" perfectionism (an ascetic piety implicitly required of all) is a hallmark of much devotional material of the era (e.g., the *Imitation of Christ*). It is a piety that stresses spontaneity and the continuously renewed turning of the will toward God, thus bypassing the hierarchies of socio-religious obligations (and the concomitant laxities) associated with the traditional system of formal religious vows. In the fourteenth and fifteenth centuries, one often finds this attitude associated with the *Devotio moderna* and the Brethren of the Common Life (Oberman 1981, 45–56; Southern 334–58), but it is apparent in the writings of trained theologians such as Matthias of Janov (III 62–65) and Gabriel Biel (Oberman 1967, 341–49) and, inarticulately, in the widespread earlier popularity of the life of the Beguines (Southern 319-31). A similar perception may be rooted in the lay piety of Wyclif and his followers with their denunciations of formal vows and the monks' "private religions" (e.g., Hudson 1983, 264-67).

So pervasive is this democratic perfectionism in Langland's era that even the Benedictine theologian, Uthred of Boldon, writing against Wyclif on this very issue of "private religions" and defending the legitimacy of monastic orders, shares some of his adversary's premises. Thus Uthred chooses to distance himself from the customary scholastic vindications. Typical of these traditional approaches is Aquinas, who readily acknowledges that all Christians are obliged to attain at least minimal degrees of perfection in charity but who still manages to defend the importance of the formal state of perfection, complacently insisting that its "perfection" derives from the taking of binding vows and has no inherent connection with actual personal sanctity (2a2ae, Q.184, Arts. 3-5). By contrast, Uthred outflanks critics of monastic vows and argues that the substance of such vows has, in a certain sense, always been binding on all people and that, therefore, *all* are required to live the life of religion. As for the matter of entering the formally "religious" life, Uthred sees this not as a choice for an objectively superior state of perfection but purely as a matter of spiritual convenience and personal temperament—a view Langland would certainly have endorsed (Pantin 376-79).

Vertical or Horizontal?

Langland's approach to ultimate reality is limited neither to the vertical, atemporal path of spiritual meditation and vision nor to the horizontal one of salvation history and apocalyptic. The former path, ascending through the purgative and illuminative stages to union with God, may perhaps be traced in the epiphanies of the Plowman, as Elizabeth Salter believed: "Over the first two sections of the poem we work . . . upwards; man, aspiring, catches a spark of the Divine, as Holy Church said firmly in Passus 1: the Truth-led man 'is a god bi the gospel agrounde and aloft.' And so we watch the metamorphosis of Piers as he becomes 'al one with him in grace . . . ʒit . . . ful fer bineþe hym in kynde. . . .' When, however, we near the third section . . . the slant of vision changes. Now seeing God 'condescending into man' to complete that union,. . . Piers must be shown as the human material, the means through which the divine works" (101-02; cf. 83 ff.). The latter path, by contrast, promises to lead us gradually through the "shadowy types" of present events to a "Truth" that only the future can reveal. This is illustrated in Will's journey through the liturgy of Lent—from Abraham to Moses to the Samaritan — as he travels toward Easter (cf. Adams 1976 and St. Jacques 1967, 1969). These two paths to God may seem mutually exclusive (hence the distance between the perspective of Vasta or Salter and that of Bloomfield), but recent scholarship has come to appreciate their fundamental kinship (McGinn 161–64; Bischoff 1976a, 13–14; and Rowland 9–72). Because they reach toward final realities, both styles of thought are eschatological; and in some admixture they co-exist in many prominent medieval thinkers. Hence not only the prophecies of future renewal (e.g., 3.284 ff.), but also the discourse of Holy Church on the treasure of Truth is eschatological. In fact, every revelation of Truth in Will's encounters with various authoritative characters has the signature of the "apocalyptic" as that term is now understood in its root sense: an unveiling of the hidden world of celestial realities.

Perhaps the strongest vertical thrust toward an immediate experience of the Divine is imparted not by the poem's specifically devotional prescriptions (e.g., the path to Truth in passus 5 as analyzed by Salter 86–88) nor by any allegory of the soul's purgation in its narrative line (Vasta 75 ff.) but by its stylistic mannerisms. These often seem neo-Platonic, *not*, in that they necessarily resemble specific linguistic devices employed by Plotinus, Proclus, or pseudo-Dionysius, but in the assumptions they rest on. The poet's apparent redundancies and logical incongruities sometimes seem to result from a deliberate rebellion against the limits of language. To the extent that he often tries to refine away the impurities of common language, stretches metaphors to the breaking point, and occasionally appeals his case to the more permanent and prestigious forum of Latin grammar — a kind of meta-language (Middleton 172, 183–85), Langland might be described as following a mystical course to illumination, the state of unknowing. But his fiction and his theology are, in themselves, firmly committed to the horizontal and the chronological. Langland sees sacred history (whose design Will enters in passus 16) as God's comprehensive means for bringing the human race to grace and finally to the Vision of Himself. This horizontal pattern clearly assimilates the vertical, whose presence is intermittent and, for the most part, implicit.

Popularized by pseudo-Dionysius, vertical eschatology pervades the theological consciousness of many early Church Fathers. It accounts in part for the anti-chronological, "spiritualized" interpretation of New Testament apocalyptic associated with the names of Origen and Augustine as well as for the general drift of nearly all patristic exegesis away from the literal and historical sense of Scripture toward tropological allegory. This static, ultra-Realist outlook may also help to explain the widespread medieval fondness for personification in visual and literary art. Langland's inability to locate completely viable personifications (e.g., the dramatized limits of Conscience and Clergy [Jenkins *passim*; Aers 6–7]) and his resultant choice of figural, time-involved characters such as Piers and the Samaritan to bear his poem's hope (Carruthers *passim* esp. 107–47) are indicative of the relative strengths of these two styles of thought in his outlook (but cf. Bloomfield 1981 on "vertical" and "horizontal" allegory). And in this respect, at least, Langland is very much a man of his time; for historians are generally agreed that, beginning in the twelfth century, there is a notable desertion from static, "spiritualizing" exegesis in favor of literal, primitive motifs with their urgently chronological appeal: Antichrist, Armageddon, Doomsday (e.g., Reeves; Bischoff 1976b).

Many readers may overlook some of the subtler hints of Langland's apocalyptic fervor (the appearance of Hunger in passus 6 or the allusion to the four ages of the Church in passus 19 [Adams 1978]); but long ago William of St. Amour (a thirteenth-century apocalypticist critic of the mendicant orders) was recognized as an important influence on Langland's somber vision, especially for the demise of Unity in passus 20 (Robertson and Huppé 7–10; Szittya 247–87; for William's career, see Dufeil). This influence may have been direct—manuscripts of William's work were readily available in late fourteenth-century England (Szittya 62–122; Hudson notes [1978, 196] that they were burnt at Oxford and Salisbury following Wyclif's condemnation)—but it probably operated also through the mediation of Richard Fitzralph (†1360; for his career, see Walsh), an Irish prelate who borrows freely from William's writings in order to criticize the friars in treatises such as the *Defensio curatorum*.

THEOLOGICAL TOPICS OF CURRENT INTEREST

Grace

Perhaps the most debated topic in current discussions of Langland's outlook is the question of his theology of grace. Certain key episodes, such as the pardon scene, the interruption of Scripture by Trajan, and the proposed marriage of Meed to Conscience, cannot be adequately discussed without reference to this matter. But in addition, Langland's understanding of grace impinges on many other passages in subtle ways often difficult to detect, and one sometimes finds that a scholar has subconsciously begged the questions raised by this issue in order to explicate some modest crux seemingly innocent of theological involvement.

Current opinion on the issue of grace is divided rather sharply between those who see Langland primarily as a moralist urging good works as a means to obtain grace (Allen; Adams 1983; Gradon 1983; Wittig; Whatley

1984b; and, for the most part, Coleman) and those who argue for a more Augustinian Langland (Woolf; Harwood 1973; and Baker). Important factors that appear to have impeded the resolution of this issue include the difficulty of access to usable editions of late medieval theologians, the problem of a nearly impenetrable theological jargon, and the persistence of historiographical and confessional biases that even today somewhat obscure the relative status of the various competing theologies of grace in the late Middle Ages. Until the terms "orthodox" and "heretical" can be restricted to a purely historical and descriptive function, and until we have a clearer sense of the theological norms of Langland's day, this debate is likely to continue.

However, at the risk of acting as judge in one's own cause, it seems fair to report that the most intensive and thorough recent work, covering a wider range of the poem's issues, appears to tilt the balance in favor of a Langland who was, roughly speaking, semi-Pelagian (for a technical definition of this term, see Adams 1983, 370–71). There are simply too many passages scattered throughout the poem that emphasize the primacy of good works and human effort for all of them to be explained away. At the same time, it is only fair to concede that those who argue for a more Augustinian view of the poem (i.e., the priority of grace to works) can make an effective case when dealing with certain passages in isolation or when dealing with the C version (surely the most conservative of the three). Thus Woolf and Baker place their greatest emphasis on explicating the tearing of the pardon, which they understand ironically as a document that incriminates mankind on account of our inability to live up to its terms. The message of the tearing, they contend, is a repudiation of a legalistic means of salvation in favor of reliance on divine grace. Woolf acknowledges that the original context of the Athanasian Creed (the pardon's source) may have been semi-Pelagian, but she believes that Langland has put it to a different use (65–66). Baker goes so far as to suggest that Langland deliberately lures his readers to entertain Pelagian hopes about pleasing God, only to smash us in the face with the words of the Athanasian Creed—which, she believes, offer no pardon whatsoever (725). Only thus can we realize that efforts to please God through human works are vain.

By contrast, Allen and Adams have argued that the pardon scene in both the A and B versions must be understood in the light of the scriptural allusions included within it. The implications of those scriptural allusions clearly cast Piers in the role of maligned virtue and the priest in that of a *detractor* or *derisor* (Allen 349–59; Adams 1983, 407–11).

As for the document itself, the terms of the pardon are meant literally; they are intended to shock our complacency, but they do not amount to a condemnation because they are conditioned by Langland's belief (one long established in medieval theology) that God will never deny his grace to one who does his best (*facienti quod in se est, Deus non denegat gratiam* [Oberman 1967, 132–45; Landgraf 1.i 249–64]). Furthermore, Langland would not have been impressed by assertions that he was falling into the classical Pelagian heresy in thus commending works as the path to salvation. A standard theological principle in his day addressed this issue by distinguishing good works from meritorious ones and by insisting on divine freedom. Absolutely speaking (*de potentia absoluta*), God owes no one anything, and good deeds, of themselves, have no salvific value. Nevertheless, God is under a self-imposed obligation (*de potentia ordinata*) in that he has freely agreed to honor good deeds as though they had either full merit (*meritum de condigno*) or half merit (*meritum de congruo*), depending on the spiritual condition of the one who performs them. Hence God has mercifully created a system whereby a sinner may "earn" his favor. In a world where our best efforts are inherently valueless apart from divine approval, his allowing us to use such means to become "friends of God" is indeed the offering of a most gracious pardon.

The same theology seems implicit in the Meed episode, where Langland appears to distinguish salvation from earthly bribery (both of which are rewards or *medes*) solely on the basis of their *mesure* or lack of *mesure*. In making God's *mede* correlative to one's deeds (it is given to "hem þat werchen wel while þei ben here" [3.233]; cf. *redde quod debes* in passus 19.182 ff. and Coleman's comments 39–41), and in characterizing earthly *mede* as *mesureless* ("lacking in moderation or correlation to merit"; cf. the gloss in Schmidt's edition of B), Langland is implying that beatitude is unlike bribery precisely because it is, in some sense, appropriate or merited by those who receive it (Adams 1983, 398–403). They have "paid what they owed" and are entitled to receive what is owed to them (5.549–52). Though this description might suggest that God's *mede* is indistinguishable from mere *permutatio* or *hire*, salvation remains a gift — because God *need not have saved anyone*. Thus what one receives from him is not something on which one has unconditional claims. Nevertheless, God has covenanted to reward with salvation those who behave appropriately, and he must remain true to his word; therefore, his *mede* is unique precisely in its *mesure* or fitness, its lack of the randomness that characterizes Lady Meed's gifts. There are a variety of views on this issue in late scholasticism, and some who could agree in a narrow sense with Langland on "merited beatitude" would still have disagreed with him on the question of "earning" grace in earlier stages of the process of salvation. Even so, his distance from the "hard" Augustinian viewpoint on this matter (i.e., belief in arbitrary predestination) is difficult to deny.

As for Trajan, the work of Gradon and Whatley succeeds in establishing beyond question what Chambers first clearly asserted: Langland's innovativeness in treating this touchy question of salvation for the righteous heathen (62–69). In his definitive survey of the Trajan legend in the Middle Ages,

Whatley cites the common medieval belief that ancient pagans (e.g., Job, Cornelius) could be saved through a special revelation. Some theologians, including Aquinas, were even willing to concede that some persons of this sort *might* be saved through implicit faith alone. But Trajan represents a significant step beyond such theories since he is a figure born in Western Europe well after the beginning of the Christian era (Whatley 1984a, 55). The standard opinion was that such persons could enter heaven only through baptism. And yet it seems clear that, in adapting the ancient legend of Trajan's deliverance, Langland was merely rendering explicit some of the implications of a theology of grace that took for granted the power of a human being, *ex puris naturalibus* (by unassisted natural effort), to discover truth and "earn" divine favor (cf. Kaulbach's discovery of an anti-Augustinian source for Langland's "vis imaginativa"). Both Gradon and Whatley agree with Wittig in finding Dunning's old theory of a "baptism of desire" for Trajan completely untenable; and Gradon characterizes Langland's actual treatment of the emperor as deriving from "a clearly Pelagian position" (1983, 101). One of the best pieces of evidence for this conclusion is the way in which Langland uses the *vix salvabitur* text from 1 Peter at 12.281–82. Where standard commentators, including Augustine, Jerome, and the authors of the *Glossa ordinaria* understand it as denoting the *difficulty* of salvation, even for the righteous, Imaginatif uses it to prove the *certainty* of salvation for the righteous. As Gradon notes, early Pelagians such as Fasticulus had used the text in exactly the same way (108).

SACRAMENTS

Because of its obvious connection with issues raised in the current debate over the poet's understanding of grace, one of the most fruitful areas for contemporary scholarship would seem to be Langland's attitude toward the sacraments. Hitherto, little direct attention has been accorded to this topic, though Russell's well-known essay and Whatley's recent remarks on the Trajan episode (1984a) offer a promising beginning for Langland's view of baptism. Similarly useful as an introduction to the question of penance in *Piers* is Hort's old account of Langland's contritionism. As for Langland's view of the Eucharist, if we limit ourselves to what he says and refrain from drawing unwarranted conclusions from his silence about matters that would assume a greater importance in later eras, his attitude seems altogether conventional and pious; and since the Eucharist is not frequently mentioned in the poem, it seems unlikely that the subject holds much promise for extensive future research. That is hardly the case, however, with baptism and penance.

With regard to the former, Russell notes that the poet appears to de-emphasize baptism in C and claims that Langland ends by endorsing (C.17.123-24) Uthred of Boldon's theory of the soul's clear vision of God at the moment of death (105 ff., esp. 112-15). According to this theory, even dying infants and pagans have such a glimpse of the divine, and one's eternal destiny hangs entirely on one's reaction to that vision. Of course such a theory—as Uthred's opponents were quick to point out (Knowles 1951)—renders the sacrament of baptism superfluous.

One need not find Russell's argument convincing in order to suspect that Langland set less store by the sacrament than did many of his contemporaries. The major discussions of baptism in *Piers* occur between passus 10 and 12, where Will argues with Scripture and Imaginatif the necessity of baptism for salvation. After having been told by Scripture that nothing worldly helps one toward heaven, Will attempts to stifle doubt about his own eternal destiny by claiming that all who are baptized are secure (10.349-51). One might suppose that what Will is defending is the objective validity of the sacrament, but what he is really defending is a mechanistic view—that baptism is efficacious regardless of one's inner condition or post-baptismal lapses. Hence Scripture responds by pointing out that baptism alone avails only for those who receive it *in extremis*, at the point of death, such as Saracen or Jewish converts. Those who live in Christian society must, in addition, display charity and obey the moral law.

Once rebuked, Will changes tactics and seeks to becloud the issue by claiming to believe in arbitrary predestination, hoping to keep the conversation away from the delicate matter of his own lack of good works. Scripture dismisses this argument with scorn (11.1-3) and the episode dissolves; but after a long exile in Fortune's kingdom, Will finds himself once more thinking about baptism. This time, almost before he realizes what he is saying, the Dreamer utters more reasonable words:

> For a baptiȝed man may, as maistres telleþ,
> Thoruȝ contricion clene come to þe heiȝe heuene.
> (11.80-81)

Thus he has now admitted what he refused to concede in the presence of Scripture: that the objective power of the sacrament is to no avail unless followed by heartfelt sorrow for post-baptismal sins. The choice of the word *contricion* instead of *penaunce* or *confession* seems deliberate. What is being urged here is not the simple necessity of one sacrament (baptism) being supplemented by another (penance). Rather, in the case of each (at least where adults are concerned) the external form of the sacrament must be rendered operative by the proper internal disposition of the recipient.

Will has thus progressed from an extremely wooden, mechanistic notion of baptism to what would pass for an orthodox formulation. Consequently, Scripture reappears to applaud his concession that something more than ritual is necessary for a Christian to be saved. However, a new crisis ensues for Will after Scripture's sermon on the parable of the wedding feast. Where earlier Will had talked glibly of arbitrary predestination, he now begins to experience genuine fear that he himself may not be among those who are chosen. But rather than allaying his fear by seeking the companionship of good deeds, Will tries to convince himself that a mere continued participation in the sacramental life of the Church through penance will prevent any final loss of grace (11.119–36). Scripture seems to endorse the dreamer's smug, stagnant orthodoxy, but just at this moment Trajan breaks in to proclaim the necessity and power of personal righteousness. This startling development disorients and disarms the reader, allowing Langland to move beyond a rhetorically satisfying dogmatism to the more mature faith of Imaginatif. The conclusion implied by his teaching is that baptism is not, in itself, necessary for salvation at all but is conditionally obligatory and required solely because Christ and the Church command it.

Still, this may not be Langland's final word on the sacrament, for Anima also raises the issue of baptism in connection with the need to evangelize Saracens and Jews. Specifically, he describes unbaptized children as "wild" (= *heþen*, which he defines etymologically so as to neutralize some of the word's more negative connotations) and "helpless" with regard to heaven. He never says that such children are damned, but it must be conceded that the note sounded here is much more conservative than that of the prior episodes. Has Langland, as Coleman has recently suggested (141–46), moderated his opinion on the sacrament by the time he reaches passus 15? Is he now more of the party of Archbishop Fitzralph (a moderate Augustinian) than that of the Dominican theologian Robert Holcot (an influential semi-Pelagian)? One's impression is that the rhetoric inherent in Anima's topic — evangelizing the heathen — has more to do with what is said here than any basic change of direction in Langland's theology. Whatley tends to agree, pointing out that this passage in passus 15 deals with "a different type of pagan, one less 'just' and more explicitly hostile to Christianity than those represented by Trajan" (1984a, 62). Moreover, the inescapable biblical imperative of preaching to and baptizing non-Christians has always constituted something of an embarrassment for Pelagians since one of their common tenets is that righteous people may be saved without explicit Christian faith. Thus Langland may be doing no more than addressing a theoretical difficulty by acknowledging that, though salvation is possible without baptism, it is much more likely to occur in the context of the entire sacramental life of the Church. In any event, Anima's words are insufficiently explicit or detailed to justify any radical revision of our understanding of this matter, but candor requires acknowledging that much remains to be done before we can hope to move beyond such tentative explanations.

The same is true for Langland's theology of penance. Long ago Hort theorized that Langland is reacting against the "attritionism" of Duns Scotus (143–54). "Attritionism" regards the penitent's mere willingness to submit to priestly absolution as sufficient, when combined with the objective (*ex opere operato*) power of the sacrament itself, to elevate the penitent's imperfect sorrow for his sin (attrition = fear of unpleasant consequences) to the quality of perfect sorrow (contrition = fear of having offended God's majesty) necessary for sin to be truly forgiven. Hort speculated that Langland may have been influenced on this issue by the more stringent and idealistic "contritionism" of Ockham (143), for it is known that the great Franciscan placed an extraordinary emphasis on the necessity of completely free volition, not only in this matter of repentance but in all areas of moral theology. Hence, for Hort, the demise of Contrition in passus 20 at the hands of Friar Flatterer and the dramatized confession of Meed in passus 3 are intended to illustrate the deficiencies of contemporary penitential *theory* as well as practice. They are intended to contrast with the confessions of the Seven Deadly Sins in passus 5, where the emphasis falls not on the objective ritual of penance but on the psychological reality of repentance.

The general drift of Hort's discussion still seems useful though it has, of course, become outdated in scholarship; yet in spite of the enormous progress of the last twenty years in our understanding of late medieval theology, only Nicholas Gray has chosen to re-examine this subject with the thoroughness that it deserves. Gray's unpublished dissertation documents exhaustively Langland's expert knowledge and use of traditional penance manuals similar to the *Memoriale Presbiterorum* (Camb. MS Corpus Christi 148) and John de Burgo's *Pupilla Oculi* (Paris, 1510). His extensive remarks (*passim*) on the confession of the sins in passus 5 are particularly valuable. While agreeing with Hort in seeing Langland as a "contritionist," Gray doubts that Langland has any knowledge of, or interest in, abstract disputes over penance among contemporary scholastics such as Scotus or Ockham. Instead, the discussions of penance that permeate his poem are of a practical and pastoral tone (83). Also, Gray insists more strongly than does Hort on the conventional orthodoxy of Langland's contritionism (86–87), though he exaggerates her opinion when he suggests that Hort saw Langland as "bordering on the heterodox." Where Gray regards Langland against the background of the confessional handbooks and tends, perhaps, to underestimate his breadth of learning and polemicism, Hort may overemphasize future developments in academic theology in her description of the poet as a self-conscious reformer: "What Langland actually said [about the relative unimportance of confession] was orthodox at the time when he said it, but it was on its way to condemnation" (155).

With the exceptions of Gray and Gradon, in recent times only Burrow has touched upon penance significantly; and even he seems rather timid when confronting the possibility — raised by his own discussion — that Langland's sermon of Reason and Confession to Repentance might be read as implicit attacks on their literal models, the sermon of a bishop and confession to a priest (212–13). Does Langland wish to suggest, with his use of an allegorical confessor and the *Deus tu conversus* prayer from the liturgy of public worship, that an open, collective acknowledgment of our sins provoked by genuine repentance is either better than or even different from the private sacrament (cf. Gray's discussion of absolution, 254–59)? Perhaps even to raise the issue is to court the danger of overreading; but it is not an easy question to answer since, for obvious reasons, any wish to say such things would necessarily have found voice in ambiguous language.

Another question that needs clarifying is how Langland's understanding of confession relates to popular attitudes among his contemporaries, especially the followers of Wyclif (Gradon 191–93 has discussed this briefly; also Gray 165–70). Nothing in the poem suggests that Langland saw confession as intrinsically harmful. That he is so concerned with the perversion of penance by the friars would seem to indicate a high regard for the benefits derivable from a proper confession. Thus at one point we are assured that oral confession, if it follows genuine contrition, will suffice to kill any sin, however deadly (14.90–92). Of course he does not think confession absolutely necessary (cf. 14.83–89 and 12.171–78) for a sin to be forgiven, but then almost no medieval theologian would have defended such a notion without making many exceptions.

In sum, Langland does not appear to question the institution of the sacrament itself, as did the Lollards, but on the other hand it is not at all clear that he would have seen it as sinful to postpone confession indefinitely if one's only available confessors offered no evidence of personal sanctity or wisdom (e.g., the implications of 12.170–85). Donatism, with its distrust of the sacramental powers of bad priests, is, perhaps, latent in several passages where he discusses the sacrament (cf. Oberman's analysis of Biel's similar tendencies, 1967, 220–22); yet, if we heed Gray, who points out that many penance manuals are likewise preoccupied with the danger of the wicked or ignorant priest (142–45), there may be nothing ominous in Langland's statements about this issue. At present, then, the only safe generalization about Langland's sacramental theology is Whatley's: "Langland's conception of Christianity is at bottom ethical and social rather than sacramental or mystical" (1984b, 11).

ESCHATOLOGY

Another topic of current relevance is the question of Langland's eschatology. Two issues were raised by Bloomfield's classic treatment of this subject (1962) that remain matters of debate among contemporary scholars: (1) the specific nature of Langland's prophetic opinions or expectations and (2) the degree of importance these opinions have for an understanding of the poem. Of course Bloomfield not only argued for the influence of Joachim of Fiore (a twelfth-century biblical exegete and prophet) on the poem's thought (cf. Frank 17–18) but also claimed that *Piers* is apocalyptic in genre. Virtually no one has accepted the generic claim, for even Bloomfield himself admitted that apocalypse was only one of six genres discernible in *Piers* (10). Likewise, the claim for Joachite and vaguely utopian models has come to seem unpersuasive to many scholars (e.g., Aers 62–63), and several recent discussions decisively reject this model in favor of a more conventional and traditional understanding of the poet's apocalypticism (Adams 1978; Emmerson 193–203; Adams 1985).

Unfortunately, one of the results of the failure of Bloomfield's arguments to sustain themselves is that some scholars now think that "Langland's apocalypticism hardly seems central to his plan" (Kean 334, n. 36). Others are willing to concede the prominence of the poem's eschatological prophecies but regard them as aesthetic or even moral blemishes. Hence Aers characterizes them as "a dramatic failure of the poet's normally powerful grasp of social and historical reality" and as "a romantically revolutionary evasion of complexities which the poem, as a whole, explores with heroic scrupulousness and energy" (67).

By contrast with these positions, Adams has recently argued that Langland's apocalypticism is both central to his thought and integral to the structure and theme of his poem. Bloomfield's perception of Langland's interest in millenarian ideologies seems correct: nevertheless, Langland's essentially traditional, Augustinian (i.e., amillennial) eschatology seems equally certain. In the light of these facts, Adams has proposed that Langland employs some of his more provocatively utopian prophecies with the same sort of rhetorical duplicity that he devotes to the description of Piers's "pardon" or the "pilgrimage" to St. Truth. Repeatedly, the poet lures us on with ambiguous promises in order to reveal to us our shallow and fallacious comprehension of the profound truths that should animate our merely conventional religious faith.

In the case of the pardon, for example, we reveal our half-hearted devotion by the sense of relief we feel on learning that this elaborately detailed instrument appears to offer a means of escape from Judgment without making any serious demand for continuous personal reform. Similarly, the prophecies of Conscience and Clergy offer ample stimulus to misreading, a stimulus that appeals powerfully to our desire to be saved from ourselves by some external means without paying any price in suffering: the Angelic Pope or Last World Emperor will set all to rights. Yet just as the actual terms of the pardon, when they finally appear, shock us out of our spiritual sloth, so the relentless attack of Antichrist in passus 20--with no royal savior in sight—gives the lie to our hopes for a mundane deliverance at the hands of a messiah made in our own image. Langland will have none of this empty triumphalism.

To say this is not, of course, to imply that the poem ends without hope. Aers is surely correct in asserting that Langland "envisaged the present as involving a massive defeat for Christianity" (77); but the poet is operating within a conventional framework of apocalyptic expectations—a framework that is, despite the darkness and urgency of the foreground, finally optimistic. Emmerson has aptly described this dual vision: "It is pessimistic in that there is no human solution for Antichrist's attack. It is optimistic in that those Christians who stand firmly against Antichrist will be rewarded ultimately when Christ comes in glory and destroys Antichrist" (200).

We have had a glimpse, during the Harrowing of Hell in passus 18, of what that moment will be like, but Langland is no escapist and will indulge no such tendencies in the reader. As Will encounters Christ in the present, at Easter Mass, he is still the suffering Son being offered sacrificially to the Father for the sins of the world. The effect of this vision is to deepen Will's entire conception of Christ's Kingship—*pacientes vincunt*. Gradually we realize that, like David, Christ (the real "king" of Langland's prophecies) must endure countless hardships between his anointing and his final, triumphant coronation. Will, and we, must prepare for that victorious future by freely embracing with him the urgent suffering of the present.

THEOLOGICAL SOURCES AND PARALLELS

MONASTICISM

It is only natural that such an idiosyncratic piece of work as *Piers Plowman* should have generated so much enthusiasm for finding its spiritual wellspring. Today we are, for good reason, a bit more cautious than scholars of the past in asserting that Langland's sources have been definitively located, but we are no less eager to find illuminating parallels. So far, some of the weightiest arguments have been those of Bloomfield, Donaldson, Vasta, and Wittig on behalf of "monastic philosophy" as the basic inspiration behind *Piers*. Unhappily, this general truth has been somewhat obscured by Bloomfield's special focus, which led him to identify "monastic philosophy" in large part with social meliorism or, more specifically, the apocalyptic utopianism of Joachim and some of his followers. Yet Langland's indebtedness to more orthodox and permanent traditions of monastic thought, such as Benedictine and Cistercian spirituality (Maisack 1953), seems indisputable. As a matter of historical necessity, any fairly orthodox, late medieval writer on spiritual subjects having a strong affective bias and standing outside the mainstream of scholasticism (and who can doubt that such a description fits Langland?) must owe something to the style of thought associated with monasticism, whatever the intermediaries or particular channels of influence. Wittig's careful study (1972) of the Bernardine psychology of conversion in passus 11 through 12 of *Piers* offers a good introduction to Langland's indebtedness, especially for those who may mistakenly regard monastic contemplation as a form of piety divorced from active charity (also see Hussey).

Of Langland's specific qualities, perhaps his anti-intellectualism is most readily attributable to monastic influences. Many examples spring to mind, such as Reason's withering rebuke to Will's prying, impious questions about the divine dispensation (11.376 ff.). Likewise, when at the beginning of passus 11 Scripture scotches Will's vain curiosity with a ponderous Latin phrase, she is quoting the opening words of a well-known, pseudo-Bernardine devotional treatise: *"Multi multa sciunt et seipsos nesciunt"* (Wittig 214). The same spirit inspires William of St. Thierry, who first alarmed St. Bernard to the dangers latent in Peter Abelard's rationalism. In a typical passage, he attacks mere *scientia* and praises monastic *sapientia* as an ideal affecting the whole person:

> Their wisdom [that of monks] comes not from the spirit of this world, nor from the prudence of this present age. Being devoid of learning, they have entered into the power of the Lord and, being poor in spirit, they are mindful only of your [God's] righteousness. Wherefore you have taught them, that in their life and conduct they may show forth your wondrous works. These are your simple servants, with whom you are wont to talk familiarly. In coming to you they do not put their trust in the chariots of their own cleverness, nor in the horses of their own strength, but only in the name of the Lord. (1:175)

The last sentence of this quotation applies to vain learning the same Scripture, Ps. 19:8, that Clergy applies to disloyal religious during his famous prophecy in passus 10.322 ff. of *Piers*. In that context, of course, the allusion has a more literal application—the materialism of lapsed monks; but much of Clergy's fury derives from his having been deserted by those whose way of life tied them to the pursuit of divine learning. Clergy's prophetic use of Ps. 19 follows close on the heels of his description of a cloister as heaven on earth (10.307–8). This passage and the lengthy reproof Will suffers from Anima (15.50 ff.) — where a distinction is drawn between wisdom of spiritual value and worthless worldly knowledge — show that Langland's anti-intellectualism, though real enough, is far from the philistine or know-nothing varieties (cf. Simpson).

Closely related to this anti-intellectualism is Langland's biblicism, an aspect of the poet's thought so strongly ingrained as to be stylistically palpable. In Bloomfield's memorable phrase, Langland often sounds as though he "speaks Bible" (1962, 37). Biblicism was in the air of the fourteenth century (a reaction, in part, against Aristotelian scholasticism — cf. Courtenay 116–17; Oberman 1967, 108–11, 361 ff.), and Langland's bias here, like his anti-intellectualism, could derive from a number of sources; still, its final inspiration is found in traditional Benedictine spirituality with its emphasis on *lectio divina* (Leclercq). That Langland appears to share with many monastic thinkers an ambivalence toward the Dionysian tradition of speculative meditation is probably attributable to biblicism. As was noted earlier, to some degree all medieval spiritual writers (including Langland) are unconscious disciples of the Areopagite since he is the principal Christian source of a neo-Platonism that had strongly affected patristic thought even before the fifth century. Yet a curious, tacit suspicion of Dionysius's own works seems to have existed in Western monastic circles, and this despite the high regard in which Dionysius himself held monasticism. Leclercq attributes this discomfort to the sense that the Areopagite's sort of contemplation was "not sufficiently biblical" (115). As for Langland, this side of the biblicist bias obtrudes when, near the end of the poem, he records that Envy

> heet freres go to scole
> And lerne logyk and lawe *and ek contemplacion*,
> And preche men of Plato, and preue it by Seneca
> That alle þynges vnder heuene ouȝte to ben in comune.
> (20.273–76)

Here the poet's aim is so broad that it fails, momentarily, to distinguish valid, affective contemplation (of the kind he has praised in Clergy's description of an ideal cloister) from the faddish, unscriptural intellectualism of friars delving into the classics.

The prominence of a literal apocalypticism and an emphatically chronological soteriology in *Piers Plowman* are sometimes put down to monastic influence. After all, the revival of the prophetic mentality in the twelfth century is undeniably connected to the renascent historicism of such monastic authors as Rupert of Deutz and Anselm of Havelberg (Bischoff 1976b; Reeves 54–55). Furthermore, many monastics (especially the Cluniacs) have seen the celebration of salvation history throughout the liturgical year as the pinnacle of their corporate existence (Knowles 1963, 148). Yet in all likelihood Langland's emphasis on the liturgical pattern of progressive redemption and his historicist bent are not directly indebted to monastic thought but are independent byproducts of the same biblicism that shaped these supposedly distinctive features of monasticism.

Ironically, the philosophy of melioristic social activism sometimes attributed to Langland and traced to monastic influences is not, in fact, prominent either in Langland or in traditional forms of medieval monasticism. Naturally one's opinion of Langland's posture on this issue will depend on a necessarily subjective reading of his poem, but no modern interpreter of classical monasticism would accept the notion that its goal was analogous to, say, the Oneida Community's — a kind of gradual spreading of economic justice and social enlightenment into the outer world. Rather, it tended to have more in common with the spirit of Thoreau — flight to the wilderness to avoid contamination and to achieve self-sufficiency. Thus Leclercq points out that "to St. Benedict, monastic life is entirely disinterested; its reason for existing is to further the salvation of the monk, his search for God, and not for any practical or social end which, incidentally, is never even mentioned" (24; on this issue, also see Flew 161–77; Peifer 40–50). Similarly, since the Cistercians aimed at nothing more than a "repristination" of earlier monasticism, it was perfectly logical that they sought to erect their first communities in remote wildernesses. Hence if Langland owes anything to monasticism on this score, it is a rigorous individualism expressed in *Piers* by means of the pilgrimage and remnant motifs (e.g., the final departure of Conscience and the resistance offered to Antichrist by a few "fooles").

The Moderni

Anti-intellectualism (of a sophisticated kind), biblicism, a sort of spiritual pragmatism, and ethical individualism are all traits that might, with equal justice, be linked to trends in fourteenth-century theology, trends associated with a rebellion against the arid Aristotelianism that some saw exemplified in Aquinas. These qualities are particularly noticeable among some of those whom we used to call "Ockhamists" and whom we are now content to call "the *moderni*" (Oberman 1981, 23–44; Coleman 23). Fascinated by epistemological and linguistic problems, and drawing their inspiration from "the mathematicism of Oxford" (Coleman 18), these theologians employed the logical innovations and methodology of the speculative grammarians in an effort to make theology more rigorously scientific than ever before. "All knowledge was resolved into propositions. Rational dialectic with its emphasis on argumentation by means of the soundly argued sophism" becomes the standard means for analyzing scriptural texts or dogmatic truths (Coleman 22). Often the result of this procedure was the disturbing discovery that much less knowledge was logically demonstrable or inferable than had previously been supposed. Of course Aquinas himself had recognized that such tenets of true religion as the existence of the Trinity or God's creation of the world could not be necessarily inferred by reason unaided. However, many other dogmatic issues that theologians of his era had dealt with as matters of natural theology (i.e., subject to resolution by reason alone) came to be classified by the *moderni* as matters of revealed theology. Thus the increased use of strict scientific criteria in the process of argument and proof tended to engender a form of fideism.

One of the hallmarks of this innovative group of theologians (possibly related to their pragmatic bias) is their obsession with sacramental and ethical problems: however, these problems are frequently discussed in the context of extreme examples or paradoxical ones — puzzles that invite the use of ever more subtle logical tools in their solution. The majority of these thinkers, influenced by Ockham's ethics as much as by his critical method, emphasize human moral autonomy to such a degree as to incur charges of Pelagianism. On the other hand, some "right-wing" *moderni*, e.g., Gregory of Rimini, are harshly critical of Ockham's ethics while continuing to make use of his distinctive approach to logic.

The first *Piers* scholar to explore at length the potential of these theologians for illuminating the poem was John F. McNamara, whose 1968 dissertation on the subject has never been published. Since that time a number of investigators have suggested the importance of the *moderni* for an understanding of *Piers* (e.g., Harwood 1971; Kirk 97–98; Murtaugh 74–91; and Adams 1983). Nevertheless, the most definitive case for this influence is made by Janet Coleman. Coleman has argued that Langland's development of such issues as grace, free will, predestination, and future contingents amounts to a popularized reflection of the questions that dominated the academic debates between the left and right wing *moderni* in the same era. She is especially effective in demonstrating the relationship of the Trajan episode to the central concerns of contemporary theology. Of course Coleman labors to prove this with a singular inherent advantage since one would ordinarily assume a philosophical poet to be aware of and reacting to the thinkers of his own period.

Still this influence seems unlikely to win, at present, the sort of universal acknowledgment accorded to monasticism. There are several reasons for scholarly skepticism. First, the theologians of Langland's day still suffer from an undeservedly bad reputation, one inflicted long ago by neo-Thomist historians eager to blame the so-called "nominalists" for the Reformation. To some degree, the reputation was invited since a major tendency of fourteenth-century theology is toward the critique and fragmenting of earlier systems. Secondly, the fact that Langland's theological contemporaries deploy a formidable technical vocabulary and are usually unavailable in modern texts or translations makes them seem, to many Middle English scholars, a rather recherché source for the thought of a man whose concerns sound so directly earnest and unsophisticated. Yet Langland need not have used the language of the schools (with its consequent narrowing of his audience) in order to have been affected by similar concerns; and one of the most effective but least noticed points in Coleman's argument is that there is ample evidence of philosophical popularization in Langland's era — that "grammar, logic and theology filtered down to the new class — the non-ecclesiastical literate" (171). Finally, scholars can scarcely be blamed for their reluctance when some of those describing a *moderni* influence see Langland reacting against it, others see him wholeheartedly in the camp of Ockham and Holcot, and Coleman herself vacillates between a Langland seemingly siding with Pelagian *moderni* at one moment and Augustinians at another. Particularly damaging for these claims is the fact that both Coleman and Adams have developed detailed readings of such central episodes as that of Meed, that of the Pardon, and that of Trajan from the common premise of *moderni* influence; and yet, their common premises do not issue in anything resembling a common interpretation. On the contrary, Adams's view is closer to that of Allen and Gradon, neither of whom accepts the thesis of *moderni* influence.

The problem appears to lie in the different interpretation of key elements in the fourteenth-century theological vocabulary: (1) the *potentia absoluta* and (2) the *potentia ordinata*. Adams has understood these concepts to refer to (1) God's (now theoretical) power, from all eternity, to do whatever does not involve self-contradiction and (2) his actualized, covenanted power (restricted by his own self-revelation) to do only what he has promised. On the other hand, Coleman has understood the *potentia absoluta* to be a mode of operation that remains always an unforeseeable possibility and the *potentia ordinata* to be no more than a customary mode of divine operation that may be overruled at any moment. Which concept corresponds to the usage of Langland's contemporaries? Unfortunately, the answer seems to be that both do (Oakley 143–45). But until those who find these terms useful for explicating Langland can agree on which meaning they should bear in this context, it should not be surprising if some scholars remain confused and doubtful.

WYCLIF AND THE LOLLARDS

The supposition that Langland was influenced by Wyclif goes back at least to Bishop Bale (Gradon 179); indeed, it has enough inherent plausibility to have occurred to some of Langland's contemporaries. Yet a sober estimate makes it seem far likelier that the undeniable similarities in certain areas derive from a shared response to contemporary conditions than from any direct influence of the Oxford theologian on the poet of Cornhill. Perhaps the most striking apparent resemblance between the two concerns the issue of a possessionate clergy and the corruption that both see rooted in excessive Church wealth. Like Wyclif, Langland appears to endorse the confiscation of ecclesiastical endowments as a cure for this condition (cf. 10.311–32 and 15.551–69). Both echo the common charge that the Church's decay began with the Donation of Constantine (Gradon 1980, 185 n. 7), and beneath their demand that priests live on tithes is the Donatist (i.e., puritanical) desire to weed out from holy orders all but the most worthy. Yet despite the modern tendency to identify all disendowment programs with Wyclif, Langland's stance on this matter links him to more conventional-minded Englishmen as well (see chapter 9; cf. Gradon 1980, 187–88).

Beyond their mutual regard for evangelical poverty, the closest link between Langland and Wyclif seems to be a shared biblicism eager to confront the individual reader with the Word of God's demands unmediated by priestly casuistry. This biblicism, which finally caused Wyclif to abandon the visible Church altogether as a source of religious authority (Leff 2:523–24), tends to lead both men to anti-sacerdotal and vaguely anti-sacramental attitudes. Langland never resorts to Wyclif's sometimes violent rhetoric, but the depiction of the priest in passus 7 and that of the vicar in passsus 19, as well as the subtle hints about baptism and penance throughout *Piers*, all have suggestive implications. Yet, as we have seen, biblicism is a hallmark of Langland's era and scarcely the private preserve of Wyclif or the Lollards. Moreover, the overlap of attitudes that one can detect on some of the matters mentioned above is probably accidental. Thus even though Langland and Wyclif may appear to share suspicions about the worthiness of the clergy and the value of some of the sacraments that they administer, they probably arrive at those opinions from different directions. Wyclif is skeptical, in part, because his belief in predestination leads him to a position where there is no need or room for the efficacy of sacramental ministrations (Pelikan 4:32–33; Gradon 1980, 201). By contrast, if Langland tends to doubt the power of priestly mediation, it is because his intense ethical commitment regards all other means than dowel as, potentially, devices for evading one's obligatory *imitatio christi*.

It is here that the significant differences between Langland and Wyclif emerge. Where Wyclif is every bit as fatalistic and "hard" Augustinian as Chaucer's "Bisshop Bradwardyn," Langland usually emphasizes the radical spiritual freedom of the human will. Indeed, Langland appears to treat the whole subject of predestination in a manner typical of Augustine's early critics when, in passus 10, he allows Will to invoke the doctrine of arbitrary predestination as an excuse for evading the demand for personal reform. And we may see, in Will's wandering in the "lond of longynge," the personal consequences of believing that God's gifts of grace and salvation have no correlation with one's efforts to please him. Likewise, as Gradon has noted, Langland shows no evidence of believing in the Wycliffite notion of "the two Churches" (the Church of Christ and that of Antichrist), which is a logical outgrowth of Wyclif's belief in the preordained separation of all souls from eternity (199–200). As for the Eucharist, Langland's attention seems purely devotional; he manifests none of the interest of Wyclif and the later Lollards in the theoretical questions regarding the mode of Christ's presence in the Host. Finally, while some of the Lollards certainly share with Langland an apocalyptic obsession (Hudson 1978, 65–66, 81, 126; Hudson 1983, 375–77), Wyclif himself cannot properly be termed an apocalypticist (but cf. Szittya 167–72). Though his biblicism encourages the use of eschatological rhetoric (so that he frequently terms the pope and his agents "antichrist"), he maintains a classical Augustinian agnosticism concerning the Last Things and explicitly rejects (with a scholastic's contempt) the "vain prophecy" of the Joachites (Leff 2:543 n. 2). In general, both Wyclif and his followers are more inclined to deploy the "plural antichrist" tradition of 1 and 2 John than that used by Langland — the single great adversary of God (the "man of sin" of 2 Thess.). The reason seems obvious: for polemical writing the "plural antichrist" tradition is very useful. One can label every opponent of one's proposed reforms as a source of ultimate evil. On the other hand, if one truly believes in the imminent advent of the Last Great Antichrist (whom Will sees approaching in his final dream), all merely human plans for ecclesiastical renewal dissolve in irrelevance.

REFERENCES

Adams, Robert. "Langland and the Liturgy Revisited." *SP* 73 (1976): 266–84.
———. "The Nature of Need in *Piers Plowman* XX." *Traditio* 34 (1978): 273–302.
———. "Piers's Pardon and Langland's Semi-Pelagianism." *Traditio* 39 (1983): 367–418.
———. "Some Versions of Apocalypse: Learned and Popular Eschatology in *Piers Plowman*." Ed. T. J. Heffernan. *The Popular Literature of Medieval England*. Knoxville: University of Tennessee Press, 1985. 194–236.
Aers, David. *Chaucer, Langland and the Creative Imagination*. London: Routledge, 1980.
Allen, Judson. "Langland's Reading and Writing: *Detractor* and the Pardon Passus." *Speculum* 59 (1984): 342–62.
Arn, Mary-Jo. "Langland's Triumph of Grace in *Dobest*." *ES* 63 (1982): 506–16.

Baker, Denise N. "From Plowing to Penitence: *Piers Plowman* and Fourteenth-Century Theology." *Speculum* 55 (1980): 715–25.

Bischoff, Guntram G. "Dionysius the Pseudo-Areopagite: The Gnostic Myth." *The Spirituality of Western Christendom*. Ed. Rozanne Elder. Kalamazoo, MI: Cistercian Publications, 1976. 13–40.

———. "Early Premonstratensian Eschatology: The Apocalyptic Myth." *The Spirituality of Western Christendom*. Ed. Rozanne Elder. Kalamazoo, MI: Cistercian Publications, 1976. 41–71.

Bloomfield, Morton W. "*Piers Plowman* and the Three Grades of Chastity." *Anglia* 76 (1958): 227–53.

———. *Piers Plowman as a Fourteenth-Century Apocalypse*. New Brunswick, NJ: Rutgers University Press, 1962.

———. "The Allegories of *Dobest* (*Piers Plowman* B XIX–XX)." *MÆ* 50 (1981): 30–39.

Burrow, John. "The Action of Langland's Second Vision." *EIC* 15 (1965): 247–68; rpt. in Blanch 1969, 209–27.

Carruthers, Mary. *The Search for St. Truth: A Study of Meaning in Piers Plowman*. Evanston: Northwestern University Press, 1973.

Chambers, R. W. "Long Will, Dante, and the Righteous Heathen." *E&S* 9 (1924): 50–69.

Coleman, Janet. *Piers Plowman and the "Moderni"*. Rome: Edizioni di Storia e Letteratura, 1981.

Courtenay, William. "Covenant and Causality in Pierre d'Ailly." *Speculum* 46 (1971): 94–119.

Donaldson, E. Talbot. *Piers Plowman: The C-Text and Its Poet*. Yale Studies in English 113. New Haven: Yale University Press, 1949.

Dufeil, M. M. *Guillaume de Saint-Amour et la Polémique Universitaire Parisienne, 1250–1259*. Paris: Editions A. et J. Picard, 1972.

Dunning, T. P. *Piers Plowman: An Interpretation of the A-Text*. 2nd ed. rev. T. P. Dolan. Oxford: Clarendon Press, 1980.

Emmerson, Richard K. *Antichrist in the Middle Ages*. Seattle: University of Washington Press, 1981.

Flew, R. Newton. *The Idea of Perfection in Christian Theology*. 1934; rpt. New York: Humanities Press, 1968.

Frank, Robert Worth, Jr. *Piers Plowman and the Scheme of Salvation: An Interpretation of Dowel, Dobet and Dobest*. Yale Studies in English 136. New Haven: Yale University Press, 1957.

Gradon, Pamela. "Langland and the Ideology of Dissent." *PBA* 66 (1980): 179–205.

———. "*Trajanus Redivivus*: Another Look at Trajan in *Piers Plowman*." *Middle English Studies presented to Norman Davis in Honour of His Seventieth Birthday*. Ed. Douglas Gray and E. G. Stanley. Oxford: Clarendon Press, 1983. 93–114.

Gray, Nicholas J. "A Study of *Piers Plowman* in Relation to the Medieval Penitential Tradition." Diss. Cambridge University, 1984.

Harwood, Britton J. "*Piers Plowman*: Fourteenth-Century Skepticism and the Theology of Suffering." *Bucknell Review* 19 (1971): 119–36.

———. "*Liberum-Arbitrium* in the C-Text of *Piers Plowman*." *PQ* 52 (1973): 680–95.

Hort, Greta. *Piers Plowman and Contemporary Religious Thought*. London: Society for Promoting Christian Knowledge, 1938.

Hudson, Anne, ed. *Selections from English Wycliffite Writings*. Cambridge: Cambridge University Press, 1978.

————, ed. *English Wycliffite Sermons* 1 (Other volumes in progress). Oxford: Clarendon Press, 1983.

Hussey, S. S. "Langland, Hilton and the Three Lives." *RES* ns 7 (1956): 132–50.

Jenkins, Priscilla. "Conscience: The Frustration of Allegory." In Hussey 1969, 125–42.

Kaulbach, Ernest N. "The 'Vis Imaginativa' and the Reasoning Powers of Ymaginatif in the B-Text of *Piers Plowman*." *JEGP* 84 (1985): 16–29.

Kean, P. M. "Justice, Kingship and the Good Life in the Second Part of *Piers Plowman*." In Hussey 1969, 76–100.

Kirk, Elizabeth D. *The Dream Thought of Piers Plowman*. Yale Studies in English 178. New Haven: Yale University Press, 1972.

Knowles, M. David. "The Censored Opinions of Uthred of Boldon." *PBA* 37 (1951): 305–42.

————. *The Monastic Order in England*. 2nd ed. Cambridge: Cambridge University Press, 1963.

Landgraf, Arthur M. *Dogmengeschichte der Frühscholastik*. 4 vols. in 8. Regensburg: F. Pustet, 1952–56.

Lawlor, John. *Piers Plowman: An Essay in Criticism*. London: Arnold, 1962.

Leclercq, Jean. *The Love of Learning and the Desire for God*. Trans. Catharine Misrahi. New York: Fordham University Press, 1961.

Leff, Gordon. *Heresy in the Later Middle Ages: The Relation of Heterodoxy to Dissent c.1250–c.1450*. 2 vols. Manchester: Manchester University Press, 1967.

Maisack, Helmut. *William Langlands Verhältnis zum zisterziensischen Mönchtum: Eine Untersuchung der Vita im Piers Plowman*. Tübingen diss. Balingen: Herman Daniel, 1953.

Matthias of Janov. *Regulae veteris et novi testamenti*. Ed. Vlastimil Kybal and O. Odlozilik. 5 vols. Innsbruck: Wagner University Press, 1908–1913 (vols. 1-4); Prague: Ceska akademie ved a umeni, 1926 (vol. 5).

McGinn, Bernard. "St. Bernard and Eschatology." *Bernard of Clairvaux: Studies Presented to Dom Jean Leclercq*. Washington, DC: Cistercian Publications, 1973. 161–85.

McNamara, John F. "Responses to Ockhamist Theology in the Poetry of the *Pearl*-poet, Langland, and Chaucer." Diss. Louisiana State University, 1968.

Mensendieck, Otto. "The Authorship of *Piers Plowman*." *JEGP* 9 (1910): 404–20.

Middleton, Anne. "Two Infinites: Grammatical Metaphor in *Piers Plowman*." *ELH* 39 (1972): 169–88.

Murtaugh, Daniel M. *Piers Plowman and the Image of God*. Gainesville: The University Presses of Florida, 1978.

Oakley, Francis. *The Western Church in the Later Middle Ages*. Ithaca, NY, and London: Cornell University Press, 1979.

Oberman, Heiko A. *The Harvest of Medieval Theology. Gabriel Biel and Late Medieval Nominalism*. 1963; 2nd ed. Grand Rapids, MI: Eerdmans, 1967.

————. *Masters of the Reformation. The Emergence of a New Intellectual Climate in Europe*. Trans. Dennis Martin. Cambridge: Cambridge University Press, 1981.

Pantin, William A. "Two Treatises of Uthred of Boldon on the Monastic Life." *Studies in Medieval History Presented to F. M. Powicke*. Ed. R. W. Hunt, W. A. Pantin, and R. W. Southern. Oxford: Clarendon Press. 363–85.

Peifer, Claude J. *Monastic Spirituality*. New York: Sheed and Ward, 1966.

Pelikan, Jaroslav. *Reformation of Church and Dogma (1300–1700)*. Vol. 4 of *The Christian Tradition. A History of the Development of Doctrine*. 4 vols. to date (1971–). Chicago and London: University of Chicago Press, 1984.

Reeves, Marjorie. "History and Prophecy in Medieval Thought." *M&H* ns 5 (1974): 51–75.

Riehle, Wolfgang. *The Middle English Mystics*. Trans. Bernard Standring. London: Routledge and Kegan Paul, 1981.

Robertson, D. W., Jr., and Bernard F. Huppé. *Piers Plowman and Scriptural Tradition*. Princeton: Princeton University Press, 1951.

Rowland, Christopher. *The Open Heaven. A Study of Apocalyptic in Judaism and Early Christianity*. New York: Crossroad Publishing, 1982.

Russell, George H. "The Salvation of the Heathen: The Exploration of a Theme in *Piers Plowman*." *JWCI* 29 (1966): 101–16.

St. Jacques, Raymond. "Langland's Christ-Knight and the Liturgy." *Revue de l'Université d'Ottawa* 37 (1967): 145–58.

———. "The Liturgical Associations of Langland's Samaritan." *MS* 25 (1969): 217–30.

Salter, Elizabeth. *Piers Plowman. An Introduction*. Oxford: Blackwell. 1962.

Schmidt, A. V. C. "Langland and the Mystical Tradition." *The Medieval Mystical Tradition in England*. Ed. Marion Glasscoe. Exeter: University of Exeter, 1980. 17–38.

Simpson, James. "From Reason to Affective Knowledge: Modes of Thought and Poetic Form in *Piers Plowman*." *MÆ* 55 (1986): 1–23.

Southern, Richard W. *Western Society and the Church in the Middle Ages*. 1970; rpt. Harmondsworth: Penguin, 1981.

Szittya, Penn R. *The Antifraternal Tradition in Medieval Literature*. Princeton: Princeton University Press, 1986.

Tavormina, M. Teresa. " 'Bothe Two Ben Gode': Marriage and Virginity in *Piers Plowman* C.18.68–100." *JEGP* 81 (1982): 320–30.

Vasta, Edward. *The Spiritual Basis of Piers Plowman*. London, The Hague, and Paris: Mouton, 1965.

Walsh, Katherine. *A Fourteenth-Century Scholar and Primate. Richard FitzRalph in Oxford, Avignon and Armagh*. Oxford: Clarendon Press, 1981.

Whatley, Gordon. "The Uses of Hagiography: The Legend of Pope Gregory and the Emperor Trajan in the Middle Ages." *Viator* 15 (1984): 25–63.

———. "*Piers Plowman* B 12.277–94: Notes on Language, Text, and Theology." *MP* 82 (1984): 1–12.

William of St. Thierry. *On Contemplating God, Prayer, Meditations*. Trans. Sister Penelope. Vol. 1 of *The Works of William of St. Thierry*. 3 vols. to date (1971–). Spencer, MA: Cistercian Publications, 1971.

Wittig, Joseph. " 'Piers Plowman' B, Passus IX–XII: Elements in the Design of the Inward Journey." *Traditio* 28 (1972): 211–80.

Woolf, Rosemary. "The Tearing of the Pardon." In Hussey 1969, 50–75.

II
GENERIC INFLUENCES
ON *PIERS PLOWMAN*

4

ALLEGORICAL VISIONS
STEPHEN A. BARNEY

THE QUESTION OF GENRE

When we first handle a literary work, we want to ask what kind of thing it is: what is its form, or mode, or type, or genre. The answer not only permits critical synthesis, as we compare a work with its kin, but disallows our asking questions inappropriate for a given type. We do not ask the same questions of an epic that we ask of a fabliau.

Yet the question of the genre of *Piers Plowman* is not easy to resolve, and in fact some of the sense of wrestling urgency every reader feels in the poem comes from its uncomfortable, uncomplacent seat among the traditional genres. Bloomfield, for example, calling the poem a quest and (with qualification) an apocalypse, finds six genres of literature that inform the poem: three literary — allegorical dream narrative, dialogue-*consolatio*-debate, and encyclopedic (Menippean) satire — and three religious — complaint, commentary, and sermon (1961; 1962, 10–34). He observes that none of the traditional forms circumscribes and entirely defines *Piers*'s genre in the way that "chivalric romance" defines the work of Chrétien de Troyes. He speaks of a "confusion and even clash of genres" (1962, 8), and most critics of the poem agree to a sense of perplexity, of shifting, elusive, kaleidoscopic poetic experience.

Some of the problems of determining the form of the poem are touched on in the opening pages of chapter 1. This essay will point to two aspects of form, probably the two most obvious matters and difficulties a reader confronts: the allegorical mode of much of the poem's presentation, and the genre of dream vision. Not all allegories are dream visions, and not all dream visions are allegorical, but by the late Middle Ages these two informing modes coincide often enough to constitute a connected tradition underlying *Piers Plowman*.

The best approach to the question of allegory and vision in *Piers* is phylogenetic rather than ontogenetic; that is, we can grasp the issues better by studying the traditions of allegory and visionary literature that precede the poem rather than by wrestling theoretically with the knotty problems of the nature of allegory and of dream vision. Nevertheless, since the publication of C. S. Lewis's seminal *The Allegory of Love* in 1936, a number of studies have attempted to describe allegory in general, and several focus on allegory in *Piers*. Before turning to the visionary tradition, we should glance at a few of the more important recent studies.

The most recent, Lavinia Griffiths' *Personification in Piers Plowman*, besides its own topic, offers a useful survey of previous scholarship on allegory in *Piers* (108-12). For preliminary orientation on allegory in *Piers*, the sketch in the introduction to Salter and Pearsall's edition of selections from the poem (3-28) is sensible and helpful: they speak of the "fourfold method" of the allegorical interpretation of Scripture as applied to the poem (see Robertson and Huppé for extended treatment of *Piers* by this approach; also B. Smith; Aers); personification (on which see especially Frank; Quilligan; Muscatine; Carruthers; and under the rubric "reification," Barney); "dramatic allegory," that is, such complex and lively allegorical scenes as the Lady Meed episode; "diagrammatic allegory" of a kind suggestive of a labeled figure, like the Tree of Charity or the Barn of Unity; "non-visual allegory" in which the allegory makes no effort to represent the visible world, like Book with its broad eyes; "allegory through exempla," of the sort found in sermons, whose moral point is central like that of a parable; and "figuralism" or typology (see Auerbach; Pépin; Charity; Carruthers; Barney).

These various categories of allegory obviously slice the subject at different angles, and in sum they by no means exhaust the poem. The more intense the examination of Langland's allegory, the more one senses that he presents as many forms of allegory as he presents instances of allegory. Critical thought is helpless before such abundance, and must give up any hope of a comprehensive description, must resign itself to various "approaches" to allegory. An approach that works for *Piers* takes its allegory in terms of the origin and development of allegory generally, and especially the tradition of allegory that accompanies visionary literature. We begin, then, with the Bible.

The biblical prophet addresses his fellow citizens in scathing, urgent social witness, because the people transgress the divine mandates and turn to false gods. He speaks in lacerated anguish, beleaguered, emphasizing his own ostracism and failure, his incompetence to speak according to God's will. Yet he is singled out and commanded to speak, even in bewilderment; at times he is instructed by God or his angel. He is inspired, given the gift of truth. What he speaks often takes the form of a series of "words" or "visions" (seeings), given by God. These words and visions are full of common things—roads, flocks, pots, seas, figs—but the language is intensely poetic, and the imagery he pours out is bizarrre, often violent (the hills were liars — Jer. 3:23), often difficult or, especially as his puns and allusions were lost in translation and time, incomprehensible: the fullness of what he sees presses at or passes the powers of language to relate. He means to rebuke Jerusalem, to elicit conversion and righteousness, to point to the divine presence, justice, and retribution. At the same time he looks to the future, to a time of desolation or, with repentance, to a messianic plenty and peace: he is apocalyptic.

If this fairly describes the prophetic stance and voice and theme, it likewise describes *Piers Plowman*. If its humor and wit distinguish the English poem's temper from the pure savage indignation of a prophetic book, still Langland's form and subject may most aptly be called prophetic. That *Piers* takes the form of a series of dream visions follows immediately from its prophetic character, and that it is allegorical is only a little less obviously a consequence of its prophetic manner of seeing.

Old Testament writers were aware that prophecy was a tradition, that God's word would be passed from mouth to mouth. Daniel refers to "the prophet Jeremiah" (Dan. 9:2), and the writer of Ecclesiasticus names and praises the prophets (chapters 48–49). Because what follows mainly attempts to trace this tradition, as it spreads and alters, and focuses on *Piers*, a few modern studies of vision allegory and *Piers Plowman* will be mentioned first. Dorothy L. Owen's study of *Piers* in relation to Old French allegories connects many of the topics and devices of *Piers* with French sources, and although she admits that no convincing evidence of the particular influence of any one poem exists, she makes a powerful case that this tradition of continental and Anglo-Norman literature, sketched below, provides an essential background for *Piers* (cf. chap. 5). Guy Bourquin's recent study augments Owen, especially by considering many more Old French poems, but his strenuous efforts to demonstrate specific sources fails to convince — the burlesque *Apocalypse of Golias* remains, outside of the Bible, the only text in the tradition of allegorical visions provably known to Langland (B.13.91; C.15.99).

Discounting unpublished dissertations, only five other studies of any length center on *Piers* and the tradition of allegorical vision. Constance B. Hieatt, in her study of *The Realism of Dream Visions*, devotes a chapter (89–97) to *Piers* in the course of her argument that medieval dream visions imitate actual dream experience as currently understood by Freud and others. Barbara Nolan's treatment of high medieval apocalyptic and visionary art and literature contains chapters on the French tradition of visionary quest and on *Piers Plowman* (124–55, 205–58). A. C. Spearing's book *Medieval Dream Poetry* is a good introduction to the whole subject, and its pages on *Piers* (138–62) present sharp observations. In *Somnium* Francis X. Newman does not focus on *Piers*, but he assembles the essential classical and patristic background on dream-lore in a wide-ranging study. The first, dense chapter of Bloomfield's *Piers Plowman as a Fourteenth-Century Apocalypse*, mentioned above, is seminal and authoritative; its remarks on "allegorical dream narrative" (esp. 10–19) have not been superseded.

BIBLICAL VISIONS

Practically all the uses of allegory and visions that occur in *Piers Plowman* may be found in the Bible, although it remained for the later tradition to compact the various topics and devices into single narratives. The importance of dreams as an access to divine truth is evident in the stories of Jacob, Joseph, and the pharaoh's servants (Gen. 28, 37, 40–41) and especially prominent in Daniel (chapters 7 and 10). These are distinctly *sleeping* visions, and the latter are enigmatic, calling for interpretation of their elements piece by piece by the gifted Joseph and Daniel. Job is told that God speaks "By a dream in a vision by night" (Job 33:15). God tells Moses, the archprophet, that he speaks to him "mouth to mouth: and plainly, and not by riddles and figures [*per aenigmata et figuras*] doth he see the Lord," but as for any other prophet: "I will appear to him in a vision [*in visione*], or I will speak to him in a dream [*per somnium*]" (Num. 12:6–8).

The later prophets aside from Daniel, in fact, do not regularly claim that their visions came to them sleeping. Perhaps mindful that dreams and visions were only second best, Isaiah and Jeremiah sometimes speak of them with scorn (Is. 56:10; Jer. 23:27–28). Yet Joel connects dreams and visions as signs of the spirit and of the apocalypse (Joel 2:28); an angel rouses Zachariah from sleep to a vision (Zach. 4:1); Judas Maccabee wins his final victory after dreaming of Jeremiah, as it were a prophecy at second hand (2 Mach. 15:11–16). The biblical writers did not trouble to explore, as medieval writers did, the different sorts of dreams and visions, and what state the visionary was in when he had his visions—asleep, entranced, ecstatic, rapt, on the verge of death or even dead but resurrected. We do best not to distinguish sharply between dreams and other visions; it is more useful to distinguish between true and false visions, between visions in which God or his angel instructs and others, between enigmatic or plain visions.

Three features of prophetic vision, found especially in Ezekial, Zachariah, and the Apocalypse (Revelation), bear special significance for the later tradition and *Piers*. First is the *serial* nature of the visions. The prophet will see one thing after another, with no connecting narrative: Zachariah will merely say, "and I turned, and lifted up my eyes, and saw, and behold. . . ." Second is the presence of an *instructive figure*, God or an angel, who guides the visionary and interprets what he sees — again, the angel whom Zachariah persistently interrogates (chapters 1–8) is the best example. In *The Visionary Landscape*, Paul Piehler treats the abundant medieval progeny of the angelic instructor, naming them *potentiae*, "active influential powers" in a vision "in the form of a divinity, personification, or figure of authority" (12). Langland's Lady Holy Church is a *potentia* whose direct ancestor is Zachariah's angel. Third is the one gesture toward narrative in the biblical visionary's experience, the *tour*. In a visionary tour, rather than seeing his whole vision at once, the prophet is led from place to place by the *potentia*. The great example is Ezekial's guided tour of the New Temple (Ezek. 40–48).

The subject of allegory in the Bible is too large to develop here: the books by Charity, Pépin, Grant, and Daniélou provide a starting point. Different people call different things allegory, and here we can only exemplify some biblical materials that at least resemble allegory. The New Testament parables, whether they are allegories or not, are interpreted within the New Testament as if they were ("The seed is the word of God" — Luke 8:11). Judges 9 presents Joatham's parable of the trees, a quasi-enigmatic political fable. The Hebrew taste for etymologizing gives us many proper names that are close to personifications. Paul interprets Sarah and Hagar as the two testaments "by an allegory [*per allegoriam*]," authorizing typological exegesis (Gal. 4:24). Many of the prophetic visions look like allegories, elicit interpretation, and sometimes provide an interpretation, like that for the Song of the Vineyard: "the vineyard of the Lord of hosts is the house of Israel" (Isa. 5:7). When Paul speaks of the "shield of faith" (Eph. 6:16) or when Jesus says, "My meat is to do the will of him that sent me" (John 4:34), their genitives (of faith) and predicates (to do the will) are not hard to turn into labels: an allegorical shield named Faith, or a food called "Thy-Will-Be-Done," a food we find in *Piers Plowman* (C.5.88; B.14.50; C.15.250). In Revelation, the rider of a white horse is named "faithful and true" and also "the Word of God" (Apoc. 19:11–13). With this we pass over into strict personification, but a fluid relationship between matter and spirit, concrete and abstract, name and thing would be expected where we are told "the Word was made flesh" (John 1:14).

THE APOCRYPHA AND THE TOURS

The orthodox Christians and the Masoretic Jews did not succeed in closing the canon of scriptural texts for five or six hundred years after the time of Jesus. Many books now relegated to apocrypha were widely read in the late Jewish and early Christian eras, and some continued to be read, even accepted as Scripture, through the Middle Ages. Most of these texts can be found translated in Charles (Old Testament apocrypha) and Hennecke or James (New Testament apocrypha). A good recent study of several apocryphal works relevant to our topic is Himmelfarb's *Tours of Hell*.

A few of these works develop the tradition of visionary allegory. Fourth Ezra and the *Shepherd of Hermas* (2nd cen. AD) adopt the series of visions and dialogues of the sort found in Zachariah. Ezra's guide and interpreter is the angel Uriel; Hermas is instructed by an angel and by Mater Ecclesia, the ancestor of Langland's Holy Church. Himmelfarb observes that the earliest apocalyptic texts, the Book of Watchers embedded in the apocryphal First Enoch and perhaps the Apocalypse of Zephaniah, contain "tours" of heaven and hell, a genre in which the speaker, asleep or at the point of death or in some other visionary state, is shown the terrors of hell or the delights of heaven. These texts were to have a formidable offspring, of which Dante's *Comedy* is of course the greatest.

The earliest full-fledged tours of hell whose date can be fixed are the Apocalypse of Peter and the Acts of Thomas, written in the second and third centuries. They were little known in the Latin West. The best known is the Apocalypse (Vision) of Paul (3rd or 4th cen.; Latin version, ?5th cen.), which claims to reveal what Paul saw when he was rapt to the third heaven and "heard secret words" (2 Cor. 12:2–4). Paul is led by the archangel Michael through a grisly survey of hell (and, in some versions, paradise). Another major influence in the Middle Ages was the Gospel of Nicodemus, to which an account of the Harrowing of Hell (see *Piers* B.18; C.20) was added by the fifth century (see D. D. R. Owen 7–9). This reports the eyewitness account of two men raised from the dead, who had viewed the Harrowing. Hell (Inferus) and Death are personified leaders, with Satan, of the legions of hell.

These texts spawned a number of visionary narratives of the other world which include the wandering or guided tour, personifications and "moralized places" (like the Castle of Care), and instructive dialogues with authoritative figures. Some of these features may be found in the three most popular Latin tours of hell, all from Ireland: the *Voyage of St. Brendan* (10th cen.?), the *Vision of Tundale* (1148 or 1149), and *St. Patrick's Purgatory* (ca. 1190; see D. D. R. Owen 22–50). These texts were all rendered into French and Anglo-Norman (D. D. R. Owen 51–141).

We shall return to this "tour" tradition, because its Old French succession lies immediately behind *Piers Plowman*. But before doing so we should follow an antique trail of allegorical vision that is pagan and philosophical rather than biblical and prophetic.

THE PLATONIC TRADITION

In antiquity, visions and allegories were not the exclusive property of the biblical writers. The Greek epic tradition gave its heroes the power to visit the world of the shades of the dead (*Odyssey* 10; *Aeneid* 6). Spiritual agents were present, in the form of the Furies or such divinities as Nemesis and Themis, to enact curses and vengeances; powers like Ate (Discordia), Furor, Fama, are close to personifications of human conditions. The Greek philosophers, who spoke of such abstract things as Beauty and Truth and Justice, could personify them. The rhetorical tradition of the ancients made the term "allegory" familiar, defining it as "continued metaphor" or "saying one thing and meaning another," with reference to such brief allegories in the poets as the Ship of State. As belief in myths broke down, the narratives were treated in a critical light as psychological or physical allegories; Kronos was Time, Venus was Love. The Neoplatonic tradition, merging with various religious gnosticisms, produced visionary accounts of the workings of the universe, hermetic soul-journeys and visions of the activities of the Demiurge and the World-Soul. (On these traditions see Pépin; MacQueen; Seznec.)

The most influential vision in Hellenistic literature is the Myth of Er, with which Plato concludes the *Republic*. It tells of Er's tour of the other world in death, and his return to life on the twelfth day to relate what he had seen. The vision includes the judgment and separation of souls, the spindle of Necessity on which the planetary spheres turn, Necessity's three daughters, the Fates, the allotment of various geniuses to the souls, a prophetic Interpreter, the plain of Forgetfulness and the river of Unmindfulness — in short, it has the features of a visionary allegory, specifically serial visions, a tour, figures of authority (*potentiae*), moralized landscapes, mythological personification, and a representation of justice at the eschaton.

In the medieval Latin West, the Myth of Er was unknown, but its indirect influence was large. Like much platonism, elements of it were transmitted through those Christian authors learned in Greek thought: Origen, Augustine, Boethius, and the fourth-century Chalcidius who commented on Plato's *Timaeus*. Cicero's Latin recension of the myth concludes his own *Republic*: the dream of Scipio. This *Somnium Scipionis* tells of Scipio's dream of a flight to the starry sphere, guided by a *potentia*, his grandfather, and instructed in ethics and the justice of the afterlife. In the early fifth century the *Somnium* was commented on at large by Macrobius, to whom Guillaume de Lorris and Chaucer refer. Of special interest is Macrobius's account of those three of the five types of dreams which are true: *somnium* (an allegory of the truth), *visio* (a plain view of the future), and *oraculum* (instruction by an authority). In the first century AD, Lucan described the ascent of Pompey's soul at death to the sphere of the moon, his vision of the semidivine shades, and his laughter at his funeral rites on earth (*Pharsalia* 9). Scipio's and Pompey's visionary flights were the precursors of the high visions of Dante, Boccaccio's Arcite, and Chaucer's Troilus.

That many of these visions represent the eschaton, the Four Last Things (death, judgment, heaven, and hell), follows from their moral and religious ancestry. Plato's Myth of Er presents a cosmography, but its main point, like that of the book it concludes, is moral. Er sees the just ascend to heaven with their sentences bound in front of them; the unjust descend on the left, carrying the symbols of their deeds on their backs, like the burden of Bunyan's Christian. Here pagan (Neoplatonic and Stoic) and Christian ethics can easily merge. In the Middle Ages, for example, the seven principal virtues consisted of the three "theological" virtues (faith, hope, and charity) from Paul and the four "cardinal" virtues (prudence, temperance, courage, and justice) from Plato, the latter allegorized as four seeds in *Piers* (B.19.276, C.21.274), the former as Abraham, Moses, and the Good Samaritan.

The enumeration and divisions of the virtues and vices became a favorite part of medieval allegory (see Bloomfield 1952), generally because of the eschatological urgency of the prophetic and platonic visions, and specifically because of the influence of the first major wholly allegorical narrative, Prudentius's *Psychomachia* (ca. 400; see M. Smith; Lewis 1936; Barney; Van Dyke).

Although not presented as a vision, the *Psychomachia*'s representation of the personified virtues and vices in battle and their final attainment of an apocalyptic New Jerusalem conditioned all later visionary and allegorical literature. In a peculiar way, the bizarre surface content of the *Psychomachia* — with characters like Worship-of-Old-Gods in battle — literalizes and demystifies the ordinary yet mysterious surfaces of the prophets, the wheels and eagles and trees of Ezekial. So when Langland says,

> Thre shypes and a schaef with an viii folwynge
> Shal brynge bane and batayle on both half þe mone
> (C.8.350–51)

he deliberately speaks prophetically, and one has no idea what he means, although the words are easy. When he names the seven sisters of Truth — Abstinence, Vmbletee, Charite, Chastite, Pacience, Pees, Largenesse (C.7.270–75) — one is not troubled at all by the representation of analysis as sorority: Allegory can be the Father of Clarity.

Along with the *Psychomachia*, the two other major influences on medieval visionary allegory, apart from the Bible, are Boethius's *Consolation of Philosophy* and Martianus Capella's *Marriage of Philology and Mercury* (late fourth or fifth century), an encyclopedic account of the seven liberal arts tricked out with personifications, a celestial journey, and an allegorical marriage. In the *Consolation* (ca. 524; see Piehler 28–45), although a mental flight is represented (Book 4, prose and meter 1), the main formal contribution is the presentation of serious philosophical matter in the form of a (platonic) dialogue with a personified *potentia*, the lady Philosophy, garbed in symbolic clothing. The *Consolation* avoids the machinery of dreaming, but powerfully develops the possibilities of representing mental conflict by personification.

The last works in the Latin development of the platonic tradition of allegory that we should notice are all of the twelfth century. Bernard Sylvestris's *Cosmographia* (before 1147) draws from the wellhead of Macrobius, the Chalcidian *Timaeus*, Martianus Capella, and Boethius, and fuses their ideas in a complex allegory of the physics of the cosmos with personified Nature, Noys, Silva, Endelechia, and Physis. The context of Bernard's work is ably summarized in the introduction to Wetherbee's translation. Directly influenced by Bernard are the two cosmographical allegories of Alain de Lille, the *Anticlaudianus* (1181–84) and the *Complaint of Nature* (?ca. 1165), the latter presented as a dream vision. Finally, the *Architrenius* of John of Altavilla (Hanville), begun about 1184, is based on the *Anticlaudianus*. Not a dream, it represents an allegorical journey, a search for Nature through a moralized landscape, and culminates in the marriage of Architrenius to the figure Moderantia (see Piehler 86–94).

From this breathless survey of the platonic tradition of visionary allegory a few common strands may be plucked. It is distinctly a tradition: the later authors deliberately imitate the earlier. As such it is learned. In the West, at any rate, it became Latinized, and hence was international, and associated with the schools. Although maintained in the hands of the clerisy, the platonic tradition often seems to avoid explicitly Christian matter. In general, the subjects are speculative, moral, philosophical. Many kinds of personifications became familiar: philosophical categories (entelechy, nous), virtues and vices, the arts, cosmic principles (genius, nature, fortune). In the later Middle Ages we find literary debates, philosophical treatises, even scientific works presented in the form of dream visions (Bloomfield 1962, 182; Hieatt 14; Bestul 24–45; Newman chap. 3). Such literary forms as the dialogue, the celestial flight, the allegorical marriage, the moralized landscape, the labeled edifice or chariot, the pilgrimage, became commonplace.

If we attempt in general to distinguish the two broad traditions outlined here, the prophetic and the platonic, we might point to their different implied audiences, their claims of authority, and their tones of voice. The prophets speak to all the children of Adam, whereas a Plato or an Alain de Lille presumes a learned elite, with a special vocabulary and an ear for literary allusions. The prophets speak the word of God; the platonizing poets wrestle with psychological and metaphysical categories. The prophetic tone is deadly earnest; in the other tradition we find an agile zest and profuse verbal wit. The one tradition is roughly Hebrew, the other roughly Greek: the platitudes about this division of Western culture are as true, and as false, when applied to the allegorical visions as when applied anywhere.

THE FRENCH TRADITION

Skeat and Jusserand (195–202) point to parallels between *Piers Plowman* and various French allegories. A number of the French works are examined in detail for parallels by Dorothy L. Owen, and several more by Bourquin, as noted above. Cornelius makes a plausible but inconclusive case for Langland's use of *Le Roman de Fauvel*. These allegories, most of them in the form of dream visions, collectively provide the immediate background for the form of *Piers*, even though none is demonstrably a source. (For Old French allegory generally see Jung; Jauss; Strubel; cf. also pp. 136–38 below.)

The first of these allegories is *Li Romans de Carité* — not a dream — written by Barthélemy, Renclus de Molliens around 1185. The pilgrim narrator searches through the world for Charity, to find that charity is in heaven only. It is sharply satirical, especially critical of the clergy, but generally full of "estates satire" of the sort treated in the next chapter. It is the first pilgrimage allegory in French — as *Piers* was to be the first in English — and sets the satiric tone for the whole tradition.

The second is a dream vision, the *Songe d'Enfer*, written by Raoul de Houdenc around 1215. It immediately descends from the tours of hell described above, and more directly than *Li Romans de Carité* gave rise to a genre of literature we may call *voie* ("way") after the titles of several of its members — a visionary account of a pilgrimage, usually to heaven or hell, often through an allegorized landscape, and usually satiric: an anagogical pilgrim's progress. Raoul dreams that he takes the broad way to hell, passing places with names like Covetise and Gluttony to arrive at Mount Despair. In hell he sits with devils at a banquet and eats such dishes as roast heretic. The motif of the banquet in the *voies*, as it becomes allegorized by personified foods, issues in the allegorical banquet of *Piers*. Attributed, perhaps wrongly, to Raoul is also a *Voie de Paradis*, a dream vision of a pilgrimage to heaven with allegorical place names comparable to those of the *Songe d'Enfer* (and compressed in Piers's directions to Truth: B.5.561–638; C.7.205–82). Because the attribution of this poem to Raoul is suspect, so is the early date, 1216, given it by its editor (see Micha).

The continuing tradition of *voies* was extensive. Among the better known, any of which might conceivably have influenced Langland, are first *La Voie de Paradis* of Rutebeuf (1270–85) in which Pity directs the dreamer to the

House of Confession, avoiding the allegorical dwellings of the seven sins (see Regalado 28–39). Like *Piers*, the poem opens in a natural setting, and is based, like the latter passus of *Piers*, on the Lenten calendar. Jehan de la Mote's *La Voie d'Enfer et de Paradis* (1340) has the dreamer lodge with the personified sins on the way to hell (see D. D. R. Owen 162–64). Guillaume de Deguileville, whose work was known to Chaucer, includes in his vast dream *voie* to the afterlife, *Le Pélerinage de l'âme* (1355–58), some tree allegory suggestive of Langland's Tree of Charity scene (Owen 1970, 165–69; Aers 1975, 47–49). The earliest pure *voie* in English seems to be the *Weye to Paradys*, identified by Owst (104–05), apparently written at the turn of the fifteenth century, although a vision of heaven, hell, and purgatory occurs in *Tomas of Ersseldoune*, treated below.

These *voies* set the pattern for most of the forms of allegory that may be found in the other French allegories and the English allegories of Chaucer, the *Pearl*-poet, and Langland. The use of dream visions, personifications, pilgrimages, debates, instructions by authoritative figures, allegorized landscapes, springtime openings, satiric reviews of the estates, allegorical banquets — all had become commonplaces by the mid-fourteenth century. We need only notice a few of the more important French allegories outside the *voie* tradition, focusing on those that share features with *Piers* and those that were best known.

Huon de Meri's *Li Tornoiemenz Antecrist* (1234 or 1235) has long been suspected as a source for *Piers* (see Bestul 37–39). Not strictly a dream, it nevertheless opens with a spring setting. It includes a psychomachia of the virtues and the vices led by Antichrist, and hence suggests the siege of Unity in the last passus of *Piers*. It likewise presents the common allegory of the body as a castle (compare the Castle of Caro), and, referring to Raoul, an allegorical banquet. Perhaps most important, it frames an allegory around a single topic — the tournament — instigating a technique that was to be used widely: we have later allegories, sometimes long ones, centered on the image of a garden, a prison, the wheel of Fortune, a marriage, a desert, a hunt, an abbey, a banquet, a chess game, a parliament, a siege, a fountain.

At about the same time Huon was writing, Guillaume de Lorris issued the first part of *Le Roman de la Rose*. We pass it by, as we pass by Dante, on the grounds that it must be familiar to readers of this book: for a recent survey of writing about it see Luria's *Guide* (1982). Its immense popularity spawned generations of allegories, many in a new genre, influenced by Ovid and chivalric romance, the love allegories, like those dream visions known to Chaucer, Froissart's *Paradys d'Amours* and Machaut's *Dit dou Vergier*.

Robert Grosseteste's *Chasteau d'Amour* is not a dream vision, and except for its architectural allegory (the body of the Virgin Mary is the castle) has little in common with *Piers*, but it is of interest because it was translated into English in the early fourteenth century (see Griffiths 76–81; Cornelius). Likewise the allegories of Nicole Bozon, an Anglo-Norman author, may well have been known to Langland (Bourquin 2:703). Perhaps a better case than for any other poem has been made for Langland's use of *Le Roman de Fauvel* (1310–14, at least partly by Gervais du Bus), a satiric allegory involving a marriage of personifications that much resembles the Meed episode, an allegorical banquet, allegorical mounts (compare those of Bozon's *Char d'Or-gueil*), and especially the name "Fauvel" itself, which may have passed directly to Langland (see Cornelius, Bourquin). Also resembling *Piers* is *Le chemin de Povreté et de Richesse*, written around 1342 by Jean Bruyant. In it the personified children of Poverty find their way to the castle of Labor, the manor of Wealth, and the figure Reason preaches a sermon about the right road, including a diatribe on the vices and virtues. Some close parallels with Langland's *Visio* are pointed out by Bourquin (774–79).

Finally, Guillaume de Deguileville's *Pèlerinage de la vie humaine* (1331, 1355) is the first of his pilgrimage trilogy that constitutes an *omnium gatherum* of religious allegory (see Tuve 145–218). In the fifteenth century Lydgate translated the 1335 version into English; Chaucer made a piece of it into his *ABC*. Guillaume dreams of a New Jerusalem, and tries to reach it by way of counseling *potentiae* and allegorized sacraments and virtues. Bourquin again enumerates specific correspondences with *Piers* (780–98); none is so close as to prove that it is an immediate source for Langland.

THE ENGLISH TRADITION

Anima berates "þise newe clerkes" who "Ne rede a lettre in any langage but in latyn or englissh" (B.15.376). This inconclusively supports what we would presume in any case, that an urban English poet with any pretensions to learning would know French. That the techniques and topics of *Piers Plowman* so closely resemble those of the French tradition sketched above merely by accident is incredible. An English tradition of visionary allegory precedes *Piers*, but its surviving remnant indicates that it was too thin to account for Langland's knowledge of the traditional material. Nevertheless the English writings reveal the penetration of continental and Anglo-Norman stuff into English, and at least one instance, *Wynnere and Wastoure*, may have been a source for Langland.

First we should observe that a substantial part of the Latin traditions of tours and other visionary works, some allegorical, were available in English (as well as French). Under the rubrics "Legends of Jesus and Mary" and "Legends of the After-Life," Frances A. Foster has summarized a number of these in the *Manual of the Writings in Middle English* (2:447–57; abundant bibliography in 2:639–49). The earliest English versions she treats are: *Gospel of Nicodemus* (before 1325); a separate *Harrowing of Hell* (late 13th cen.); the *Vision of St. Paul* (late 12th cen.); *St. Patrick's Purgatory* (early 13th cen.); *Vision of Tundale* (early 13th cen.); *Vision of Fursey* from Bede (early 14th cen.). Of the originally French works, only *Le Roman de la Rose* was englished in Langland's time, by Chaucer (and perhaps others); Chaucer's translation of Boethius was probably too late (ca. 1380) for Langland to have used it.

A substantial body of English allegory takes the ancient form of a debate between (often personified) characters (see Utley in *Manual* 3:669–745, 829–902). One of these, the "Debate between the Body and Soul" (691–95), in many versions, derives ultimately from the *Visio Philiberti* (possibly written by Grosseteste). The most important version (Utley's "e," p. 693), of the late thirteenth century, takes the form of a vision. Likewise derived from a Latin legend is *The Gast of Gy*, whose earliest English form is mid-fourteenth century (698–700), an unusual form in which a haunting ghost acts as the *potentia*. There are a number of Middle English versions of the (widespread) Debate Between the Four Daughters of God (see Mader 1971; Traver 1925) that precede the version in *Piers*; among them is the early fourteenth-century translation (ed. Sajavaara) of Grosseteste's *Chasteau*.

The sermon literature of Europe, including sermons in English, may well account not only for theological precepts and local motifs in *Piers*, but for some major allegorical structures. Chapter 6 gives general guidance. The work of Owst mentioned there remains the fullest account of the genre in connection with literature. So many of the allegorical devices and episodes in *Piers* find their counterparts in the sermon literature that it is possible that most of the material of the allegorical visions came to Langland immediately from sermons heard or read.

In English also appears the curious genre of political prophecy, treated by Robbins (*Manual* 5:1516–36, 1714–25). These are often enigmatic — a favorite device is to represent a powerful noble as an animal or flower — and crudely allegorical, and they clearly have some bearing on *Piers* (see Bloomfield 1962, 91–94; Bestul 59–65; Reeves; *Piers* B.3.320–30). The most like *Piers*, *Tomas of Ersseldoune*, is too late (after 1388 in its present form: Robbins 1526–27) to have been used by Langland, but parts of it seem to date from before mid-century. It contains a May opening in which the poet wanders into the countryside, and a vision of the underworld. *Adam Davy's Five Dreams*, "probably written soon after 1308" (Robbins 1529), may be the only English allegorical prophecy explicitly a dream.

Besides *Tomas of Ersseldoune*, several other English visionary allegories have springtime openings reminiscent of *Piers*. Of these, *Somer Soneday* and *The Parlement of the Thre Ages*, alliterative poems clearly in a poetic tradition that Langland knew (see Blamires), are, like *Pearl* and the four dream poems of Chaucer, probably too late to have influenced the conception of *Piers*, although *Parlement* may be early enough (see Turville-Petre on the date of *Soneday*). The closest poem to *Piers* is *Wynnere and Wastour* (before 1366, probably 1352–53), a satiric, political allegory in the form of a debate which opens with a poet who dreams on a river bank on a sunny day (see Bestul). Langland seems to allude to it in his earliest version: some laborers "Wonne þat þise wastours wiþ glotonye destroiȝeþ" (A.Prol.22); Wastour is personified at the Half-Acre (A.7.139 ff.).

From Jeremiah to *Wynnere and Wastoure* is a long way, but clearly the two works form part of a tradition, a tradition which the Bible continued to influence directly through the centuries. The developing presence and even "story" of the visionary speaker himself, and the abundant use of personification, are post-biblical; many readers have seen in *Piers* a movement from an obtrusive narrator in a highly "moralized" landscape toward an increasingly voiceless narrator in an increasingly apocalyptic, typological world (Kirk; Carruthers; Anderson), a movement that constitutes a return to the ancient prophetic way of telling the truth.

REFERENCES

Aers, David. *Piers Plowman and Christian Allegory*. London: Arnold, 1975.

Alain de Lille. *Anticlaudianus*. Ed. R. Bossuat. Paris: J. Vrin, 1955. Trans. James J. Sheridan. Toronto: Pontifical Institute of Mediaeval Studies, 1973.

———. *De Planctu Naturae*. Ed. N. M. Häring. *Studi Medievali*, 3rd ser. 19:2 (1978): 797–879. Trans. James J. Sheridan. *The Plaint of Nature*. Toronto: Pontifical Institute of Mediaeval Studies, 1980.

Anderson, Judith H. *The Growth of a Personal Voice: Piers Plowman and The Faerie Queene*. New Haven: Yale University Press, 1976.

Apocalypsis Goliae. Ed. Karl Strecker. Texte zur Kulturgeschichte des Mittelalters 5. Rome: Regenberg, 1928. Anonymous trans. "The Revelation of Golias the Bisshoppe" in Jeanne Krochalis and Edward Peters, eds. *The World of Piers Plowman*. Philadelphia: University of Pennsylvania Press, 1975. 39–55.

Auerbach, Erich. "Figura." *Scenes from the Drama of European Literature: Six Essays*. New York: Meridian, 1959.

Barney, Stephen A. *Allegories of History, Allegories of Love*. Hamden, CT: Archon, 1979.

Barthélemy, Renclus de Molliens. *Li Romans de Carité*. Ed. A. G. Van Hamel. Paris: Vieweg, 1885.

Bernardus Sylvestris. *Cosmographia*. Ed. Peter Dronke. Leiden: Brill, 1978. Trans. Winthrop Wetherbee. New York: Columbia University Press, 1973.

Bestul, Thomas. *Satire and Allegory in Wynnere and Wastoure*. Lincoln: University of Nebraska Press, 1974.

Blamires, Alcuin G. "Mum & the Sothsegger and Langlandian Idiom." *NM* 76 (1975): 583–604.

Bloomfield, Morton W. *The Seven Deadly Sins*. East Lansing: Michigan State University Press, 1952; rpt. 1967.

————. "*Piers Plowman* as a Fourtccnth-Ccntury Apocalypse." *Centennial Review of Arts and Sciences* 5 (1961): 281–95; rpt. Vasta 339–54.

————. *Piers Plowman as a Fourteenth-Century Apocalypse.* New Brunswick, NJ: Rutgers University Press, 1962.

Boethius. *De Consolatione Philosophiae.* Ed. Ludwig Bieler. CCSL 94. Turnhout: Brepols, 1957.

Bourquin, Guy. *Piers Plowman: Etudes sur la genèse littéraire des trois versions.* 2 vols. University of Lille dissertation. Paris: Champion, 1978.

Bozon, Nicole. *Le Char d'Orgueil.* Ed. J. Vising. Göteborg: Göteborgs Högskolas Årsskrift 25, 1919.

Bruyant, Jean. *Le chemin de Povreté et de Richesse.* J. Pichon, ed. *Le Ménagier de Paris.* Paris: de Crapelet, 1846. 2:4–42.

Carruthers, Mary. *The Search for St. Truth.* Evanston: Northwestern University Press, 1973.

Charity, A. C. *Events and Their Afterlife: The Dialectics of Christian Typology in the Bible and Dante.* Cambridge: Cambridge University Press, 1966.

Charles, R. H. *The Apocrypha and Pseudepigrapha of the Old Testament.* Oxford: Oxford University Press, 1913.

Cornelius, Roberta D. *The Figurative Castle.* Published Bryn Mawr thesis, 1930.

————. "Piers Plowman and the Roman de Fauvel." *PMLA* 47 (1932): 363–67.

Daniélou, Jean. *Sacramentum Futuri: Etudes sur les origines de la typologie biblique.* Paris: Beauchesne, 1950. Trans. Dom Wulstan Hibbard. *From Shadows to Reality.* Westminster, MD: Newman Press, 1960.

Foster, Frances A. "Saints' Legends." *A Manual of the Writings in Middle English 1050–1500.* Ed. J. Burke Severs. Hamden, CT: Archon, 1970. 2:441–57.

Frank, Robert Worth, Jr. *Piers Plowman and the Scheme of Salvation.* New Haven: Yale University Press, 1957.

Gervais du Bus. *Le Roman de Fauvel.* Ed. Arthur Långfors. SATF. Paris: Didot, 1914–19.

Grant, Robert M. *The Letter and the Spirit.* London: S. P. C. K., 1957.

Griffiths, Lavinia. *Personification in Piers Plowman.* Cambridge: Brewer, 1985.

Grosseteste, Robert. *Le Chasteau d'Amour.* Ed. J. Murray. Paris: Champion, 1918. Middle English trans. ed. K. Sajavaara. Helsinki: Mémoires de la Société Néophilologique de Helsinki 32, 1967.

Guillaume de Deguileville. *Le Pélerinage de l'âme.* Ed. J. J. Stürzinger. Roxburghe Club. London: Nichols, 1895.

————. *Le Pélerinage de la vie humaine.* Ed. J. J. Stürzinger. Roxburghe Club. London: Nichols, 1893.

Hennecke, Edgar. *New Testament Apocrypha.* Trans. R. McL. Wilson. Philadelphia: Westminster, 1963–65.

Hieatt, Constance B. *The Realism of Dream Visions: The Poetic Exploitation of the Dream Experience in Chaucer and His Contemporaries.* The Hague: Mouton, 1967.

Himmelfarb, Martha. *Tours of Hell: Apocalyptic Form in Jewish and Christian Literature.* Philadelphia: University of Pennsylvania Press, 1983.

Huon de Meri. *Li Tornoiemenz Antecrist.* Ed. G. Wimmer. Ausgaben und Abhandlungen aus dem Gebiete der romanischen Philologie 76. Marburg: Elwert, 1888.

James, M. R. *The Apocryphal New Testament.* Oxford: Oxford University Press, 1924.

Jauss, Hans Robert. *Genèse de la poésie allégorique française au moyen âge (De 1180 à 1240).* Heidelberg: Carl Winter, 1962.

————, with Uda Ebel. "Entstehung und Strukturwandel der allegorischen Dichtung." *La Littérature didactique, allégorique, et satirique.* Grundriss der romanischen Literaturen des Mittelalters 6:1,2. Heidelberg: Carl Winter, 1968. (Includes bibliography.)

Jean de Hanville (Altavilla). *Architrenius.* Ed. Thomas Wright. *The Anglo-Latin Satirical Poets.* Rolls Series 59 (1872); rpt. New York: Kraus, 1964. 1:240–392.

Jean de la Mote. *La Voie d'Enfer et de Paradis.* Ed. Sister M. Aquiline Pety. Washington, DC: Catholic University of America Press, 1940.

Jung, Marc-René. *Etudes sur le poème allégorique en France au moyen âge.* Romanica Helvetica 82. Bern: Francke, 1971.

Jusserand, J. J. *Piers Plowman: A Contribution to the History of English Mysticism.* Trans. M. E. R. 1894; rpt. New York: Russell & Russell, 1965.

Kirk, Elizabeth D. *The Dream Thought of Piers Plowman.* New Haven: Yale University Press, 1972.

Lewis, C. S. *The Allegory of Love: A Study in Medieval Tradition.* Oxford: Oxford University Press, 1936

————. *The Discarded Image: An Introduction to Medieval and Renaissance Literature.* Cambridge: Cambridge University Press, 1964.

Luria, Maxwell. *A Reader's Guide to the Roman de la Rose.* Hamden, CT: Archon, 1982.

MacQueen, John. *Allegory.* The Critical Idiom 14. London: Methuen, 1970.

Macrobius. *Commentary on the Dream of Scipio.* Trans. William H. Stahl. New York: Columbia University Press, 1952.

Mäder, Eduard Johann. *Der Streit der 'Töchter Gottes': Zur Geschichte eines allegorischen Motivs.* Bern: Lang, 1971.

Martianus Capella. *De Nuptiis Philologiae et Mercurii.* Ed. A. Dick. Stuttgart: Teubner, 1969. Trans. William H. Stahl. New York: Columbia University Press, 1977.

Micha, A. "Raoul de Houdenc est-il l'auteur du 'Songe de Paradis' et de la 'Vengeance Raguidel'?" *Romania* 68 (1944–45): 316–60.

Muscatine, Charles. "The Emergence of Psychological Allegory in Old French Romance." *PMLA* 68 (1953): 1160–82.

Newman, Francis Xavier. "*Somnium*: Medieval Theories of Dreaming and the Form of Vision Poetry." Unpub. diss. Princeton University, 1962.

Nolan, Barbara. *The Gothic Visionary Perspective.* Princeton: Princeton University Press, 1977.

Owen, D. D. R. *The Vision of Hell: Infernal Journeys in Medieval French Literature.* Edinburgh: Scottish Academic Press, 1970. New York: Barnes & Noble, 1971.

Owen, Dorothy L. *Piers Plowman: A Comparison with Some Earlier and Contemporary French Allegories.* London: University of London Press, 1912.

Owst, G. R. *Literature and Pulpit in Medieval England.* 1933; 2nd rev. ed. New York: Barnes and Noble, 1961.

The Parlement of the Thre Ages. Ed. M. Y. Offord. EETS 246. Oxford: Oxford University Press, 1959.

Pépin, Jean. *Mythe et allégorie: Les origines grecques et les contestations judéo-chrétiennes.* Paris: Montaigne, 1958.

————. *Dante et la tradition de l'allégorie.* Montreal: Institut d'études médiévales, 1970.

Piehler, Paul. *The Visionary Landscape: A Study in Medieval Allegory.* London: Arnold, 1971.

Plato. *Timaeus, a Calcidio Translatus Commentarioque Instructus.* Ed. J. H. Waszink. London: Warburg; Leiden: Brill, 1962.

Prudentius. *Carmina.* Ed. J. Bergman. CSEL 61. Leipzig: Hoelder, 1926.

Quilligan, Maureen. *The Language of Allegory: Defining the Genre*. Ithaca: Cornell University Press, 1979.

Raoul de Houdenc. *Le Songe d'Enfer suivi de La Voie de Paradis*. Ed. Philéas Lebesgue. La Rochelle: Texier; Paris: Sansot, 1908.

Reeves, Marjorie. *The Influence of Prophecy in the Later Middle Ages: A Study in Joachimism*. Oxford: Clarendon, 1969.

Regalado, Nancy Freeman. *Poetic Patterns in Rutebeuf*. New Haven: Yale University Press, 1970.

Robbins, Rossell Hope. "Poems Dealing with Contemporary Conditions," *A Manual of the Writings in Middle English 1050–1500*. Ed. Albert Hartung. Hamden, CT: Archon, 1975. 5:1385–1536.

Robertson, D. W., Jr., and Bernard F. Huppé. *Piers Plowman and Scriptural Tradition*. Princeton: Princeton University Press, 1951.

Rutebeuf. *La Voie de Paradis*. Ed. E. Faral and J. Bastin. *Oeuvres complètes de Rutebeuf*. 2 vols. Paris: Picard, 1959–60. 1:336–70.

Salter, Elizabeth and Derek Pearsall, eds. *Piers Plowman*. York Medieval Texts. London: Arnold, 1967.

Seznec, Jean. *La Survivance des dieux antiques*. London: Warburg, 1939. Trans. B. F. Sessions. *The Survival of the Pagan Gods*. New York: Pantheon, 1953.

The Shepherd of Hermas. Ed. and trans. Kirsopp Lake. *The Apostolic Fathers*. Loeb Classical Library. London: Heinemann, 1912–13. 2:1–305.

Smith, Ben H. *Traditional Imagery of Charity in Piers Plowman*. The Hague: Mouton, 1966.

Smith, Macklin. *Prudentius' Psychomachia: A Reexamination*. Princeton: Princeton University Press, 1976.

Spearing, A. C. *Medieval Dream Poetry*. Cambridge: Cambridge University Press, 1976.

Strubel, Armand. "La littérature allégorique." *Précis de littérature française du moyen âge*. Ed. Daniel Poirion, Paris: Presses Univ. de France, 1983. 236–71.

Thomas of Erceldoune, The Romance and Prophecies of. Ed. James A. H. Murray. EETS 61. London: Trübner, 1875.

Traver, Hope. "The Four Daughters of God: A Mirror of Changing Doctrine." *PMLA* 40 (1925): 44–92.

Turville-Petre, T. "'Summer Sunday,' 'De Tribus Regibus Mortuis,' and 'The Awntyrs off Arthure': Three Poems in the Thirteen-Line Stanza." *RES* ns 25 (1974): 1–14.

Tuve, Rosemond. *Allegorical Imagery: Some Mediaeval Books and Their Posterity*. Princeton: Princeton University Press, 1966.

Utley, Francis Lee. "Dialogues, Debates, and Catechisms." *A Manual of the Writings in Middle English 1050–1500*. Ed. Albert Hartung. Hamden, CT: Archon, 1972. 3:669–745.

Van Dyke, Carolynn. *The Fiction of Truth: Structures of Meaning in Narrative and Dramatic Allegory*. Ithaca: Cornell University Press, 1985.

Visio Sancti Pauli: The History of the Apocalypse in Latin, Together with Nine Texts. Ed. H. T. Silverstein. Studies and Documents 4. London: Christopher, 1935.

Wynnere and Wastoure. Ed. Israel Gollancz. *Select Early English Poems*. London: Milford, 1920.

5

SATIRE

JOHN A. YUNCK

Most early critics of *Piers Plowman* (for example, Puttenham [1589], Warton [1774]) called it simply a "satire," but critical fashions change. In 1956 J. D. Peter, distinguishing between satire and complaint, could deny that Langland, or any Middle English poet except Chaucer, wrote satire (3–13; but see Lawlor 1957, 121; Heiserman 292–94). Admittedly, medieval satire tended to shade into comedy and grotesquerie in one direction or sermonizing and lament — "complaint" — in the other. In the vernaculars it usually functioned as a literary mode rather than a genre, a stance that writers in any genre — epic, romance, lyric, sermon — could assume, when it suited their purposes. We may describe it, warily, as disparagement or censure viewed as a verbal art, sometimes using complex fictions, sometimes simple invective, usually with the professed purpose of reform. Neither Langland nor Dante, as Kane has pointed out (214), was a "satirist," but both converted to their purposes the satiric themes, devices and imagery they had inherited, as cautery to promote the healing of Christendom. Langland censured, as Lawlor remarked (1957, 122), only to pass "from censure to inquiry." Though rooted in satire, his poem is in essence visionary, homiletic, propaedeutic.

Virtually all recent critics treat the art of Langland's satire. Lawlor's extensive comments are especially perceptive, as are the brief but important remarks scattered through the books by Kane, Donaldson, Bloomfield and Kirk. Wesling and Knight have devoted essays to it, and Norton-Smith a chapter. The art and significance of the crucial episode of Lady Meed have been discussed by Frank (21), Mitchell, Yunck (10–11, 290–92), Benson, and Stokes (99–154).

In keeping with the plan of this volume, the present chapter is concerned less with Langland's satirical art than with influences on the poet — with his position in the satirical milieu of his period. It will take up in order opinions concerning Langland's sources, his relation to medieval moral-satirical traditions (including his affinities with contemporary writers of satire), the spiritual and intellectual intertext of fourteenth-century satire, and the principles that sustain it in *Piers Plowman*. All comments, unless otherwise indicated, are based on the B text.

SOURCES AND TRADITIONS

Attempts to identify sources for Langland's satire have been largely surmises based on similarities of idea or language, but essentially unprovable. Specific fourteenth-century alliterative satires or complaints have been mentioned. For example, Yunck (269–70) and Hussey have observed a likeness between *Wynnere and Wastoure* and *Piers Plowman*. Salter has suggested that "Langland had read *The Simonie* and used it to good effect" (243), and that he might also have drawn on "The Song of the Husbandman" and "Thomas of Erceldoun's Prophecy." Despite clear similarities, there are no verbal echoes; and even apparent echoes, in a literature filled with proverb and commonplace, can deceive.

The earliest and most long-lived surmise concerns the French religious-allegorical tradition, whose visionary aspects have been discussed already in chapter four. In 1774 Warton suggested that Langland, describing the attack by the forces of Antichrist on Unity in B.20, probably "had his eye on" Huon de Meri's *Tournoiement de l'Antechrist* (ca. 1235). Skeat, however, found "no close resemblance of the language, but only a certain similarity of ideas" (1886, 2:276). In 1912 Owen detailed the parallels and similarities between the two works, without claiming direct influence. In 1983 Norton-Smith again proposed influence, when he found "traces of Langland's actual reading of Huon" (52) and amusingly reworked a few of Huon's octosyllabics into neo-Middle English alliterative verse to press his point. But direct influence is not clear. As Pearsall notes, "the [psychomachia] motif is perhaps too commonplace to make it worthwhile looking for parallels in particular OF [Old French] allegorical poems. . ." (365 n. 70).

The *Voie de paradis* or *Songe de paradis*, doubtfully attributed to Raoul de Houdenc, has been mentioned (Owen l05) as a possible source of the Doctor of Divinity scene in B.13. The dreamer in the French poem, dining with Confession, consumes an allegorical meal of sighs and laments, tears and anguish of heart. Again, there is no verbal echo or other indication that Langland knew the poem. In the Doctor of Divinity episode, however, Langland mentions the friars' "Pocalips" (B.13.91), that is, the "Apocalypse of Golias," indicating his familiarity with that most famous of all Latin "goliardic" satires (in Wright 1841, 1–20). We should also note here Marcett's widely accepted identification of William Jordan as the original of the Doctor of Divinity (49–64).

Cornelius has suggested that the satiric French *Roman de Fauvel* may have influenced *Piers Plowman*. She notes, among other similarities, the parallel between the attempted marriage of its allegorical horse-hero, Fauvel, to Fortune, and the attempted marriage of Lady Meed to False Fickle-Tongue (363–67). Bourquin, the latest to pursue possible French influences, has expanded Cornelius's proposal, suggesting a number of other French and Latin works not previously discussed in connection with Langland (1:178–93; also 1:353–58, 2:737–98). Some of these are strongly satirical; for example, the early (ca. 1185) *Romans de carité* of the Renclus de Molliens, which, as Barney remarks (above, p. 126), "sets the satiric tone for the whole tradition," or the later (ca. 1290) non-allegorical *Lamentationes* of Matheolus, a Latin work translated into French around 1370. Bourquin sees close parallels between Langland and Matheolus, but here as in other cases, proof is impossible. The conclusions of Owen's cautious study of *Piers Plowman* and seven French allegories — she calls it only a comparison — deserve repetition. She notes that of the seven only the *Roman de la rose* is known to have been copied in Langland's England, and observes (1) that there is no proof that Langland had borrowed directly from any of them; (2) that similarities suggest but do not prove that Langland had read and remembered some of them; and (3) that he probably knew and used the *Roman de la rose* (127–28). On that last universally influential work we may note Kirk's observation: "Whether or not the poet knew the *Roman* itself is difficult to discern and is of no practical importance, since it is certain that his world was full of its offspring" (16 n.).

In fact, the progeny of the entire lively tradition of French moral-religious-allegorical verse seems to have filled Langland's world. We can hardly deny his familiarity with its techniques and imagery, but the vehicles by which they reached him remain obscure. Late medieval writers were as prone in satire as in epic or romance to *topos* or commonplace. Who cast the first satirical stone at a hypocritical friar? Or at a cheating craftsman, a swindling merchant, a venal judge, a grasping lawyer? We are not likely to discover; by Langland's time they were everybody's targets. Or who first personified the power of money over venal man? Horace made money a queen (*Epistulae*, I, vi, 36–38); Juvenal made her a goddess (*Saturae*, I, 109–14); and in the century of Lady Meed, Dan Michel of Northgate made Dame Avarice a schoolmistress (Morris 35, 38). Or who invented Langland's satirical image of the cross on the coin (B.15.538–47; 15.500–09)? Goliards used it in the twelfth and thirteenth centuries (Yunck, 177–78), Gower (*MO*, 18577–18600, 25269–25272) and Bromyard (*SP*, "Crux") in the fourteenth. Owen noted that the chief result of her work was "to show that there was a common stock of allegorical material of which the writer, or writers, of 'Piers Plowman' made use" (127). By Langland's time satire subsisted chiefly on such inherited flotsam, which (along with a variety of other literary, devotional and liturgical texts) formed an important part of what Bourquin calls the poet's *effectif culturel* (2:737–38).

Hence the wisdom of examining satirical tradition rather than attempting to uncover evasive specific sources. With no proof of the direct influence of any single French moral-religious allegory on the satire of *Piers Plowman*, we can yet recognize the influence of that tradition. Jauss provides an excellent terse survey and bibliography of it; Owen's and Bourquin's studies demonstrate its richness and the nature of its influence on Langland and others. But until Jean de Meun's portion of *Le Roman de la rose* (ca. 1275) this tradition was incidentally rather than primarily satirical. The same is true of the ancient moral-devotional-homiletic tradition of the Seven Deadly Sins, which filled devotional and penitential literature after the Fourth Lateran Council (1215) and provided some of *Piers Plowman*'s most vivid satirical moments. The entire tradition is surveyed by Bloomfield (1952), with extensive bibliography. Wenzel has written a survey of the sin of sloth alone, richly documented and narrower in historical scope, hence more detailed in its treatment of Langland and fourteenth-century England.

Here we may group together a number of moral-satirical traditions that played significant parts in the composition of *Piers Plowman*, however unclear their channels of influence. The development of medieval venality satire and its various personifications of avarice, graft and the power of money—all central to Langland's satire—have been treated in detail by Yunck. Bloomfield (1962, 80) has suggested that False's charter at the espousal of Meed (B.2.73–114) was inspired by the parodic Devil's Letter or Devil's Charter (Lehmann 85–101). Heiserman, exploring the backgrounds of Skelton's satire, has examined a number of medieval traditions—satiric allegory, the "nowadays" *topos*, satire against courtiers and clerics, the peasant/plowman as satiric spokesman, among others—which cast light on Langland's satire. The tradition of medieval estates satire has been treated at length by Mohl and, with special reference to Chaucer, by Mann. Although *Piers Plowman* is not strictly estates satire (Mohl 102–04; Mann 2), the genre's materials are "clearly recognizable," especially in the *Visio*. The new understanding of Christian doctrine and discipline fostered by the Fourth Lateran Council produced numerous devotional works, very influential on fourteenth and fifteenth century English satire, which have been examined by Arnould, Pantin, and Braswell.

Although Will's invective is scattered throughout *Piers Plowman*, the tradition of the satirist-satirized, associated with Menippean satire, has received less attention than it deserves. Bloomfield considers encyclopedic or Menippean satire, along with the allegorical dream narrative and the debate, one of the three genres that form the basis of *Piers Plowman*; in that genre "a figure, somewhat foolish or at the least ingenuous, is chosen to pass through various, often ridiculous situations for the purpose of satire on current events, foibles, or sins" (1962, 10, 23–25). Martin notes that this Fool-hero is combined in *Piers Plowman* with the Wanderer, a motif usually not inimical, and often helpful, to satire. He sees Langland's antagonism toward vagrant scoundrels like his hypocritical friars, false hermits and lying pilgrims as clashing with the conventional image of the peripatetic seeker after Truth, and hence obscuring his satire. Lawlor notes the satirical effectiveness of the Dreamer's stubborn slowness to understand in his heart what he had long formally "known," his laborious ascent from "the doctrines so long accepted" to "the significances at last apprehended" (1957, 124). The satirical undercutting of the narrator by his human or personified interlocutors, while he himself heaps invective on the *canaille* he observes, effectively establishes Langland's humble posture, depriving his narrator of any haughty Juvenalian detachment that might defeat his wider purpose.

But for Langland the most important satirical tradition is that of the medieval sermon. Wenzel has discussed the sermon's general influence on *Piers Plowman* elsewhere in this volume. For an understanding of Langland's satire Owst's three well-documented chapters on "The Preaching of Satire and Complaint" (210–470) are indispensable. More important than his frequent references to Langland is the full picture of the satirical milieu that emerges from his discussion and quotation. Owst's polemics and hyperbole have at times offended scholars (see p. 157 below), but the depth of his evidence and the force of his conclusions cannot be ignored. One of Langland's finest achievements was to capture in an essentially learned narrative the tang and color of popular literature without its inanity and chaos. He learned this art largely from the preachers. It is likely, though it cannot be proved, that traditional satirical imagery, attitudes and fictions such as those of French religious allegory usually reached Langland through the sermons of the ubiquitous friars, who were quick to adopt useful literary aids, as a review of Bromyard or Bozon will testify.

SATIRICAL AFFINITIES WITH OTHER FOURTEENTH-CENTURY AUTHORS

The breadth and uniformity of Langland's fourteenth-century satirical world is most conveniently experienced through contemporary poets, Chaucer and Gower (in his *Mirour de l'omme* and *Vox clamantis*), and preachers (represented here by the *Summa praedicantium* of the Dominican John Bromyard), whose satirical objects and images are surprisingly similar to his. These span a broad literary spectrum: Chaucer's inscrutable, ironic evasiveness, Langland's moral (often highly poetic) intensity, Gower's meticulously ver-

sified ethical sternness, and the entirely practical (though often imaginative) diligence of Bromyard the homilist. They are of different creative
worlds: one can hardly imagine Gower's narrator shaping himself into the
shrouds of a shepherd or a hermit; his verse is always in dinner jacket. But
all deal in satire, and each writer's satire can usually be documented by one
or all of the others. For example, Langland's *bêtes noires*, the pretentiously
indigent friars, weave in and out of the *Canterbury Tales* from the General
Prologue through the brief, caustic animadversions of the Wife of Bath to
the revolting friar of the Summoner's Tale; and their vices are lengthily
retailed by Gower (e.g., *MO* 21181–21780; *VC* IV, 677–1182; cf. Fisher
265–69), though understandably they are absent from Friar John Bromyard's *Summa*. Most of the other targets of Langland's wrath also appear
in these contemporaries: the minstrels and sturdy beggars; the pardoners,
petty-simonist parish priests, grand-simonist bishops and officers of diocesan chanceries and courts; judges, lawyers and others associated with civil
law, such as sheriffs and beadles and jurymen; physicians; the entire courtly spectrum — sycophant courtiers, rowdy knights, wasteful lords, occasionally a king; the Roman Curia's grasping cardinals, sometimes the pope
himself; lying pilgrims and palmers; those high priests of finance, the Lombards and Jews; the great merchants whose lives are money, and their petty Cheapside counterparts — small tradesmen, drapers, weavers, brewers,
bakers, grocers. They crowd the literature.

The guild dramas, probably little different from the later redactions that
we have today, also contributed to Langland's satirical world. Like the sermons, they were composed by the learned for popular audiences. Their frequently satirical tone is typified by the corrupt Judases of all the cycles, the
Pilates of York and Towneley, and various jibes in the *Second Shepherds' Play*.

Many short satires and complaints, English and Latin — also a significant
part of the fourteenth-century satirical ambiance — can be found in volume
1 of Wright's collection of *Political Poems and Songs*, as well as in his earlier
collection of *The Political Songs of England*, these latter in Latin, Provençal,
Anglo-Norman and English, with translations. Those interested in pursuing medieval English satirical traditions to their twelfth and thirteenth century roots will find good translations of Nigel de Longchamps' tale of Dan
Burnel the Ass (*Speculum stultorum*, 1180), of John of Salisbury's *Policraticus*
(1159) and of Walter Map's *De nugis curialium* (ca. 1185), all of which develop satirical themes still commonplace in Langland's day. Readers of Latin will find satire scattered through the extensive works of the eccentric and
chatty Giraldus Cambrensis, but especially in his *Speculum ecclesiae* (*Opera*,
IV) and *Gemma ecclesiastica* (*Opera*, II). Also rewarding are the important long
pieces collected by Wright (1832) and the shorter, "goliardic," satiric poems
of his 1841 collection. Though the editions of many pieces in both collections have been superseded, the books are convenient, and the editions ade-

quate for the exploration of major satirical themes. Donaldson (11), citing Wright's contention that Langland "not infrequently imitates" the goliards, notes (more cautiously) "a number of things reminiscent of the goliardic tradition," while granting that the tradition is "worlds apart" from *Piers Plowman* (cf. also p. 136 above).

This older moral-satirical literature demonstrates vividly the traditional nature of the satire in *Piers Plowman*. There were changes, to be sure. The bourgeoisie — great merchants, petty shopkeepers, city craftsmen and apprentices — are rarely objects of satire before the mid-fourteenth century, and the mendicants make their first appearance only around 1250, some decades after their establishment. The changes in the spiritual climate of Western Europe, which gave a new character to satire and its spiritual bases, strongly influenced Langland and his contemporaries.

SATIRE: THE SPIRITUAL INTERTEXT

The uniformity of fourteenth-century satire reflects the relatively homogeneous, broadly-accepted ethical standard produced by the great thirteenth-century religious renewal, a watershed in the history of Western Christendom, which affected profoundly the average Christian's understanding of his spiritual life in the thirteenth and fourteenth centuries. Though the forces that produced it are complex and often obscure, the major events through which it was manifested are well known: first, the Fourth Lateran Council (1215), with its insistence on a trained clergy and a religiously educated laity, as well as its famous requirement of annual private confession to one's parish priest and annual communion at Easter time — a canon that produced a torrent of devotional and penitential writing with incalculable literary influence;* second, the founding of the mendicant orders; third, the rise of the universities and a concomitant scholarly class. These three separate developments became inextricably associated during the thirteenth century. If Lateran IV decreed urgent reforms, the universities provided their intellectual support, and the friars were the first shock troops to carry them out. The friars especially became essential parts of both the popular and the learned aspects of the renewal, important throughout Christendom as preachers and confessors (cf. Grosseteste's letter, pp. 142–43 below), but also dominant in the universities. Members of the regular clergy, they served popes and bishops as a convenient means of bypassing local or parochial

---

*The importance of Lateran IV to medieval literature was described in 1940 by Arnould (1–59), who also noted the contributions of the universities and the friars. Pantin gave the subject wide currency. Burrow (106–07), Fisher (137–41), Wenzel (68–69), Bloomfield (1952, 91), and Yunck (189, 201–02), among others, have noted briefly its importance. Braswell's volume is entirely devoted to it.

resistance to the new canons — certainly one reason for their growing un-
popularity among the secular clergy.

English bishops actively promoted the aims of Lateran IV, as the consti-
tutions of their councils and synods indicate. Their activity encouraged the
religious literature that contributed to the period's characteristic cultural ambiance (Cheney; Pantin 189–262). Braswell (127–29 and passim) concludes
that penitential literature, mandatory confession, and the habitual examination of conscience gave fourteenth-century writers new instruments for
characterization in narrative. To Langland they gave a firm ideological
matrix for his satire; their concern with sin, penance and penitence produced
images of private and public misconduct in ready menu, adapted to the
satirist's hand.

Based on the formulations of Lateran IV, the revival produced a new understanding of Christian doctrine and discipline, soon developed and scrutinized
in the universities. It was preached by the friars, applied by confessors, and
widely explained in a profusion of devotional and penitential literature to aid
laymen and simple priests in the understanding of their duties and the examination of their consciences (Pantin 192–235). Of interest to preachers and
satirists were certain specific reforming goals of Lateran IV: improving the
conduct of the clergy (Canons 7, 14–17, 62–66), religious education of both
clergy and laity (Canons 7, 10–11, 27, 30–31), and annual confession and
communion for all (Canon 21) (Hefele-Leclercq V, ii, 1316–98).

These developments form a significant part of the broad intertext of the
period from 1230 through 1400 and beyond. To poets the penitential focus
of the post-Lateran revival offered the model of a weak and sinful human
nature (Arnould 1–59; Braswell passim), which after 150 years of preaching and writing produced the grotesque, naturalistically sketched scoundrels
of all estates who fill the pages of Langland, Chaucer and Gower. The chief
villains of the fourteenth-century satirists were the friars. Their growth in
numbers, their popularity as preachers and confessors, and their rise to
supremacy in the universities, had been phenomenal; so was the fourteenth-
century decline in their reputation, at least among poets and secular clerics. The complex truth about these friars may be forever out of reach. Williams, whose discussion remains the best brief treatment of the subject, warns
that anti-mendicant polemic of the fourteenth century should be interpreted cautiously (499–513), and Szittya argues persuasively that such attacks
had a largely "symbolic rather than social function" (287–313). Our concern here is with the nature and traditions of the satire, not its truth or justice;
yet its contrast with Grosseteste's earlier evaluation of the friars is striking.
In 1238 the bishop had written to Pope Gregory IX:

> . . . inestimable benefits have been produced by the friars; for they illuminate
> our whole country with the light of their preaching and learning. Their holy con-

versation excites vehemently to contempt of the world and to voluntary poverty, to the practice of humility in the highest ranks, to obedience to the prelates and the head of the Church, to patience in tribulation, abstinence in plenty, in a word, to the practice of all virtues. If your holiness could see with what devotion and humility the people run to hear the word of life from them, you would indeed say that *they that dwell in the land of the shadow of death, upon them hath the light shined.* (*Epistolae*, trans. Luard, xxii. Text on 180; cf. also 120-22, 133-34, 181-82)

The difference between Grosseteste's friars of 1238 and Langland's friars of 1380-or Chaucer's or Gower's—is a good measure of the fourteenth-century reaction against them.

But the revival also provided writers with a new image of the devout layman and saturated their devotional experience with the devices and imagery of the new religious education; it familiarized many with dialectic and commentary—disputation and gloss—those major instructional methods of the universities that so delighted Langland's dreamer. Preaching, clerical vice and incompetence, confession, penitence and penance became part of everyone's daily experience, reacquainting clergy and laity with one another in revolutionary fashion, educating laymen in the Christian cult to a degree almost unknown for centuries. Religious devotion was no longer the function of a single estate; now clergy and laity were in regular meeting or confrontation, in confession, at sermons, even in the routine begging of the friars. All estates were daily reminded of personal religious obligations. It was a remarkable "democratization" of religion.

PIERS PLOWMAN AND THE SPIRITUAL INTERTEXT

Langland was influenced by all three elements of the thirteenth-century religious renewal. His poem is full of acts and images derived from the canons of Lateran IV, especially those concerned with the sins, preaching and confession. Ancient imagery, renewed by the Council, had filtered into satire. For example, Canon 21 uses a medical image as old as the fourth century: sin is illness, the confessant the patient, the confessor his physician (McNeill 14-26). The confessor is told to be "discreet and careful, so that like an experienced physician he may pour wine and oil into the wounds of the injured person (*superinfundat vinum et oleum vulneribus sauciati*)" (Hefele-Leclercq V, ii, 1350). The echo of Luke 10:34 (*infundens oleum et vinum*) was clearly intended to associate the priest-confessor with the healing Christ, who had long been typified by the Good Samaritan and his charity (see St. Jacques 217-30), a typology exploited by Langland (B.17.51-124). But the physican-image was easily subverted. The vision of venal friars probing the spiritually ill for gain suited the profane spirit of anti-mendicant satire well.

Chaucer's Summoner's friar thus calls Thomas's curate "ful necligent and slowe / To grope [i.e, to probe, medically] tendrely a conscience / In shrift ..." (*CT* .III.1816–1818); but soon the friar is himself "groping" elsewhere, for profit: ". . . this sike man felte this frere / Aboute his tuwel grope there and heere" (*CT*.III.2147–2148), where he discovers the indivisible gift of the peasant.

In passus 20, with Unity under attack, Langland uses the image of the soul-physician in grim satirical earnest. The sin-wounded defenders are treated by Shrift with his sharp salve:

> Shrift shoop sharp salue and made men do penaunce
> For hir mysfetes þat þey wroȝt hadde,
> And þat Piers pardon were ypayed, *redde quod debes.*
>
> (B.20.306–08)

This therapy of *redde quod debes*, "pay what you owe," proves so painful that sinners beg for gentle Friar Flatterer—glib, venal, interloping soul-physician, whose physic is of course entirely subversive. He too "gropes" the patient's wounds in hope of meed:

> And gooþ grope Contricion and gaf hym a plastre
> Of "a pryuee paiement and I shal praye for yow
> And for hem þat ye ben holden to al my lif tyme,
> And make of yow *memoria* in masse and in matyns
> As freres of oure Fraternytee, for a litel siluer."
>
> (B.20.363–67)

Contrition is lulled to sleep by this servant of Meed, and the spiritual betrayal is complete.

Nor could passus 5, centered on preaching and confession, have been written before Lateran IV. Its scenario derives from Canon 21 and in part from Canon 10, requiring non-preaching bishops to appoint diocesan preacher-confessors. Reason and Repentance (B.5.10–62) might well have been a pair of Grosseteste's friars. In the confessional vignettes that follow, allegory is almost submerged, not by a systematic "realism" but by the often grotesque *realia* of life in an inglorious, comic/satiric world, exactly the sort of drab world of misconduct daily visible to the clergy who carried out the requirements of Canon 21. The characters in these vignettes are less personifications than incarnations, material creatures bodying forth the immaterial, men fleshing out ideas, in a sort of sacramental *figura*: sin peopled into action. Coveitise, for example, is first incarnate in a shabby, filthy miser, who will spend no money even to feed and clothe himself. But he confesses to a past that could not have belonged to one man: from his master Symme he learned false weights and faulty merchandise; from the drapers how to stretch cloth for false measure; from his wife the weaver how to cheat employees, and then (she becomes a brewer) how to brew watery ale. As a youth he had been a usurer, a student of the Lombards and Jews, coin-clipper, cheater of the poor and of his neighbors (B.5.188–259).

The space given the different sins varies widely. Lechery, sensational favorite of both preachers and entertainers, gets a mere four lines; more surprising, Pride, ancient chief of all, receives only eight; Anger gets 50 and the closely related Envy, 59; Gluttony and Sloth (also closely related), 88 and 75 respectively; and Avarice, a heavy 107 lines (in the C text all are enlarged by the relocation of Haukyn's sins). But the thorough treatment of Avarice, source of Lady Meed's power, is revealing. Pride may confess first, but the root-evil for Langland, as for St. Paul (1 Tim. 6:10), is avarice. If Pride is the great epic sin, of Ajax or Achilles or Ganelon, and Lust the great romantic one, of Lancelot and Gueneuere or Tristan and Iseult, Avarice is the great, tawdry sin of Langland's increasingly commercial, unheroic world, the sin that sells other sins and then sells absolution from them (Yunck 314–17).

The art of this sawdust-trail penitential procession is highly sophisticated, its effects bizarre, surrealistic — "modernist" effects not uncommon in dream literature. It draws composites, multiple exposures in the fashion of the mature Picasso, views of each sin from several sides, variously incarnate. It is a complex art: not simple "personification allegory" decked out in patches of roguish naturalism, but polished homiletic satire, fleshing out sin in gross humanity. Though scholars do not agree on Langland's view of the sacrament of penance (see p. 101 above) the confessional theme fills Langland's satire throughout, from the false friar-confessor of Meed to the false friar-confessor of Unity; it dominates the scene of the Deadly Sins (passus 5), and Haukyn's confession of *his* deadly sins (passus 13–14).

Langland's attitude toward the second element of the religious revival — the friars — has already been dealt with at length. Friars appear throughout *Piers Plowman*, venal in their mendicancy, hypocritical in their shameless perversion of Scripture and dogma for the aggrandizement and enrichment of their orders, and offensively pretentious in displaying their university learning. They betray their vows, as well as the souls committed to their care and teaching. His hatred of the friars, associated with the struggle between seculars and mendicants (Williams 499–513), is complicated by his admiration for poverty as a way of life. Perhaps he saw the friars as *corruptio optimi*, the corruption of the best. He hates them, remarks Donaldson, "because, given the highest of ideals, they have sunk to the vice most destructive of charity, namely, avarice" (126).

The third element of the revival, the university, provides the dialectical atmosphere of the *Vita*, in particular Will's multifarious confrontations with figures concrete and abstract, when he "as a clerc . . . comsed to disputen"

(B.8.20). Disputation appears even in the Meed episode, as a dramatized *quaestio disputata* between Meed and Conscience (B.3.101–4.181), or more accurately, perhaps, as a dramatic conflation of university disputation and legal trial before the king. It is a deft satiric instrument, allowing Conscience to anatomize, then reject with finesse, the specious attractiveness of the economic argument. But the other major teaching method of the universities, commentary on a text, probably taught many friars the habit of the scriptural gloss, and thus gave Langland his glozing friars with their suave exegetical evasions of Scripture's harsh literalities.

But in the end it is their servitude to Meed that makes friars the poet's prime satirical targets. Langland does not reject the apostolic (and Franciscan) ideal of poverty or even the mendicancy it entails (B.14.216–29). What he hates is mendicancy for profit. He hates it in the lazy hermits and beggars of his time (e.g., B.Prol.40–45), but far more in the professed religious, where it enslaves religion to Meed.

Their common slavery to Meed also associates lawyers with the friars as satirical targets. Langland tags them with two memorably mordant lines, compounded of local color and scorching contempt (B.Prol.215–16):

> Thow my3test bettre meete myst on Maluerne hilles
> Than gete a mom of hire mouþ til moneie be shewed.

Venality is their manifest essence throughout the poem, notably in the preface to Piers's Pardon (B.7.40–61), where of all men they "leest pardon hadde," since they demanded meed from innocents (cf. Ps. 14:5). Most of the rich medieval satire against venal lawyers canon and civil (Yunck 153–59, 205–11, 251–52) reflects a conservative principle, that for lawyers to demand pay for their tongues and talents was simony: *scientia donum Dei est, unde vendi non potest*, "knowledge is the gift of God, hence cannot be sold" (Post, Giocarnis and Kay 195–234; Yunck 153–59; Stokes 62–64, 218–19). The principle had been long abandoned by canonists and theologians, but the half-forgotten feudal assumption that all living should come from the land — that spiritual and intellectual activities were of the Holy Spirit — had been versified by Latin poets in the twelfth and thirteenth centuries (Yunck 119, 157–58) and still lingered on. Langland speaks in this tradition. Having just asserted that only those lawyers who had spoken freely for the poor and innocent would be safe from hell-fire, his narrator affirms the *donum Dei* principle:

> Ac to bugge water ne wynd ne wit ne fir þe ferþe,
> Thise foure þe fader of heuene made to þis foold in commune;
> Thise ben truþes tresores trewe folk to helpe,
> That neuere shul wexe ne wanye wiþouten god hymselue.
> Whan þei drawen on to þe deþ and Indulgences wolde haue,

His pardon is wel petit at his partyng hennes
That any Mede of mene men for motyng takeþ.
(B.7.53-59)

LANGLAND'S LILLIPUT: SATIRE BY BELITTLEMENT

The grasping vices of friars and lawyers are mean sins, grimy but universal, perhaps a large part of the confessions with which the clergy were newly burdened. They reflect exactly the anti-heroic current that Robertson (284-85) and Burrow (106-09) find in Ricardian literature, and which the latter also attributes in part to the confessional requirement of Lateran IV. Langland is here true to the Ricardian type, leaning strongly toward satire by belittlement, by exposing the sort of human pettiness encountered in confession. The deadly sins in passus 5 are a crowd of such base sinners. Even Pride, in the person of Pernele Proud-herte, is reduced to mere vanity; shriveled Envy and the puking glutton are demeaned into comic gargoyles. Their collectivity later becomes Haukyn, in whom the sins are treated contrapuntally, developed *fugato* into a single image, not unlike the far cruder sample confessant in Robert of Flamborough's *Liber poenitentialis* (179-99; discussed by Braswell 38-45). Though formally a mere congeries of the sins, whom Langland later dismantles in the C text, Haukyn is a fine comic-satiric creation, a perversely attractive human figment whose warped vision of himself is shattered in an utterly demeaning confession.

The function of the dreamer as satirist-satirized and Menippean hero has been mentioned above. "Doted daffe," dull of wit (B.1.140) and unheroic, he likewise plays a major part in Langland's satire by belittlement, browbeaten repeatedly throughout the *Vita* by most of the abstractions he meets, but especially by Dame Study upon his initiation into the world of scholarship (B.10.1 157). Living out a *Bildungsroman*, he provides his various interlocutors opportunity to demean him, but also to attack the vices of the day, as in Study's invective against the frivolity of great men, who turn Scripture and theology into dinner-table chat, and (in that unforgettable satiric line) "gnawen god in þe gorge whanne hir guttes fullen" B.10.58), or her reactionary lament over the current unwillingness of great lords to dine charitably in hall with their households and dependents (B.10.96-103). But Will (the allegorical overtones of his name should never be ignored) is even further demeaned when Elde slashes at him, leaving him glumly bald, deaf, toothless, gouty and impotent, so that his imperfectly solicitous wife wishes him in heaven (B.20.183-216). To the defeat of his mind is added the disgrace of his body, belittled even as he bids for salvation.

Yet Will (poet, dreamer, or faculty—it is most difficult to distinguish) is undercut not merely by his interlocutors and by circumstance, but also, devastatingly, by his own insecurity. Donaldson has canvassed thoroughly in all three texts "the strange self-revelations . . . where the poet half-bitterly, half-humorously, emphasizes his own disreputability" (153 and passim; also Norton-Smith, passim). Possibly those glimpses are calculated attributes of the dreamer as Menippean hero, a further extension of the poet's satirical purpose.

The anti-heroic is thus basic to Langland's satire. His one true hero is superhuman: Jesus, tried Master of *redde quod debes*, quaestor of Piers's pardon, who jousts in Jerusalem in the armor of Piers. Other characters, allegorical or real, are at best earnest fumblers like the dreamer, at worst fatuous hypocrites like the gluttonous Doctor of Divinity. Though Piers is the highest potential of mankind, the ideal of the dreamer who faints with joy at the sound of his name (B.16.18–19), and an authority for Clergy (B.13.124–30), even he suffers repeated defeats and perplexities. The knight in Piers's half acre (B.6.164–69) is earnest and cooperative but unable to keep order. The King at Meed's trial (B.4) is blind to her inevitable evil. And Conscience, right in so many spiritual crises, finally errs and admits a venal friar into besieged Unity.

Langland fabricates his satire from these details of failure and bumbling, expressed in colloquial, caustic, even snarling verse, in slashing side-glances and satirical vignettes. A lazy Breton in Piers's creaking commune tells him to "go pissen with his plouʒ" (B.6.155). "Baw!" shouts a brewer in Unity,

> I wol noʒt be ruled
> By Iesu! for al youre Ianglynge, wiþ *Spiritus Iusticie*,
> Ne after Conscience, by crist! while I kan selle
> Boþ dregges and draf and drawe at oon hole
> Thikke ale and þynne ale; þat is my kynde,
> And noʒt hakke after holynesse; hold þi tonge, Conscience!
>   (B.19.396–401)

And Conscience can merely continue the endless cycle of search.

Thus the fourteenth-century world view anatomized by Burrow (94–111), in large part a spiritual construct of Lateran IV, dominates Langland's satire. It is a sardonic, withering view of a mankind petty even in its mortal sins. In the final scene at Unity, for example — that great opportunity for celebrating the heroic defense of a narrow passage in the epic manner of *Maldon* or *Roland* — the hero, Piers, as Burrow observes, is absent; the villain, Antichrist, merely a shadow in the distance; the narrator discredited by the humiliating ravages of Elde; and the fortress betrayed by a sneaking infiltration of friars. "The age of persecutors," he adds, "has given way to the age of hypocrites, in which the heroic virtues of courage and physical endurance no longer have any meaning" (97). Both Burrow (106–07) and

Braswell (61–100) see the pervasive influence of Lateran IV in the confessional scenarios of Ricardian narratives and in the "moral psychology" of some of their characters. The just man, the dreamer observes to two friars, falls seven times a day (Prov. 24:16; B.8.21–22). This stumbling humanity fills the poet's satiric vision.

THE POSITIVE BASIS OF LANGLAND'S SATIRE

Langland's friars and lawyers, then, stand as extreme representatives of the tarnished race, busy with petty lusts and treacheries, which the poet sees around him. But two positive principles — moral-satirical commonplaces linking man's duty to God with his duty to society — support this satiric vision and order the poet's social thought.

The first principle — that by which Langland judges educated men, especially the lawyers — has been mentioned already: learning is the gift of God, hence cannot be sold (cf. p. 146 above). Simony in its broadest sense — the sale not only of church offices, the sacraments and other priestly functions, but also of talent and education — constitutes the Treason of the Clerks. Its cure, as preached to Haukyn by Patience, is perfect poverty, a true *donum Dei* (B.14.297–300). Langland broadens the theme eloquently, as Grace himself explains that every man's craft is his own gift of God, carrying a Divine dignity:

> Loke þat noon lakke ooþer, but loveþ as breþren;
> And who þat moost maistries kan be myldest of berynge.
> And croune Conscience kyng and make craft youre Stiward,
> And after craftes conseil cloþeþ yow and fede.
>
> (B.19.254–57)

The second principle that governs Langland's satire is sounded tentatively after the confessions of the sins, when "Roberd þe Robbere on *Reddite* loked" (B.5.461), but could make no restitution. In broader form it rises to a major theme in passus 19 and 20: *Redde quod debes!* The words are the threatening demand of the evil servant in Matt. 18:38, who will not imitate his master's compassion; but here *Redde* is demanded by Christ himself as prerequisite to Piers's Pardon (B.19.186–87, 258–59; Bloomfield 1962, 132). And *redde* indeed resembles the harsh demand for works that closes the Athanasian Creed. Langland himself connects the two when Conscience remarks that the faithful can receive the Sacrament "as often as þei hadde nede, þo þat hadde ypaid / To Piers pardon þe Plowman *redde quod debes*" (B.19.389–90). And *redde* is the active ingredient of Shrift's "sharp salue" for the sin-wounded inside Unity (cf. p. 144 above).

Frank (106–09) and Bloomfield (1962, 130–32) have demonstrated the centrality of *redde quod debes* to Langland's thought. It implied for him a highly detailed program of Christian justice which provided the major positive basis for his satirical stance. Piers's principle of *redde quod debes*, handed down from Truth by Grace, counters Coveitise's principle — nowhere formulated but everywhere implied — of *rape quod potes*, "grab what you can," which enslaves men to Meed.

Bromyard's *Summa praedicantium* conveniently condenses the richness of the *redditio* principle. Under that heading he summarizes the individual's obligations to God, to society and to self, in effect presenting a commentary on the nature of justice and setting forth, with dense scriptural support, an entire program of conduct. The entry is a lengthy series of the triads so favored by devotional writers. We are all obligated, he states, to repay three debts to three different creditors: to our God, to our neighbors and to ourselves; and for three goods, those of Nature, Fortune and Grace (this last a familiar commonplace; cf. Owst 308). We should render to God (*reddere debemus*), says Bromyard, for each of these goods in three different ways; for the goods of nature by act of the heart (loving and believing), of the mouth (confessing and praising), and of the body (preaching and obeying His precepts). Later he treats (more briefly) obligations to self: purity of heart, decency (*honestas*) of speech, and sobriety or rationality in deeds; all three of which are *propter Deum*, whose purity we receive into our hearts, in whose presence we always speak, and in whose rational image we were created. Finally he treats obligations to neighbor, again *secundum triplicem actum cordis oris et operis*, and stresses the rewards for observing our obligations and the penalties for neglecting them.

This sketchy summary shows Bromyard's *redditio* as a dense network of obligations surrounding all individuals throughout their lives. It is a view that Langland seems to share entirely. Both men see these obligations as *interpersonal*, rooted in the divine and natural laws, hence antecedent to positive law. Both associate them with feudal obligation (see pp. 33–34 above). For each individual the nexus is personal: to God, to neighbor, to self. When the personal nexus fails anywhere in this complex, feudally conceived reticulation, the cash nexus takes over. Obligation succumbs to negotiation, exploitation, or worse; and *redde quod debes* falls victim to Meed. It appears, then, that the unsalability of the *donum Dei*, of intelligence and education, is simply a rigorous application of the *redde* principle to the learned. But Langland's surly brewer in besieged Unity likewise recognizes no obligations, and will water his beer to what the market will bear, for "it is my kynde" (p. 148 above). Thus the tongue-vending Westminster lawyers, and thus the unspeakable friars who cling in act to the meed which they have forsworn in word. *Rape quod potes!*

Redditio is thus the touchstone of Langland's satire. His poem is full of people like the brewer or the Breton Waster (B.6.152-70), or the tradesman-servants of Meed, who place personal gain above the common weal, rejecting *redditio* and hence all social order. Disorder flares openly in the Breton's snarls and threats; but it is latent even in tractable Haukyn, who assures Conscience that society has not treated him justly (B.13.226-70). The Field of Folk early in *Piers Plowman*, and Unity at its close, both harbor these subversives: Fortress is a reprise of Field (see pp. 58-61 above), but the first scene is the dreamer's Song of Innocence, the last his Song of Experience. He has gained in vision. The milling, meaningless crowd of the Field he sees at the close undisguised, as an apocalyptic confrontation between those who pay what they owe and those who seize what they can. "In the last dream," remarks Wittig (75-76), "[the Field Full of Folk] is portrayed with all the conceptual clarity of a morality play," revealing "the failure of human choice to live up to 'redde quod debes.'" As an image of justice, *redde quod debes* is both private and public, secular and religious; it orders and elucidates the Field Full of Folk, which concerns the poet first and last. It recapitulates in practical terms Jesus's commandments of love (Matt. 23:37-41), and, with Romans 13:7, asserts our duties to others, requiring each to render to each his due.

Langland does not preach the Social Gospel, that souls are saved by rectifying social organization. His theology is concerned traditionally enough with the individual soul's (Piers's, the dreamer's) pilgrimage to God (cf. pp. 88-90 above). But he is a social satirist: the unstable, self-seeking crowd, which once shouted "Crucify Him," is always at hand, first and last a danger to the progress of the soul. His satire is not an essay *de contemptu mundi*, rejecting an ugly world for the bright, distant prospect of the the Church Triumphant; rather it bears on the duties and potentialities of the Church Militant, the Christian individual submerged in the grimy turmoil of *nowadaies*. Jerusalem the Golden, with milk and honey blessed, is man's final end, but remote. Chill and muddy England, with her plagues, famines and unrest, is at hand, immediate; her social wrongs, products of myriad individual failures in *redditio*, absorb the satirist's attention. Of the preachers' traditional targets, "the World, the Flesh and the Devil," Langland shows the truly satanic only in defeat, and treats the Flesh almost incidentally. But his satire rakes those who endanger social order: the unproductive, the crooks and the fraudulent, the simonists and brain-peddlers, Meed's train. Pride and Lust weigh little against Avarice and Sloth. In the individual Christian's fulfillment of his personal obligations lies the hope for English society. Langland draws his weapons from the common arsenal of fourteenth-century satire, but he selects his targets by the social principle of *redde quod debes*.

He aims at all who deny the triple obligation to God, neighbor, self, imposed by their gifts. These are the hectic seekers after more than their deserts, after "Mede mesurelees þat maistres desireþ" (B.3.246), the enemies of *redde quod debes*. But Conscience has described another meed, beyond all human deserts,

> That oon god of his grace gyueþ in his blisse
> To hem þat werchen wel while þei ben here.
> (B.3.232–33)

Here is the meed supreme, the spoils of the joust on the cross, the fruit of Truth's pardon to Piers. Through Christ's joust the harsh lines of the Athanasian Creed that express the pardon are enfranchised, for Heavenly Meed is beyond the reach of the human *redde*. Satire fades; the boundless human debt is forgiven, just as the compassionate lord of Matthew 18 forgave the debt of his servant.

REFERENCES

Arnould, E. J. *Le Manuel des péchés: étude de littérature religieuse anglo-normande*. Paris: E. Droz, 1940.

Benson, C. David. "The Function of Lady Meed in *Piers Plowman*." *ES* 61 (1980): 193–301.

Bloomfield, Morton W. *The Seven Deadly Sins*. East Lansing: Michigan State University Press, 1952; rpt. 1967.

————. *Piers Plowman as a Fourteenth-Century Apocalypse*. New Brunswick, NJ: Rutgers University Press, 1962.

Bourquin, Guy. *Piers Plowman: Etudes sur la genèse littéraire des trois versions*. 2 vols. Paris: Champion, 1978.

Braswell, Mary Flowers. *The Medieval Sinner: Characterization and Confession in the Literature of the English Middle Ages*. Rutherford, NJ: Fairleigh Dickinson University Press, 1983.

Bromyard, Johannes. *Summa praedicantium*. 2 vols. Venice: Dominicus Nicolinus, 1586.

Burrow, J. A. *Ricardian Poetry: Chaucer, Gower, Langland and the "Gawain" Poet*. London: Routledge & Kegan Paul, 1971.

Cheney, C. R. *English Synodalia of the Thirteenth Century*. London: Oxford University Press, 1941.

Cornelius, Roberta D. "*Piers Plowman* and the *Roman de Fauvel*." *PMLA* 47 (1932): 363–67.

Donaldson, E. Talbot. *Piers Plowman: The C-Text and Its Poet*. New Haven: Yale University Press, 1949.

Fisher, John H. *John Gower: Moral Philosopher and Friend of Chaucer*. New York: New York University Press, 1964.

Frank, Robert Worth, Jr. *Piers Plowman and the Scheme of Salvation*. Yale Studies in English 136. New Haven: Yale University Press, 1957.

Giraldus Cambrensis. *Opera*. Ed. J. S. Brewer and James F. Dimock. 8 vols. Rolls Series. London: Longman, Green, Longman, and Roberts, 1861–91.

Gower, John. *The Major Latin Works*. Trans. Eric W. Stockton. Seattle: University of Washington Press, 1962.

Hefele, Charles-Joseph and H. Leclercq. *Histoire des conciles d'après les documents originaux*. Paris: Letouzey et Ané, 1913.

Heiserman, A. R. *Skelton and Satire*. Chicago: University of Chicago Press, 1961.

Hussey, S. S. "Langland's Reading of Alliterative Poetry." *MLR* 60 (1965): 163–70.

Jauss, Hans Robert. *Genèse de la poésie allégorique française au moyen-âge (de 1180 à 1240)*. Heidelberg: Winter, 1962.

John of Salisbury. *Policratici sive de nugis curialium et vestigiis philosophorum libri VIII*. Ed. C. C. J. Webb. 2 vols. Oxford: Clarendon, 1909. Trans. John Dickinson. *The Statesman's Book* (books 4–6, selections from 7, 8). New York: Knopf, 1927. Trans. Joseph Pike. *Frivolities of Courtiers and Foot-prints of Philosophers* (Books 1–3, selections from 7, 8). Minneapolis: University of Minnesota Press, 1938.

Kane, George. *Middle English Literature*. London: Methuen, 1951.

Kirk, Elizabeth. *The Dream Thought of Piers Plowman*. New Haven and London: Yale University Press, 1972.

Knight, S. T. "Satire in *Piers Plowman*." Hussey 279–309.

Lawlor, John. "The Imaginative Unity of *Piers Plowman*." *RES* ns 8 (1957): 113–26.
———. *Piers Plowman: An Essay in Criticism*. London: Arnold, 1962.

Lehmann, Paul. *Die Parodie im Mittelalter*. Munich: Drei Masken, 1922; 2nd ed. rev. and expanded, Stuttgart: Hiersemann, 1963.

Mann, Jill. *Chaucer and Medieval Estates Satire*. Cambridge: Cambridge University Press, 1973.

Marcett, Mildred E. *Uhtred de Boldon, Friar William Jordan and Piers Plowman*. New York: the author, 1938.

Martin, Jay. "Wil as Fool and Wanderer in *Piers Plowman*." *TSLL* 3 (1962): 535–48.

McNeill, John T. "Medicine for Sin as Prescribed in the Penitentials." *Church History* 1 (1932): 14–26.

Mitchell, A. G. *Lady Meed and the Art of Piers Plowman*. Third Chambers Memorial Lecture. London: Lewis, 1956.

Mohl, Ruth. *The Three Estates in Medieval and Renaissance Literature*. New York: Columbia University Press, 1933.

Morris, Richard, ed. *Dan Michel's Ayenbite of Inwyt*. EETS 23. London: Trübner, 1866.

Nigel de Longchamps. *Speculum stultorum*. Ed. John H. Mozley and Robert R. Raymo. Berkeley and Los Angeles: University of California Press, 1960. Trans. John H. Mozley. *A Mirror for Fools: the Book of Burnel the Ass*. Notre Dame: University of Notre Dame Press, 1963.

Norton-Smith, John. *William Langland*. Leiden: Brill, 1983.

Owen, Dorothy L. *Piers Plowman: A Comparison with Some Earlier and Contemporary French Allegories*. London: University of London Press, 1912.

Owst, G. R. *Literature and Pulpit in Medieval England*. 1933; 2nd rev. ed. Oxford: Blackwell, 1961.

Pantin, W. A. *The English Church in the Fourteenth Century*. Cambridge: Cambridge University Press, 1955; rpt. Notre Dame: University of Notre Dame Press, 1962.

Pearsall, Derek, ed. *Piers Plowman by William Langland. An Edition of the C-Text*. London: Arnold, 1978.

Peter, J. D. *Complaint and Satire in Early English Literature.* London: Oxford University Press, 1956.

Post, Gaines, Kimon Giocarnis, and Richard Kay. "The Medieval Heritage of a Humanistic Ideal: 'Scientia Donum Dei Est, Unde Vendi Non Potest.'" *Traditio* 11 (1955): 195–234.

Powicke, F. M., and C. R. Cheney. *Councils and Synods, with Other Documents Relating to the English Church.* Vol. 2 (AD 1205–1313). Oxford: Clarendon, 1964.

Robert of Flamborough. *Liber poenitentialis.* Ed. J. J. F. Firth. Toronto: Pontifical Institute of Medieval Studies, 1971.

Robert Grosseteste. *Epistolae.* Ed. Henry R. Luard. Rolls Series. London: Longman, 1861.

Robertson, D. W., Jr. *A Preface to Chaucer: Studies in Medieval Perspectives.* Princeton: Princeton University Press, 1962.

Salter, Elizabeth (see Zeeman).

St. Jacques, Raymond C. "The Liturgical Associations of Langland's Samaritan." *Traditio* 25 (1969): 217–30.

Stokes, Myra. *Justice and Mercy in Piers Plowman: A Reading of the B Text Visio.* London and Canberra: Croom Helm, 1984.

Szittya, Penn R. "The Anti-Fraternal Tradition in Middle English Literature." *Speculum* 52 (1977): 287–313.

Walter Map. *De nugis curialium: Courtiers' Trifles.* Ed. and trans. M. R. James, rev. C. N. L. Brooke and R. A. B. Mynors. Oxford: Clarendon, 1983.

Wenzel, Siegfried. *The Sin of Sloth: Acedia in Medieval Thought and Literature.* Chapel Hill: University of North Carolina Press, 1967.

Wesling, Donald. "Eschatology and the Language of Satire in *Piers Plowman.*" *Criticism* 10 (1968): 277–89.

Williams, Arnold. "Chaucer and the Friars." *Speculum* 28 (1953): 499–513.

Wittig, Joseph S. "The Dramatic and Rhetorical Development of Long Will's Pilgrimage." *NM* 76 (1975): 52–76.

Wright, Thomas. *The Political Songs of England.* London: Camden Society, 1839.

———. *The Latin Poems Commonly Attributed to Walter Mapes.* London: Camden Society, 1841.

———. *Political Poems and Songs.* 2 vols. Rolls Series. London: Longman's and Trübner, 1861.

———. *The Anglo-Latin Satirical Poets and Epigrammatists of the Twelfth Century,* 2 vols. Rolls Series. London: Longman's and Trübner, 1872.

Yunck, John A. *The Lineage of Lady Meed: the Development of Mediaeval Venality Satire.* Notre Dame: University of Notre Dame Press, 1963.

Zeeman (Salter), Elizabeth. "*Piers Plowman* and 'The Simonie.'" *Archiv* 203 (1967): 241–54.

6

MEDIEVAL SERMONS

SIEGFRIED WENZEL

PROLEGOMENA

Langland's concern with man's spiritual destiny and the question of how one may save one's soul; his lengthy condemnation of vices and failings in nearly all classes of society; and his introduction of allegorical figures who preach (Reason at B.5.11; Scripture at B.11.107), obviously relate *Piers Plowman* closely to preaching. The poem of course is not a sermon, but it appears to owe contemporary sermons a great deal.

Before surveying major investigations into this debt, it is well to stress that the influence of contemporary preaching is less easy to grasp than might appear. Preaching is an oral act, but the documents that have survived to tell us about it are more or less self-consciously literary and hence may record only part of what was actually spoken from the pulpit. Their majority, at least in the period with which we are concerned, are in Latin rather than English. And the texts that can enlighten us about the medieval art of preaching are diverse in nature — not only actual sermons but also handbooks and preaching aids that differ widely in content and form (see Pfander; Von Nolcken).

In addition it is not always easy to clearly distinguish preaching from other influences. Late medieval sermons harvested and garnered crops that had been grown in quite separate fields, as for instance venality satire (Yunck 239–58), or the liturgy (e.g., St. Jacques), or the meditative tradition (e.g., Hill). One must therefore be prepared to reckon with preaching as a channel through which images reached Langland that originated, and can now be found, in a number of quite different genres. This caveat applies especially to two areas of medieval intellectual and literary activity that were closely connected with preaching, namely, penitential literature and biblical commentary.

Penitential literature included such handbooks as *Oculus sacerdotis, Hand-lyng Synne, The Book of Vices and Virtues,* or *Livre de seyntz medicines,* which were intended to aid both priests and penitents in their preparation for confession. Such literature has occasionally been cited as a source or analogue for Langland's "social satire" and moral criticism, and evidently furnished the precise model for Langland's confession of Sloth (B.5.385–440, see Wenzel 1967, 137–40). One may distinguish the authors of such treatises from preachers by calling them "moralists" (Frank 82–83), but of course the term fits both categories. Penitential literature is excluded from special consideration in the following review because in comparison with sermons it does not occupy a significant place in *Piers Plowman* scholarship (cf. p. 101).

Quite the reverse is true of the tradition of biblical commentary. There is no doubt that in both its substance and its form *Piers* owes much to medieval exegesis of the Bible. Again, it is likely that a good deal of this influence reached Langland through sermon literature. Now and then one can demonstrate that even though one of Langland's images or quotations had its remote origin in Scripture and was further developed by biblical exegetes, an exact parallel cannot be found except in contemporary sermons. For example, the metaphor "þat loue is triacle of heuene" (B.1.148) may well derive ultimately from the biblical account of Moses' erecting the serpent of brass to ward off the desert snakes, which in medieval exegesis led to the statement that *thyriaca,* a serpent's poison, is the fitting antidote to the poison of sin (Smith 22–23). But more plausibly Langland's direct source was sermon literature, where the image occurs as a commonplace, as for instance in a Middle English sermon which will be quoted below. Similarly, Langland's tag "Omnis iniquitas quantum ad misericordiam dei est quasi sintilla in medio maris" (B.5.283) has been traced to Augustine's commentary on Psalm 143. But Augustine's text lacks the image of the spark, whereas the quotation, in the form in which it appears in Langland, is a commonplace in fourteenth-century preaching: it occurs, for instance, in Robert Holcot's sermon 53 (Cambridge, Peterhouse MS 210, fol. 73ᵛ), in John of Grime-stone's collection of sermon commonplaces, under "Misericordia" (Edinburgh, Advocates' Library MS 18.7.21, fol. 84), and in *Fasciculus morum* (Canterbury, Cathedral Library MS D.14, fol. 124ᵛ; on the nature and content of this work see Wenzel 1978). We must, therefore, recognize that sermons handed on and popularized a good deal of the verbal material and even the thought processes developed and applied in biblical exegesis.

MAJOR CONTRIBUTIONS

The first — and lastingly fundamental — investigation of the sermon background of Langland's poetry is the work of Gerald R. Owst. Following an earlier find by Gasquet, Owst in 1925 pointed to a sermon by Thomas Brinton, bishop of Rochester, which was preached during the Good Parliament of 1376 and contains the fable of "belling the cat" (also B.Prol.146 ff.) together with some criticism of contemporary conditions. These similarities led Owst to identify Langland's "Aungel of heuene" (B.Prol.128) with Brinton and the "Goliardeis" (139) with Peter de la Mare, then spokesman of the Commons. But these specific suggestions were only a byproduct of Owst's reading widely in the extant sermon literature produced in England between roughly 1350 and 1450, which had led him to realize that contrary to "the superior scorn of our modern men of letters [and] the negligences and ignorances of professors" — among whom he singled out W. P. Ker, Jusserand, Skeat, and Manly — , the medieval sermon provided a most influential background to Middle English literature and especially to *Piers Plowman*, without whose study and comparison "Langland's work will never be correctly estimated or understood" (1925, 271). This view Owst documented fully in two volumes (1926 and 1933) larded with references to Langland's poem. Especially the second volume, *Literature and Pulpit in Medieval England*, builds an impressive case. It cites over 170 mostly unedited sermon manuscripts and quotes repeatedly from a handful of works that in the meantime have become household words in *Piers Plowman* scholarship: Brinton, Bromyard, Wimbledon, Rypon, and the Middle English sermons since then edited by Ross. What emerges is the view that the qualities hitherto so greatly admired in Langland's poetry had their inspiration and actual sources in the work of contemporary preachers. Again and again Owst quotes sermon analogues to such dominant topics in the poem as the cupidity of the clergy, oppression of the poor, the venality of lawyers, and much else (1933, passim). Occasionally he points to the sermon background of literary *topoi*, such as the marriage of the devil's daughters (93–97) or the allegorical castle (84). And here and there he can even cite sermon parallels for specific smaller images and similes, as for instance, penance as a laundress in B.15.186–94; C.16.333–36 (36), or the *stella comata* of C.20.248 (506). This wealth of parallels gave Owst sufficient ground to react against the "professors" who had been praising *Piers Plowman* for the supposed originality and uniqueness of its lively satire, reforming passion, allegory, and realistic imagery, and instead to claim that the poem "represents nothing more nor less than the quintessence of English mediaeval preaching gathered up into a single metrical piece of unusual charm and vivacity" (1926, 295).

This often repeated remark — itself quintessential of Owst's view — has a hyperbolic ring that at once signals a possible oversimplification and distortion in Owst's understanding of Langland's poetry. No wonder that in due time he would be severely if wittily taken to task for it (Donaldson 143–44 n. 6). One critic went just as far in the opposite direction, claiming that "there is no proof that Langland took anything from the homilists of the age" (Bloomfield 1939, 232). Yet upon further reflection the same critic reversed himself. Noting that "the tricks of the trade" — namely, such homiletic devices as the use of quotations, everyday detail, moral personifications, satire directed at classes and groups in society — "are scattered throughout the work," Bloomfield concluded that "the sermon is a dominant mode of the literary background of *Piers*, and a knowledge of its structure and conventions is essential in uncovering the literary forebears of the poem" (1962, 34). This more mature appraisal served to rectify Owst's claims in two important respects: it ranked sermons as only one out of several "literary forebears" that influenced *Piers* (Bloomfield listed six: 1962, 10), and it emphasized that "Owst's fine study" had analyzed the sermon influence "mainly from the point of view of its *content* rather than *form*" (32, italics added).

Hence it is chiefly the *formal* influence of sermons that has occupied critics of the poem since Owst.* Thus, Salter considered the spirit and techniques of the medieval sermon, together with alliterative poetry and the vision genre, as the major aspects of Langland's *ars poetica*. Assuming that, just as in preaching, Langland's "art of rhetoric" is functional and subservient to his religious purpose, she argues that "the driving force, the real centre of energy in his work is spiritual" and that "poetry serves this dedication" (1962, 31). Such figures as *adnominatio, contentio, similiter cadens, commutatio, traductio*, and metaphor are therefore used to create "a lucid, emphatic text which will both instruct and move" (41). Concerning the apparent lack of structure and consistency, she similarly proposes that the poem's unity is not that of a narrative but is instead subordinated to "the development of theme or themes" as in sermon literature. "Langland is constantly distracted by fresh objects of interest," and the resulting "elusive 'logic of the plan' " is understandable by reference to medieval pulpit oratory (47–48).

Salter's fresh approach to the sermon background of *Piers*, whose main points were summed up again in her edition of selections from the poem (Salter and Pearsall 48–51), further inspired a rich essay by Spearing (1964). Sharing his predecessors' conviction that *Piers Plowman* is close to sermons in both content and form, Spearing addresses particularly the problem of

---

* An exception is Coleman, who frequently refers to sermons in order to show that the theological concerns of the *moderni* were echoed in preaching as they, supposedly, were by Langland. Similarly, Aers (33–51) uses sermons for his analysis of biblical exegesis. The studies by Swieczkowski and Ryan are exclusively concerned with, respectively, syntactic matters and alliterating word pairs which the poem may share with sermons, and the latter subject has been explored further by Tristram. Salter (1978) suggests a strong influence on *Piers* from alliterative practices found in some contemporary Middle English Sermons.

the poem's arrangement or *dispositio*. Starting from the admiring comment made by a contemporary listener about the preaching of Gilbert Foliot, bishop of London, whose sermon "ran backwards and forwards on its path from its starting point back to the same starting-point," Spearing argues that Langland employs just such sermon art by choosing a sermon text (the *thema*), developing it by means of dividing it into a number of parts (the *divisio*), and restating it at the end of his work. In Spearing's view, therefore, the poem deals with the *thema breve* of "What good thing shall I do?" (cf. Matt. 19:16, though the question does not occur in the poem in this form), which is restated, as Spearing claims, in C.21.195-98. The theme is developed at length with the help of "the threefold *divisio* of the 'university' sermon," namely, by extending the Dreamer's search for Do-well into Do-better and Do-best (116-19). The main principle of the poem's order and coherence, therefore, is its "thematic organization," which Spearing further illustrates by analyzing the sermon preached by Reason in C.5 (119-22). That such development should include digressions is not astonishing, for both Gregory the Great and later medieval writers of handbooks on the art of preaching (the *artes praedicandi*) permitted the preacher to digress if it was done for the spiritual profit of his audience (122-27). Lastly, Spearing points out that verbal repetition and "thematic interweaving" are two more stylistic features which, as part of "an essentially oral rhetoric," closely link *Piers* to contemporary preaching (127-31; and also Spearing 1963, 736).

With Spearing's work *Piers Plowman* scholarship took fuller cognizance of the techniques of sermon-building that were formulated and taught in the *artes praedicandi*, by considering such basic features of the "university sermon" as its *thema* and *divisio*. Alford (1977) explores the relevance of a third fundamental aspect of sermon making, that of verbal concordance. In an attempt to answer the question what relation the hundreds of Latin quotations sprinkled throughout *Piers* might have to the rest of the poem, Alford argues that rather than tacking the quotations onto his alliterative lines as confirming authorities, Langland "*began* with the quotations, and from them, using the standard aids of a medieval preacher, derived the substance of the poem" (82). In late medieval preaching, "concordance" had become a major technique of "inventing" material for the sermon and developing it; a preacher would amplify his points with the help of scriptural and other "authorities" which contained the key word (*concordancia verbalis*) or at least the key idea (*concordancia realis*). Such "authorities" could be easily found in a large number of different preaching aids, from collections of *distinctiones* to alphabetical encyclopedias of preaching matter. Authoritative quotations, therefore, function as primary elements in establishing the structure of a sermon (86). Alford then shows in detail that the same procedure underlies passus 14 of the B text (86-96) and concludes that "the picture [of Langland] that emerges is that of a man eking out his poem slowly, even tediously, while poring over a variety of commentaries and preachers' aids" (99).

This sobering and provocative view of Langland's process of composition serves at least as a needed corrective to earlier views of Langland as "impulsive and even violent" (Kane, quoted by Alford 1977, 97) or as wandering in digressions (Salter 1962, 44–57; Spearing 1964, 126), and it anchors Langland's prominent use of verbal repetition and word play more firmly in technical instructions. It is well to recall, however, that in the "university" sermon biblical and other quotations do primarily serve as *confirming* authorities. According to formal instructions on sermon making (see Charland; Ross xliii–li; and Murphy 269–355), a preacher was first to select his *thema*: a word or string of words usually taken from Scripture, from which the entire verbal construct of his sermon would derive. After some introductory steps, such as *antethema* (protheme or "fore-theme"), prayer, *introductio thematis* (introduction of the *thema*), all of which could and did vary a great deal, the preacher would divide his verbal *thema* into a number of concepts or aspects inherent in the *thema* or suggested by it. The members of this *divisio* or *partitio* then furnished the topics for the sermon's principal parts. The most important element in the genesis of a sermon's structure was, therefore, the main division, whose importance was not only taught by arts of preaching but can still be seen in the pages of some extant sermons where the entire introductory section leading to the division is elaborated in detail and with care, whereas the remainder of the sermon is dealt with only cursorily (see Wenzel 1984b, 28–29, and Wenzel 1986, chapter 3). Now, the meanings which a preacher extracted in the division from his *thema* — no matter how topically far-fetched they might be — had to be confirmed with scriptural authorities (see Charland 279–82). Arts of preaching, preachers' handbooks, and actual sermons thus demonstrate page after page that sermon construction progressed from choosing a *thema* to dividing it and then to finding confirming authorities. In this progression, "concordance" in thought or — even better — in the actual wording was indeed a fundamental requirement.

All this indicates not only that in the scholastic sermon *thema* and *divisio* were of fundamental structural importance but also that fourteenth-century sermon making was a tightly structured verbal art. Even if we realize that not all sermons preached in Langland's time were of the sophisticated "modern" or "thematic" or "university" or "scholastic" sermon type as sketched above, it is this type which was taught in the arts of preaching and which in fact fills the major collections of fully developed Latin sermons made after about 1250. The preceding survey suggests that literary critics have not always understood these principles. Especially the technical term *thema* — not meaning "theme" in the sense of topic (as Spearing's discussion implies) but referring to the "text" of the sermon, that is, the verbal basis on which the sermon is built — represents a major stumbling block in assessing how closely related to sermons *Piers Plowman* is. A more serious shortcoming is the continuing unfamiliarity with the vast amount of actual sermons, mostly preserved in Latin. In fact, the material basis on which one might come to appraise Langland's indebtedness to sermon literature has not been much extended since the publication of Owst's works. In contrast to Owst's wide acquaintance with unpublished sermons, his successors have, in this respect, limited their work to quoting from what little sermon material is now in print: Brinton's sermons, Bromyard's *Summa*, Mirk's *Festial*, the Middle English sermons edited by Ross, the Wycliffite sermons, half of *Jacob's Well*, and Wimbledon's sermon on *Redde quod debes.** Yet the great collections of Latin sermons made in England between 1250 and 1450, whether anonymous or by known authors and compilers, remain unread. One may hope that the currently resurgent interest in medieval sermon studies will bear fruit for *Piers Plowman* scholarship as well (see Wenzel 1984b, 20).

SUGGESTIONS FOR FURTHER RESEARCH

But can further perusal of medieval sermon literature really produce new insights commensurate with the pains of deciphering the unfamiliar language and crabbed handwriting of the documents? The answer is affirmative, and the following paragraphs will support it with a number of cases that elucidate Langland's text and help us evaluate the poet's craftsmanship and genius.

Owst's attempt to show the sermon background of Langland's poem was fairly much limited to shared topics. But the poem's closeness to sermons extends to its diction and to precise images and quotations. For example, the Latin verse: "Precepta Regis sunt nobis vincula legis" (B.Prol.145), which has so far not been found elsewhere in exactly this form (cf. Alford 1975, 392), occurs thus in the *Summa* that Richard of Wetheringsette made early in the thirteenth century for the use of the parish clergy.† Similarly, the

---

* See bibliography under Devlin, Erbe, Arnold, Hudson, Brandeis, Knight. To these can be added Bradwardine's *Sermo epinicius* (Oberman and Weisheipl) and the Worcester sermons edited by Grisdale. Wenzel's edition and translation of *Fasciculus morum* is ready for publication. With regard to Bromyard it should be noted that his *Summa* is not a collection of sermons as several critics seem to believe but of sermon material arranged in alphabetical articles (Bromyard's "sermons" are his *Distincciones* preserved in Oxford, Bodleian Library, MS Bodley 859); that the *Summa* dates from before 1349 (see Leonard E. Boyle, *Speculum* 48 [1973], 533-37); and that the printed editions omit some material in French and English.

† "Congrua, commissa, suscepta, statuta, remissa,/ Et precepta regis sunt nobis vincula legis," London, British Library, MS Royal 4.B.viii, fol. 235ᵛ. Some manuscripts read *Hec*

observation "On fat lond ful of donge foulest wedes groweth" (C.12.223) was, as in *Piers*, used by preachers to condemn superfluity and luxury (*Fasciculus morum*, V.25, fols. 159ᵛ–160). More interesting is Langland's metaphor of Christ as the nurse of mankind who "bad hem souke for synne saufte at his breste" (B.11.121). The *topos* of "Christ our Mother" had some currency among late medieval mystics and may indeed be generally linked to Old Testament passages that liken God to a mother nursing her babe and to the image of the pelican (Pearsall 213). But the specific image of "souk[ing] . . . at his breste" can once again be found in *Fasciculus morum*, which teaches that as soon as the sinner runs to God, "Christ is at once present and ready like a nurse to suckle (*allactans*) him, now on one side from his breast (*mamilla*) of grace, now on the other from his breast of pity and mercy" (*Fasciculus morum*, V.7, fol. 124).

Langland's borrowing of sermon language extends even to preaching verses. Pearsall has pointed out that "poems of complaint" (which recur in sermons) "are important as the raw material of Langland's inspiration" (31). A different sermon verse is quoted or alluded to in the *sermo ad status* (a sermon treating the obligations and failings of certain social and professional groups) by Reason, who —

> chargede Chapmen to *chastiȝen hir children*:
> "Late no wynnyng forwanye hem *while þei be ȝonge*,
> Ne for no poustee of pestilence plese hem noȝt out of reson.
> My sire seide to me, and so dide my dame,
> 'Lo, þe *leuere child* þe moore *loore bihoueþ*.' "
>
>   (B.5.34–38)

The italicized phrases are identical with lines in a stanza preserved in *Fasciculus morum* (Wenzel 1978, 146, Verse 12).

But enough has been said to demonstrate Langland's debt to sermon language. More illuminating are instances in which the sermon use of a specific image clarifies the lexical meaning of a word and its associations in *Piers*. Thus, when Satan rouses his crew to defend the castle of hell at Christ's coming, he ends with the command: "With crokes and kalketrappes acloye we hem uchone" (C.20.294). Pearsall glosses *kalketrappes* as "spiked iron balls used to impede and maim horses in battle" (p. 332; compare *OED* under "calketrap"), but a passage in Bromyard's *Distincciones* shows that this devilish implement is not reserved for horses:

---

for *Et* (e.g., Oxford, Bodleian Library, MS Digby 103, fol. 25ᵛ). Notice that this form, a hexameter, agrees with Langland's calling it a "vers of latyn" (B.Prol.144), as his own quotation does not.

> *Calketrap* . . . is an instrument consisting of four sharp iron spikes which are so arranged that as three fall to the ground, the fourth sticks out upward, so that when an unwary traveler puts his foot on it, it gets pierced and he cannot go any further.*

Another of Langland's words whose use can be similarly elucidated from sermon texts is "Gobelyne," the name of a devil (or another name for Satan, according to Pearsall 334), who in the same Harrowing-of-Hell scene discusses Christ's beguiling the beguiler (B.18.292–306; C.20.322–40). Why Langland should have chosen this curious name has so far been unclear. A passage in *Fasciculus morum* reveals that to medieval preachers Gobelyne's particular nature was to beguile wayfarers and lead them astray:

> In ancient times, I have heard, the following often happened to little boys as well as to people who at night went to see their lovers and to gratify other desires. When they set out on their way toward a premeditated place, they suddenly wandered all night long in a circle around a grove or a manor house as if led astray by some illusion, thinking all the time they were proceeding on a straight path. . . . But when at last dawn came, they realized that they had made no progress on the way they originally planned to go. And as in their astonishment they reflected that they were being deceived, they heard a noise close by as if it were the laughter of some invisible being. According to some, this is a demon popularly called "goblin." (VII.16, fol. 210$^{\text{r-v}}$)

Langland's selection of this puckish sprite as the devil that attempted to lead Jesus in the desert, as it were, in a circle from sin to sin (as Gobelyne does in the moralization in *Fasciculus morum*), is apt, witty, and ironic, especially in the C text with its word-play on *going*, the activity especially subject to this demon's machinations:

> "Forthy y drede me," quod þe devel, "laste treuthe wol hem fecche.
> And as thowe bigyledest godes ymage in *goynge* of an addre,
> So hath god bigiled vs alle in *goynge of a weye*."
> "For god hath *go*," quod gobelyne, "in gome liknesse. . . ."
> (C.20.325–28; italics added)

Even the teaching propagated in sermons can often help solve the bafflement that *Piers* occasionally causes its modern readers. For instance, in

---

* "Calketrap, quod est instrumentum compositum ex quatuor acutis stimulis ferreis, qui sunt sic facti quod quando tres ad terram cadunt, quartum superius eminet, cum quo cum pes viatoris perforatus fuerit qui super eum pedem incaute vadens ponit, non poterit ultra progredi"; MS Bodley 859, fol. 159^{v}. In Bozon's *Contes moralisés* (ed. L. T. Smith and P. Meyer [Paris: Didot, 1889], 182 ff.), the instrument is used to catch a stag.

C.17.56 ff. Langland authenticates the parents' obligation to provide for their children by quoting the fourth commandment, "Honor your father and mother." On this passage Donaldson has commented: "With a rather desperate effort the poet does succeed . . . in reversing the sense of the [fourth] commandment so that it will apply to the atttitude of parents toward their children" (Donaldson 83; cf. Pearsall 281). But one will become less certain that Langland's logic "goes the wrong direction" as soon as one realizes that in sermons (e.g., Ross 120) and sermon handbooks (e.g., *Fasciculus morum*, I.11, fol. 9ᵛ) the fourth commandment did, as in Langland, include the parents' obligation toward their children, especially that of teaching and chastizing them. If the logic of this passage is faulty or questionable, the blame need not be laid at Langland's doorstep.

Sermon literature can thus clarify notoriously obscure lines and images. For example, when after the great confession scene Repentance makes his prayer for mercy, he recalls:

> And siþþe wiþ þi selue sone in oure sute deidest
> On good fryday for mannes sake at ful tyme of þe daye;
> . . . .
> The sonne for sorwe þerof lees siȝt for a tyme.
> Aboute mydday, whan moost liȝt is and meel tyme of Seintes,
> Feddest wiþ þi fresshe blood oure forefadres in derknesse.
>
>   (B.5.487–93)

The general reference of this passage to Christ's death at "mydday" and the subsequent Harrowing of Hell is clear enough, but the "mealtime of saints" has remained "cryptic" (Bennett 185). Perhaps a longer passage used in preaching on Christ's Passion can bring some light. Here the preacher asks in what hour Christ suffered, and he explains:

> He suffered at the ninth hour, that is, at the time when men commonly take a rest and allow themselves some refreshment in food and other bodily comforts. This hour rightly occurs at midday, when the sun is at its highest point. If a devout soul calling to Christ said the words from Canticles: "Show me where you feed, where you lie at midday," the Psalmist can answer that, as he was about to return to his Father, he first nourished mankind with his miracles and teaching, and then his disciples with his own flesh and blood. . . . If we skillfully consider how midday brings the greatest heat of the day, it is at that time that a shepherd is glad if he can find a pleasant place for his rest. . . . And in summertime one finds it particularly delightful to rest beneath the hawthorn, whose flowers give a sweet smell and its leaves shade. In the same way, beloved, after that banquet of eternal memory which we have mentioned, in which Christ fed his disciples with himself, there followed a very hot noon, namely on Good Friday, on which the greatest heat occurred. You know that it seems to be hottest when one cannot stand to have clothes on but throws them off. But Christ sustained such heat of

love and charity on that day that he threw off his clothes and wanted to lie and rest naked on the cross for our salvation; Daniel 13: "For it was hot weather." The pleasant and lush place which Christ chose before all others was the wood of the cross. This place indeed had flowing water on one side— when "one of the soldiers opened his side with a spear and at once blood and water flowed forth," John 19. . . . This, then, is the hour in which Christ not only fed but also rested, and in which he suffered death for us.

Used twice in *Fasciculus morum* (III.12, fols. 49–50, and V.8, fol. 126^{r-v}) as well as in Holcot's sermon 96 (Cambridge, Peterhouse MS 210, fol. 153^v), this passage may well have served as the background for Langland's "meel tyme of Seintes," by applying Canticles 1:6 with its reference to feeding ("Ubi pascas, ubi cubes in meridie?") and the image of the shepherd in the *locus amoenus* at noon to the crucifixion. It also suggests that the poet's "whan moost liȝt is" (line 492) was derived from the preacher's remark that "midday brings the greatest heat of the day," and that here Langland changed "heat" to "light" in anticipation of the darkness-vs.-light image of the following lines.

If some of Langland's images thus originated in contemporary sermons, may the same be true of structural features as well? Can any of his structural units be convincingly related, not just to general techniques taught in the arts of preaching, but to their use in an actual sermon? Perhaps the best candidate for which this may be claimed is Lady Holy Church's reply in B.1.85–209 to the Dreamer's question, "How can I save my soul?" The speech falls into two equal halves, which are separated by another request from the Dreamer (lines 138–39). It is unified by Holy Church's *thema*, "Whan alle tresors arn tried, treuþe is þe beste," which is announced at the very beginning (85) and, at the end (207). Parts of the verbal string are further repeated throughout the speech. This first half develops the notion of *Treuþe*; this is not only the quality or habit of *speaking* truthfully (88) but, beyond that, of *being* true, meaning obedient to God's will (110 and ff.). A life spent "in treuþe," by "working well" and in conformity with God's will, will lead to heaven "Ther Treuþe is in Trinitee" (133), that is to say, to the union with Truth that is God (cf. B.1.12 ff.). This explication is developed by giving an initial definition with scriptural confirmation (88–91) and by applying the notion of "treuþe" to two classes of society (clergy and knights, 92–104). The mention of the order of knights leads Langland to the ten orders of angels (conceived as Christ's knights, 105–10) and their virtue of obedience, which is then contrasted with the disobedience of "Lucifer wiþ legiounes" (111–27). These opposing examplars of being "true" and being "untrue" then yield the general principle that "alle þat werchen with wrong" will go to hell, "ac þo þat werche wel" will "wende to heuene" (128–32).

In similar fashion, the second half develops the notion of love, a topic already announced in line 86 and there implicitly set in relation to *treuþe*.

Now the relation between the two is succinctly formulated: "treuþe" is to love the Lord and "no dedly synne to do" (143–44). The nature of love is then defined, or rather illustrated, by the image of healing remedies (*triacle, spice, plante of pees*, 148–52), and by a further associative development which implies that "love" has two aspects: it is both a remedial virtue in man and a major characteristic in God which led to Christ's incarnation and redemptive death (153–74). A specific "example" of God's love is that Christ was mighty yet meek and prayed for mercy for his torturers (169–74). The moral application of such a model is then developed in a longer passage that shows — and confirms with three scriptural quotations — that God's love and mercy require man to respond in kind, that virtuous behavior without charity is as useless as a lamp without light,* and that love must be directed to one's fellow man (175–203). In the course of this development, Langland again expresses the relation between "treuþe" and love, now more sharply and with a recapitulation of his earlier thought: speaking the truth and being true are worth nothing unless accompanied by love (179–84). This second half then closes with a restatement of its topic, "Loue is leche of lif" (204) and soon thereafter the entire speech ends with the repetition of the *thema* (207) and a final blessing (209).

The rhetorical terms used so far — *thema*, definition, development, illustration and example, confirming quotations, and recapitulation — already suggest the sermon-like quality of Holy Church's speech. But in addition the speech is surprisingly similar in a number of ways to part of a Middle English sermon on *Diliges Deum tuum* ("Thou shalt love thy God," in Ross, sermon 36). The sermon begins with the *thema* that to love God "is þe pryncipall comaundement" because it "fordoþe all maner synnes" (199/21–26). The *thema* is repeated at midpoint: "loue distrowes all maner of synne, as I told you before" (200/18–19) and again at the end of the section: "þis is þe principall wey, as I seid at þe begynnynge" (201/1–2). Though the two repetitions are only partial, the preacher's explicit references to what he had "said before" clearly establish their function as structural markers. In the two halves which are thus created, the preacher then develops two separate but logically related topics. The first is that the love of God destroys all sins (199/21–200/20). It is introduced with a quotation attributed to Chrysostom (199/23–27) and then "proven" (199/28) with the example of Mary Magdalene (199/28–200/7) and with a quotation attributed to Saint Bernard

---

* The image of the lamp without *oil* is biblical (Matt.25), but its extension to being without *light* occurs in *Fasciculus morum*, III.8, fol. 41ᵛ: "sicut lampas clarissima sine oleo et igne non lucet. . ., sic omnia opera coram Deo sine caritate vilia sunt et nichil prosunt."

(200/8-15). In the second half the preacher develops the point that love keeps a man from evil and spiritual harm ("myschewes") by pointing to what can be "seen openly" in people who love God in prosperity as well as those who love him in adversity (200/19-31); this appeal to general experience is in turn confirmed with a biblical quotation (200/31-37).

Although this section from the sermon on *Diliges* may not be the actual source of Langland's speech of Holy Church, the two texts share the same circular structure created by repetitions of the *thema* and by back-references, a development of the *thema* in two equal halves, various similar modes of "proof" and amplification, and even the same metaphor and phrasing that love is a "goostely tryacle" (199/23 and 26; cf. B.1.148). The prose passage is not a full "sermon" but merely the formal *introductio thematis* preceded by a short *antethema* (198/14-199/13) and followed by the sermon's main *divisio* (201/4-8) and development (to 206/29). It is intriguing to note that Holy Church's speech similarly serves as an *introduction* to the action of Langland's poem: The Dreamer's question "What shall I do to save my soul?" elicits from Holy Church the answer "Do good," in the form of "Those who do good will go to heaven," etc. (B.1.128-33), which is verbally repeated in the "pardon" of passus 7 and then sets the Dreamer off on his continuing search for Treuthe and the unfolding of doing good into Dowel, Dobet, and Dobest — such unfolding of a term being another device taught by the arts of preaching (see Charland 276). Crafted as it is with unusual care, Holy Church's speech thus bears a startling similarity to a structural unit in a contemporary sermon.

EVALUATION

The specific instances offered above, together with Langland's use of such common sermon techniques as confirming statements with biblical and other "authorities" or illustrating theological and moral doctrine with a proverb (B.17.321 ff.), a parable (B.15.462 ff.), a natural object (B.12.235-63), or an *exemplum* (*forbisne*, B.8.28 ff.), which are then subjected to point-by-point moralization, and finally his constant urge to criticize the failings of various classes in society — all these add up to a strong argument for his debt to contemporary preaching. Nonetheless, to date no case has been made that shows that Langland drew from a specific source or preacher. Names like Brinton and Bromyard appear again and again in the critical literature because their works are in print and relatively familiar. But it has not been demonstrated that any specific passage in *Piers* is unmistakably derived from such sermon texts or handbooks (see Gallemore passim), in the way that some fourteenth-century sermons derive from Bromyard (see Von Nolcken).

We must therefore think of the poem's sermon background as a diffuse and widely dispersed influence, furnishing commonplaces and perhaps even structural patterns that floated from pulpit to pulpit and settled in many written texts.

At the same time, such definite though general parallels allow us to see how profoundly different Langland's poetry is from sermon style. *Piers* never uses the rigidly schematic progression of scholastic sermons and handbooks, with its points and numbers, so well-known to Chaucer readers from the tales of the Parson ("The causes that oghte moeve a man to Contricioun been sixe. First. . . . The secounde cause. . . . The fourthe point. . . . The fifthe thyng . . .," X.133 ff.) or of the Pardoner ("And now that I have spoken of glotonye, / Now wol I yow deffenden hasardrye. . . . Now wol I speke of othes false and grete," VI.589–90, 629). In remarkable contrast, Langland's thought progresses in a far more free-flowing manner by association (see also Spearing 1964, 122–27, on Langland's "digressive style"). Thus, in Holy Church's speech the point that anyone who is true "is a god by þe gospel" leads the poet to remark, evidently with some implied criticism, that clerics should make this truth known. The clerical obligation in turn takes Langland to the obligation of knights to "keep" truth in the realm, and the topic of knighthood triggers a sequence of further associations, from David's establishing knighthood to Christ's founding an order of knight-angels whose main virtue is "to be buxom," which virtue was refused by Lucifer and his legions, who thereupon fell out of heaven into "helle depe," where now "alle þat werchen with wrong" will go, whereas "þo þat werche wel" will "enden . . . in truþe"—with which Langland has returned to his initial topic. While the *structure* of Holy Church's speech is very much like that of the Middle English sermon analyzed, its *mode of progression* and development—the "burr-like quality of [Langland's] arguments by association," in Pearsall's happy phrase (238)—is not at all characteristic of fourteenth-century sermons; it is much more reminiscent of the meditative prose one finds, for instance, in book 3 of *Ancrene Wisse*.

Holy Church's speech also illustrates two other fundamental differences. One is the poem's dramatic nature. The Dreamer's request for more knowledge (B.1.138–39) not only dramatizes the fictional situation but also serves to characterize himself as limited in understanding, a "doted daffe" whose wits are dull (line 140). Both features are of course central to the progression of *Piers Plowman* and make it a poem. The other difference is the fascinating association and compression of images, especially in the second half of Holy Church's speech (lines 146–56). This stylistic feature, too, runs through all of Langland's poem, in spite of its *longueurs* and repetitions. A good example occurs in Anima's elaboration on the hypocrisy of priests:

For ypocrisie in latyn is likned to a loþly dongehill
That were bisnewed wiþ snow and snakes wiþInne,
Or to a wal þat were whitlymed and wer foul wiþInne;
Right so preestes, prechours and prelates manye,
Ye aren enblaunched wiþ *bele paroles* and wiþ *bele* cloþes
Ac youre werkes and workes þervnder aren ful wolueliche.

(B.15.111–16)

Langland's images of the dunghill covered with snow, the whitewashed wall, and the wolf-like behavior of priests, all of biblical origin, can be found clustered in a passage on hypocrisy in the thirteenth-century *Summa virtutum de remediis anime*, which was used by Chaucer and by the anonymous compiler of *Memoriale credencium* (Wenzel 1984a, 94–96). In Langland, the material is condensed to the point of allusion. Moreover, his "in latyn" suggests that he was thinking of an "etymology" of *hypocrisis* such as is given in the just mentioned *Summa*, first in Greek and then in Latin (the qualifiers "Greek" and "Latin" are actually used in another "etymology" of this type: Wenzel 1984a, 54–55 and variants). Unless some of Langland's original text has been lost at this point, the phrase "in latyn" may have been intended to serve as a highly curtailed allusion, a signal to learned readers to recall standard commonplaces and images of the topic under discussion, of which only a few are selected. The short passage, thus, illustrates well a major characteristic of Langland's poetic strength.

Such compression can of course turn into obscurity, but it does indicate Langland's impulse, not to write a sermon but to produce imaginative poetry, following dictates other than those motivating a preacher. The difference can be clearly perceived in passages where Langland deals with such theological or moral "set pieces" as the seven deadly sins, the seven remedial virtues, the Ten Commandments, and the like. Not only is, in such cases, the extent of his dramatization and use of imagery unparalleled in contemporary sermons, but his freedom to order and even to omit members of set lists reveals his obedience to demands that differ profoundly from that of accurately teaching basic matters of faith and morals. Part of these demands derives from his chosen alliterative verse form. Critics may find good theological reasons why, for instance, Hope carries a horn (B.5.506: for the same reason as Peace has a pipe, B.18.408, and Truth a trumpet, B.18.422) or why Plato is labeled a poet (B.10.178 and 11.37), or why the cardinal virtues are called *spiritus* when any parish priest would know that the gifts of the Spirit and the virtues, though overlapping, are not the same (B.19.274 ff.). But the more obvious reason is rhetorical and linguistic or prosodic, namely the need to find alliterating collocations. As a result, the language of *Piers Plowman*, in its compression, associative wealth, and alliterative measure, is often glorious, whether exalted ("The lord of lif and of light þo leide hise eighen togideres," B.18.59) or more down-to-earth ("And bad hym go pissen with his plow3," B.6.155). Such lines have no parallels in the written sermons of Langland's time. In this, we should see the poet's conscious attempt to *distance* his language and work from the everyday commonplace. Here our attention to the dependency of *Piers Plowman* on contemporary sermons reveals to us more than sources and analogues, namely, the poet's achievement and his urge—which he surely shares with poets of all ages— to be imaginatively extra-ordinary.

REFERENCES

Aers, David. *Piers Plowman and Christian Allegory*. London: Arnold, 1975.

Alford, John A. "Some Unidentified Quotations in *Piers Plowman*." *MP* 72 (1975): 390–99.

———. "The Role of the Quotations in *Piers Plowman*." *Speculum* 52 (1977): 80–99.

Anhorn, Judy Schaaf. "*Sermo Poematis*: Homiletic Traditions of *Purity* and *Piers Plowman*." Ph.D. dissertation, Yale University, 1976. Abstract in *DAI* (1976) 37: 3605A.

Arnold, Thomas, ed. *Select English Works of John Wyclif*. 3 vols. Oxford: Clarendon, 1869–71.

Bennett, J. A. W., ed. *Piers Plowman. The Prologue and Passus I-VII of the B text as found in Bodleian MS. Laud 581*. Oxford: Clarendon, 1972.

Bloomfield, Morton W. "Present State of *Piers Plowman* Studies." *Speculum* 14 (1939): 215–32; rpt. Blanch 3–25.

———. *Piers Plowman as a Fourteenth-Century Apocalypse*. New Brunswick, NJ: Rutgers University Press, 1962.

Brandeis, Arthur, ed. *Jacob's Well. An English Treatise on the Cleansing of Man's Conscience*. EETS 115. London: Kegan Paul, Trench, Trübner, 1900.

Charland, Th.-M. *Artes praedicandi. Contribution à l'histoire de la rhétorique au moyen âge*. Paris: De Vrin, 1936.

Coleman, Janet. *Piers Plowman and the "Moderni"*. Letture di Pensiero e d'arte. Rome: Edizioni di Storia e Letteratura, 1981.

Devlin, Sister Mary Aquinas, ed. *The Sermons of Thomas Brinton, Bishop of Rochester (1373–1389)*. Camden Third Series 85–86. London: Royal Historical Society, 1954.

Donaldson, E. Talbot. *Piers Plowman. The C-Text and Its Poet*. Yale Studies in English 113. New Haven: Yale University Press, 1949.

Erbe, Theodor, ed. *Mirk's Festial: A Collection of Homilies by Johannes Mirkus (John Mirk)*. EETS es 96. London: Kegan Paul, Trench, Trübner, 1905.

Frank, Robert Worth, Jr. *Piers Plowman and the Scheme of Salvation*. Yale Studies in English 136. New Haven: Yale University Press, 1957.

Gallemore, Melvin A. "The Sermons of Bishop Thomas Brinton and the B Text of *Piers the Plowman*." Ph.D. dissertation, University of Washington, 1968. Abstract in *DA* (1968) 27:3008A.

Gasquet, Francis Aidan [Cardinal]. *The Old English Bible and Other Essays*. 1897; rpt. Port Washington, NY: Kennikat Press, 1969.

Grisdale, D. M., ed. *Three Middle English Sermons from the Worcester Chapter Manuscript F. 10.* Leeds: School of English Language, 1939.

Heffernan, Thomas J. "Sermon Literature." *Middle English Prose. A Critical Guide to Major Authors and Genres.* Ed. A. S. G. Edwards. New Brunswick, NJ: Rutgers University Press, 1984. 177–207.

Hill, Thomas D. "Christ's 'Thre Clothes': *Piers Plowman* C.XI.193." *N&Q* 223 (1978): 200–03.

Hudson, Anne, ed. *English Wycliffite Sermons* 1 (Other vols. in progress). Oxford: Clarendon, 1983.

Hussey, S. S. "Introduction." *Piers Plowman. Critical Approaches.* Ed. S. S. Hussey. London: Methuen, 1969. 1–26.

Knight, Ione Kemp, ed. *Wimbledon's Sermon "Redde Rationem Villicationis Tue": A Middle English Sermon of the Fourteenth Century.* Duquesne Studies, Philological Series 9. Pittsburgh: Duquesne University Press, 1967.

Longère, Jean. *La prédication médiévale.* Paris: Etudes Augustiniennes, 1983.

Murphy, James J. *Rhetoric in the Middle Ages.* Berkeley: University of California Press, 1974.

Oberman, Heiko A., and James A. Weisheipl. "The *Sermo epinicius* Ascribed to Thomas Bradwardine (1346)." *AHDLMA* 25 (1958): 295–329.

Owst, G. R. "The 'Angel' and the 'Goliardeys' of Langland's Prologue." *MLR* 20 (1925): 270–79.

————. *Preaching in Medieval England.* Cambridge: Cambridge University Press, 1926; rpt. New York: Russell & Russell, 1965.

————. *Literature and Pulpit in Medieval England.* 1933. 2nd rev. ed. Oxford: Basil Blackwell, 1961.

Pearsall, Derek, ed. *Piers Plowman by William Langland. An Edition of the C-text.* London: Arnold, 1978.

Pfander, Homer G. "The Mediaeval Friars and Some Alphabetical Reference-Books for Sermons." *MÆ* 3 (1934): 19–29.

Ross, Woodburn O., ed. *Middle English Sermons.* EETS 209. London: Oxford University Press, 1940.

Ryan, William M. *William Langland.* New York: Twayne, 1968.

St. Jacques, Raymond C. "Langland's Christ-Knight and the Liturgy." *Revue de l'Université d'Ottawa* 37 (1967): 146–58.

Salter, Elizabeth. *Piers Plowman. An Introduction.* Cambridge, MA: Harvard University Press, 1962. 2nd ed. Oxford: Blackwell, 1969.

————. "Alliterative Modes and Affiliations in the Fourteenth Century." *NM* 79 (1978): 25–35.

————, and Derek Pearsall, eds. *Piers Plowman.* York Medieval Texts. London: Arnold, 1967.

Smith, Ben H., Jr. *Traditional Imagery of Charity in Piers Plowman.* The Hague: Mouton, 1966.

Spearing, A. C. "Verbal Repetition in *Piers Plowman* B and C." *JEGP* 62 (1963): 722–36.

————. "The Art of Preaching and *Piers Plowman*." *Criticism and Medieval Poetry.* London: Arnold, 1964. 68–95. 2nd ed. New York: Barnes and Noble, 1972. 107–34; rpt. *Chaucer and His Contemporaries.* Ed. Helaine Newstead. Greenwich, CT: Fawcett, 1968. 255–82.

Swieczkowski, Walerian. *Word Order Patterning in Middle English: A Quantitative Study Based on "Piers Plowman" and Middle English Sermons.* Janus Linguarum 19. The Hague: Mouton, 1962.

Tristram, Hildegard L. C. "Intertextuelle *Puns* in *Piers Plowman*." *NM* 84 (1983): 182–91.

Von Nolcken, Christina. "Some Alphabetical Compendia and How Preachers Used Them in Fourteenth-Century England." *Viator* 12 (1981): 271–88.

Wenzel, Siegfried. *The Sin of Sloth: Acedia in Medieval Thought and Literature*. Chapel Hill: University of North Carolina Press, 1967.

———. *Verses in Sermons. "Fasciculus Morum" and Its Middle English Poems*. Cambridge, MA: The Mediaeval Academy of America, 1978.

———, ed. *Summa virtutum de remediis anime*. Chaucer Library. Athens, GA: University of Georgia Press, 1984.

———. "Medieval Sermons and the Study of Literature." Piero Boitani and Anna Torti, eds. *Medieval and Pseudo-Medieval Literature. The J. A. W. Bennett Memorial Lectures, Perugia, 1982–1983*. Tübingen: Gunter Narr; and Cambridge: D. S. Brewer, 1984. 19–32.

———. *Preachers, Poets, and the Early English Lyric*. Princeton: Princeton University Press, 1986.

Yunck, John A. *The Lineage of Lady Meed. The Development of Mediaeval Venality Satire*. Publications in Mediaeval Studies 17. Notre Dame, IN: University of Notre Dame Press, 1963.

III

THE TEXT AND LANGUAGE
OF *PIERS PLOWMAN*

7

THE TEXT

GEORGE KANE

Our poem exists by virtue of the imperfect survival of an assemblage of linguistic norms or structures of language put together by a man in the fourteenth century and transmitted, until relatively modern times, by scribal copying. Those structures of language we call the "text" of *Piers Plowman*. All study of the poem, to have any validity, should manifestly relate as closely as can be to that text which he put together. But scribal copying is notoriously erratic and inefficient. Because of that circumstance there are, in one sense, as many texts of *Piers Plowman* as there are ancient copies, all more or less distanced from the one the author fashioned.

We know of 52 manuscripts, a black-letter edition of 1550 that represents at least a fifty-third, lost manuscript, and three fragments of lost manuscripts. None of these derives from another surviving copy. All differ, more or less widely, in their content, in how this is arranged, and in the particulars of language by which it is expressed. We have no information to account for those various kinds of difference other than that afforded by the language of the texts themselves.

EARLY STUDY

"Modern" interest in the text began with the antiquary John Bale, who described it as *pium opus*, produced *sub amoenis coloribus et typis* (Bale 1557, 474). The poem was respectfully edited by Robert Crowley, who, in 1550, issued three impressions of which at least the second was actually reset (Kane-Donaldson 15). Crowley's edition, except for the single word *renk* which he invariably printed *reuke* or *reuk*, is in impeccable Middle English, which he could evidently read and must have believed his public could read. But one contemporary, who produced the Sion College translation of *Piers Plowman* into Tudor English, did not have the same competence: his modernization makes clear how much he failed to understand (Kane-Donaldson 15).

Crowley's text was for a long time accepted as authoritative. In 1737 in the first volume of *The Muses Library* (Cooper 7–18), and in 1761 by Thomas Percy citation was from Crowley. But it had already been discerned that there were variant forms of the text. By 1725 Thomas Hearne, in the course of editing Robert of Gloucester's *Chronicle*, had come upon the *Piers* text in Cotton Caligula A XI, with components from all three versions (Kane-Donaldson 5). Hearne had already identified *Pierce the Ploughman's Crede* as a separate work; of the longer poem he wrote, "This is certain, that this Work hath been much altered at different times" (395).

Readers in the antiquarian tradition to which these scholars belonged also looked at the text in detail. The Crowley variant in line 1 of the Prologue, *set* for *softe*, which is meaningless in its context, caught Thomas Warton's eye, and he proposed the emendation *hotte* following a conjecture *caleret* by John Bale (Bale *Scriptorum* 474; *Index* 383, 509). Thomas Percy, replying to Warton, accepted the suggestion, but preferred a spelling *hette* (15, 16).

As more and more manuscripts came to light in the Bodleian Library and in the British Museum, the antiquaries compared their texts with Crowley's. For these men, trained in the classical tradition, and aware that editors were then active in the textual criticism of classical texts and of the New Testament, the differences they found raised the question of authenticity, of the quality of texts. Thomas Tyrwhitt in his 1775 edition of *The Canterbury Tales* proclaimed that Crowley's and Rogers's texts (see p. 261) were so much corrupted "that the Author, whoever he was, would find it difficult to recognize his own work" (4:74). He was evidently comparing them with a copy of C, probably Q (C.U.L. Addl. MS 4325). A generation later Ritson, having examined copies of the three main forms of the poem, expressed a radical insight: he found it "highly probable that the author had revised his original work, and given, as it were, a new edition; and it may be possible for a good judge of ancient poetry, possessed of a sufficient stock of critical acumen, to determine which was the first and which the second" (29–30).

Here now were two issues, of the quality of texts and of authorial changes. Both soon became matters of lively discussion. In 1813 Thomas Whitaker brought out the first edition of *Piers Plowman* since the 1550s, with the argument that Crowley's text was from a bad, late manuscript and that the copy he himself had used (a C manuscript now Huntington Library MS 137) preserved the author's original version (p. xxxi). In 1824 Richard Price, in his re-edition of Warton's *History of English Poetry*, proposed that there were not two, but three forms of the poem (2:482). In 1832 Thomas Wright brought out a rival edition to Whitaker's from a B manuscript (Trinity College Cambridge B.15.17). He presently supported this with a review of Whitaker in *The Gentleman's Magazine*. Whitaker had chosen his base text for wrong reasons. He had not seen enough copies. And he was mistaken in the opinion that what he had printed was the author's first version (Wright 1834, 386). Eight years later still, in a re-edition of his own text, Wright proposed that Whitaker's form of the poem embodied changes by someone else than the poet, the reviser having been "gradually led to produce a revision of the whole," possibly for reasons of political discretion. His own text was, by contrast, the "best and oldest" of the manuscripts (Wright 1842, xli–xlii, xlvii–xlviii). Here was the third main issue raised by the text of *Piers Plowman*, namely authorship (see Introduction). The recovery of manuscripts and especially their comparison had raised the three great questions.

SKEAT'S ACHIEVEMENT

The pattern for solving them, and to a large extent their solution, we owe to the brilliantly organized intellect of Walter Skeat. In 1866, as one of the earliest issues of the Early English Text Society (of which he was a founder), he published a volume of parallel extracts from 29 manuscripts of *Piers Plowman*. That he himself had brought many of those manuscripts to light was overshadowed by his demonstration that they represented five forms of the poem of which three (he argued on good critical grounds) were authorial (Skeat 1866). In 1867 appeared his edition of the first of these forms: he called it the "A text" (Skeat 1867). He presumed a sequence of revision from that form, until then not generally known, to the form printed by Crowley and Wright, and thence to the one printed by Whitaker. In his judgement the shortest form of the poem, the A text, with only a prologue and eleven sections, had not been completed by the poet (Skeat 1867, xxvi, xxvii). In 1869 he followed this with an edition of the form of the poem printed by Wright, but from another manuscript than Wright's, namely Laud Misc. 581, which, from the correction marks in it and its good quality, he thought possibly the author's autograph (Skeat 1869, ix). This he called the "B text." In 1873 he brought out the third form of the poem, the "C text," based on examination of 21 copies. He also, in this edition, dealt briskly with the sequence of composition of the forms of the poem (Skeat 1873, xiv). Here indeed was Ritson's "good judge of ancient poetry, possessed of a sufficient stock of critical acumen."

SEQUENCE OF THE VERSIONS

Skeat's argument about the sequence of versions has stood up well to specification and extended application. The antecedence of A is argued by more extensive development in B and C of notions that occur in its text. As to B, this resembles A more than C does and also resembles C more than A does: that its respective affinities with A and C are very substantially greater than those between A and C argues its medial position. With no significant exceptions critical readers have found Skeat's sequence acceptable, as revealing a development of imaginative conception in the poet, and a deepening and refinement of meaning in the poem (Kane-Donaldson 71–74). Except for some of his opinions about the development of A (Skeat 1886, 2:xxii–xxiii), most of Skeat's conclusions about the three main forms of the text have held good in outline, although there has been much discrepant detail to account for.

Thus Skeat's A, B and C texts, attested respectively by ten, by fourteen and by eighteen copies, seemed solidly based. But the texts of the ten A copies differed in length, ranging from seven to twelve sections after the prologue. And ten other copies contained texts that appeared to be composites: one a combination of B with A; six a combination of A with C; and three a brief combination of C and A with a long B completion. The following lists illustrate the situation.

MANUSCRIPTS OF THE A VERSION*

Bodley Ashmole 1468 (A): Prologue–XI
      Douce 323 (D): Prologue–XI
      Rawlinson Poet. 137 (R): Prologue–XII
      Vernon: English Poetry a. 1 (V): Prologue–XI.183
British Library Harley 875 (H) : Prologue–VIII.142
Lincoln's Inn 150 (L) : Prologue–VIII.185
Pierpont Morgan Library M 818 (J): Prologue–XII.88
Society of Antiquaries 687 (M): Prologue–XI
Trinity College Dublin D.4.12 (E): Prologue–VII.213
University College Oxford 45 (U): Prologue–XII.19
Pembroke College Cambridge fragment

MANUSCRIPTS OF THE B VERSION

Bodley Laud Misc. 581 (L)
      Rawlinson Poet. 38 (R)
British Library Additional 35287 (M)
Cambridge University Library Dd. 1. 17 (C)
                        Gg. 4. 31 (G)
                        Ll. 4. 14 (C^2)

---

* For the sake of clarity, roman numerals are used in this table, rather than arabic as in the rest of the book.

Corpus Christi College Oxford 201 (F)
Crowley's manuscript (Cr)
Huntington Library 128 (Hm)
Newnham College Cambridge Yates-Thompson MS (Y)
Oriel College Oxford 79 (O)
Sion college MS (S)
Trinity College Cambridge B. 15. 17 (T)

MANUSCRIPTS OF THE C VERSION

Bodley Digby 102 (Y)
  Digby 171 (K)
  Douce 104 (D)
  Laud Misc. 656 (E)
British Library Additional 34779 (P²)
    Additional 35157 (U)
    Cotton Vespasian B xvi (M)
    Harley 2376 (N)
    Royal 18 B XVII (R)
Cambridge University Library Additional 4325 (Q)
      Dd. 3. 13 (G)
      Ff. 5. 35 (F)
Corpus Christi College Cambridge 293 (S)
Huntington Library 137 (P)
    143 (X)
London University Library S.L.V.17 (A)
    S.L.V.88 (I)
Trinity College Dublin 212 (D.4.1) (V)
Caius College fragment 669*/646 (Ca)
John Holloway's fragment (H)

CONJOINT AC MANUSCRIPTS

Bodley 851 (Z of C): A Prologue–VIII.192 + C XI–XXII
  Digby 145 (K of A, D² of C): A Prologue–XI + C XI.296–XXII
British Library Harley 6041 (H² of A and C): A Prologue–XI + C
 XI.295–XIV.200, XVI.24–XXII.286
Liverpool University Library F.4.8 (Ch of A and C): A Prologue–XI +
 C XI.295–XXII
National Library of Wales 733ᴮ (N of A, N² of C): A I.176–VIII.184 +
 C XI–XXI.425
Trinity College Cambridge R. 3. 14 (T of A and C): A Prologue–XI +
 C XI.295–XXII
The Westminster Manuscript (W of A and C): A Prologue–XI + C
 XII–XXII

CONJOINT BA MANUSCRIPT

British Library Harley 3954 (H³ of A, H of B): B Prologue–V.127 + A V.106–XI

CONJOINT CAB MANUSCRIPTS

Bodley 814 (B of B and C): C Prologue–II.131 + A II.90–198 (expanded) + B III–XX

British Library Additional 10574 (Bm of B, L of C): C Prologue–II.131 + A II.90–198 (expanded) + B III–XX

Cotton Caligula A xi (Cot of B, O of C): C Prologue–II.131 + A II.90–198 (expanded) + B III–XX

CONFLATED ABC MANUSCRIPT

Huntington Library 114 (Ht)

AUTHORIAL AND SCRIBAL DIFFERENTIATION OF TEXTS

The immediate question is why these other forms of the text should not be treated as authorial: if revision is an acceptable explanation of difference in some cases, why not in others? One reason is critical and discriminative. The three main forms of text were judged to be differentiated by revision because it seemed possible to discern authorial intention in their differences: the second and the third forms of the text appeared as products of changed conceptions of a comprehensive subject (Skeat 1866; 1886 2:vii–xiv; Donaldson *passim*; Russell 1966, 1969). Conversely, in the largest number of combinations of two forms of text, that is of A supplemented by C, the effect of the combination at the point of juncture seems forced. On comparison with the corresponding passages in the accepted versions, the C-text portion of these manuscripts proceeds as if from another beginning than the A text before it (Kane 1965, 28, 40–42). The third reason is that in all instances of AC combination the two sets of text severally belong to A or C manuscript traditions, where they can be genetically placed. Thus Ch, H² and T fit successively into an A and a C family of manuscripts; N and W, with texts of seven and eleven A passus respectively, are a genetic pair in their A portions. There is a further consideration, that if a medieval text was current in a long and short form, the short form was almost sure to be augmented. The differences of length of copies of the A text are most likely to be results of physical loss: three of the shorter manuscripts, E, H and N, are genetically related to manuscripts with a prologue and eleven passus (see below, p. 189).

The one special case is Harleian MS 3954. Its first part is from the second version, and the text of this part cannot be confidently placed in the genetic scheme of B. Moreover its text has a number of B readings which have seemed more likely original than the corresponding ones in the other B manuscripts (Kane-Donaldson 59–81). That the B part of this manuscript records a moment in the A>B revision when, in whatever circumstances, someone had access to Langland's working copy cannot be ruled out. All other conjoint copies reflect the availability of exemplars.

These conjoint texts postulate readers concerned with the completeness of the work they very likely called "The book of Piers Plowman" (Kane 1965, 46–48). The conjoint texts are not, strictly speaking, "scribal" unless we understand their scribes to have been critical readers who, having the short text as an exemplar, and knowing or learning that the poem existed in a longer form, took steps to make and so own or disseminate a more extended form. The AC combinations — especially that of the exclusive common ancestor of TH²Ch, and the ancestors of W and N, on the indication of correction in both sets and of intercalated B and C readings (Kane 1965, 29–36) — very likely originated in copying centres, whether commercial or monastic. The striking exception is Digby 145, where the combination left physical traces, and is thus directly attributable to the amateur who copied the poem in 1532 (Kane 1960, 9, 10). In the case of Bodley 851 the difference of hands between the A and C components is unmistakable indication of the artificiality of the combination. The almost invariable choice of a C text for the supplement may be an accident of local availability, but could just possibly reflect the compilators' awareness that in some senses C was more "complete" than B (below, pp. 186 ff.).

There are two other texts of *Piers* that fit poorly into Skeat's classification. One is the part of Bodley 851 (Z) that corresponds to A Prologue–VIII, and the other is Huntington Library MS 114 (Ht).

The A text of Z is distinctive because it reads more than 200 lines not found in any other copy of the poem, lacks more than 300 lines found in other A manuscripts, presents some of its content in a different order than that of A, and divides two of its passus at other points than does the A text (Rigg-Brewer 45–46, 76–77). The Huntington text is of a longer form of the poem and concurs most often with B. It also contains many lines like those distinctive of the A text. Like C it reads the long passage sometimes called "autobiographical" before the Confession of the Sins, and like C it incorporates Haukyn's self-revelations in that Confession. Unlike C it also reads these latter in its equivalent of B passus 13. It contains, otherwise, many lines and passages from various parts of the C text, some of them deftly set in new positions. And it contains 50 lines peculiar to itself (Russell and Nathan 126–29).

It has been seriously proposed that the A text in Bodley 851 is a copy of an authorial draft of the poem antecedent to Skeat's A, on the grounds of the "Langlandian" quality of the lines and passages which it uniquely attests; its deficiencies are the consequence of its being a draft (Rigg-Brewer *passim*). The argument against the proposition is that where this text runs with that of A it has the character of a copy well down the A tradition; that the "Langlandian" quality of many of its distinctive lines comes from their being pastiches of A, and that the incoherence and inconsequence of the passages peculiar to it reflect intelligence and sensibility inferior to those pervasively manifest in *Piers Plowman* (Kane 1985).

No one has yet proposed an authorial origin for the Huntington text, but an argument of similar reasoning and comparable force for this being an uncompleted authorial harmonization of the three versions could be mounted. Its composition testifies to phenomenal knowledge of all three. Its content is unmistakably Langlandian. And the occurrence of the Haukyn self-exposure in two places is explicable by the revising author's failure to cancel material that he had moved (cp. Rigg-Brewer 14). But as with the Z text of A, where the content of this manuscript is not recognizably pastiche it is both intellectually and poetically inferior.

These two texts most strikingly instance the capacity of *Piers Plowman* to elicit response, to generate active participation in the literary and social experience it evidently constituted for near-contemporary readers. That capacity was what prompted the poetaster John But to write an ending for what he saw as the unfinished A Version (Kane 1960, 431; 1965, 32–34); a scribe in the tradition of Lincoln's Inn MS 150 to augment the alliteration of his copy (Kane 1960, 141, 142); a scribe in the immediate tradition of Corpus Christi College Oxford 201 to rewrite many lines of an excellent exemplar (Kane-Donaldson 165–72), to add some 50 lines of his own to it (Kane-Donaldson 222–23), and to rearrange some passus divisions (Kane-Donaldson 8 n.49); a scribe in the tradition of London University Library MS V.88 to modify the content and organization of his C original (Skeat 1873, xxxiii, xxxiv; Russell 1969, 28, 29; Pearsall 1981); and a marginal commentator in the Westminster manuscript to add a pious ending in the poet's voice.

> And when I was wytterly awakyd I wrote all thys dreame
> And theys marvellys þat I met on mawlverne hyllys
> In a seyson of sommer as I softe nappyd
> For þe people after ther power wold persen after dowell
> That þe tresure moost tryed and tryacle at neede
> now god gravnt hys grace to make a good ende
> And bryng vs all to þe blysse as he bowghte vs on þe Roode
>   Amen   R H

MANUSCRIPT TRADITIONS

The strongest support for the occurrence of two authorial revisions and for the authorial character of three distinctive texts of *Piers Plowman* comes from the existence of three manuscript traditions.

A manuscript tradition identifies itself when a number of manuscripts agree so substantially in the texts they present as to make evident their descent from an exclusive common ancestor, while at the same time they differ enough in details of text to indicate the intervention of a number of stages of copying in that descent. The system of stages of copying by which the surviving copies are descended from that presumed common ancestor forms the character of the tradition. Depending on circumstances a greater or lesser amount of information can be got about those stages by the process called classification, that is analysis of agreements between manuscripts in readings presumed not to be authorial (Kane 1960, 53–114; Kane-Donaldson 16–69).

Theoretically a manuscript tradition would originate when an author caused or permitted his personal text of his work to be reproduced. Inevitably before long he would lose control of the reproduction he had sanctioned, and this reproduction would generate successive descendants increasingly differentiated from their authorial progenitor by the inaccuracy axiomatically inherent in copying by hand, not to mention other causes. The "quality" of a tradition would depend upon the accident of scribal efficiency, the number of stages of transmission, and external circumstances such as the existence of other forms of the same work, or indeed its public relevance.

In the case of *Piers Plowman* three manuscript traditions exist, with abundant representation (pp. 178–80 above). If, as seems commonly accepted, Langland worked at *Piers Plowman* for a number of years, those three traditions originated on occasions when he caused or permitted the poem in his hand to be copied, unless, as seems likely, it was incapacity or death that left the B>C revision unfinished, in which case the sanction of the copy from an incompletely revised text—the origin of the C tradition—was by a "literary executor."

The manuscript traditions have a direct bearing on the philosophical concept of the texts of the poem. They are evidence that the authorial texts are not modern editorial ideas. Each tradition exists because there was once a tangible, readable object to which the poet (or in one instance a literary executor) was willing to allow access for the purpose of copying. There were thus, for however long or short a time, definitive points in the poet's realization of the artistic conception which drove him to write. The texts copied at those points are the respective progenitors, at however many removes, of the exclusive common ancestors of the surviving manuscripts of the three traditions.

The existence of the manuscript traditions also has a bearing on the smaller differences between manuscripts. It implies that whether Langland revised ruminatively or impulsively (the latter is suggested by the sense of urgency his poem communicates) he did not constantly or at frequent intervals make his working text available for copying. Therefore it is very unlikely that the smaller differences between the manuscripts of any tradition record his revisions, rearrangements, exclusions and reinsertions as, in effect, a succession of minutely differentiated "versions" of his poem. In any event, from the otherwise known circumstances of manuscript copying, and from the visible effect of the immediate relevance of this poem upon its copyists, there is a very strong *a priori* likelihood that such differences between the manuscripts of a tradition are not to be attributed to the poet. The probability is that the text of any manuscript of any version of this poem is a record of generations of substitutions, unconscious or conscious.

DATES OF ORIGIN OF THE VERSIONS

When the versions originated is roughly indicated by references in their texts to historical events and situations. In each case the significant reference is the one to the latest event or situation, for the date of this establishes a point when Langland was still working on that version, and therefore a date necessarily before he authorized the first copying in which its manuscript tradition was generated.

In the A text the latest date seems implied in the activity of the *rome renneris* of 4.111, intent on buying benefices and pluralities, which requires the presence of a pope in that city, as he was from October 1367 to September 1370 (Bennett 1943a, 568). So 1367–68 looks like a *terminus a quo* for the first copying of A. The *terminus ad quem* is, correspondingly, the earliest reference after 1367–68 in the B text where it is revised or goes beyond the text of A. That reference is pretty certainly to an outbreak of the plague and the pope's compassionate grant of a plenary indulgence in 1375–76 (B.13.246–49: Skeat 1886, 2:xi–xiii; Devlin 23). From these indications the manuscript tradition of the A version originated in the period 1368–1374.

In the B text the latest unmistakable reference is to the coronation of Richard II in July 1377 (Bennett 1943b, 64; Donaldson 116–18). It has been asserted that B.Prol.100–111 which raise the question of the right of the cardinals in the Curia to elect a pope, B.13.173–76, which refer to the possibility of peace between the pope and his enemies, and B.19.428, 429, 445, 446, which represent the pope as making or promoting war against Christian folk, must refer to the Schism of 1378 and to the warfare between the rival popes which broke out in 1379 (Bennett 1943b, 62–63). Carefully read, however, the text of the Prologue passage appears concerned not with the right of one or another clique of cardinals to elect a pope, but with the issue of dominion (110), that is, the actual right itself (108). This was being questioned by Wyclif as early as 1374–1376, in lectures at Oxford which lie behind his *De Dominio Divino* (McKisack 511). The concept *nichil falsius quam quod humana electio facit papam, . . . solus dominus facit papam*, was abroad in the land before Wyclif published it in *De Potestate Papae* in 1379/80 (Leff 2:531 n. 4; 536 n. 1). As for the later B passages, the papacy had been involved in territorial wars since 1353, particularly from 1362–64 and 1367–78 against Barnabo Visconti. A shocking episode in those wars was the sack of Cesena in February 1377 by the papal forces under Cardinal Robert of Geneva (Devlin 80–83; Gwynn 11–13). So it appears that 1377, not 1378 or later, is the likely *terminus a quo* for the origin of the B tradition.

Two changes Langland made in the B > C revision point to a *terminus ad quem*. The first change is to the end of the passage about the right to papal election (B.Prol.111) where, in revision, the Dreamer's pointedly ambiguous posture of reticence is replaced with a clear injunction by Conscience: "For the sake of Holy Church, do not dispute it" (C.Prol.135). This clearly shows the poet in the orthodox position, and suggests that the issue of papal election has come to a head in the publication of *De Potestate Papae*. The second change is to the Prologue account of the royal procession, which in B reads *Thanne kam þer a kyng; knyȝthod hym ladde; Might of the communes made him to regne* (Prol.112–13). C substitutes *Myght of tho men made hym to regne* (Prol.137: v. 1. *The muche myȝte of the men*). The reference of *tho men* is clearly to the escorting knights. This replacement of the traditional concept that the royal power derives from the common people of England with the realistic one that he rules by military force is best explicable as the poet's reaction to the rising of 1381 (but cp. Donaldson 108). So too may be the exclusion from C of B.Prol.143–45, lines sympathetic to the common people. Depending on how these two indications are read the *terminus ad quem* for the origin of the B tradition is 1379 or 1381.

For dating the origin of the C tradition there is no comparable evidence. There are, to be sure, striking new references in C to royal misgovernment, tolerance of favourites, growing hostility to the king at home and abroad, and his financial straits (C.3.208–10, 4.189–94). Skeat thought they referred to 1392 (1886, xxxiv). But since Langland was dead by 1387 their latest plausible reference must be to some point leading up to the concert of lords and commons against the king in 1386. So the C tradition originated in the period 1379/1381–c.1385.

The brackets of time suggested above are not to be seen as the periods during which the three versions were severally being written. When Langland began and when he left off working on each version we cannot know precisely. To illustrate this: in the A version there are allusions to Edward III's Norman wars and to the treaty of Bretigny in 1360 and to a great storm in 1362 (3.176–95, 5.13–14: Skeat 1886, ix, x; Bennett 1943a, 568). To read those dates as evidence that he did not begin to write until after 1362 would require a presumption of sequential composition for which we have no evidence. It would also presume that Langland made only immediately applicable topical allusions, and there is evidence to the contrary of this. For instance, in B.19.247 he referred to the Folvilles, a family of outlaws last active in 1347 (Stones 1956), and in A.5.140 to a woman charged with forestalling in 1350 (Richardson 1939). In B and C he let stand a passage that seems to allude to a time when the Black Prince was still alive and in health (B.4.45, C.4.43). In C, albeit for good dramatic reasons, he expanded what must have begun as an allusion to Edward III's failure to exert his right to the kingdom of France (3.234–58). The king in the early passus of all versions comes to embody Langland's hopes and disappointments of government: as soon as made, his topical allusions become in essence generic. What they tell us, at best, is that he thought his first version worth having copied sometime in 1368–75, and his second sometime in 1377–79/80. Of the third version we can reasonably presume that he was no longer working on it in 1386. And the early currency of C manuscripts suggests that the generative copy of C was made some time before that date.

DISSEMINATION OF THE VERSIONS

The dissemination of *Piers Plowman* texts was very rapid. All three forms of the poem were already current and being copied by the early 1380s. It seems that while Langland was revising A to B the A tradition was taking shape, and that B copies were being multiplied while he was about his second revision. As it happens the oldest surviving copies, to judge by handwriting, are not of A but of B (Laud Misc. 581) and of C (T.C.D. 212). Even these, on the indication of the classification of manuscripts in their respective traditions, must be at least five removes from any authorized exemplar.

There is no indication of a "final" text having driven out earlier ones. The conjoints with C supplements may as likely reflect availability of exemplars as preference for C. That their A beginnings were less developed treatments seems not to have been noticed, or not to have been a matter of concern. What was clearly wanted was a longer, more "complete" text. None of the medieval copies of *Piers* known to us descends from a surviving copy: there must, at least in the fifteenth century, have been many more copies in existence than have survived.

SCRIBAL "CORRECTION"

Interest in the completeness of text was accompanied by interest in detail of content and expression. This appears from the amount of visible "correction" in practically all manuscripts. When correction is in the hand of the main scribe it must reflect a sense of obligation to follow the exemplar stronger than his care for the appearance of his page, something not to be taken for granted. Very often corrections are in another hand, sometimes evidently as a formal part of the process of book production, sometimes, just as evidently, by enthusiastic amateurs. An instance of the former is Huntington MS 128 (Hm of B) where the hands of two correctors who made more than a thousand changes, apparently checking the copy against the exemplar, have been identified (Kane-Donaldson 9, 10). C.U.L. Dd. 3.13 (G of C) was heavily corrected, apparently by the main scribe; Huntington Library 143 (X of C) was systematically corrected by someone whose mark appears on many pages. An extreme instance of the second kind is B.L. Additional 35287 (M of B) (Kane-Donaldson 11 n. 75). Amateur "correction" usually catches the eye more readily. It is heavy in B.L. Harley 6041 (H[2] of A), in Oriel College 879 (O of B), and in the C tradition, notably in Douce 104 (D), in B.L. Additional 35157 (U), and above all B.L. Additional 34779 (P[2]). Both kinds of correction must be presumed to have occurred at all stages of transmission, the second especially in the later stages of the traditions as the poem gained in popularity and general interest. Amateur correction , which would most likely introduce readings from another strain of descent, their intrusiveness to be concealed at the next stage of copying, will have been one source of the random variational groups brought to light in the classification process (Kane 1960, 83; Kane-Donaldson 22, 63).

Correction was especially frequent in the C tradition, on the showing of both the manuscripts just cited, and the classification of C. Some explanations suggest themselves. One is implied in the circumstance that many C manuscripts come from a relatively small region (Samuels) not far from the poet's birthplace (Kane 1965, 28, 29 n. 1, 38). This is a situation that suggests heightened interest in the poem among the copyists of C, and also a proximity where consultation of other copies was not difficult. Another explanation may lodge in the circumstance that the C revision was not completed, and that the initiating copy of the C tradition was prepared by someone else than the poet. This again, if it was known to copyists in some proximity, might well reduce the sense of authority of any particular text as exemplar and prompt consultation and comparison.

The term "correction" in this situation must be rightly understood. It certainly implies that the agent of change, scribe or reader, believed himself to be improving his text. What needs to be qualified is the source of his alternative reading, the value of his judgement, and the degree of his perceptiveness. One finds formal correction in manuscripts produced in a copying centre where, also, slavishly copied nonsense readings were let stand (Kane-Donaldson 42, notes 62, 63). The two correctors of Hm 128, again apparently professionals, register no perception of massive dislocations that destroy the sequence of discourse (Kane-Donaldson, 10). Time and again both scribes and their correctors show no sign of noticing omissions of text from their exemplar: C's S, Corpus Christi College Cambridge 293, had an exemplar which lacked 21.8–322; the exemplar of the Westminster manuscript lacked 13.110–175, and that of the genetic pair London University Library S.L.V.17 and T.C.D. 212 (AV of C) lacked 7.237–84. When the correction was from another copy the quality of the alternative reading was a matter of luck, and the "corrector's" judgement of its quality is likely to have been formed by the same criteria which directed his own subconscious or deliberate substitutions as a scribe.

THE A TRADITION

These are the general circumstances in which the three manuscript traditions of *Piers Plowman* developed. Each is, however, distinctive in character. The least coherent is the tradition of A. The A manuscripts have resisted general classification. Among the sixteen only one unmistakable family and a couple of genetic pairs are confidently identifiable (Kane 1960, 83 ff.). To go by its presence in the Vernon manuscript this version evidently had canonical status, but supplementation, by both insertion of B or C or BC lines (Kane 1960, 29–38), and the attachment of the C conclusion on four evidently distinct occasions, may imply that the A tradition developed in awareness that a fuller, therefore more desirable, form of "The book of Piers Plowman" existed: a factor in the history of the A tradition seems to have been availablility of exemplars. A question is raised by the difference in length of the A manuscripts. Three copies, R, U and J— whether they are genetically related is obscure (Kane 1960, 14)—have a twelfth section after the prologue. The latter part of this at least is avowedly by a continuator, John But. Where does his continuation begin? The whole of A.12, notwithstanding some engaging lines, may be a pastiche. Or some of its earlier lines may represent an abortive start by Langland (Kane 1960, 51). Then there is the circumstance that some copies have eleven passus, some only seven or eight (Kane 1960, 27, 40). There is a sense of ending in the last lines of A.11, but the same has been claimed for the end of 8 (Rigg-Brewer 29, 30). Were there once, as Skeat believed (1886, 2:xxii, xxiii), "shorter versions" of A? Did the poet once or twice allow his working text of A to be copied? This cannot be physically resolved, since all the manuscripts with the shorter form break off within passus, E at 7.213, H at 8.142, L at 8.155 and N at 8.184. Thus there are no helpful colophons. Loss from the end of a text (as from the beginning) was more than likely in a time when manuscripts were not generally bound and would readily account for these shorter forms, as well as for the changes of exemplar in passus 8 of N and of Z. Moreover the length of the A copies does not correspond to their genetic relation, as far as this is determinable. Another intriguing problem is raised by A's H[3] (B.L. Harley 3954) which is a B copy to about 5.150, then completed from A; this was discussed above (pp. 180–81). When these unknowns are set aside there is still a distinctive A form: the positive evidence is for a poem with a prologue and eleven passus (Kane 1960, 19–52).

Its representatives are regionally dispersed (Samuels 1963, 94; p.207 below). The Vernon copy was evidently a pious work; to go by their hands, the Antiquaries' and Pierpont Morgan Library copies were made for own use; the exclusive common ancestor of TH²Ch, T itself, and the Westminster manuscript are professional work; Bodley 851's "A" text is the work of an eccentric. Nevertheless in their various degrees of purity and completeness they are our evidence for the first form of *Piers Plowman* authorially sanctioned for copying. Although the quality of the text in these A manuscripts varies hugely, the archetypal manuscript, their exclusive common ancestor, is generally reconstructable. It proves to have readings which, on comparison with the corresponding ones of B and C, have a scribal look (Kane-Donaldson 205, 210–11). This could indicate that the author improved his poem at such points on his first revision. But that is a speculation, whereas it is known that scribes corrupted texts.

THE B TRADITION

The B tradition, by contrast, is well defined. All the manuscripts (except, of course, Huntington 114) attest a poem of a prologue and twenty passus lacking some 240 lines found in A and some 1300 found in C, but with about 1400 distinctive lines (Kane-Donaldson 16, 17 n. 4). The tradition is also close: classification reveals two clearly distinct families, therefore a probable bifid stemma. One family is constituted by two copies, R and F, the other by the remaining manuscripts (but H, it must be recalled, *may* be an outsider). Each family reads a total of about 170 lines not found in the other (Kane-Donaldson 61 ff.). It has been argued that the differences created by the presence or absence of this material are authorial, that RF might preserve a form of the poem intermediate between B and C or, conversely, that the text of the large family might incorporate changes by the poet (Skeat 1886, lxviii; Kane-Donaldson 64 n. 101). The essential weakness of either argument is the presence of additional material of unmistakable authorial quality in *both* families, which excludes the concept of augmentation: there is no direction of progression. The situation seems best explicable as differentiation by scribal omission from a group ancestor of each family (Kane-Donaldson 66–69).

The quality of the B manuscripts is such that the B archetype, their exclusive common ancestor, can in general be confidently restored. But that archetype must have been at least two and possibly more removes from the authorially sanctioned B exemplar. It was at least twice subjected to extensive prosifying substitution, some of this careless and unconscious, some (its character suggests) designed to make meaning more accessible, all at the expense of technical excellence and poetic energy (Kane-Donaldson 74–97, 98–127). Thus, notwithtanding the integrity of the B tradition, the text of *Piers* that it preserves is seriously defaced. None of the copies has any lines recognizably from the C version. The few A lines found in B manuscripts are probably there by memorial contamination. Otherwise the manuscripts of this tradition register no awareness that other forms of the poem existed. The distribution of the surviving B manuscripts is divided (Samuels 94). Taking into account the bifid stemma of the manuscripts, this seems to indicate both a western and an East Midland centre of dissemination.

THE C TRADITION

The tradition of the C manuscripts is also integral. The C completions of the conjoint manuscripts are shown to belong to it by their congruency in the C classification, as is the Ilchester manuscript (L.U.L.S.L.V.88) except where it inexplicably diverges from the traditional text (above p. 182). But the character of the C tradition is distinguished by three circumstances in its history.

The first is that Langland used a scribal copy of B for his revision to C. The second is that this revision was unsystematic and local and was not completed. The third is that the "authorized," formal copy of C seems very likely to have been made under direction of someone else than the poet.

The scribal copy Langland used for revision to C was a better text than the archetypal copy of the B manuscripts (Kane-Donaldson 123–24). Nevertheless it contained many scribal readings. It represents an earlier stage in the archetypal tradition of B than does the exclusive common ancestor of the surviving B copies. The latter was differentiated from it simply by further variation: thus the archetypal tradition of B had two phases, a first which ended with the copying of the B manuscript Langland used for his revision to C, and a second — during which further error was introduced — which ended with the copying of the exclusive common ancestor of the surviving B manuscripts.

That the consideration why Langland might have used a scribal copy must remain a matter of speculation does not alter the evidence of the C text that he did so (Kane-Donaldson 121, 122, 98–121). What is quite clear is that he did not begin by checking the B copy before him. Beyond that, the differences between the B and C text show his revision to have been anything but slow and careful. He did, to be sure, apply himself to it intently at some points. The recasting of the Confession of the Sins (B.5) by incorporating Haukyn's self-revelations from B.13 and 14, and the replacement of Haukyn with Liberum Arbitrium have this character (Russell 1966, 1969). Otherwise the indication is of local changes, not serial review. Some statements are moderated, others sharpened. Some have a look of being remedial, where an archetypal B error did catch his eye as something he had not written. At such points he did not restore, but rewrote (Russell 1969, 30 ff.; Kane-Donaldson 124–27). From the look of about twenty rewritten passages he never completed the process of substituting these for the supplanted material. In some instances the text incorporates both old and revised forms (Russell 1966, 103, 104).

These are the features of the text of the C tradition which indicate that it was not Langland himself who sanctioned or oversaw the copying of the progenitive C text. There was apparently what we would call a "literary executor," whose knowledge of the poet's intentions was necessarily imperfect. His attitude toward the poem will certainly have included a large measure of piety. The dialectal and chronological cluster of so many C manuscripts (Samuels 1963, 94; p. 207 below) suggests more: a proprietary pride in this poet and his poem; exceptional concern for its text, implied in the unusual amount of consultation; a possible intensification of this concern by knowledge that here was the latest, therefore the author's preferred form of the poem. There is one more feature of the C tradition to be noted: in the last two passus the C manuscripts present an unrevised text and join with those of B in forming a single, richly attested tradition (Russell 1969, 47, 48; Kane-Donaldson 124).

SCRIBES AND THE TEXT

Within each tradition the texts of *Piers Plowman* preserved by individual manuscripts vary considerably in detail of expression, with greater or lesser effect on the sense and quality of expression. The variation reflects the character of the three traditions only to this extent, that disagreements about crucial

readings in A manuscripts more noticeably cut across such genetic align-
ments as can be discerned than they do in the other traditions. Aside from
that difference, the text of every copy is a compounded stratification of diver-
gencies from the exclusive common ancestor of the tradition of its version
and, *a fortiori,* from the authorially sanctioned exemplar which generated
this tradition. Viewed as the ultimate reflexes of three authorial originals
the fifty-odd *Piers Plowman* manuscripts we know of are differentiated, essentially, only by the amount of scribal defacement, and by the proportion
of one or another type of this which they exhibit.

Three types of differentiation of extreme character need only to be noticed. One is translation, identifiable as such because the target language
cannot have been the author's. The clear and striking instances are the A
copy T.C.D. MS D.4.12 of the late fifteenth century, in the dialect of the
Durham region (Samuels 94), and the Sion College manuscript (from its
hand mid-sixteenth-century) in Tudor English (Kane-Donaldson 15).
Another type is systematic conflation, as in Huntington 114 (Russell and
Nathan). The third type is "creative" modification, as in the A portion of
Bodley 851 or John But's coda to A (above p. 182). The object of the translations is evident. The other activities imply eccentricity in the agents of
another order than scribal departure from an exemplar.

In this latter, more usual situation, texts are differentiated by variants
of two broad classes. One class is formed by those variants which, because
they do not make sense, or make bad sense, or are not real language, were
evidently mechanical (Kane 1960, 116–24). The second is formed by variants which, if they were not subject to comparison, that is, to critically discriminative evaluation, would pass muster, but which, on such comparison,
are seen to affect the style and meaning of the text.

Whether a variant in the second class was consciously substituted or subconsciously induced is not necessarily determinable. But a likelihood of subconsciously induced variation is present in the method by which scribes
copied Middle English vernacular verse. That they did not copy word by
word, or even, *pace* Windeatt (28, 32), line by line, is evident from the classes
of mechanical error, in particular larger omissions, to which they were subject. They took up blocks of text, groups of lines such as a stanza or a verse
"paragraph," into the memory by eye and ear both and then, writing from
that memory, put their eyes to the page and their hand to the forming of
letters: the medieval pen did not "flow" in the writing of most scripts.

In this process the accuracy of the signal from memory to hand could
be affected by many factors. Simply the attempt to understand what he was
copying could distract the scribe. Distraction and disturbance of nerve-
messages could originate as the scribe's subconscious mind measured the
sense of the immediate text against his own experience. His sense of gram-

mar, that is his expectation of grammatical fulfilment of an expression, or imprinted common collocations and forms of language, or his own habitual locutions, could result in his consciously or unconsciously "normalizing" Langland's text like a modern copy-editor. Distraction could originate in his emotional or intellectual preoccupation with text just before or just after the expression he was actually writing. These are some reasons why it is not always, or even generally, possible to classify a variant absolutely as deliberate or unconscious. What editors do learn from experience, from extended observation of variants, is the various inducements to substitution. These fall into two broad classes.

One is the language or sense of the immediate context. In *Piers Plowman* more often than not language and sense are in a highly complex rhetorical relation where the actual form of expression is a prime factor of meaning. That circumstance was inherently conducive to scribal prosification, simplification of expression, loss of compression, debasement of the style by the reduction of poetic energy. Often a local passage contains within itself inducements to particular kinds of substitution, so that the character of its variants would be predictable, and coincidence of variation not surprising (Kane-Donaldson 31, 32, 63). "Historical" variation, from the language of the 1370s to that of the earlier fifteenth century was absolutely likely. Other variation almost as predictable was generated by the topicality of *Piers Plowman*. A recent edition of *Troilus and Criseide* shows how another, radically different text with a high emotional charge has similar capacities (Windeatt 25–33).

The other broad class of substitution originated in distraction by elements of a wider context than immediate expression and subject. Here for a start the continual relevance of the discourse to *topoi* of estates satire, and its recurrence to crucial theological issues, would engage and distract. But actually everything that the scribe had ever copied or even read was a potential source of disturbance of message from eye to brain to hand because of the possibility of his subconsciously associating it with the copy in hand. Specifically the experience of having previously copied *Piers Plowman*, in whatever version, would be calculated to disturb accuracy, if only because the occasional, quasi-formulaic quality of its style would promote association between different parts of the poem, with an overlay of small differences of expression in the memory. Expecially in the regionally concentrated C tradition there are likely to have been scribes who copied the poem more than once; their accuracy is likely to have been affected by differences between successive exemplars.

Where these two classes of substitution through distraction are more than apparently random disturbances of nervous messages, they exhibit patterns of copyist response to text that have been known for centuries (Kane 1960,

125–36). These are abundantly illustrated in all versions of *Piers Plowman*. Examination of variation in Chaucer manuscripts shows them present there as well (Kane 1983; 1984, 213–27). The recent editor of *Troilus* has identified them in the copies of that poem, although he feels called upon to give them new names (Windeatt 27–35). The more explicit, the grammatically, or lexicographically, or stylistically easier, the more emphatic substitutions, the censorship, the substitution of favoured instances, whether deliberate or subconscious, are predictable forms of reaction by inferior but nevertheless engaged intelligences to major literary experience.

To sentimentalize such scribal response or to dignify it by calling it "criticism" (Windeatt 28) is unrewarding. Most often it is predictable conditioned reaction, often, in the case of *Piers Plowman* scribes, to some component of estates satire or to a theological sore spot. At the level of style it is the response of mediocrity to distinction. By its nature as variation it damages the work of art that evoked it. Scribal variation from the text of such a work cannot have "intrinsic" value (but cf. Windeatt 26). The scribal variant is a deplorable circumstance of the manual transmission of texts. It has value only as evidence for the authorial reading it supplanted.

There were in the Middle English period exceptional scribes like the man who copied Harleian MS 2253 (Revard 1979). And there were, to go by handwriting and grammatical usage, a small number of educated scribes active in the London area round about 1400, copying *Piers* and *Troilus* and *The Canterbury Tales* and *Confessio Amantis* (Kane-Donaldson 215 n. 184; Doyle-Parkes). Langland's initial scribes must have been good. Behind the archetypes of B and C there were texts of these poems of which the quality shines through the damage done at the archetypal stage. But these seem exceptions. Most *Piers Plowman* scribes seem to have been more typical of the craft, literate in being able to form letters, but not necessarily much more so, capable of response; but in the character of this response they appear essentially mediocre, and they were, above all, for whatever reasons, inaccurate transmitters.

THE TEXTUAL PROBLEM

So there remain as many texts of *Piers Plowman* as there are manuscripts. Any of these, if it were the only copy, would "be" the poem, a unique arrangement of linguistic norms, a major literary event. We would know, from the axiomatic damage to texts in manual transmission, that it was necessarily inaccurate, an imperfect reflex of the author's intention (Thorpe 467, 481). But we would have no alternative to accepting it. As things are, we have the many copies. Again, axiomatically, none of these accurately represents the combination of language assembled by authorial intention called the true poem. How, if we wish to attain the ideally authentic experience of that poem, do we proceed?

The direction of the history of the subject is that we should proceed as before, by critical comparison and evaluation. It was by those means, by an initial assessment of the poem in terms of literary experience, that its excellence was perceived. Then followed the identifying definition of the work: it was by literary and critical comparison that three successive forms of the work were recognized, each supported by a manuscript tradition which, again, was established by comparison and critical evaluation.

The authentic experience of *Piers Plowman* must be, in this consideration, the one most directly and wholly generated by the poet's own words. For, philosophically, the author must be allowed the final say (however he exercised it) "over which words constitute the text of his literary work" (Thorpe 467), and thus over the work itself. "It is the author who is the ultimate goal of our intention" (Windeatt 33). Here is the logical imperative to extend the comparison and critical analysis to those differences between the texts of manuscripts which have been caused by scribal variation. It ought to follow that the same critical faculty that recognized the excellence of *Piers Plowman* and identified its authorial forms should go on to distinguish between authorial and scribal readings in the texts of the manuscripts.

That conclusion is, however, not accepted in all quarters. Disagreement in the field of textual criticism is no novelty: the history of the activity is one of controversy. But the ground of this has changed. Once the issue was whether someone was a good or bad editor, or whether this or that method or procedure was sound. Now the situation has a deconstructive element: is textual criticism actually an effective activity? This development reflects the unhappy history of editing Old French texts, from which emerged the notion that the right procedure is to select a manuscript in the poet's own dialect, which is relatively old, which is physically intact, and print this, with correction only of its "manifest errors." But it also has a psychological basis. "The average man, if he meddles with criticism at all, is a conservative critic. . . . He believes that the text of ancient authors is generally sound, not because he has acquainted himself with the elements of the problem, but because he would feel uncomfortable if he did not believe it" (Housman 43).

So he rationalizes his need for a secure text. Simply the fact that textual criticism can be badly conducted appears reductive of its intellectual status. The textual critic is self-indulgent, rewriting his poem in a version that never was: Bentley's "improvement" of Milton is recalled. And however plausible the textual critic's arguments may seem there is no way of being "sure" that his emendation actually restores authorial language. And in any event textual critics disagree among themselves: whom is one to believe? In textual criticism "there are too many unknowns." And after all Middle English writers were not much concerned about the minutiae of their texts or about their grammar.

Each of these criticisms except the last has some substance. There *have* been bad editions of Middle English texts which invoked, though they did not observe, good rationale. Undoubtedly they discredit the discipline: whether they invalidate it is a matter of logic. That the textual critic may be carried away by his activity is a genuine risk, but unless he is a fool he will be safeguarded by his respect for the poet. Bentley was lacking in this quality (Housman 29). When William Empson maintained that he could improve on the text of Rupert Brooke (Thorpe 465) he was writing not as a textual critic but as a better poet. It is undeniable that textual criticism cannot produce "absolute proof." Neither can most literary studies; people who have a psychological need to be "sure" have no business with literature. But the notion that medieval writers were careless about the details of their language is pure nonsense. It discounts the correcting that Chaucer describes in his epigram to Adam, his anxiety about the metre of *Troilus*, Langland's abuse of clerks who cannot *formalliche endite*, Scogan's description of Chaucer's language as *curious*, that is, "carefully chosen." The few holographs we have from the period argue the concern of their authors for detail. Even the minute changes made by "correctors" of manuscripts point to this. A better explanation of the vagaries of language in later Middle English texts is the perplexity of successive generations of scribes with earlier forms of English, from which their own had changed.

The first and paradoxical feature of the sceptical view of textual criticism is that it induces a complacent acceptance, most often unthinking, of existing printed texts of medieval works: the deconstructive scepticism is converted to a blind faith. This does damage to scholarship. The consequence of pious acceptance of scribal error sanctioned by print, of using indeterminately corrupt texts, could be illustrated from most Middle English glossaries, and studies of rhyme and metre, and syntax and style and phonology. Kenneth Sisam once wrote in respect of Anglo-Saxon studies, "To support a bad manuscript reading is in no way more meritorious than to support a bad conjecture, and so far from being safer, it is more insidious as a source of error. For, in good practice, a conjecture is printed with some distinguishing mark which attracts doubt; but a bad manuscript reading, if it is defended, looks like solid ground for the defence of other readings. So intensive study with a strong bias toward the manuscript reading blunts the sense of style, and works in a vicious circle of debasement" (Sisam 39; cp. Maas 13). But in Middle English scholarship he has not been heeded, and we find solemn exegesis of scribal error, solemn translation of scribal garble into good sense, language study actually based on texts with modernized spelling. Worst of all, acquiescence in the sanction of scribally corrupt texts is a failure of respect for the poet, whose achievement, if its excellence shines through the "haze" of scribal damage (Windeatt 32–33), must necessarily have once been greater than it now seems to us, and should be so perceived.

THE CHARACTER OF TEXTUAL CRITICISM

To put the issue as it applies to *Piers Plowman* in perspective it is necessary to consider the esential character of textual criticism, understood to mean the removal of damage, or the identification and signalling of damage, done by scribes to the language and sense of the poem as the author left it. For that the damage occurred and was considerable is not deniable. The question is whether and how its effect can be reduced.

Textual criticism is, first, essentially comparative and evaluative, based on differentiation between the mode of writing of the great artist and those of his copyists, betweeen the *usus scribendi* of poet and scribes. It can be effectively applied to *Piers Plowman* because the high, and highly distinctive, excellence of that work implies sensible differences between the structures of language and meaning created by the poet and those substituted by his scribes. Textual criticism is, second, analytical, a process of close stylistic criticism. It applies the criterion of appropriateness to the linguistic texture of the poem, identifying the language of the poet in the reading which, on comparison, carries the larger charge of poetic energy, and the language of the scribe in the reading which reduces this. To this comparison it applies consideration of Langland's rhetoric, those particulars by which his writing is distinguished from the prosaic or from prose and is in itself distinctive. Textual criticism is, third, practical in its application, dependent for its effectiveness on, above all, the experience of scribal substitution afforded by extended collation. For during that activity analysis of visible variation, that is variation by the single manuscript from a majority or group reading, is unavoidable. Here the variant, rarely a serious competitor for authorial status, illustrates in a controlled situation typical substitution and its critical difference as a functional element in the linguistic texture of the poem. So for the textual critic the historically accumulated generalizations about scribal proclivities become real. He identifies and classifies the "reader response" of scribes (Windeatt 32, 33), acquires some degree of psychological insight into their reaction to the text of *Piers*. Textual criticism is, fourth, diagnostic, when, on the basis of a developed critical judgement, it identifies a reading supported by all the manuscript evidence as not authorial, corrupt (Maas 33; Kane 1969, 167, 168). It is, finally, not "privileged."

Although it has an unmistakable intuitive element, it is accountable, especially for explanation of any reading identified or rejected as scribal.

It is an avowedly intricate process of reasoning which, by its very intricacy, may fail to inspire confidence. Its proponents must acknowledge that their propositions about detail of readings stand or fall by their individual intellectual quality. That is their only authority. But textual critics rightly arrogate to themselves a cautionary function: to keep the fact of the scribal corruption of texts before the eyes of those who occupy themselves with the great literary monuments of the past.

Their activity is traditionalist and progressive both. Every acceptance of a disputed reading of a *Piers Plowman* text by competent judgement replicates the laborious process by which, over something like half a millenium, the texts of classical literature were restored (Maas 11–13). Their negative function, the questioning of received texts, is equally important, and constantly so. For it is calculated to keep in view that while there are as many texts of any version of *Piers Plowman* as there are manuscript copies, there was only one authorial text of each. To make that consideration the beginning of any study of our poem may seem the more responsible and scholarly attitude.

REFERENCES

Bale, John. *Scriptorum illustrium maioris Brytannie . . . Catalogus*. Basel: Oporinum, 1557.
———. *Index Britanniae Scriptorum . . . John Bale's Index of British and Other Writers*. Ed. R. Lane Poole and M. Bateson. Oxford: Clarendon Press, 1902.
Bennett, J. A. W. "The Date of the A-Text of *Piers Plowman*." *PMLA* 58 (1943): 566–72.
———. "The Date of the B-Text of *Piers Plowman*." *MÆ* 12 (1943): 55–64.
[Cooper, Elizabeth]. *The Muses Library, or a Series of English Poetry from the Saxons, to the Reign of King Charles II*. Vol. 1. London: Wilcox et al., 1737.
Devlin, Sister Mary Aquinas. "The Date of the C-Version of *Piers Plowman*." University of Chicago Ph.D. dissertation, 1925.
Donaldson, E. Talbot. *Piers Plowman: The C-Text and Its Poet*. Yale Studies in English 113. New Haven: Yale University Press, 1949; rpt. Hamden, CT: Archon Books, 1966.
Doyle, A. I., and M. B. Parkes. "The Production of Copies of the *Canterbury Tales* and the *Confessio Amantis* in the Early Fifteenth Century." *Medieval Scribes, Manuscripts and Libraries: Essays Presented to N. R. Ker*. Ed. M. B. Parkes and Andrew Watson. London: Scolar, 1973. 163–210.
Gwynn, Aubrey. "The Date of the B-Text of *Piers Plowman*." *RES* 19 (1943): 1–24.
Hearne, Thomas. *Remarks and Collections of Thomas Hearne*. Vol. 8 (September 23, 1722–August 9, 1725). Ed. C. E. Doble et al. Oxford: Oxford Historical Society, 1907.

Housman, A. E. *Selected Prose*. Ed. John Carter. Cambridge: University Press, 1961.

Kane, George, ed. *Piers Plowman: The A Version*. London: Athlone. 1960.

———. *Piers Plowman: The Evidence for Authorship*. London: Athlone, 1965.

———. "Conjectural Emendation." *Medieval Literature and Civilization, Studies in Memory of G. N. Garmonsway*. Ed. D. A. Pearsall and R. A. Waldron. London: Athlone, 1969. 155–64.

———. "The Text of the *Legend of Good Women* in CUL MS Gg.4.27." *Middle English Studies Presented to Norman Davis in Honour of His Seventieth Birthday*. Ed. D. Gray and E. G. Stanley. Oxford: Clarendon Press, 1983. 39–58.

———. "John M. Manly (1865–1940) and Edith Rickert (1871–1938)." *Editing Chaucer: the Great Tradition*. Ed. Paul G. Ruggiers. Norman: Pilgrim Books, 1984. 207–29.

———. "The 'Z-Version' of *Piers Plowman*." *Speculum* 60 (1985): 910–30.

Kane, George and E. Talbot Donaldson, eds. *Piers Plowman: The B Version*. London: Athlone, 1975.

Leff, Gordon. *Heresy in the Later Middle Ages*. 2 vols. Manchester: Manchester University Press; New York: Barnes and Noble, 1967.

Maas, Paul. *Textkritik*. 3rd. revised impression. Leipzig: Teubner, 1957.

McKisack, May. *The Fourteenth Century 1307–1399*. Oxford: Clarendon Press, 1959.

Pearsall, Derek. "The 'Ilchester' Manuscript of *Piers Plowman*." *NM* 82 (1981): 181–93.

Percy, Thomas. *The Correspondence of Thomas Percy and Thomas Warton*. Ed. M. G. Robinson and Leah Dennis. Vol. 3. *The Percy Letters*. Ed. David Nichol Smith and Cleanth Brooks. Baton Rouge: Louisiana University Press, 1951.

Revard, Carter. "Richard Hurd and MS Harley 2253." *N&Q* 224 ns 26 (1979): 199–202.

Richardson, M. E. "Piers Plowman." *TLS*, March 11, 1939, 149–50.

Rigg, A. G., and Charlotte Brewer, eds. *Piers Plowman: The Z Version*. Toronto: Pontifical Institute of Medieval Studies, 1983.

Ritson, Joseph. *Bibliographia Poetica: a Catalogue of English Poets of the Twelfth, Thirteenth, Fourteenth, Fifteenth and Sixteenth Centurys, with a Short Account of Their Works*. London: Nicol, 1802.

Russell, G. H. "The Salvation of the Heathen: the Exploration of a Theme in *Piers Plowman*." *JWCI* 29 (1966): 101–16.

———. "Some Aspects of the Process of Revision in *Piers Plowman*." In Hussey 1969, 27–49.

———, and Venetia Nathan. "A *Piers Plowman* Manuscript in the Huntington Library." *HLQ* 26 (1963): 119–30.

Samuels, M. L. "Some Applications of Middle English Dialectology." *ES* 44 (1963): 81–94.

Sisam, Kenneth. *Studies in the History of Old English Literature*. Oxford: Clarendon Press, 1953.

Skeat, W. W. *Parallel Extracts from Twenty-nine manuscripts of Piers Plowman, with Comments, and a proposal for the Society's three-text edition of this poem*. EETS 17. London: Trübner, 1866.

———. *The Vision of William concerning Piers Plowman . . . by William Langland. . . . The "Vernon" Text; or Text A*. EETS 28. London: Trübner, 1867.

———. *The Visions of William concerning Piers the Plowman, Dowel, Dobet and Dobest, by William Langland. . . . The "Crowley" Text; or Text B*. EETS 38. London: Trübner, 1869.

―――. *The Visions of William concerning Piers the Plowman, Dowel, Dobet and Dobest.* . . . *The "Whitaker" Text; or Text C.* EETS 54. London: Trübner, 1873.

―――. *The Vision of William Concerning Piers the Plowman in Three Parallel Texts.* 2 vols. Oxford: Clarendon Press, 1886.

Stones, E. L. G. "The Folvilles of Ashby-Folville, Leicestershire, and their Associates in Crime, 1326–1347." *TRHS* 5th ser. 7 (1957): 117–36.

Thorpe, James. "The Aesthetics of Textual Criticism." *PMLA* 80 (1965): 465–82.

Tyrwhitt, Thomas. *The Canterbury Tales of Chaucer to which are added, An ESSAY upon his Language and Versification; an Introductory Discourse; and Notes.* 5 vols. London: Payne, 1775.

Warton, Thomas. *The History of English Poetry from the Close of the Eleventh to the Commencement of the Eighteenth Century: A New Edition Carefully Revised* [by Richard Price]. 4 vols. London: Dodsley, 1824.

Whitaker, Thomas, ed. *Visio Witti de Petro Plouhman . . . ascribed to Robert Langland. . . . Printed from a MS Contemporary with the Author, Collated with two others of Great Antiquity and exhibiting the original text.* London: Murray, 1813.

Windeatt, B. A., ed. *Troilus & Criseyde: a new edition of 'the Book of Troilus'.* London: Longman, 1984.

Wright, Thomas. *The vision and the creed of Piers Ploughman, newly imprinted.* 2 vols. London: Pickering, 1832.

―――. "The Visions of Piers Plowman." *Gentleman's Magazine* ns 1 (1834): 385–91.

―――. *The Vision and the Creed of Piers Ploughman newly imprinted.* 2 vols. London: Pickering, 1842.

8

DIALECT AND GRAMMAR

M. L. SAMUELS

ENGLISH IN THE LATER FOURTEENTH CENTURY

Langland, Chaucer and their contemporaries wrote in the period of the language known as Middle English (c.1100–1500), and for most of this period no standard form of the language existed. The official languages of government, law and learning and many other spheres of activity were Latin and French, and the result is that, lacking any unifying model, written Middle English is a vast kaleidoscope of different dialects from all parts of the country. It was not until 1430 that English began to replace Latin and French for official purposes, and from then on the type of English used in Chancery documents was available as a model (Samuels 1963); but even so, and in spite of the introduction of printing in 1475, great variation remained, and personal spelling remained virtually idiosyncratic until well into the sixteenth century (Samuels 1981).

THE DIALECTS OF MIDDLE ENGLISH

The evidence for Middle English dialects must obviously be in written form, and that written form consists of features that (a) definitely reflect differences of pronunciation, e.g. *driveth* and *driven*, *thurgh* and *thorugh*, (b) probably reflect them, e.g. *fuyr* and *fyr*, *stan* and *ston* or (c) reflect no such differences and are purely orthographic, e.g. *though* and *þouh*, *goed* and *good*. Since all these features are clearly correlated in the regional spelling of each Middle English writer, the term *dialect* will, in what follows, be used to express any or all of them (cf. McIntosh 1956, 1974 and 1975).

The written dialects of Middle English, thus defined, form a continuum of minute differentiations over the whole country, in much the same way as can be observed in modern spoken dialects. This must not, of course, be understood in the literal sense that "each writer wrote as he spoke" but rather that (i) each writer's spelling-system was idiosyncratic and, when analysed today, can be recognised as such in the same way as a fingerprint, (ii) groups of such idiosyncratically adopted spellings varied from centre to centre and even from village to village (Benskin 1981, xxxi), and (iii) within each spelling system there is always a proportion of spellings that definitely reflect pronunciation and demonstrate sufficiently the correlation between the continua of written and spoken dialect (Brunner 1; Strang 224-25; Kristensson 6-10). Hence, starting from texts for which there is *non*-linguistic evidence for localisation, one can not only localise any other consistently written text but also, in a text that is not consistently written, isolate the "layers" of dialect contributed by past copyists (McIntosh 1962; Samuels 1969; Benskin and Laing 82-85).

THE COPYING OF LITERARY WORKS

Any standardisation of spellings in Middle English is exceptional before 1430; the main exceptions are Wycliffite tracts and Bible-translations, written in a standard language of the Central Midland region (Samuels 1963). The rest of the vast surviving output of Middle English scribes is manifested in idiosyncratic, regionally differentiated spelling systems, and this great diversity radically affected the copying of literary works. The practice of exact copying letter by letter certainly still existed in the fourteenth century, but it was decidedly rarer than the opposite process by which the scribe, for the benefit of his destined local reader, "translated" his exemplar into his own dialect and spelling, usually leaving only rhyming words in their original form. In addition, there was a whole range of scribes who must be classed somewhere between these two extremes in that they only partially translated their exemplars (Brunner 2; McIntosh 1973, 61; Benskin and Laing 56). This could result in unpredictable mixtures of the scribe's and the exemplar's forms, or in copies that consisted largely of the scribe's forms but with just occasional forms preserved from the exemplar (hereinafter termed "relict forms" or "relicts").

What happened to the linguistic shape of an author's original text was thus largely a matter of chance. With the possible exception of the Wycliffite Bible, no text could be guaranteed an unbroken succession of exact copyists: if it were subjected to a series of partial translations, it would contain not just two "layers" or "strata" of language, but numerous layers; on the other hand, if it were next copied by a scribe who translated it fully, all trace of those previous layers would disappear, including the few remaining authorial forms. In short, the more a text was copied, the less chance that the author's forms would be preserved. Exceptions to this are rare, and virtually limited to cases where an author personally organised, and retained some control over, the copying of his work. There is some evidence that this applies to Gower (Burrow 32, 149, and references there quoted).

METHODS OF RECOVERING THE AUTHOR'S LANGUAGE

If, as is more usual, no author's holograph or archetypal copy survives, the most likely sources of authorial forms will be manuscripts copied at only a few removes from their archetype. If only one such manuscript survives, it may still be difficult to distinguish between the author's and the copyists' forms; but if a number of them survive, each in the hand of a different scribe copying his own dialect and spelling system, it may then be possible to detect a layer of relict authorial forms that is common to them all.

Failing the evidence of relict forms, the recovery or reconstruction of the author's language will depend on a number of secondary sources of evidence:

(i) External or internal indications of the author's place of upbringing will also indicate his dialect. Then, if an early and textually reputable manuscript is written in the dialect of the same place, it is likely to give a better idea of the author's forms than those written elsewhere.

(ii) The dialects of all the surviving manuscripts can be plotted on a map to show the areas of regional circulation of the work. If the map shows a heavier concentration of these dialects in a single area, that may be an indication of the author's home or place of work.

(iii) The use of a regional vocabulary, provided it can be established from a consensus of the manuscripts, may give a general indication of provenance.

(iv) In the case of verse texts, the author's rhyming or alliterating practice may give a similar indication.

SOME CASE-HISTORIES

For most Middle English authors other than Langland, a combination of the above types of evidence has yielded positive results, though the methods employed often have to be adapted to suit the individual circumstances of each case. A fairly straightforward example is provided by the manuscripts of Trevisa's works, which, even when translated into some type of London English, usually contain relict southwestern forms. Since we know that he spent his working life at Berkeley, S. Gloucs., it is reasonable to assume that the two manuscripts that are in the pure dialect of that area will provide the best evidence for his language. In the case of Gower, the evidence is more complex but also more revealing. In general, there is no lack of relict forms in manuscripts of his work, but in two manuscripts the same forms appear to be integral, not relict. Yet the identical language of these manuscripts cannot be reconciled with the dialect of any single place, and turns out to be an entirely idiosyncratic mixture of two separate dialects, each vouched for by metrically proved forms. When we find that these dialects are the ones expected for two places in Kent and Suffolk associated with the Gower family, the only possible conclusion is that Gower, as a result of his upbringing, must have written in the same idiosyncratic mixture of two local spelling systems. Then, since no scribe could have fabricated that precise mixture, the two manuscripts in question can be regarded as virtually equivalent to holographs (Samuels and Smith 304). It should be noted that such a combination of two dialects in one person results in an entirely consistent spelling system (as seen throughout the *Confessio Amantis*), and that this is wholly different from the unpredictable mixtures of scribal origin which are found, as we shall see, in many A and B texts of *Piers Plowman* (Benskin and Laing 75–77).

For Chaucer, more detective work has to be used on rather less evidence. The key factor is that the scribe of the Hengwrt and Ellesmere manuscripts of *The Canterbury Tales* also copied a portion of Gower's *Confessio Amantis* (Doyle and Parkes 170). By comparing this scribe's treatment of his two very different exemplars, it is possible to define which forms are his own and which are the Chaucerian and Gowerian relicts. This evidence, corroborated by that of documents from the exact area of Chaucer's upbringing in London, enables us to identify which of the various current types of London language Chaucer must have used (Samuels 1983a).

THE PROBLEM OF LANGLAND'S DIALECT

In the above and many other cases, it is the manuscripts and manuscript traditions that provide the primary evidence; but in Langland's case all the more obvious sources of evidence are either lacking or debatable and inconclusive. It is usually accepted that he was a West-Midlander, born in southeast Shropshire (Kane 1965a). Yet of all the 52 surviving manuscripts only one is in the dialect of that area (P^2, British Library Additional 34779), a manuscript that is not likely to be close to the archetype (Chambers 1935, 22; Donaldson 230). Another possibility would be to assume from the setting of the poem that he was brought up in the Malvern area (Southwest Worcestershire). Here, as we shall see, there is more agreement, for the better C manuscripts have linguistic connections with that area; but this particular correspondence would need further corroboration, without which we might run the risk of an autobiographical fallacy (Kane 1965b). When we look to the manuscripts for potential relict forms, we do not find any pervasive common ground. The A and B manuscripts show every sign of having been repeatedly recopied and either re-translated or half-translated, so that there is no common core of relicts that is obvious in all three versions. It is true that there is a quite persistent scatter of western relict forms in eastern manuscripts, whereas the opposite is rare; but these forms are either not sufficiently specific, or, if they agree, they do not all point to any single locality.

The evidence of the vocabulary yields still less: Langland seems to have avoided most specifically regional words, presumably in order to make his work accessible to a wider readership (Turville-Petre 45). A clear difference from Chaucer is to be seen in his use of certain words like *ac* "but," *myd* "with," *follouht* and *fullen* "baptism" and "baptise," which would have been regarded as old-fashioned in later-fourteenth-century London, but they do not indicate a specific area. The western words in his vocabulary have probably been underrated (Kittner 122 ff.; Elliot 242), but, even so, the total evidence from this source is no more specific or conclusive than that of any of the others so far mentioned.

We are thus left with the only two remaining, and usually less hopeful sources of evidence: the regional distribution of the dialects of the surviving manuscripts, and the alliterations.

The Scribal Dialects of the Manuscripts

Piers Plowman survives in the language of scribes from many different parts of the country. Some contain so many relicts from previous copyings that they are difficult to localise, but the remainder are either in a fairly consistent dialect or show sufficiently predominant features from one dialect to enable them to be localised, as in the following lists (see further Samuels 1985).

A texts

    A Bodl. Ashmole 1468: S.W. Norfolk.
    E Trinity Coll. Dublin D.4.12: Durham or Northumberland.
    H BL Harley 875: N.W. Warwickshire.
    H³BL Harley 3954: S. Norfolk.
    J Pierpoint Morgan M818 (olim Ingilby): Lincolnshire.
    L Lincoln's Inn 150: S.W. Shropshire.
    M Society of Antiquaries 687: N.W. Suffolk.
    R Bodl. Rawlinson Poetry 137: S.W. Sussex

U University Coll. Oxford 45: S. Cambridgeshire.

V Bodl. English Poetry a.l (olim Vernon): N. Worcestershire.

B texts

C²Cambridge Univ. Libr. L1.4.14: Cambridgeshire.

F Corpus Christi Coll. Oxford 201: Essex.

H BL Harley 3954: see H³ above.

HtHuntington HM 114 (olim Phillipps 8252): S. Essex.

O Oriel Coll. Oxford 79: N. Herts.

W Trinity Coll. Cambridge B.15.17: London.

Y Newnham Coll. Cambridge (olim Yates Thompson): probably London, with diluted Western forms.

C texts

D Bodl. Douce 104: Hiberno-English.

E Bodl. Laud Misc. 656: N. Oxfordshire.

F Cambridge Univ. Libr. Ff.5.35: mid-Oxfordshire.

G Cambridge Univ. Libr. Dd.3.13: S.E. Herefords. and N.W. Gloucs. borders.

I London Univ. Libr. V.88 (olim Ilchester): copied in London from a S.W. Worcs. exemplar.

K Bodl. Digby 171: S.E. Herefords.

M BL Cotton Vespasian B.XVI: W. Warwickshire.

N BL Harley 2376: S.E. Herefords.

P Huntington HM 137 (olim Phillipps 8231): Gloucs.-Monmouths. border.

P² BL Add. 34779 (olim Phillipps 9056): S.E. Shropshire.

Q Cambridge Univ. Libr. Additional 4325: N.W. Gloucs.

S Corpus Christi Coll. Cambridge 293: S. Herefords.

St London Univ. Libr. Sterling MS V.17 (olim Clopton): W. Worcs.

U BL Add. 35157: copied by a N. Worcs. scribe from a S.W. Worcs. exemplar.

V Trinity Coll. Dublin D.4.1 (212): N.W. Gloucs.

X Huntington HM 143: S.W. Worcs., but with some slight signs of interference typical of a London copying.

Y Bodl. Digby 102: S.W. Worcs.

When these localisations are plotted on a map (p. 207), it can be seen that the surviving A texts are peripheral: they demonstrate a situation that is found elsewhere, in which the oldest manuscripts of a work (or their descendants) are found on the periphery of a culture (Reynolds and Wilson 248). The B texts are predominantly eastern, and, to judge from the numerous mixtures in their forms, it is *a priori* likely that a majority of them were written in London, some by immigrant scribes. But the most noticeable con-

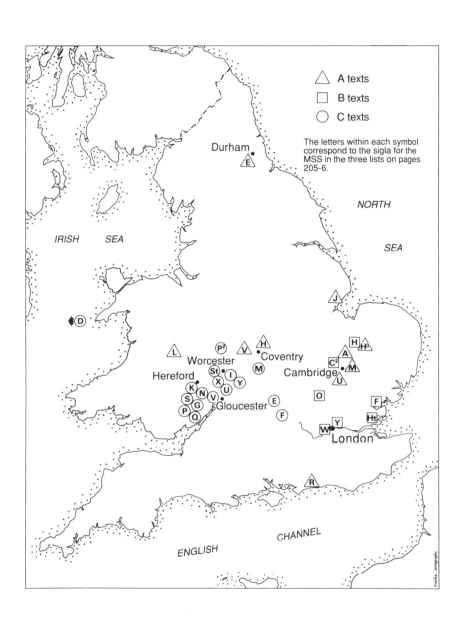

A texts

B texts

C texts

The letters within each symbol
correspond to the sigla for the
MSS in the three lists on pages
205-6.

Durham

NORTH

IRISH   SEA

SEA

Worcester

Coventry

Hereford

Cambridge

Gloucester

London

ENGLISH   CHANNEL

centration is of C-text dialects in the areas surrounding the Malvern hills
(S.W. Worcs., S.E. Herefords. and N.W. Gloucs.). The significance of this
clustering is debatable: it might be taken to support Skeat's view (1873, lxxiv)
that Langland returned to Malvern in later life; there is the counter-argument
that it is simply due to scribal dialect, but even that implies, at the very
least, that the poet was well known in the area and had special connections
with it.

To sum up so far: the texts were recopied too often to yield a consensus
of potentially authorial relict forms; and the clustering of the dialects of the
C manuscripts in the Malvern area, though suggestive, is somewhat circumstantial and therefore, to the sceptic at least, inconclusive. What is needed at this point in the search is some further clue to provide a catalyst for
the different kinds of inconclusive evidence encountered hitherto; and it
comes from an unexpected quarter — Langland's alliterative practice.

The Evidence of the Alliteration

Alliteration generally provides less useful evidence for localising an author
than end-rhyme, since it indicates only the initial consonants, not the stressed
vowels. For example, it could be expected to tell us whether or not a northern author's dialect had merged Old English *hw-* and *cw-* (ME *wh-* and *qu-*),
but that would yield only a rather general indication of regional provenance.
Moreover, because Langland's alliterative practice undoubtedly includes
some traditional northern variants, critical opinion has hitherto tended to
regard it as eclectic and mixed (Kane-Donaldson 132; Kane 1981, 43 ff.),
and its possible dialectal significance has been overlooked. Before conclud-
ing that it is mixed, however, there are two points to be borne in mind:

(i) Alliterative practices vary from poet to poet, and, both in the particular combinations of features used and in their incidences, they are largely
idiosyncratic to each poet. Langland is no exception to this (Donaldson 43;
Schumacher 212 ff.; Oakden 162–64). Furthermore, it is evident from analysis of each poet's alliterative practice that it is the result of applying the
rules of alliterative poetry to his *own* dialect system (cf. Schumacher 62–94).

(ii) We normally assume, as a sound critical canon, that poetic practices
are founded on a natural and consistent linguistic system, and that any additions or mixtures must have special justification (as, for example, in the
case of Spenser). Langland's use of *k-* as in *kirke* "church" or *g-* as in *gar* "cause"
can be justified in this way: they are simply lexical borrowings from Northern or N.W. Midland alliterative poets, and their stylistic purpose is evident. But phonology and grammar are far more deepseated than lexis in
the individual's linguistic system: the notion that Langland availed himself

of extraneous grammatical and phonetic variants purely *metri gratia* is not one to be lightly accepted if it can be shown to be unnecessary. The extent to which such mixtures occur in Middle English rhyming poets has certainly been overestimated in the past. For example, it was once thought that Chaucer used "Kentish" rhymes for convenience; but we now know that these rhymes were normal in the London of Chaucer's youth (Smithers 42–47; Samuels 1963, 87; Burnley 127).

It so happens that Langland alliterates on small grammar-words like pronouns to a greater extent than his contemporaries. The habit has been both criticised and praised (Kane-Donaldson 134; Kane 1981, 53–55; Schmidt 294); but, irrespective of aesthetic considerations, it is for our present purpose a lucky accident which enables us to find out more about the particular dialect forms that occurred in the grammatical system of the author's language. The relevant forms are those used in alliteration for "she" and "are." For "she" the alliteration demands the form *heo* (less probably *he*) more frequently than the form *sche* or *scheo*, and this restricts the area of provenance to the western and southern dialects, and excludes London. For "are," the alliteration demands *ar(e)n* as well as forms in *b-* (*beþ, beoþ, buþ, ben*), and this, when taken in combination with the previous criterion, further restricts the area to the West Midlands only.

Now, in addition to the above two grammatical criteria, there are the usual phonological criteria that are available for any alliterative text. Although, as mentioned above, these rarely give more than a general indication, it is in this case a very fortunate coincidence that they combine with and complement the grammatical criteria in such a way as to narrow down the area of provenance to what is virtually a single locality. The alliteration of *f-* with *v-*, within the West Midlands, restricts the possible area to Herefordshire and Southwest Worcestershire; and the alliteration of *h-* with vowels excludes Herefordshire.

If a map is now constructed for the above total of four criteria, it shows how the possible area is limited by each from a different direction: from the east by *heo* "she," from the south by *ar(e)n* "are," from the north by *f/v-* alliteration, and from the west by alliteration on *h-* with vowels. The resulting small area is the *southwestern portion of Worcestershire, including Malvern*. (For a map and evidence see Samuels 1985, 234–37, 242 ff.)

So much for the indications which, for want of corroboration from the texts themselves, might be termed circumstantial: the setting of the poem, the distributions of the extant manuscripts, and, especially, the alliterations when regarded as dialectally significant. We have here a problem that calls for the exercise of some logic in judgment: the sceptic can claim that each of these indications can for one reason or another be discounted, that each can be otherwise explained, and that they are all non-significant. But even the sceptic will have to admit that, if they are allowed to tell us anything, it then becomes a very curious coincidence that they all point to the same place: Malvern.

We now, therefore, have a choice: we may, with the sceptic, give up and decline to follow the trail any further; or we may accept the challenge and attempt to deal with the mass of seemingly inconclusive evidence contained in the manuscript spellings. But this time there is a difference: we have a clue to tell us which relict spellings to look out for.

ISOLATING THE RELICT SPELLINGS

We know what the local spellings of S.W. Worcs. texts were like: especially prominent as a diagnostic criterion is the *oe*-spelling as in *goed* "good," and the C texts written in the dialect of this area naturally show it. As already pointed out (p. 208), if these texts are considered on their own, it would be difficult to prove that their S.W. Worcs. dialect was not that of a local scribe who copied the C text either in the closing years of Langland's life or even after his death. However, there is some powerful further evidence to indicate that the S.W. Worcs. language in these manuscripts is, in basis at least, Langland's own. It consists of a relict stratum of exactly the same dialect forms in two important and otherwise not closely connected B manuscripts, L and R: *oe* as in *goed* "good," *heo* "she," *a* "he" and "she," *noyther* "neither," *no* "nor," *ar* conj. "ere, before," *ȝut* "yet," together with the usual western *u*- and *uy*-spellings in words like *buggen* "buy" and *pruyde* "pride." There is, furthermore, good reason to believe that such forms in MSS L and R go back to the B-text archetype (Samuels 1985, 241).

It is this occurrence of the same combination of S.W. Worcs. dialect features as a relict stratum in two eastern B manuscripts that provides us with the essential link for our conclusion: that the dialect of Southwest Worcestershire, already pinpointed for us by Langland's alliterative practices, was in fact the one that he used in his holographs.

LANGLAND'S PHONOLOGY

On the basis of the above evidence, it is reasonable to assume that Langland's phonology (and grammar, for which see further below) was a somewhat anterior form of that found in the C manuscripts X, U, Y and I. Some idea of it can be established by a process of extrapolation, aided by comparison with other S. Worcs. texts (Samuels 1985, 242 ff.). The main differences from Chaucerian phonology are:

(i) The typically West Midland rounding of *a* before nasals, as in *mony*, *mon*, *con*, was recessive in Worcestershire, and is likely to have survived only in *mony*, though the other texts from the area do also show *mon* as a minority-variant to *man*.

(ii) The rounded front vowel descending from Old English *y* usually survived in all positions except before nasals, e.g. *muys* "mice," *fuyr* "fire," *pruyde* "pride," *hulles* "hills," *buggen* "buy," compared with *synne* "sin," *kynde* "nature," "natural."

(iii) The survival of a rounded vowel from Old English *eo* may have been less extensive. Fifteenth-century texts from the area show quite frequent spellings like *seo* "see," *treo* "tree," *deop* "deep," and though by that time they may have been largely traditional, it is likely that Langland's fourteenth-century spelling system would have included it. This is supported by the fact that even the London B tradition shows a few spellings like *heo* "she," *leode* "man."

(iv) Whereas in Chaucer's language the endings *-ir*, *-is*, *-id* were giving place to *-er*, *-es*, *-ed*, S. Worcs. texts show some proportion of *-ur*, *-us*, *-ud*. Relicts in the B tradition suggest that this applied also to Langland's spelling.

All the above westernisms would normally be translated by London scribes to their own forms (though even in the London MS W, printed by Kane and Donaldson as their base text, a few forms like *buggen* remain untranslated).

Now, although such translation was normal in the fourteenth century, the question arises as to how Langland's text would fare when translated by scribes into an eastern dialect which had long since merged the rounded vowels [y(:)] and [ɸ(:)] with their respective unrounded counterparts [i(:)] and [e(:)]. Such mergers naturally involve some homophony and ambiguity, of which Langland would not necessarily have been aware unless actually faced with one of the scribal translations of his work. It is therefore of interest to speculate on whether this factor could have played a part in some of those minor revisions which the modern reader finds so puzzling. An example is provided by A.1.25 and the corresponding lines in B and C. In the A text this appears variously as the impersonal *And drink whanne þe driȝeþ* or the personal *And drink whanne þou dryest*. For this Langland would originally have written the western *druy(ȝ)eþ* or *druy(ȝ)est*; but we know that the C revision was made from a corrupt B text (Kane-Donaldson 98–127), i.e. one that is most likely to have been in London spelling and to have had the translated form *dry(ȝ)est* that is common to all the surviving B manuscripts. But to Langland that form would naturally convey the wrong and inappropriate meaning "endurest" instead of his intended "art thirsty." Obviously we have no means of fathoming the working of the author's mind on such a point, but it is at least worth considering as one of the factors that might have triggered the rather less impressive C revision with the change to *And drynke þat doth the good*. Such changes are usually explained as part of a general aim in the C version of simplicity for greater universal appeal (Salter and Pearsall 55); but there are many cases where the impression of needless meticulousness remains, and one way of explaining it is to assume that the stimulus for such alterations might have been a more immediate and direct one: the simpler and less elaborate the language, the less liable to misunderstanding and corruption by scribal translators. The misgivings are the same as Chaucer's as shown in his rebuke to Adam Scriveyn; and if Chaucer, the native Londoner, could be assailed by such doubts, it is reasonable to assume that Langland, the immigrant, would have found the problem even more intractable.

GRAMMAR

PRONOUNS OF THE THIRD PERSON

Overall, the most prominent feature to differentiate the dialects of Middle English is the pronouns of the third person. The variation was due to a restructuring of these pronouns, partly of functional origin, which is typical of the whole Middle English period. Its origin lies in the fact that the Old English forms *he* "he" and *heo* "she" merged to *he* by normal sound-change in Early Middle English in eastern areas; in the north, the new form *scho* arose from *heo* via the stress-shifted **hjo*, and then, spreading southwards to the East Midlands, blended with *he* to give *sche*. Only in western areas did *heo* survive as a distinctive feminine form with rounded vowel (Wright 161 ff.; Samuels 1972a, 115).

The forms for "she" in the many different scribal dialects of the *Piers Plowman* manuscripts naturally mirror these complex developments and indicate the stage reached in each dialect; we find *heo, hue, he, scheo, sche, she, ʒhe, ʒo* and *scho*, and, were it not for the evidence of the alliteration and the relict forms in the B manuscripts, we would find it difficult to decide which were Langland's. From that evidence, however, we can be fairly certain that he used the three forms *heo, sche* and *a* for "she," and *he* and *a* for "he."

It is perhaps difficult for the educated modern reader, brought up on Standard English, to grasp the fact that in Middle English two or more variants of the same personal pronoun, differentiated by functions of stress, markedness or style, could exist in a single dialect system. But that is still the case in certain modern dialects, and we know from localised Middle English texts from Worcestershire that the forms *heo, hoe, hue, ho, he, a, s(c)he* and *s(c)heo* were all used in that area, in varying combinations in the different texts. There are therefore no grounds for the view that Langland was combining his provincial *heo* with London *she* (Chambers 1919, 149).

The Middle English developments of the forms for "they" were only slightly less complex than those for "she," and, in the Midlands, closely connected with them. In the North, Old English *hie* was early replaced by *þei, they* etc. of Norse origin. In the East Midlands, the Old English form *heo* "they" was unrounded to *he* and was thus indistinguishable from "he" and "she" except by the accompanying verb endings (e.g. *he is*, singular, but *he arn*, plural); and in the West Midlands, the surviving *heo* "they" had the same form as *heo* "she." It is therefore not surprising that the northern *they* spread southwards in the thirteenth and fourteenth centuries, eventually also largely ousting the surviving southern form *hy (hij)*. For this pronoun South Worcestershire was a border area between midland *heo* and southern *hy*, but in the later fourteenth century *heo* had been largely replaced by *þey*, and Langland's forms, as shown by both the alliterations and the relict forms, were *þey* and *hij*. Here again, the co-occurrence of these two forms in a single system is well-evidenced (Samuels 1972a, 117).

Pronouns of the Second Person: *Thou* and *Ye*

The changes in the pronouns of the third person were largely functional in origin, affecting different areas at different times, and for them, Langland started from a different linguistic threshold from that of Chaucer. For the pronouns of the second person, that difference does not apply; here, a change of sociolinguistic origin was affecting the courtly language and gradually entering the system at other levels. In later Middle English, the plural *you/ye/your* was often used instead of the singular *thou/thee/thy*. In its origins from Latin and French this was basically a polite or respectful usage, typical of courtly style, but it was open to many nuances, which, as shown in Chaucer and works like *Sir Gawain and the Green Knight*, could be very complex. Depending on the status and relationship of the speakers, a switch from *thou* to *ye* could imply formality and distancing, whereas the opposite switch from *ye* to *thou* could imply a change towards reproof, insult, defiance or scorn, or, in different circumstances, rapprochement or conspiracy (Mustanoja 127; Burnley 21). However, *thou* was not limited to familiar and colloquial use, but was also, under the influence of literal translation from the Bible, normal in didactic and religious language; and this explains why Langland's language was less affected by the change. His themes are moral and religious, his style didactic, and his sources largely biblical; and, in the allegorical characters at least, there are no obvious indications of superior or inferior status. The result is that his use of *thou* and *ye* is firmly based on the normal grammatical distinction between singular and plural.

The difficulty of attempting to assess the extent of singular *ye/you/your* in Langland is the lack of certainty in the manuscript traditions as to what he actually wrote; since the feature is sociolinguistic in origin, the dialect criterion cannot provide the same guidance as it does elsewhere. Variation in the manuscripts shows that it was liable to continual alteration by scribes according to their own notions of propriety, and it can therefore be judged only by certain preponderances both within and across the three manuscript traditions. In general, a comparison of the three traditions shows a preponderance of *thou* in A, a considerable increase of *ye* in B, and in C either a continuation of B's use of *ye* or a return to the *thou* of A; but the interpretation of this distribution is beset by further problems. Certainly there are a number of passages where a consensus of the manuscripts produces the normal contrasts expected for the feature: for example, Holy Church addresses the Dreamer as *thou*, but the Dreamer uses mostly *ye/your* to Holy Church; and Meed uses *ye* to the King but *thou* to Conscience (A.3.162 ff. and correspondingly in B and C). But elsewhere there is much more mixture, the B text in particular showing switches to *ye/you* which seem to have been conditioned by polite phrases like *I preie yow . . . par charite* (B.6.253) and *ye profre yow so faire* (B.6.24). Such changes from *thou* in A are likely to have been scribal, even when, as in the former of these two instances, they were seemingly accepted by Langland when revising for C.

A more difficult problem is posed by passages which may show more complex contrasts, as at B.6.37 ff. Here A shows *thou* throughout, but B and C, as they stand, show alternations of *ye* and *thou*, starting with the polite request of *I preye yow of moore* and moving towards warning (*how shalt ȝelde it ayein . . . in . . . Purgatorie*) and prohibition (*mysbede noȝt þi bondemen*). Here again on the evidence of A, it is tempting to assume that these alternations in B are merely scribal; but the corresponding passage in C — even though it shows other signs of revision — retains them, and this might suggest that Langland saw nothing wrong with them. Then, if that hypothesis is accepted, it might be extended to the view that Langland might even have been responsible for them (or something like them) in B.

It thus remains an open question whether such nuances are scribal or authorial: we can either assume that Langland maintained the *thou* of preaching and biblical style throughout all three versions, with acceptance of only the simpler features of the later polite and courtly usage; or we can prefer to think that he might occasionally, in B and C, have availed himself of some of its nuances. As will appear below (p. 219), he would, as an educated cleric, have been perfectly well aware of them; but the distinctions were complex, and governed by stylistic as well as sociolinguistic choice. To speculate on that stylistic choice without firm textual evidence is merely to raise the spectre of the intentional fallacy.

Nouns and Adjectives

The ending *-es*, descending either from Old English *-es* (genitive singular) or *-as* (nominative plural), is the normal surviving inflection in Middle English nouns, but in the West Midland dialects it often appears as *-us*, *-is* or *-ys*, and it seems likely that Langland would have used a high proportion of such endings. But apart from the occasional survival of a genitive plural in *-ene* (OE *-ena*) as in *kingene kyng, for no lordene loue*, the Middle English reflex of the remaining Old English inflections is the written final *-e* in both nouns and adjectives.

Past controversy as to whether this *-e* was sounded as a syllable (Southworth; Robinson) has largely overlooked the fact that in many late-fourteenth- and early-fifteenth-century manuscripts there is a clear distinction in what can be proved to be the scribes' *own* usage, not that of their exemplars, between the strong adjective (without *-e*) and the weak (with *-e*). The claim that the *-e* in such cases is merely a traditional scribal relic, or that it was induced by a knowledge of formal grammar cannot be upheld, for (i) the distinction is specific to Germanic languages, and the only grammar taught in the fourteenth century was that of Latin, not English, and (ii) the conditioning of its distribution was extremely complex, being partly etymological, as in the adjectives *swete* and *grene*, and partly syntactical, as in *this olde man* compared with *an old man*. We can therefore be quite certain that if a scribe distinguishes between *old* when it follows "a(n)" "any," "each," "every," "some," "is," "was" and *olde* when it follows "the," "this," "that," the only possible basis for the usage must be a corresponding inherited distinction in his spoken language.

The fact that this *-e* can be proved to have been syllabic in Chaucer's time both agrees with the most likely interpretation of Chaucer's metre and casts further light on it (Samuels 1972b). Nevertheless, this usage of Chaucer's was a formal one, and there is much evidence from other scribes that the use of *-e* depended on varying conditions of stress, style and register; the individual usage of an author cannot be established simply on the evidence of when and where he lived. If there is no holograph, the only other possible evidence is the author's practice in writing syllabic metre. But the conclusions that can be drawn from stressed metre are much less certain. One possible indication is from half lines that would, with *-e*, have a common and normal rhythmical pattern, but without it become rare and unusual. Thus, at B.9.19 manuscripts which show *-e* (whether due to their scribe or his exemplar) give *bĭ hĭs fĭrste wy̆ue*, with a normal pattern of xx|/x|/x, whereas MS L (Skeat's text) has *bĭ hĭs first wy̆f*, with xx|/|/. Such a half-line, consisting of anacrusis ("prelude") plus two monosyllabic feet, is of course perfectly consonant with the timing of the four-stress line; but provable cases (i.e. those that have this pattern but could not, historically, admit grammatical -*e*) are decidedly rare, and are likely to have been used only for special effect. For example, the *Gawain*-poet used this pattern at 928 *and þe dér(e) úp* (with -*e* elided, as normal in mid-line), an effective use of it with excellent semantic motivation. Since it is a rare and remarkable pattern, there seem to be no good grounds for presupposing it in semantically unremarkable cases where grammatical -*e* would produce a correspondingly unremarkable and normal pattern. Such cases suggest that Langland is likely to have made at least some use of grammatical -*e*.

The Verb

For the forms of the verb, the Southwest Midland dialects in Middle English are to be classed with the Southern rather than the West Midland dialects. The main reason is that, whereas in the Midlands there was normally a distinction between -*eþ* (-*eth*) in the third singular present indicative and -*e(n)* in the plural, the Southwest Midland area, like the Southern, possessed no distinction between singular and plural, with -*eþ* for both except for the greater use of contracted forms like *fint* "finds," *chit* "chides" in the singular (Brunner 70; Wright 175).

The spread of Central Midland influences in the fourteenth century and later had a similar effect on the verb in both the London and the Southwest Midland areas, but reached London earlier than South Worcestershire. Langland's usage in verbs, therefore, would have been more conservative than Chaucer's: in the London English of Chaucer, -*eþ* had been virtually replaced by -*en*, but in South Worcestershire this change did not occur till after Langland's death. The result is that there is great mixture of -*eþ* and -*en* in both western and eastern manuscripts of *Piers Plowman*, but for different reasons. In western manuscripts the mixture would occur as a natural concomitant of the dialect at the turn of the century; but in London and other eastern manuscripts the expected distribution would be -*en* with only occasional -*eþ*, and the fact that these manuscripts show quite frequent -*eþ* is a strong indication that it was a feature of the scribes' exemplars. It therefore seems likely that Langland wrote predominantly -*eþ*, and, by the same token, *beoþ, buþ* or *beþ* "are" rather than *ben*, though, as already pointed out on p. 209 above, he also used the rarer variant *ar(e)n*.

There are a number of other ways in which Langland's verb-forms were more conservative than Chaucer's. Some of the more prominent are:

(i) Survival of the older metathesized forms for "run" from Old English *(ge-)yrnan, (ge-)ernan*, as seen in the infinitives *erne* and *ȝerne* as well as in the past singular *ȝorn*. These forms are well attested by alliteration, both on *e-* (B.19.378; C.18.163) and on *ȝ-* (B.15.188; C.12.12), though the later form *renne* is similarly attested.

(ii) Survival of the ending *-ye*, *-ie* or *-y* from Old English *-ian* in classes 1 and 2 of weak verbs, as in *louye* "love," *wonye* "dwell," *tilye* "cultivate," *erye* "plough" (Brunner 80; Wright 175). This feature survived in Southern and Southwest Midland dialects into the fifteenth century (and survives today in Somerset and Devon), whereas in London English it died out before Chaucer's time (Chaucer has it only in *herie* "praise"). As it is an inflection it cannot, like *(ȝ)erne* above, be proved by the alliteration, but it is another of the features that are attested by their preservation in the eastern manuscripts L and R.

(iii) Retention of double consonants in the infinitive and present stems of *habbe(n)* "have," *libben* "live," *buggen* "buy" and *seggen* "say." These, again, would be normal in southwestern dialects, but in London, though understood, would have been regarded as old-fashioned (they had occurred in the mid-fourteenth-century type of London English that preceded that of Chaucer, but even there were outnumbered by the modern forms; for texts see Samuels 1963, 87).

VARIABLE *-E* AND *-EN* IN VERBS

A grammatical feature that admits of especially wide variation is the Midland and Southern *-en*, which can vary both with *-e* and, according to dialect and context, with *-yn*, *-un* and *-on*, and occurs:

(a) in the infinitive, as in *fynde(n)*, *fyndyn*;
(b) in the past indicative and subjunctive plural as in *fo(u)nde(n)*, *-yn*, *-un*, *-on*;
(c) in the plural of preterite-present verbs, as in *schulle(n)*, *-yn*;
(d) in the present subjunctive plural, as in *ȝif þey fynde(n)*, *-yn*;
(e) in the present indicative plural, if *-eþ* is not used (cf. the preceding section).

In all these parts of the verb, the retention of *-n* would mean an extra syllable if the next word began with a vowel, as in *riden away*, whereas without *-n* that same syllable would be liable to elision, as in *rid(e) away*. Furthermore, in the preterite plural of weak verbs, there were three possible variants: *-ed*, *-ede* and *-eden*.

As has been shown recently by Smithers, Chaucer's use of these variants has been much misunderstood. Because the scribe of the Hengwrt and Ellesmere manuscripts of the *Canterbury Tales* often used longer forms than those intended by Chaucer, it has been wrongly assumed that Chaucer allowed hypermetric syllables in all such cases; but in fact Chaucer's metrical practice proves that -*e* and -*en* were in free variation, and that he regarded the addition of the extra syllable as optional. However, only syllabic metre, not stressed metre, will show which was intended. Thus in B.Prol.56 *cloped(en) hem in copes* it is impossible, on historical, dialectal or metrical grounds, to tell whether the first sequence of unstressed syllables should number three or four. The metrical question here may seem similar to that of -*e* in adjectives discussed above (pp. 215–16) but in fact differs, for whereas in adjectives the -*e* normally constitutes the only following unstressed syllable before the stressed noun, verbs are usually followed by a sequence of them, as in the example just quoted and others like *putten hem to plouȝ* (B.Prol.20), *to kissen his bulle* (73), *comen to a conseil* (148), *wasten þat men wynnen* (B.6.133). Most exceptions to this are of heavier lines which are no more revealing, e.g. *Beren beiȝes ful briȝte* (B.Prol.161), *And holpen ere þe half acre* (B.6.116). It is only in the rarer cases like *comen knelyng* (C.21.151) that we can be fairly certain that the -*en* is syllabic.

The Negatives *Ne* and *Not*

Whereas for a number of the grammatical features discussed above Langland appears more conservative than Chaucer, his use of negatives is more progressive.

The Old English negative was *ne*, as in *he ne cymþ* "he does not come." It continued to be used alone in Middle English, but mainly in subordinate clauses with a subjunctive verb. In main clauses it was strengthened by addition of the further negative adverb *nouȝt, nat, not*, etc. from Old English *no wiht* "no whit, not at all" (cf. Fr. *ne . . . pas*), placed after the verb, as in *he ne comeþ nouȝt*. Then, at varying periods according to dialect, *ne* was dropped, to give the normal late Middle English *he cometh not*; and in southern dialects this loss was taking place in the later fourteenth century. But whereas Chaucer's frequent *ne . . . nat* or *ne . . . noght* was, even for the London of his day, conservative, Langland normally used the simple *nauȝt* or *nat*, except that *ne* still survived in contracted forms like *nis* (= *ne is*), *nere* (= *ne were*), *nolde* (= *ne wolde*). It seems likely that, within each dialect system, the loss of *ne* took place first in colloquial register and entered formal register slightly later; but since the chronology of these changes may have differed in Worcestershire and London, they cannot be taken as proof that Langland's style is more colloquial than Chaucer's.

THE SOCIOLINGUISTIC STATUS OF LANGLAND'S WRITING

A question remaining from the preceding discussion is: How "dialectal" was Langland's language? As was shown above (p. 210), its regional character is vouched for by the presence of a specifically localisable combination of spellings. But the use of regional spellings must not, at this period, be taken to imply rusticity or lack of culture; other fourteenth-century writers like Rolle, Trevisa and the *Gawain*-poet all used regional spellings and were obviously educated men. Since no written standard yet existed, even London spellings of this period can be clearly identified and as yet carried no superior status (Samuels 1983b, 53 ff.). As with other Middle English writers, Langland's spellings can be regarded simply as his hallmark, and as of equal social status to those that we recognise as typical of Gower or Chaucer (cf. p. 203–04 above).

The answer to the question posed, therefore, could be judged only by comparison with the language of other texts from South Worcestershire (Samuels 1985, 242). That area, like London, was affected by the spread of innovatory and more prestigious features from the Central Midlands: an example is the form *þouȝ* "though," which was replacing the original S. Worcs. forms *þauh*, *þeih* and variants. Here, the consensus of the B manuscripts L and R with Worcestershire C manuscripts suggests that Langland's forms were *þouh* and *þeih* rather than *þauh*, that is, he seems to have avoided the more dialectal form. Similarly, there are a number of other features of "broader" dialect which do not appear in these B and C manuscripts: *ant* "and," *myt* "with," *-et* and *-ut* in past participles, addition of unhistorical *h-*, and omission of historical *h-*. On this evidence, Langland's written language could be placed fairly high in the sociolinguistic scale. On the other hand, it could be argued that Langland's holographs could actually have contained a higher proportion of dialect spellings than is vouched for by the B and C manuscripts in question, and that these were all later replaced by copyists.* Here, the very nature of our evidence seems to preclude an answer.

*In this connection it is relevant to note that the "Z text" (ed. Rigg and Brewer 1983) would answer well to this description: apart from a slight veneer of features deriving from a later copyist, this text shows all the characteristics typical of S. Worcs. texts in "broader" dialect. Of especial interest is the addition and omission of *h-* (as in *hasket* "asks," *ast* "hast"), since this both agrees with, and shows the basis of, Langland's practice of alliterating *h-* with initial vowels.

REFERENCES

Benskin, M. "The Middle English Dialect Atlas." Benskin and Samuels xxvii–xli.

―――, and Margaret Laing. "Translations and *Mischsprachen* in Middle English Manuscripts." Benskin and Samuels 55–106.

―――, and M. L. Samuels. *So Meny People Longages and Tonges: Philological Essays in Scots and Medieval English Presented to Angus McIntosh.* Edinburgh: The Editors, 1981.

Brunner, K. *An Outline of Middle English Grammar.* Trans. G. K. W. Johnston. Oxford: Blackwell, and Cambridge, MA: Harvard University Press, 1963.

Burnley, David. *A Guide to Chaucer's Language.* London: Macmillan, 1983.

Burrow, J. A. *Ricardian Poetry: Chaucer, Gower, Langland and the Gawain Poet.* London: Routledge & Kegan Paul, 1971.

Chambers, R. W. "The Three Texts of *Piers Plowman* and their Grammatical Forms." *MLR* 14 (1919): 129–51.

―――. "The Manuscripts of *Piers Plowman* in the Huntington Library, and Their Value for Fixing the Text of the Poem." *HLB* 8 (1935): 1–25.

Donaldson, E. Talbot. *Piers Plowman: The C-Text and Its Poet.* Yale Studies in English 113. New Haven: Yale University Press, 1949.

Doyle, A. I., and M. B. Parkes. "The Production of Copies of the *Canterbury Tales* and the *Confessio Amantis* in the Early Fifteenth Century." M. B. Parkes and A. G. Watson, eds. *Medieval Scribes, Manuscripts and Libraries: Essays presented to N. R. Ker.* London: Scolar Press, 1978. 163–210.

Elliot, R. W. V. "The Langland Country." Hussey 226–44.

Gray, Douglas, and E. G. Stanley, eds. *Middle English Studies Presented to Norman Davis.* Oxford: Clarendon Press, 1983.

Hussey, S. S., ed. *Piers Plowman: Critical Approaches.* London: Methuen, 1969.

Kane, George. *Piers Plowman: The Evidence for Authorship.* London: Athlone Press, 1965.

―――. "The Autobiographical Fallacy in Chaucer and Langland Studies." Chambers Memorial Lecture. London: H. K. Lewis, 1965.

―――. "Music 'Neither Unpleasant Nor Monotonous.'" *Medieval Studies for J. A. W. Bennett.* Ed. P. L. Heyworth. Oxford: Clarendon Press, 1981. 43–63.

―――, and E. Talbot Donaldson, eds. *Piers Plowman: The B Version. Will's Visions of Piers Plowman, Do-Well, Do-Better and Do-Best.* London: Athlone, 1975.

Kittner, H. *Studien zum Wortschatz William Langlands.* Diss., Universität Halle. Wurzburg: K. Triltsch, 1937.

Kristensson, G. "On Middle English Dialectology." Benskin and Samuels 3–13.

McIntosh, Angus. "The Analysis of Written Middle English." *Transactions of the Philological Society* (1956): 26–55.

―――. "The Textual Transmission of the Alliterative *Morte Arthure*." *English and Medieval Studies Presented to J. R. R. Tolkien.* Ed. Norman Davis and C. L. Wrenn. London: Allen & Unwin, 1962. 231–40.

―――. "Word Geography in the Lexicography of Medieval English." *Annals of the New York Academy of Sciences* 211 (1973): 55–66.

―――. "Towards an Inventory of Middle English Scribes." *NM* 75 (1974): 602–24.

―――. "Scribal Profiles from Middle English Texts." *NM* 76 (1975): 218–35.

Mustanoja, Tauno F. *A Middle English Syntax. Part I, Parts of Speech.* Mémoires de la Société Néophilologique de Helsinki 23. Helsinki: Société Néophilologique, 1960.

Oakden, J. P. *Alliterative Poetry in Middle English*. 2 vols. Manchester: Manchester University Press, 1930.

Reynolds, L. D., and N. G. Wilson. *Scribes and Scholars: A Guide to the Transmission of Greek and Latin Literature*. 2nd. rev. and enlarged edition. Oxford: Clarendon Press, 1974.

Rigg, A. G., and Charlotte Brewer, eds. *Piers Plowman: The Z Version*. Toronto: Pontifical Institute of Mediaeval Studies, 1983.

Robinson, Ian. *Chaucer's Prosody: A Study of the Middle English Verse Tradition*. Cambridge: Cambridge University Press, 1971.

Salter, Elizabeth, and Derek Pearsall, eds. *Piers Plowman*. York Medieval Texts. London: Arnold, 1967.

Samuels, M. L. "Some Applications of Middle English Dialectology." *ES* 44 (1963): 81–94.

———. "The Dialects of MS Bodley 959." *MS Bodley 959: Genesis-Baruch 3.20 in the Earlier Version of the Wycliffite Bible*. Ed. C. Lindberg. 6 vols. (1959–73). Stockholm: Almqvist & Wiksell, 1969. 5:329–39.

———. *Linguistic Evolution, with special reference to English*. Cambridge: Cambridge University Press, 1972.

———. "Chaucerian Final -*e*." *N&Q* 217 ns 19 (1972): 445–48.

———. "Spelling and Dialect in the Late and Post Middle English Periods." Benskin and Samuels 1981, 43–54.

———. "Chaucer's Spelling." Gray and Stanley 1983, 17–37.

———. "The Scribe of the Hengwrt and Ellesmere Manuscripts of *The Canterbury Tales*." *SAC* 5 (1983): 49–65.

———. "Langland's Dialect." *MÆ* 54 (1985): 232–47.

———, and J. J. Smith. "The Language of Gower." *NM* 82 (1981): 295–304.

Schmidt, A. V. C. "The Authenticity of the Z-Text of *Piers Plowman*: A Metrical Examination." *MÆ* 53 (1984): 295–300.

Schumacher, Karl. *Studien über den Stabreim in der mittelenglischen Alliterationsdichtung*. Bonner Studien zur englischen Philologie 11. Bonn: Peter Hanstein, 1914.

Skeat, W. W., ed. *The Vision of William concerning Piers the Plowman: The "Whitaker" Text; or Text C*. EETS 54. London: Trübner, 1873.

Smithers, G. V., ed. *Kyng Alisaunder*, 2. EETS 237. London: Oxford University Press, 1957.

———. "The Scansion of *Havelok* and the Use of ME -*en* and -*e* in *Havelok* and by Chaucer." Gray and Stanley 195–234.

Southworth, J. G. *Verses of Cadence: An Introduction to the Prosody of Chaucer and his Followers*. Oxford: Blackwell, 1954.

———. *The Prosody of Chaucer and his Followers: Supplementary Chapters to Verses of Cadence*. Oxford: Blackwell, 1962.

Strang, Barbara M. H. *A History of English*. London: Methuen, 1970.

Ten Brink, Bernhard. *The Language and Metre of Chaucer*. Trans. M. Bentinck Smith. London: Macmillan, 1901.

Turville-Petre, Thorlac. *The Alliterative Revival*. Cambridge: D. S. Brewer, 1977.

Wright, J., and E. M. Wright. *An Elementary Middle English Grammar*. London: Oxford University Press, 1928.

9

ALLITERATIVE STYLE
DAVID A. LAWTON

ALLITERATIVE POETRY AND THE MODERN READER

Modern readers of traditional English verse-forms are used to the idea that poetry is a contest between form and language, metre and rhythm. *Rhythm* is unavoidable in all language: everyone has a speech-rhythm that is partly idiosyncratic, reflecting the metabolism and temperament of the individual speaker, and partly conditioned by culture and place, the time and social context of the speaker and the utterance. Rhythm varies not only from speaker to speaker but from language to language; it also varies among geographic areas of one language, and from one historical period to another. Any written discourse will reflect the rhythm of the language more or less self-consciously; more so, generally, in the case of literary discourse, and with a greater than usual degree of formalisation. Churchill's famous tribute to the airmen who fought in the Battle of Britain is a clear example: "Never in the field of human conflict was so much owed by so many to so few." This is not the word-order of casual conversation: its rhythm is selected in the interests of balance (two adverbial phrases around the inverted verb/subject cluster, "was so much owed"), repetition, parallelism, variation and contrast ("by so many to so few"). These effects are the devices common to self-conscious rhythmical organisation; such rhythm is a characteristic of literary discourse, whether poetry or prose. *Metre* however, is an extra pattern generally distinctive to poetry, a deliberate overloading of the circuits of the language, an abstract sound-pattern (the x / x / x / x / of the iambic pentameter, for example) played on and against the rhythms of the language (the actual sound and meaning of the words used). This sort of metre is a genuine *measure*: it creates a temporal expectation of the intervals between stressed syllables.

With Langland's sort of poetry, however, the situation is a little different. There is no device that measures the intervals between stresses with anything like the notional predictability of the iambic pentameter. Rhythm therefore appears less constrained, and the reader is struck equally by insistent rhythmicality and by the intrusive use of alliteration:

a-verse		*b-verse*
13 [Ac] as I biheeld into þe Eest,	/	an heiȝ to þe sonne,
14 I seiȝ a tour on a toft	/	trieliche ymaked,
15 A deep dale bynéþe	/	a dongeon þerinne
16 Wiþ depe diches and derke	/	and dredfulle of siȝte.
17 A fair feeld fùl of folke	/	fond I þer bitwene
18 Of alle manere of men,	/	þe meene and þe riche,
19 Werchynge and wandrynge	/	as þe world askeþ.

(B.Prol.13–19)

These seven long lines consist of fourteen half-lines, or *verses*, each of which has its own rhythmical structure and integrity. In the standard terms for describing this structure (see Oakden 1:175 and Davis 148, after Sievers 1887, 1893), most verses consist of two *lifts* and two *dips*: a lift is a *stressed* syllable (/) and a dip one or more *unstressed* syllables (x..). The lifts and dips may be arranged in different ways and produce different rhythms: *falling*, where the verse generally begins with a lift and ends in a dip (15b, 17b, 19a); *rising*, where the verse begins with a dip and ends in a lift (13a, 14a, 18a), or *rising-falling*, where the verse begins and ends with a dip (13b, 15b, 16b, 18b, 19b). This last type is most common in *Piers Plowman*. Some verses, however, may have *three* lifts with either two or three dips (15a, 16a, 17a): these will usually be a-verses. The rising rhythm is more common in a-verses, and the falling in b-verses, in part because final -e is elided within the long line when followed by a vowel but probably sounded at the line's end. It should also be noted that the fairly frequent loss of final -e and decay of inflexions in later Middle English led to a type of verse, / x(x)(x) /, which begins and ends on a lift ("wenten forth in hire wey," B.Prol.48a): what was originally a falling pattern has developed what might be called a falling-rising rhythm. Finally, while lifts are usually separated by dips, in some verses they stand together in what is known as a *clashing* rhythm (15a, 16a, 17a, 19b). This terminology, though conventional, is of limited usefulness. It could be summarised as saying that in two-stress phrases, all combinations of two stressed and three unstressed positions occur; there is also, generally in the a-verse, a three-stress pattern. There is considerable variation in the duration of verses, but only that variation which the language permits among two-stress (and sometimes three-stress) phrases. It is from this narrow range of choices that Langland assembles his permutations of varied rhythmical types. The criteria for judging their effect are again balance, repetition, parallelism, contrast and skilful variation. For the form has these properties in abundance.

Tabulation of *alliterative patterns* shows another set of relations and differences, this time across rather than within the two verses that make up the long line. The notation is simplicity itself: in the most common case (lines 13, 14, 18, 19 above) *aa/ax*, where *a* stands for the fall of *primary* alliteration (i.e. the alliteration that binds the long line, in which there may also be secondary alliteration) and *x* for a prominent syllable without alliteration. Since the *aa/ax* pattern is normative, the last stress of most long lines is without alliteration; but there may be other prominent syllables within the line that do not bear alliteration, and these should also be marked *x*. Here *x* is always used to mean non-alliterating. (Some scholars, however, resort to both *x* and *y* if there are two prominent non-alliterating syllables: this is potentially confusing.) Line 14 could be classified *aa/ax* or *(x)aa/ax*, if one "hears" a stress on *seiȝ*; line 15 could be classified *aa/ax* or *aax/ax*, if one hears a stress on *byneþe*, or even *aaa/ax* if one claims a sufficient similarity, as some scholars do, between *d* and *n*. The oblique stroke in *aa/ax* divides the line into two verses and stands for the caesura, marked by many scribes (thus "$\overset{a}{w}$erchynge and $\overset{a}{w}$andrynge / as þe $\overset{a}{w}$orld $\overset{x}{a}$skeþ"). The letters marked *a* are conventionally called *staves*, i.e. sounds bearing primary alliteration. Secondary alliteration is marked *b*, and so on. Lines with three-stave a-verses, such as 16a, are classified *aaa/ax*, even though there is some possibility of stress-levelling, here between *depe* and *diches*—a possibility that cannot be ignored in line 17a, in which one should not acknowledge four stresses. Lines with the same alliterative pattern may be rhythmically contrasting (compare, for example, lines 18 and 19 above), for alliterative patterns establish a purely formal relationship.

The evidence of alliteration no doubt influences judgments about rhythm. In an adjective/noun combination, one would normally expect the noun to carry greater stress; acceptance above of verses 16a and 17a as having three stresses, not two, acknowledges the weight of alliteration in this context. Nevertheless, rhythm and alliteration have different functions and are two principles of composition, not one. The rhythm does not depend on the alliteration. Alliteration usually falls on stressed syllables, but in *Piers Plowman* does not always do so; and not all syllables unmarked by alliteration are unstressed (particularly, and normatively, the last lift of the b-verse, the *x* of the *aa/ax* pattern). As a principle of composition, rhythm does not extend beyond the verse. It is the alliteration, in various patterns, that knits the two verses together into a long line. The organising principle of the long line, therefore, is alliteration; and it is in this sense, it will be argued here, that alliteration deserves to be called the *metre* of alliterative poetry, even though — unlike most other metres — it does not *measure*. Yet, like other metres, it is an artificial regulation, a pattern, superimposed on rhythm. The question is how well the regulation and the rhythm work together, whether and to what extent they make a whole greater than the sum of its parts.

Admittedly, the collaboration of rhythm and alliteration has served to keep *Piers Plowman* on the fringes of the main tradition of English metres and metrical analysis. To Derek Attridge, for instance, who has given us the best modern account of the rhythms of English poetry, Langland's verse-form seems anomalous. It contradicts his central argument that "Four-Beat Verse" distorts the rhythms of English speech in a way that five-beat patterns do not: it "is not language raised to a higher pitch of orderliness, but speech granted extra force by the highlighting of significant words, and cumulative power by the succession of discrete but parallel units of rhythm, sound and sense" (326); "the metre has a rhythmic character quite different from that of the regular four-beat line" (325). The reason is the range and relative unpredictability in the number of unstressed syllables between two lifts (or, as Attridge calls them, beats), "too great a range to create the alternating rhythm by which we identify regular verse. The 'beats' of this metre are not peaks of energy balanced against equivalent valleys, but isolated alps jutting up from foothill ranges" (324–25). All this is shrewd, but it leads Attridge to offer some disappointing advice: "The wisest course for the modern reader is probably to concentrate on the vigorous speech-rhythms, and let the metre fend for itself; the rhythmic strength of Langland's verse lies in its energetic freedom, not in the tight control of metrical form" (325).

Attridge omits any possibility that there may be both aesthetic and semantic enrichment in the way Langland plays rhythm against metre: "no firm metrical set is established, and the verse lacks the expressive potential of variation from a strict norm. . . . [It] often requires something of a conscious effort — at least for the modern reader — to place the beats on the alliterated syllables and not on the supernumerary stresses" (325). The problem should be evident from the scansion of the seven lines presented above; for it is not the only possible scansion. Why not, for instance, place a stress on the verb in line 14a, "I seiȝ a *t*our on a *t*oft"? Because, rightly or wrongly, the alliteration has been allowed to determine the scansion. But it is not always feasible to do this: there are lines in *Piers Plowman* where alliteration and stress are dramatically at odds. Where Attridge would simply follow the stress and ditch the alliteration, others claim that "a conscious effort" would yield an insight similar to those we have on discovering iambic pentameters with four or six stresses rather than five: an insight, that is, into the counterpoint, or *modulation*, of metre and rhythm, pattern and sense.

George Kane finds in *Piers Plowman* a kind of modulation that he implicitly compares to iambic pentameter by calling it "tension" (50). Perhaps "tension" is better reserved for stricter metres; for the tension in iambic pentameter is generated by the frustration of a temporal expectation, in the deviation from a very tight notional pattern, and the metre of alliterative poetry is too variable a pattern, and too loose in its intervals, ever to capture a quality of modulation such as we find, say, in the opening of *Paradise Lost*. Yet in *Piers Plowman* there is a different quality of modulation, and it is a potentially meaningful resource (see below, p. 232). Langland's poetry does stage a contest between rhythm and metre, though neither rhythm nor metre behaves, or can be defined, quite as in "regular verse." What, then, is the expressive potential of Langland's verse-form? This is the question addressed in this chapter. The author will not approach it by means of quantitative analysis: there is a need for such work, but it could scarcely be done intelligibly, if it can yet be done at all reliably, in less than a weighty monograph. (For the best example of older quantitative analysis, see Schumacher.) The primary task here is to help readers to make informed judgments for themselves, and to introduce them to the issues they must take into account in arriving at an understanding of the interaction between pattern and meaning in *Piers Plowman*. In this aid to self-help, the first three sections are general, with few examples; the fourth section is an analysis of one passage, laid out for ease of cross-reference to the first three sections; the fifth section deals briefly with the central literary-historical issues. The discussion initially is technical in nature. Yet it can be said, in defence, that what may strike some readers as jargon is nothing of the kind, but a specialised vocabulary indispensable to a study of metre and style, each term of which is defined on its first occurrence. The focus and direction of this study embrace technique, not technicalities — the technique that enabled Langland to write a great poem.

THE UNRHYMED ALLITERATIVE LONG LINE

Historically, studies of the unrhymed alliterative long line of *Piers Plowman* have been complicated by two related factors. The first is its resemblance to that of Old English poetry. The second is that *Piers Plowman* at least coincides, in the second half of the fourteenth century, with a considerable number of other poems such as the *Gawain* group, composed in the same basic metre but quite different in subject and style. One consequence has been that questions of provenance and literary relations have cast a long shadow over those of metre. A second consequence has been that Old English poetic practice has influenced the terms of analysis for the metre of Middle English alliterative poetry. The influence has not gone without protest, from earlier prosodists who claimed an exception, six or seven beats to a line, as the norm of the Middle English line (Kaluza; Leonard; see Lawton 1980a), or more recently from those concerned that the method prejudges questions of provenance (Matonis 1981). The real objection is perhaps contingent: more and more readers of *Piers Plowman* approach the poem without benefit of Anglo-Saxon. Moreover, analyses based on the standard treatments of Old English metre (Sievers; Heusler) move freely between two classes of evidence: language patterns and alliteration. Following McIntosh (1982) the first of these is here called the *rhythmical system* (i.e. the structure of the individual verses), and the second the *metrical system* (i.e. alliteration, the formal principle that binds the verses into a long line).

THE RHYTHMICAL SYSTEM

A useful distinction again comes from McIntosh (1982, 21–22). Rhythmically, English metres come in one of two forms. They are *homomorphic*, that is, all the feet partake of the same basic nature and are genuine metrical feet (as in iambic poetry, whether rhymed couplets or blank verse, where each foot is an iamb or a permissible variant such as trochee or dactyl). Or they are *heteromorphic*, as in accentual or free verse, where the rhythmical units constituting the line are many and varied in type. Alliterative poetry is heteromorphic.

Standard ("prose") English discourse does not confine itself happily to iambs, trochees or dactyls. It need not follow that heteromorphic forms are closer than homomorphic ones to standard, spoken English discourse. Indeed, a highly regular four-stress metre may interact with heteromorphic forms in such a way as to distort normal speech-rhythms, as in nursery rhymes. But in poetry using homomorphic forms, like the iambic pentameter, an effect of easy colloquial informality is a product of high art, whereas a looser metre, like that of *Piers Plowman*, using heteromorphic forms, may achieve a similar result altogether more naturally. That is why alliterative poetry has been described as "a sort of talking style" (P. F. Baum, quoted in Salter 1969, 15) and demands from the engaged reader a spoken performance. English is also a characteristically *phrasal* language: we write, think, and speak in distinct phrases. These are composed of two or three stresses: a one-stress phrase is a single word, and anything over three would split into smaller units. The *verses* (i.e. half-lines) of alliterative poetry are not artificial "feet" but standard English phrases.

For this reason alone, ignorance of Old English poetry and late nineteenth-century German scholarship need not handicap modern readers of *Piers Plow-*

man. The five types of Anglo-Saxon verses proposed by Sievers constitute a taxonomy of the stress-pattern of every half-line of Old English poetry. They can be adapted, with some morphological strain (as in Stobie), to the verses of *Piers Plowman*; but the exercise might be academic if one agrees with Daunt that the five types "are language patterns, not metrical patterns" (291).

Less happily, Daunt added: "Old English verse is really conditioned prose, i.e. the spoken language specially arranged with alliteration, but arranged in a way that does no violence to the spoken words" (290). This certainly explains why we find the five types — the rhythmical and phrasal patterns of alliterative poetry — in the prose of Ælfric (see Pope), and the history of late Old English prose style(s) provides several possible lines of transmission to Middle English alliterative poetry (McIntosh 1982, 1949). But there are grounds for caution here. How can "conditioned prose" be the same as "the spoken language"?

The danger is twofold. General prosodists might be led to argue that alliterative poetry is "a very heavily accentual prosody in which sense rhythm rather than any abstract metrical imperative tends to supply the meter" (Fussell 75); scholarly advocates of alliterative poetry might answer that all poetry is based on natural speech stress (Bliss 1962a, b). Both these extremes would imply that alliterative poetry is all rhythm and no metre. Lawlor has stated that the phrase "alone constitutes the principle of this verse-making" (198). If this were so, both *Beowulf* and *Piers Plowman* would be better still in blank verse or prose, and alliteration is nothing but a nuisance. Norton-Smith comes close to saying just this (29).

The role of alliteration can be understood only if we understand what it acts upon. "Sense rhythm" or "natural speech stress" signify *phrasal stress*, which is the *verse-stress* of alliterative poetry. It must be distinguished from *lexical* stress. Lexical stress is straightforward: every English word has one primary stress, and except in rare cases of compound words or certain foreign names (e.g., *Nabugodonosar*) where two equal stresses are conventionally sanctioned, that is all readers of *Piers Plowman* need recognise. Phrasal stress is complex: Halle and Keyser come up with 154 rules and four different degrees. For phrasal stress, while it does not violate lexical stress, overrides it.

"Any stressed syllable bears a potential for accent; whether that potential is fulfilled will depend on broader conditions of meaning and emphasis" (Chatman 58). By *accent* Chatman means the interaction of metrical norm and phrasal stress; and he argues for its definition not in terms of loudness or amplitude but as a kinaesthetic feeling of muscular sympathy induced by pitch, frequency, duration, intensity and perhaps vowel quality. Accent is not *isochronous* (i.e. recurring as if by metronome at exactly equal time

intervals) but predictable. In the last resort, it is not a percept, a phonological given, but a concept, a semantic (and phonological) recognition. The
judgment of qualified readers as to where it falls will therefore vary: otherwise all good Shakespearean actors should sound the same. McIntosh (1982,
30) acknowledges this contextual subjectivity by calling accent *prominence*,
which is really a competent judgment on semantic weight. Phrasal stress
is the verse-stress of alliterative poetry. But it is by no means always its verse
accent. The phrasal patterns of alliterative poetry are regulated by a purely
formal device — alliteration; and because it is so regulated, the poetry of *Piers
Plowman* is not exactly "natural speech"; nor, given the limited number of
rhythms employed, is it exactly "prose rhythm." All English poetic metre
demands a subtle distortion of "natural speech rhythm." That is what metrical
systems achieve, and what they are there for. They make for greater density of semantic emphasis than unregulated discourse.

THE METRICAL SYSTEM

"Alliteration is no more the whole secret of this verse than rhyme is the
whole secret of syllabic verse. It has, in addition, a metrical structure, which
could stand alone, and which would then be to this system as blank verse
is to the syllabic" (Lewis 305). The point made here is unimpeachable, but
what Lewis calls "metrical structure" is the *rhythmical* system described above.
Skeat (1868) saw alliteration as the metrical *ictus*, i.e. the driving force, of
the unrhymed alliterative long line; without it the poetry of *Piers Plowman*
would in fact be a short-line form, for it is the alliteration that binds the
verses across the (fixed, hence metrical) medial caesura.

It must not be assumed that phrasal stress and the *ictus* of alliteration always coincide: the frequency with which the two diverge in *Piers Plowman*
is discussed below. This divergence sets *Piers* apart from other alliterative
poems, but the case may have been overstated by scholars consulting the
extensive but unreliable tabulation of alliterative patterns by Oakden. Oakden is reluctant to admit the feature outside the *Piers Plowman* tradition. He
scans this line from *William of Palerne* (2033) as *aa/bb* — i.e. as two verses each
with internal but without linking alliteration: "On þe *b*oldest *b*arn þat euer
bi*s*trod *s*tede." Clearly, however, the line can also, and should, be scanned
aa/abb if the alliteration on the unstressed syllable "*b*istod" is accepted as
primary, leaving a normal pattern with secondary alliteration and requiring modulation. Langland offers many comparable examples (Kane 1981).

In order to assess the effect of such lines, it is best to reserve the term
accent for instances where phrasal stress and *ictus* incontrovertibly coincide:
lines in which there is a conflict between the two challenge the reader to

resolve a tension between rhythmical and metrical systems by assigning prominence. The final stress in an *aa/ax* pattern should be called the *x-stress*: it is without ictus but in this it follows the design of the metrical system. What if there is a non-alliterating but prominent syllable before the first stave of either verse? This is where Old English systems prove misleading. Followers of Heusler (such as Sapora) discount these as *anacrusis*, that is, as preliminary to the metrical system of the verse; followers of Sievers (Borroff), and in effect those who employ musical notation (Hieatt), allow the existence of anacrusis in some rhythmical types while rejecting it in others. Since examples of this kind from *Piers Plowman* (Kane 47 n.11) clearly belong with other verses requiring resolution — as do verses in which Langland uses the occasional licence of exempting speech formulae ("quod he") from the metrical system of the line — they are best treated together.

This all introduces *modulation*, but some other comments must first be made:

(i) Because the first stave of the b-verse cements the bond of the long line, it is generally regarded as the "head" stave (or "chief-letter"): Bliss (1958, 110) rightly calls this a "convenient fiction," since the first stave of the a-verse usually alerts the reader to the alliteration of the line.

(ii) The primary alliteration of *Piers Plowman* is structural in that it is the main part of the metrical system. There is much less room than in other poetry for lyrical appreciation of its phonological appropriateness or onomatopoeic effect, and such other comments on alliteration that sometimes mark, though they rarely distinguish, "practical" criticism of post-medieval poetry, in which the alliteration is not a structural feature.

(iii) The line admits secondary alliteration and some complex patterns of cross-alliteration (for all these see Kane 1981; also Matonis 1981, 1984). They are secondary to the metrical system marked as *a*-staves, but like the *a*-staves they are of mainly lexicogrammatical, rather than phonological, weight. It is unhelpful to classify these as "ornamental."

(iv) Whereas disparity between phrasal stress and ictus requires resolution, variable treatment of *lexical* stress is an acceptable alliterative licence. For this see Kane-Donaldson 133–34.

(v) Kane-Donaldson establish beyond doubt that Langland regarded three staves as normative, and their edition uses, as a fundamental principle for approaching an "authorial" text, the preference for the *aa/ax* pattern displayed by Langland as by all other poets of fully worked Middle English unrhymed alliterative poems (Oakden 1:181–200; for apparent exceptions see Lawton 1982, 12). Henceforth, these will be referred to here as *aa/ax* poems. Clearly, Langland accepted some variant patterns: *aa/aa* is common, especially in moments of formality like the poem's opening line: "In a somer seson whan softe was þe sonne" (B.Prol.1). He also employed a three-stave a-verse, to which the evidence of alliteration points unambiguously (B.Prol.16; see above, p. 224). Sometimes such an a-verse is allowed to break the bond of the line: Kane-Donaldson accept both *aaa/xx* and *aaa/bb* as authentic. Here it is as if three identical staves matter more than the bond across the caesura. Kane-Donaldson also put up a strong case for rejecting other patterns as spurious, including any patttern that gives only two identical staves (e.g., *aa/xx*, *ax/ax*, *aa/bb*, *ab/ab*), though they are often compelled to let such readings stand, especially *ax/ax*. A. V. C. Schmidt (1984, 296) admits both *axax* and *abab*, together with *axaa*, into his type III ("reduced") of alliterative patterns in *Piers Plowman*, though he concedes that the type is rare. Schmidt's type II ("clustered") consists of *aaaxx* and *aaabb*, and his type I ("standard") of *aaax* ("normative"), enriched (*aaaa*) and extended (*aaaax*) variants, another that is both enriched and extended (*aaaaa*) and a "blank extended" variant (*aaxax*). Schmidt shows that these ten types cover all the long lines of *Piers Plowman*, though he may have economised by not marking the caesura.

(vi) Most significant is the persuasive Kane-Donaldson rejection of *aa/xa*, which would place an alliterative stave on the final stress. According to Schmidt's notation (1984), most patterns leave the final stress unmarked by alliteration. This is of vital importance to the question of provenance, for it marks the style of *aa/ax* poetry as radically different from Middle English examples of heavily alliterating prose (Stone 109) and all Middle English *rhymed* alliterative poems, in which alliteration habitually falls with rhyme on the final stress: see the examples provided by McIntosh (1982) and Matonis (1981), who seem to underrate this difficulty. Similarly, the overwhelming preference for the *aa/ax* type as normative marks a substantial departure from Old English poetic practice, though in Old English poetry too the final stress of the line is generally unalliterated.

MODULATION

Traditionally, Langland's permissiveness towards alliteration on unstressed syllables has been censured as a fault (since Skeat 1868). Yet what has been described so far are the conditions for a fruitful interplay between rhythmical and metrical systems: "The two patterns might coincide: lines where this occurred . . . would be normative. To make the patterns coincide only partially was to modulate the line" (Kane 48). Modulation is a semantic resource, fraught with potential meaning. Kane has provided a strong and detailed defence of Langland's practice, and his essay is essential reading (though the reader should note that Kane calls "metrical accents" what are here called phrasal stress and assigned to the rhythmical system). With copious examples that cannot be repeated Kane demonstrates that

> The interest . . . generated by modulation is at least as much intellectual as it is sensory. Expert modulation implies for the reader/hearer the question why the poet undertook it, which directs him to the meaning of the line. (50)

It sets up a "competition for prominence between the two patterns" that supplies the extra semantic weight, the quickening we expect from poetic discourse: the elevation of language by metre and phrasal patterning, where stress, accent and ictus are potentially out of alignment, each making slightly different demands, in order to accommodate a concentration and density of meaning. Schmidt (1984) talks about the same phenomenon in terms of "blank" (stress without alliteration) and "mute" (alliteration without stress).

Kane's essay corrects a traditional failure, by both general prosodists and too many specialists, to take seriously the alliterative verse form of *Piers Plowman*. It can no longer appear "a delightfully simple subject" (Fraser 14). On the one hand, we should be careful not to view metre as "an ideal and thus invariable formal pattern" (Fussell 4), for either we may then doubt the desirability of attaining the ideal—hence the frequent claim that a metrically perfect line in which metre and "prose" rhythm correspond would be a weak line, when one can in fact point to any number of excellent "perfect" pentameters, or indeed of *aa/xx* lines in *Piers* where there is no divergence of any kind between rhythmical and metrical demands; or we may elevate it, as an ideal, to an overblown status: "Meter is . . . meaning" (Gross 2). On the other hand, modulation is significant because it is a marked departure from an established metrical norm, in heteromorphic and homomorphic poetry alike (in many iambic pentameters we rightly hear four not five main stresses). Its resolution is a matter not for scansion but for competent performance, critical judgment on meaning, by the reader. Readers respond to the deviation because they have been made aware of the norm. The importance of modulation in Langland's poetry, therefore, does not detract from but enhances the key role of alliteration.

STYLE AND *aa/ax* FORM

Metre is not meaning; but it is one of its prime exponents. To appreciate the style of alliterative poetry, we must realise how much follows from the verse form. Modulation is the smallest and most easily grasped example of the interaction of rhythmical and metrical systems in the normatively *aa/ax* line; but that interaction has other larger consequences. Norton-Smith, who views the *Piers Plowman* line almost wholly in terms of its rhythmical system ("phraseological emphasis"), has noted its effect on syntax: "The effect of phraseological emphasis is not primarily rhythmic . . . but grammatical" (29). Skeat, who concentrated on the metrical system, testified succinctly to alliteration's lexical foregrounding: "It may be said that alliteration draws attention rather to the *words* themselves than to their initial syllable" (xxii). Similarly, Huppé ascribed to metre Langland's tendency to wordplay. Lexicogrammatical features of the style follow the potential of the verse form.

Just as there are differences between Langland's handling of the verse form and that of contemporary or slightly later alliterative poets, so there are too in style. One must recognise at least two distinct styles within the *aa/ax* corpus, "classical" and "non-classical" (Pearsall 1977, adapting McIntosh 1949) or "formal" and "informal" (Lawton 1982). The informal group consists of *Piers* and other poems in the Langland tradition (such as *Mum and the Sothsegger*), the formal group virtually the rest of *aa/ax* poems — mainly, but not exclusively, "alliterative romances." Neither group is at all monolithic in style, and there are many differences from poem to poem within each group as well as similarities between poems in different groups. The distinction is inadequate, then, but necessary — if only because Langland's informal style has mostly been described quasi-historically as a conscious deviation from that of formal *aa/ax* poetry. This issue will be deferred until the discussion of "Affiliations" below.

Syntax

(i) *Word-order*. This subject invites a far fuller treatment than can be accommodated here. Suffice it to say that both rhythmical and metrical types of patterning in alliterative poetry drastically affect word-order: the rhythmical, in the limited number of formalised patterns available and the apparent preference for placing rising types in the a-verse and falling types in the b-verse, and the metrical, in the need to arrange the alliterating lexical sets of each line so that, normally, two of its three elements fall in the a-verse. Balance, contrast, repetition, parallelism and variation make further demands. The most common sign of all these influences is syntactic inversion. "A fair feeld ful of folk fond I þer bitwene" (B.Prol.17): this is unlikely to be "natural" or "prose" word-order, either in the sequence of object-verb-adverbial across the line or in the inversion of subject and verb in the b-verse. As with any other verse-form, the reader needs to be constantly aware of the many effects that arise from meeting such demands. That said, it must be admitted that detailed study is made difficult by the absence of a body of contemporary texts that manifestly demonstrate, for purposes of comparison, "natural" word-order. Other Middle English poetry reveals other metrical demands, and much Middle English prose, especially translation, is sometimes painfully unidiomatic where Langland is always inventively idiomatic.

(ii) *The paragraph and end-stopping*. Most scribes divide *Piers Plowman* into paragraphs, and these are the building-blocks of Langland's discourse. They are irregular in length, not quatrains (see Day) or other regular units sometimes proposed for *aa/ax* poems; the length of the scribal paragraphs is determined by subject-matter and sense. *Piers Plowman* is therefore *stichic*, not *strophic*: its sense flows freely without being channelled into stanzas of regular length. Yet when one looks at these verse-paragraphs, in *Piers* and formal *aa/ax* poems, the lines appear to be predominantly end-stopped and enjambement relatively rare. This impression, though exaggerated by modern editorial over-punctuation, is valid. It arises partly from the stichic form: where no larger predictable interval exists, the metrical unit itself, the long line, tends to assume the syntactic function of the strophe. This is a departure, however, from the syntactic practice of Old English poetry, where alliterative poets countered this tendency by frequent enjambement, making a syntactic unit out of the b-verse (or the whole of one line) plus the a-verse of the next. This sort of syntactic enjambement, regularly forming a syntactic unit across two lines, is rarer in Middle English alliterative poetry. The most drastic examples occur in an informal poem, *Mum and the Sothsegger*: "Full woo for I ne wiste what was my best / Reed . . ." (572–73). This is unparalleled in *Piers*; but enjambement is more common in *Piers* than in formal *aa/ax* poems (see e.g. B.3.176–79).

Two explanations exist for the syntactic difference between Old English and Middle English unrhymed alliterative poetry. One has to do with linguistic, especially morphological, change: the line in Middle English is significantly longer, allowing for more grammatical activity within it. Moreover, Langland — unlike most formal poets — is relaxed in his attitude to variations in line-length. Lines such as Sloth's are over-stretched for dramatic effect (B.5.395–96):

> But I kan rymes of Robyn hood and Randolf Erl of Chestre,
> Ac neiþer of oure lord ne of oure lady þe leeste þat euere was maked.

Secondly, the *x*-stress in Middle English, falling even more regularly than in Old at the end of the line, seems to encourage a coincident syntactic termination: syntax now complements the alliterative pattern, rather than running against it. The *x*-stress again distinguishes unrhymed from rhymed alliterative poetry, which is generally strophic and in which enjambement falls more frequently (if only across rhyming couplets).

However, the degree and effect of end-stopping should not be overrated. Syntactic co-ordination in unrhymed alliterative poetry is generally looser than that of modern expectations or, say, Chaucerian rhymed poetry (Lawton 1981b, 618). Narrative especially tends to be relatively paratactic in construction, and many speeches, being more propositional in character, are correspondingly more hypotactic. It is in fact very difficult to mark longer syntactic periods consistently except in the way the scribes did, by the paragraph following sense. The relation between the metrically end-stopped line and the larger irregular paragraph unit of syntax and sense establishes a crossplay comparable to modulation.

(iii) *The syntactic function of alliteration.* Stone usefully distinguishes three types of alliteration in Middle English prose: "pairing" (*a* + *a*); "consecutive words" (*a . . . a*); and "grammatical alliteration," requiring a grammatical relation between the alliterating words (Verb-Noun, Adverb-Verb, etc.). Stone's example from Margery Kempe (104) — "perfeccyon of prechyng / spred & sprong / wondyr wyde" — shows all three types: the first grammatical, the second pairing, the last consecutive (and grammatical). The rhythmical and metrical systems of the *aa/ax* line coincide in giving unusual prominence to the grammatical. The poets seek alliterating words with either an inbuilt syntactic relation (a formula) or, more often, one that is quickly assembled: the reader can parse alliterating patterns more easily than scan them. One need not look to adaptations of oral-formulaic theory (Waldron) for an explanation: this feature is the relation within the line of grammar and ictus in which either may dominate or prompt the other, and is again assimilable to modulation. The syntactic significance of modulation lies in Langland's readiness to mark by alliteration the unstressed "grammar words" that maintain the continuity of the line and paragraph.

(iv) *The relative weight of a- and b-verses.* Caesura in unrhymed alliterative poetry, being in an invariable position between a- and b-verses, is properly a metrical feature. Such a caesura is "a device for emphasizing the formality of the poetic construction and for insisting on its distance from colloquial utterance" (Fussell 30); but it is a measure of Langland's modulation that he can also manipulate his caesura to gain the opposite, "something of the informal movement . . . of ordinary speech." This is partly a syntactic achievement, balancing the a-verse and b-verse. In much formal *aa/ax* poetry the a-verse is dominant, and the b-verse is reduced to a basically temporising function, often filled by empty tags. Langland avoids this effect with remarkable consistency, not least by converting potential a-verse main clauses into b-verse subordinate clauses, and by inversion, placing the main verb in the b-verse. His success in this respect points beyond syntax to a difference in subject-matter. The b-verse is often used for a bitter contrast or in an ironic reverse, for example Sloth's "I haue maad auowes fourty and foryete hem on þe morwe" (B.5.397). What in a romance context would be empty tags are made satirically mordant (e.g., B.5.396 quoted already, or B.Prol.18–19, "Of alle manere of men, *þe meene and þe riche,* / Werchynge and wandrynge *as þe world askeþ*").

(v) *Rhetoric*. Overall, Langland's syntactic structure lends itself, in a sophisticated poetic mode, to types of repetition, balance, parallelism and variation susceptible of rhetorical analysis. One of the few scholars to attempt such analysis, Spearing suggests that Langland's rhetoric derives from *artes predicandi*. A more common source should not be overlooked: "Grammar, þe ground of al" (B.15.372), from which the more specialised rhetorical arts of preaching and poetry are relatively late and eclectic medieval developments. (See Kaske on Langland's use of the simple figures.)

LEXIS

Familiar lexical and rhetorical devices such as metaphor are abundant in Langland's poetry. His imagery is often of a conceptual and thematic kind (Schmidt 1980). Since modern readers are unlikely to overlook these, lexical features closely related to the metrical contract will be the focus here.

(i) *Synonyms*. Since *aa/ax* lines are predominantly end-stopped yet can contain only a certain amount of narrative information, there is a frequent need in formal alliterative poetry for synonyms: "A bolde beryn one a blonke bownne for to ryde, / A hathell on ane heghe horse with hauke appon hande" (*Parlement of the Thre Ages* 110–111; Burrow 1957 comments over-harshly on these lines). This process can be seen clearly in *aa/ax* poems with Latin prose sources (see Lawton 1982), and it is sanctioned by medieval poetic theory (*idem sit, sed tamen varius*): it is as if the syntax has to begin all over from one line to the next with a change of alliteration. In Langland, this seldom occurs. What occurs instead is the feature which this sort of use of synonyms in formal poems also serves: repetition and variation of information, conforming to *amplificatio*. But there is another reason for synonyms in alliterative poetry. One key word will often determine the alliteration of the line, and if the remainder is not to be semantically inert, synonyms will frequently be needed, especially for nouns and verbs. The more common the field, the greater the incidence of synonyms: it is unsurprising that synonyms for "man" and for verbs representing recurrent activities such as motion or (characteristically in Langland) speech are numerous. Even the most humble traveller to Rome in alliterative poetry may well ride there, and find himself called a *"renk"* en route. A *"wye"* will probably *"wend"* and a *"freke"* will *"fare"* to appropriately alliterating destinations. Such synonyms may be drawn from sources other than their "standard" prose utterance or the poet's own dialect (e.g., Langland's use of *cairen* and interchange of *chirche/kirk* to suit alliterative need).

There are no fewer than ten high synonyms for man in *Gawain*, used in all 263 times, and they occur almost invariably on the staves; most but not all are found in Old English poetry. Langland uses six: *freke, gome, lede, renk, segge,* and *wye* — also mainly on the staves, but much less frequently than in formal poetry. Borroff, after Brink, argues that these words have an archaic, poetic or idealising quality. However, in Langland — and probably in the formal poems too — they are above all technical expedients. Each of the synonyms for man begins with a different initial sound. Their use increases in direct proportion to the amount of extended linear narrative and elevation of style. It is therefore predictable that we should find a relatively low incidence in *Piers Plowman*, and this cannot logically be used to prove Langland's ignorance of more formal modes. Nor can it be shown that he raided formal *aa/ax* poetry to find them.

What can be said is that the verse form is lexically heuristic. One suspects that "*Paternoster*" began as the keyword of the line made so memorable by its verb (and verb's destination): Will's reference to poor and "lewed luttes" who "Percen wiþ a Paternoster þe paleys of heuene" (B.10.468).

(ii) *Wordplay*. Langland is always sensitive to the possible range of a word's meaning, and the (sometimes bilingual or even trilingual) pun is a common device (Schmidt; Tristram): the friar of the feast of Conscience, for example, is a "dyuynour" (B.13.115) — that is, a theologian (a doctor of divinity), a quack (as in water-diviner), and an over-imbiber (one who speaks *de vino*). But *aa/ax* poetry, with its long lines arranged in irregular paragraphs and with its metrically derived balance and parallelism, is an ideal medium for more extended wordplay (Huppé; for an example see Dillon). This potential of the verse form is most perfectly realised in *Piers Plowman* and the poems of the *Pearl*-manuscript, for it is a conceptual as well as a merely poetic resource. It is centred not upon elevated or esoteric diction but upon more common vocabulary (e.g., *clene* in *Cleanness*) of great *impact* (Gradon 397: "the emotional intensity or semantic depth of a word"). A celebrated example in *Piers Plowman* occurs in the poetic heightening of Christ's speech at the Harrowing of Hell. Both B and C versions are given:

365   For I þat am lord of lif, loue is my drynke,
       And for þat drynke today I deide vpon erþe.
367   I fauȝt so me þursteþ ȝit for mannes soule sake;
       May no drynke me moiste, ne my þurst slake,
369   Til þe vendage falle in þe vale of Iosaphat,
       That I drynke riȝt ripe Must, *Resureccio mortuorum*.
                                                      (B.18.365–70)

403   For y þat am lord of lyf, loue is my drynke,
       And for þat drynke today y deyede as hit semede.

405   Ac y wol drynke of no dische ne of deep clergyse,
        Bote of comune coppes, alle cristene soules;
407   Ac thy drynke worth deth and depe helle thy bolle.
        Y fauht so me fursteth зut for mannes soule sake:
            Sicio.
409   May no pyement ne pomade ne preciouse drynkes
        Moiste me to þe fulle ne my furst slokke,
411   Til þe ventage valle in þe vale of Iosophat,
        And y drynke riht rype most, *resureccio mortuorum.*

                            (C.20.403–12)

The play on "*drynke*" is fully realised in B, as both noun and verb (370). The C passage brings the verb-form forward to the newly introduced 405–6, and 407 is introduced to contrast Christ's drink with Satan's (as in B 364), which is "*deth.*" As the drink-passage is extended in C, so, for balance, is the play on thirst — again, as in B, as noun and verb. Without introduction of much new content (unlike the "*clergyse*" of C 405), B 368 is amplified into C 409–10; in both B 368 and C 410 modulation occurs, the ictus stressing the uniqueness of the speaker (*me, my*), and the rhythmical system favouring the keyword *þurst* (given secondary alliteration in C, and balanced against *drynke* in B). Modulation also occurs in B 370, C 412, with its triumphant overstress (*xaab/ab*). In both passages *drynke* begins and ends in a stressed but non-alliterating position, but otherwise falls with the stave — thus signalling the wordplay. The C passage is well analysed by Spearing, who discusses its spare and emphatic linking of drink and thirst with life and death (and, in the outer lines, love and resurrection).

This example brings the study of style to the semantic level.

THE SEMANTIC SYSTEM AND *aa/ax* FORM

Much careful research on the meaning of individual words in *Piers Plowman* can be flawed by a failure to take alliterative style into account. Some words are a habitual part or transform of alliterative collocations; other are not. Thus *Imaginatyf*, for example, or "*Liberum Arbitrium*" can be examined in isolation. They are words that play no part in the poem except where personifications so named are given prominence; where they form part of *alliterative collocations* (i.e. the a-staves of a single sound), these are evidently designed to serve the names as headword. On the other hand, words such as *clergie* and *kynde* (and formations such as *kynde knowyng* or *kynde wit*) permeate the entire poem. These words are neither meaningless nor indefinable, but they are semantically stretched in the process by the host of diverse alliterative collocations in which they appear over numerous lines. We must be able to detect the presence of ghosts — the ghosts, as it were, of other words with which they commonly collocate. Salter writes perceptively of "echoes" and "forewarnings" which may not always be part of the poet's conscious intention, but always have some effect on the reader (52). The best work in this area, like Kean's on love, law and leauté and Burrow's on words, works and will, treats a full collocation of both alliteration and sense. Every alliterative line helps form a nexus of cross-references.

One might add that for all the attention paid to various triads in the poem, little work has so far been done to relate them to their obvious correlative: the staves of the *aa/ax* line. The *aa/ax* line is itself triadic (Thompson 108). Alliterative poets were probably conscious of this: if we accept Gollancz's masterly emendation, the poet of *Wynnere and Wastoure* condemns other poets "þat neuer wroghte thurgh witt three wordes togedere." Often in *Piers* it is as if the key alliterating words of a particular line have a semantic interaction wholly apart from, and more important than, their immediate syntactic context.

Until we can explore such connections, we will continue to draw arbitrary distinctions between "style" and "content," and see *Piers Plowman* criticism that could be based on a prose crib. The fact is that there is little or no difference in Langland's poetry between *pattern* (Gradon 398, "thematic linking of repeated themes") and *texture* ("the exploitation of lexical sets [which] gives close texture or semantic density"). Sets of words alliterating on the same sound, alliterative collocations, give semantic range through their intricate network of cross-references. On another level, the principle underlying synonymy establishes an abecedary pattern of repetition and variation, which gives semantic reinforcement. In Langland's poetry, these two poetic features — the one similar giving semantic range and the other giving semantic reinforcement — have a prominence similar to that accorded in modern canons of taste to metaphor and metonymy. However unfamiliar they are to us, they are central to his poetic and his semantic systems, and his meaning is inalienable from them.

Both features are directly attributable to Langland's use of the unrhymed alliterative long line. They make for what may be an educative mode (Norton-Smith); but it is not in their poetic nature to assume the form of linear exposition. (Recognition of this is what prompts modern comparisons between Langland and the Middle English mystics, or at least with affective or meditative composition such as Rolle's.) They are not good didactic techniques because they are not straightforward. In a poem both colloquial and cerebral, they make for something more valuable — a challenging teaching mode, a sort of medieval instress.

Everything described above follows from Langland's choice of metre and his poetic expertise. The phonetic device of alliteration is indispensable to

Langland's meaning, and inseparable from it. Every level of his poem —
phonological, lexicogrammatical, semantic — is profoundly conditioned by
its poetic form.

A SAMPLE ANALYSIS

Space has so far permitted few examples. But let us now analyse a passage from early in the poem, B.Prol.58–67. The reason for the selection
will become evident.

58	I fond þere Freres	alle þe foure ordres
59	Prechynge þe peple	for profit of þe wombe
60	Glosed þe gospel	as hem good liked
61	For coueitise of copes	construwed it as þei wolde
62	Manye of þise maistress	mowe cloþen hem at likyng
63	For hire moneie and hire marchaundiȝe	marchen togideres
64	Siþ charite haþ ben chapman	and chief to shryue lordes
65	Manye ferlies han fallen	in a fewe yeres
66	But holy chirche and hij	holde bettre togidres
67	The mooste meschief on Molde	is mountynge vp faste

Metre, Rhythm, Modulation

Lines 59, 63 and 65 are standard *aa/ax* lines without tension between metrical and rhythmical systems. Of the rest, 58 and 60 are *aa/ax* but depart slightly from the norm: there is secondary vocalic alliteration in 58 on "alle" and
"I," balancing the subject-object relation of the a-verse, and in 60b the pejora-
tive sense of the b-verse, which could be read neutrally were it not preceded
by 59b, is reinforced by the possibility of a stress on "hem." The alliterative
pattern of 61, 62, 64 and 66 remains *aa/ax*, but in each case the b-verse is
somewhat swollen, and in the first three examples the extra information
around the x-stress highlights what the friars would keep hidden: "as þei
wolde," "at likyng," "to shryue lordes." In 66, the tension in "holding together"
is reflected in the extra length of the b-verse. While "construwed" in 61 may
not be an example of modulation but of stress-shift in Modern English (it
is Langland's standard lexical stress on this word), there is no doubt about
62b, where the alliteration falls on the modal "mowe," and the drastic modulation underscores the friars' disruption of religious discipline, their "bad
habits." In 67 (*aaa/ax(x)*), the overstress corroborates the superlative of the
a-verse, as the rhythm of the b-verse mimics its meaning.

Syntax

(i) The word-order is almost thoroughly idiomatic. The sole example of metrical conditioning occurs in 58, where "I found there all four orders of friars" would fit in neither with the rhythmical organisation nor with alliterative patterning (*aa/xa* is avoided); but Langland's immediate introduction of friars in the a-verse is singularly effective, and "alle þe foure ordres" makes an appropriately expansive b-verse. The pressure of thought and the demands of metre support one another strikingly.

(ii) This is a self-contained unit of sense, a paragraph. It is reproduced as if in a manuscript format without modern editorial punctuation in order to demonstrate that the reader is guided to the major syntactic breaks at the end of 61, 63 and 65 by the obvious introduction of a new grammatical subject in the subsequent a-verse. Syntactic co-ordination is marked in 63, "For," and subordinate clauses — corresponding to lines — in 64 ("Siþ . . .") and 66 ("But . . ." = unless). Each pair of lines from 62–67 could be said to show enjambement, while 58–61 are "end-stopped"; but the distinction has little meaning when 59–61 are clearly parallel, taking as their subject the object, "Freres," of 58a.

(iii) The syntactic function of alliteration is clearly demonstrated here. Of the a-verses only 63a and 66a show pairing, and here each a-verse becomes the subject of the verb in the b-verse.

(iv) The equivalence in weight of a-verse and b-verse is remarkably sustained. Of the ten verb forms in the passage, five occur in a-verses (58–60, 64–65) and five in b (61–63, 66–67). Indeed, the modulation in 61, 62 and 64 gives the b-verse a slight edge in semantic weight to make up for its grammatically inferior position. 67 has an extra stress in both verses. The only notably long a-verse, 63 (long only because the length of the words puts the caesura, as it were, out of vertical alignment) is an index of the importance of the collocation, as is the consecutive alliteration from 62: "maistres," "moneie" and "marchaundiʒe," religious life and commerce, are brought together in the key 64a, "charite . . . chapman."

(v) Rhetorically, 64a is located in a key position, as it marks the move from particular to general in the opening of a *sententia*, a quasi-proverbial statement of a general truth.

Lexis

(i) There are few actual synonyms, and they are common words: freres, maistres; glosed, construwed. But their presence is enough to signal a larger principle of artful variation, whereby a common sense in 59–61 accumulates through new information. 59b and 61a, for example, are near parallel, as are the whole of 60 and 61b. 65 and 67 are significantly parallel. The most striking feature here is again the taking up of the collocation from 62/63 in the new alliterative collocation of 64a.

(ii) There is very little wordplay compared to the highly wrought passage discussed under *Wordplay* above. But what there is is unobtrusively witty: chief/meschief (64, 67); fallen/mountynge (65, 67); the possible modulation mentioned in 60b; the repetition of "togidres" in 66 where the hope it expresses is ironically undercut by its very different context in 63; and, above all, the mordant (and discordant) personification of "charite" in 64a.

SEMANTIC ANALYSIS

(i) There are five major recurrent lexical sets in the passage, with some overlap:

Religious: Freres, ordres, prechynge, peple, gospel, maistres, charite, chief, shryue, holy chirche, Molde. "Copes" (like "maistres," with its discordant hint of grandeur) is marginal, and "lordes," confirming the hint of grandeur, is discordant in its supernumerary *x*-stress placement.

People's needs: (Again: prechynge, gospel, charite, shryue); "wombe," "cloþen" and "glosed" are marginal, given that they refer to "Freres," not their flock.

Friars' appetites: (Again, wombe); coueitise; liked/likyng; wolde.

Commercial: profit, moneie, marchaundiȝe, chapman (always referring to "Freres").

Unnatural events: ferlics, meschief on Molde.

There are seven different sets of staves, alliterating phonemes. Both lexical sets and alliterative collocations are arranged in the passage so as to conflict. This happens from a-verse to b-verse, as in 59 and 60, and within a verse, as in 62b, where it is one thing for friars to clothe themselves and another for them to do so "at likyng." This is perhaps what Lawlor meant by saying that Langland's poetry is built on a "principle of contrast" (208). The most violent contrast occurs in 64a, when within one alliterative collocation two conflicting lexical sets — religious and commercial — are joined by use of the verb "to be," triggering the prophetic language and fears of 65–67.

(ii) The headword of the passage is "Freres," and one should consult the standard contemporary meaning: friars were supposed to be physically needy and to minister to people's spiritual needs. Langland uses conventional anti-mendicant complaint to pervert this standard meaning: friars have exploited people's spiritual needs in order to minister to their own appetites and profit. This is what all the semantic information tells us: religion has gone commercial, and from this unnatural event others will follow. The key line, as syntax and lexis testify, is 64: "charite" cannot be "chapman," yet this is the way of the world of Langland's poem.

(iii) This nexus, spun out of the incompatibility of "charite" and "chapman," will be developed by repetition, variation and cross-reference throughout the poem; but it is firmly in place by Prol.67. So, indeed, is the outcome, the end—of the world, the poem, the dream, the "ferly" with which friars are linked: the friars penetrate Unity, and Holy Church falls. The prophecy of 64–67 is fulfilled: Conscience leaves, wishing "þat freres hadde a fyndyng" (B.20.383) in order that "charite" need not be "chapman." It is a complex, sustained and impressively coherent production on every level of style.

LANGLAND'S METRE AND ITS AFFILIATIONS

Did Langland make his own metre or remake what was already there? In either case, what models were available to him?

The notion of an "alliterative revival" in the fourteenth century still has many adherents (see Turville-Petre) though none quite agrees with another on what revived and how. The complementary notion of an "alliterative survival" faltered for a whole on the paucity of evidence (for further references see Pearsall 1982), on the implausibility of oral transmission (which would not tend to keep a metre strict as the *aa/ax* line), and on the difference between the *aa/ax* norm in Middle English and the alliterative patterns of Old English verse (see pp. 231–32 above). The "revival"/"survival" argument has been renewed by a subtle appeal to "lost literature" (Pearsall 1981), which hardly admits refutation or proof.

Since the question is unanswerable, it may be better to revise it. When R. W. Chambers wrote on "the Continuity of English Prose" he unnecessarily doubled his burden of proof by claiming a revival of alliterative poetry that "was kept alive by oral tradition through nine generations, appearing in writing very rarely, and then usually in a corrupt form, till it suddenly came forth, correct, vigorous, and bearing with it a whole tide of national feeling." The "corrupt form" is as tell-tale an index of argumentative strain as the "whole tide of national feeling" (generally, see Pearsall 1982 and 1977). The fact is that Chambers did not need alliterative poetry for his argument at all—and very nearly avoided the encumbrance when he claimed that for alliterative poetry to be written in the fourteenth century alliteration must have been strong *in the spoken language* (lxvii).

The key is that *aa/ax* poetry is heteromorphic (see p. 228 above), and so open to an extraordinary variety of influences and lines of provenance. The evidence that alliterative and rhythmical patterns were pervasive in English prose in 1066 is a lot stronger than that for "good command of the old technique of alliterative verse" (Chambers lxvi). Evidence for the prominence of alliteration in both verse and prose persists through the early Middle English period, and becomes commonplace not long after 1300. Yet there is nothing even in Laȝamon's *Brut* to explain the standard use of the *aa/ax* pattern after about 1350. In this situation we should accept the possibility of almost every influence proposed, from manuscripts of Old English poetry in Worcester Cathedral Library to many forms of rhymed poetry (Salter 1967; Matonis 1981; Lawton 1980a), rhythmical prose (Morgan 1952a, b) and devotional composition (Salter 1978; generally, see Pearsall 1982). We should concede that alliteration is not the sole evidence, for lightly alliterating works in prose and verse may well have influenced the rhythmical system of *aa/ax* poetry. We should also allow for "the innovatory work of a single individual" (McIntosh 1982, 25).

On no plausible dating was that individual likely to have been Langland. At least, of the *aa/ax* poems *William of Palerne* probably antedated the *Piers Plowman* A text: it comes from the Southwest Midlands, close to Langland's part of the world, its author identifies himself as one William, and lovers of *Piers Plowman* have been stupendously silent about any slight chance that his surname was Langland. What then was Langland's acquaintance with formal *aa/ax* poetry?

Writers on Langland's style have generally differentiated it from that of formal *aa/ax* poetry by rather broad strokes (e.g., Donaldson 44). It is only one step to claim extant formal poems as particular models for *Piers Plowman*, and Langland's style as a conscious departure from them (e.g., Hussey; Burrow 1957; Salter 1969). The present writer has dissented from this view and speculated on whether the *Piers Plowman* A text may have been a major influence on the writing of other *aa/ax* poems, if only by virtue of its success and currency (Lawton 1983). What is certain where so much is conjectural is that no argument from metre and style sheds any light whatever on this question: they merely emphasise that Langland was not trying to write an alliterative romance, and to judge from the C revisions was not much interested in the style of writers who were. They redirect us to differences in intention and meaning.

We may never be sure of the relation between *Piers Plowman* and the formal *aa/ax* poems. We do not know, and probably never shall, whether to admire *aa/ax* poetry as the work of creation or evolution. In assessing Langland's affiliations and artistry, however, we should never forget that metre, style and meaning are inseparable: together, they realise — or frustrate — a writer's intention. Two conclusions can be drawn from this.

First, the *aa/ax* corpus is heterogeneous; so must have been the influences upon it. In Langland's case, we should cast our net widely. It will include not only an "alliterative tradition" or three, but also works, however humble, with an intention akin to whatever we judge Langland's to have been: for example, penitential manuals and partly macaronic preaching books like John of Grimestone's, where the topics treated read like a resumé of Langland's mental universe: Abstinence, the Wise Heart, the Love of God, Thought, Charity, Confession, Riches, Doctrine without Grace, Law, Sin, the Passion of Christ, the Deadly Sins, Truth, the Way of Christ, Will. The questions of provenance and literary affiliation cannot be kept to the areas of metre and style.

Secondly, there can be no reason to doubt that Langland *chose* to write alliterative poetry, and did so because it seemed to him an ideal medium (Kane 43). Certainly, he achieves a real semantic originality. There has been too much critical notice of his supposed lack of poetic "art": "Only a very prejudiced reader could fail to be persuaded that Langland does not consistently — nor, I believe, fundamentally — feel the need to communicate as a poet" (Salter 1969, 31); "One cannot supply Langland's form and style from the author's own consciousness of his art" (Norton-Smith 28), for all the world as if Langland should have anticipated more modern poets in providing a preface and footnotes. Beneath such criticism lurks a modern, not a medieval concept of the Poet — one that would have prompted Chaucer to identify himself gratefully as a civil servant. There also lurks the provocative misjudgment of C. S. Lewis in *The Allegory of Love*: Langland "is confused and monotonous, and hardly makes his poetry into a poem" (161). This distinction between "poetry" and "poem" conceals another frustrated attempt to separate form and content. It is hoped that the foregoing account helps to show how impossible this is, for in *Piers Plowman* the one is the condition of the other. "As for Langland, his alliterative line works" (Kane 62). So, therefore, does his poem.

REFERENCES

Attridge, Derek. *The Rhythms of English Poetry.* London: Longman, 1982.

Bessinger, J. B., and S. J. Kahrl, eds. *Essential Articles for the Study of Old English Poetry.* Hamden, CT: Archon, 1968.

Bliss, A. J. *The Metre of Beowulf.* Oxford: Blackwell, 1958.

———. *An Introduction to Old English Metre.* Oxford: Blackwell, 1962.

———. "The Appreciation of Old English Metre." *English and Medieval Studies Presented to J. R. R. Tolkien.* Ed. Norman Davis and C. L. Wrenn. London: Allen and Unwin, 1962. 27–40.

Borroff, Marie. *Sir Gawain and the Green Knight: A Stylistic and Metrical Study.* New Haven: Yale University Press, 1962.

Brink, August. *Stab und Wort im Gawain: eine stilistische Untersuchung.* Studien zur englischen Philologie 59. Halle: Niemeyer, 1922.

Burrow, J. A. "The Audience of *Piers Plowman.*" *Anglia* 75 (1957): 373–84.

———. "Words, Works and Will: Theme and Structure in *Piers Plowman.*" Hussey 111–24.

Chambers, R. W. *On the Continuity of English Prose from Alfred to More and his School.* EETS 191a (1937), rpt. from his preface to EETS 186 (1932).

Chatman, Seymour. *A Theory of Meter.* The Hague: Mouton, 1965.

Daunt, Marjorie. "Old English Verse and English Speech Rhythm." *Transactions of the Philological Society* (1946): 56–72. (Cited in text from reprint in Bessinger and Kahrl 289–304.)

Davis, Norman. Appendix ("Metre") to *Sir Gawain and the Green Knight.* Ed. J. R. R. Tolkien and E. V. Gordon, 2nd ed. (rev. by Norman Davis). Oxford: Clarendon, 1967. 147–52.

Day, Mabel. "Strophic Division in Middle English Alliterative Verse." *Englische Studien* 66 (1931–32): 245–48.

Dillon, Janette. "*Piers Plowman*: A Particular Example of Wordplay and its Structural Significance." *MÆ* 50 (1981): 40–48.

Donaldson, E. Talbot. *Piers Plowman: The C-Text and Its Poet.* New Haven: Yale University Press, 1949.

Duggan, Hoyt. "Notes toward a Theory of Langland's Meter." *YLS* 1 (1987): 41–70.

Fraser, G. S. *Metre, Rhyme and Free Verse.* London: Methuen, 1970.

Fussell, Paul. *Poetic Meter and Poetic Form.* New York: Random House, 1965.

Gradon, Pamela. *Form and Style in Early English Literature.* London: Methuen, 1971.

Gross, Harvey. *Sound and Form in Modern Poetry.* Ann Arbor: University of Michigan Press, 1964.

Halle, M., and S. J. Keyser. *English Stress: Its Form, Its Growth, and Its Role in Verse.* New York: Harper and Row, 1971.

Heusler, Andreas. *Deutsche Versgeschichte mit Einschluss des altenglischen und altnordischen Stabreimverses.* 2 vols. Berlin and Leipzig, 1925; rpt. Berlin: De Gruyter, 1956.

Hieatt, Constance B. "The Rhythm of the Alliterative Long Line." *Chaucer and Middle English Studies in Honour of R. H. Robbins.* Ed. Beryl Rowland. London: Allen and Unwin, 1974. 119–30.

Huppé, B. F. "*Petrus, id est, Christus*: Word Play in *Piers Plowman,* The B-Text." *ELH* 17 (1950): 163–90.

Kaluza, Max. *A Short History of English Versification.* Trans. A. C. Dunstan. London: George Allen, 1911.

Kane, George. "Music 'Neither Unpleasant nor Monotonous.' " *Medieval Studies for J. A. W. Bennett.* Ed. P. L. Heyworth. Oxford: Clarendon, 1981. 43–63.

———, and F. Talbot Donaldson, eds. *Piers Plowman: The B Version.* London: Athlone, 1975 (esp. pp. 130–40).

Kaske, R. E. "The Use of Simple Figures of Speech in *Piers Plowman* B." *SP* 48 (1951): 571–600.

Kean, P. M. "Love, Law and *Lewte* in *Piers Plowman.*" *RES* ns 15 (1964): 241–61; rpt. Blanch 132–55.

Lawlor, John. *Piers Plowman: an Essay in Criticism.* London: Arnold, 1962.

Lawton, David. "Middle English Unrhymed Alliterative Poetry and the *South English Legendary.*" *ES* 61 (1980): 390–96.

―――. "Larger Patterns of Syntax in Unrhymed Middle English Alliterative Verse." *Neophil.* 64 (1980): 604–18.

―――. "Middle English Alliterative Poetry: An Introduction." *Middle English Alliterative Poetry and Its Literary Background.* Ed. D. A. Lawton. Cambridge: D. S. Brewer, 1982. 1–19.

―――. "The Unity of Middle English Alliterative Poetry." *Speculum* 58 (1983): 72–94.

Leonard, W. E. "The Scansion of Middle English Alliterative Verse." *University of Wisconsin Studies in Language and Literature* 11 (1920): 58–104.

Lewis, C. S. "The Alliterative Metre." *Lysistrata* 2 (1935). (Cited in text from reprint in Bessinger and Kahrl 305–16.)

―――. *The Allegory of Love: A Study in Medieval Tradition.* Oxford: Oxford University Press, 1936.

McIntosh, Angus. "Wulfstan's Prose." *PBA* 35 (1949): 109–42.

―――. "Early Middle English Alliterative Verse." Lawton 1982, 20–33.

Matonis, A. T. E. "An Investigation of Celtic Influences on MS Harley 2253." *MP* 70 (1972): 91–108.

―――. "Middle English Alliterative Poetry." *So meny people longages and tonges.* Ed. M. Benskin and M. L. Samuels. Edinburgh: The Editors, 1981. 341–54.

―――. "A Reexamination of the Middle English Alliterative Long Line." *MP* 81 (1984): 339–60.

Morgan, Margery. "*A Talking of the Love of God* and the Continuity of Stylistic Tradition in Middle English Prose Meditations." *RES* ns 3 (1952): 97–116.

―――. "A Treatise in Cadence." *MLR* 47 (1952): 156–64.

Norton-Smith, John. *William Langland.* Leiden: Brill, 1983. Esp. chaps. 3 and 7.

Oakden, J. P. *Alliterative Poetry in Middle English.* 1: *The Dialectal and Metrical Survey*; 2: *A Survey of the Traditions*, with assistance from Elizabeth R. Innes. Manchester: Manchester University Press, 1930/1935; rpt. (2 vols in 1) Hamden, CT: Archon, 1968.

Pearsall, Derek. *Old and Middle English Poetry.* London: Routledge and Kegan Paul, 1977.

―――. "The Origins of the Alliterative Revival." *The Alliterative Tradition in the Fourteenth Century.* Ed. B. S. Levy and P. E. Szarmach. Kent, OH: Kent State University Press, 1981. 1–24.

―――. "The Alliterative Revival: Origins and Social Backgrounds." Lawton 1982, 34–53.

Pope, J. C., ed. *Homilies of Ælfric: A Supplementary Collection.* EETS 259. London: Oxford University Press, 1967. Esp. Intro., "Ælfric's Rhythmical Prose," 105–36.

Salter, Elizabeth. "*Piers Plowman* and *The Simonie*." *Archiv* 203 (1967): 241–54.

―――. *Piers Plowman: An Introduction.* 2nd ed. Oxford: Blackwell, 1969.

―――. "Alliterative Modes and Affiliations in the Fourteenth Century." *NM* 79 (1978): 25–35.

Sapora, R. W., Jr. *A Theory of Middle English Alliterative Meter with Critical Applications.* Speculum Anniversary Monographs 1. Cambridge, MA: Medieval Academy of America, 1977.

Schmidt, A. V. C., ed. *The Vision of Piers Plowman.* London: Dent, 1978. Esp. Appendix, "Langland's Alliterative Verse," 359–60.

―――. "Langland's Structural Imagery." *EIC* 30 (1980): 311–25.

―――. "*Lele Wordes* and *Bele Paroles*: Some Aspects of Langland's Word-Play." *RES* ns 34 (1983): 137–50.

————. "The Authenticity of the Z text of *Piers Plowman*: A Metrical Examination." *MÆ* 53 (1984): 295–300.

Schumacher, Karl. *Studien über den Stabreim in der mittelenglischen Alliterationsdichtung.* Bonner Studien zur englischen Philologie 11. Ed. K. Bülbring. Bonn: Hanstein, 1914.

Sievers, Eduard. "Der angelsächsische Schwellvers." *Beiträge zur Geschichte der Deutschen Sprache und Literatur* 12 (1887): 454–82.

————. *Altgermanische Metrik.* Sammlung Kurzer Grammatiken germanischer Dialekte 2. Halle: Niemeyer, 1893.

————. "Zu Cynewulf." Neusprachliche Studien, Festgabe für Karl Luick. *Die Neueren Sprachen* 6 Beiheft (1925): 60–81.

————. *Altenglische Grammatik.* 2nd ed. rev. by Karl Brunner. Sammlung Kurzer Grammatiken germanischer Dialekte 3. Halle: Niemeyer, 1951.

————. "Old Germanic Metrics and Old English Metrics." Trans. Gawaina D. Luster in Bessinger and Kahrl 267–88.

Skeat, W. W. "An Essay on Alliterative Poetry." *Bishop Percy's Folio Manuscript.* Ed. J. W. Hales and F. J. Furnivall. London: Trübner, 1868. 3:xi–xxxix.

Spearing, A. C. "Verbal Repetition in *Piers Plowman* B and C." *JEGP* 62 (1963): 722–37.

Stobie, M. M. R. "The Influence of Morphology on Middle English Alliterative Poetry." *JEGP* 39 (1940): 319–36.

Stone, R. K. *Middle English Prose Style.* The Hague: Mouton, 1970.

Thompson, Claud A. "Structural, Figurative and Thematic Trinities in *Piers Plowman*." *Mosaic* 9:2 (1975–76): 105–14.

Tristram, Hildegard L. C. "Intertextuelle *Puns* in *Piers Plowman*." *NM* 84 (1983): 182–91.

Turville-Petre, Thorlac. *The Alliterative Revival.* Cambridge: D. S. Brewer, 1977.

Waldron, R. A. "Oral-Formulaic Technique and Middle English Alliterative Poetry." *Speculum* 32 (1957): 792–804.

EPILOGUE

THE LEGACY OF *PIERS PLOWMAN*

ANNE HUDSON

John Schep, som tyme Seynt Marie prest of 3orke, and nowe of Colchestre, greteth welle Johan Nameles and Johan the Mullere, and Johan Cartere, and biddeth hem that thei ware of gyle in borugh, and stondeth togiddir in Goddis name, and biddeth Peres Plou3man go to his werke, and chastise welle Hobbe the robber, and taketh with 3ou Johan Trewman, and alle his felaws, and no mo, and loke scharpe 3ou

　　　　　　　　　to on heued, and no mo.
　　Johan the Muller hath ygrownde smal, smal, smal;
　　The Kyngis sone of hevene shalle pay for alle,
　　Be ware or ye be wo,
　　Knoweth 3our frende fro 3oure foo,
　　Haveth ynowe and seythe 'Hoo';
　　And do welle and bettre, and fleth synne,
　　And seketh pees, and holde therynne.
And so biddeth Johan Trewman and alle his felawes.

Few works of literature can match the record of *Piers Plowman* in having been used within twenty years of their composition as the rallying cry for a serious civil rebellion. Yet in their accounts of the Peasants' Revolt of 1381 (Dobson) both the chroniclers Thomas Walsingham and Henry Knighton record the production by one of the leaders of the revolt, John Ball, of propaganda that seems to have alluded to the poem to incite support. The version of the material above is that of Walsingham in his *Historia Anglicana* (2:33–34), where the form is a letter, sent under the name of John Sheep to the poor men of Essex; according to Walsingham, Ball admitted that this was one of his pseudonyms. Knighton's story (2:138–40) is more obscure: he gives brief addresses (the last in two forms) by four of those he calls leaders of the revolt, one of which mentions *Peres the Plowman*, *Hobbe robbyoure* and the phrase *doþ wele and ay bettur*, and several of which include phrases found in Walsingham's account. The names of the leaders given are Thomas

Baker (the prime mover but not apparently the author of any pamphlet), Jack Straw (likewise mute), *Jakke Mylner, Jakke Carter, Jakke Trewman* and later *Johannis Balle*. Here Knighton seems to be mixing fact with fiction: Baker, Straw and Ball were real rebels, but the three others are known only to Knighton and Walsingham, and to the latter as fictional pseudonyms for Ball. The names of Milner (or Miller) and Carter are credible generic terms for the honest labourer; *Jakke Trewman* is a comparable name, but here there may be the further complication of a possible allusion to the personification *true men*, regularly found in Lollard texts for those sypathetic to the Lollard causes (Hudson 1981, 16–17, 26). The mixture of the real with the fictional has gone even further in the *Dieulacres Abbey Chronicle* (Clarke and Galbraith 164–65), where the leaders of the revolt are said to be *John B*, presumably John Ball, Jack Straw and *Per Plowman*. The notion that Piers was a real person is also seen in the scribe's additional line in BL MS Harley 3934 of the A version *Preyit for pers þe plowmans soule* (Kane 1960, 48).

It seems impossible to avoid the conclusion that *Piers Plowman* had by 1381 gained sufficient fame amongst those likely to favour the Revolt to act as a rallying cry. The name might on its own possibly have been traditional; but the addition to it of apparent allusions to two of three lives, Dowel and Dobet, and to the figure of Roberd the Robber from the *Visio* (B.5.461) would seem to require familiarity with some form of the poem as we know it. That form must, on the usual dating of the versions, have been either A or B; if it were the former, it must have been in a copy that had the material after the tearing of the Pardon episode. Although modern research has shown that the title of the Revolt is something of a misnomer (Hilton 1–8), since many of the participants, or at least of the leaders, were artisans, often of some substance, it seems plain from the story that the poem, in so far as it was understood, was perceived as an expression of sympathy with, if not of instigation to, action by such participants towards bettering their lot. Even clearer is it from the story that the poem must have been familiar — such is a prerequisite for such allusive references to have any meaning or, more importantly, any effect.

The obscurity of this story is paradigmatic of much of the later history of *Piers Plowman*'s fortunes. The number of surviving manuscripts is, taking all three versions together, considerable: only *The Prick of Conscience* and *The Canterbury Tales* significantly exceed it (Robbins and Cutler 521). As John Burrow has shown, ownership of copies of the poem indicate that it gained some favour amongst clerks of relatively humble station and amongst the literate laity; but equally, the work is not mentioned often in wills, and marks of ownership in extant manuscripts are infrequent. The other items to be found in manuscripts that contain the poem in any of its versions are equally uninformative. The most common travelling companion, and that is found only five times, is Mandeville's *Travels*; otherwise the most that can be perceived by way of identifying mode amongst the other items is an interest in pseudo-historical romance — works such as *The Wars of Alexander, The Siege of Jerusalem, Kyng Alisaunder, The Sege or Batayle of Troy* and *Troilus and Criseyde* (cf. Middleton 104–08). But this may tell us more about the relative popularity of these other works than about the medieval understanding of Langland's poem. As the story of John Ball indicates, *Piers Plowman*, unlike most other poems of the "alliterative revival," was not geographically limited in its distribution (Samuels 1963, 94; Middleton 101; Samuels 1985; Doyle 1986). Tentatively it may be possible to trace a discrepancy between the different versions in their continuing popularity: whilst the B version appears from extant copies to have been relatively neglected after c. 1450, the A version continued to be copied throughout the fifteenth and into the sixteenth centuries at a fairly constant rate (dating from Kane 1960, 1–18; Kane and Donaldson 1–15). This may be relevant to the fact that the sixteenth century seems to have seen Piers as essentially a communal figure, voicing concern about the welfare of society rather than the salvation of the individual.

If John Ball and his associates interpreted *Piers Plowman* in its A or B versions as a rallying cry for reform, Thomas Usk is thought to have been immediately impressed by the C version and to have imitated it in his *Testament of Love* (Skeat 1897, 1–145). Indeed, Usk's execution in 1387 has been taken as providing the *terminus ante quem* for the C version (Donaldson 19). Some of the parallels produced seem unconvincing (e.g., those cited to *Test.* II.2.35–69 in Skeat 1897, 465–66), but the echoes of the Tree of Charity are more persuasive (*Test.* III.7.9–85, B.16.1–52 or C.18.1–52). Recently the case has been reopened for the possibility that Chaucer knew *Piers Plowman* and was influenced both in his literary strategies as well as in his satire by Langland (Bennett 310–24; Mann esp. 208–12; Cooper). Here the case depends upon broad questions rather than upon the minutiae that earlier commentators examined; the question must, however, probably be regarded as an open one.

Perception of the influence of *Piers Plowman* has been modified in recent years by a growing understanding of literary and ideological traditions in the later fourteenth and fifteenth centuries (Hussey; Turville-Petre 31–32, through cf. Lawton 1983). Early critics tended to suggest that any echoes of the verbal patterns of Langland's poem were to be understood as evidence of literary borrowing from the work that to a modern critic appears to tower over the bulk of medieval English poetry outside Chaucer. Hence parallel phrases or lines in works such as *Wynnere and Wastoure* (Hulbert 31–40) must be reassessed in the light of the probable earlier date of this poem than Langland's (Steadman 211–19). The same readjustment of earlier assessments may be needed for *The Parlement of the Thre Ages* (Gollancz 2; Lawton 1982,

10; but compare Offord xxxvii). Such an easy way out is not available for works such as *The Crowned King, Death and Liffe*, or *Scottish Feilde*. The case for the influence of *Piers Plowman* on *Death and Liffe* was set out by Hanford and Steadman (246–48, following Skeat 1868, 49–55), and has been accepted by more recent critics (Gollancz and Day xiii–xiv, and Lawton 1982, 10–11). But it perhaps depends on general similarities in certain allegorical figures and literary conventions, and on comparable alliterative collocations rather than on irrefutable borrowings. Parallels, for instance, in the description of the harrowing of hell (*Death and Liffe* 408–29, *PP* C.20.269–449) are, given the inherited story with its scripturally-based phraseology combined with the demands of a similar metre, not altogether convincing of close relationship. Likewise, the combination of an alliterative metre, albeit much less strict than Langland's work, with a dream vision in *The Crowned King* inevitably recalls *Piers Plowman*. The short poem dates from 1415, and addresses a king to be identified from fairly precise allusions with Henry V. The advice given to the king is unremarkable, but some lines contain perceptible echoes of Langland (Robbins no. 95; Turville-Petre 32). Another historical poem, *Scottish Feilde*, written between September 1513 and March 1515 (Oakden viii; but compare Lawton 1978, 43–44), probably echoes alliterative tradition generally rather than *Piers Plowman* specifically (cf. Manly 40–41).

Similar reliance upon tradition, albeit tradition of another kind, is probably the explanation for apparent reminiscences of Langland's anticlericalism and other satire in prose of the Wycliffite school. Langland's discussion of issues also important to Wyclif himself has recently been the subject of major reinvestigation (Gradon). Editions of *Piers Plowman* tend to include in their notes numerous references to English Wycliffite texts (Skeat 1886, 2:9, 12, 41 etc.; Pearsall 33, 34, 35 etc.), without any regular indication of what the comparison is meant to signify. Dating of Wycliffite texts is notoriously difficult, but it seems hard to see such texts as in any way the source of *Piers Plowman* (Gradon 184–97), since few if any can have been written by the usual date given to the A or B versions or even, unless the latest dating is accepted for it, the C text. It is tempting to suggest that the influence was the other way round, from *Piers Plowman* to the Wycliffite texts. Sadly, writers were drawing upon a common tradition, sometimes proverbial, often anticlerical, occasionally anti-intellectual (cf. Coleman 58–156). Thus the proposal that a section of one version of the English *Lay Folks' Catechism* (Lambeth version, lines 877–91) thought to have Lollard background (but see Hudson 1985, 249–58) derived from *Piers Plowman* A.8.149–84 (Coulton 372–73) cannot be sustained; both derive from long-standing criticism of papal indulgences. Similarly, though C.5.164 "To religious þat haen no reuthe thow it ryne on her auters" may be set against the criticism of friars who take no care *þof hit rayne on þo auter of þo parische chirche* (Arnold, *Select English Works* 3:380), both probably drew on the common phraseology of satire (cf. C.Prol.131–38 and Matthew *English Works* 472, where the same is likely to be true). As Lawton has said (1981, 793), "The issue is really that Lollards had Langlandian sympathies." Even if trial material produces no evidence of the confiscation of *Piers Plowman* from suspected heretics, and manuscript juxtaposition little sign of affiliation, later texts confirm that Langland's poem was perceived by many fifteenth and sixteenth century reformers, great and small, as favourable to their cause.

The first literary case where influence of *Piers Plowman* seems irrefutable is the work whose title proclaims its background, *Pierce the Ploughman's Crede*. The *Crede* mentions the trial of the Lollard Walter Brut (lines 657–62), and hence is probably to be dated shortly after 1393 when that trial ended. The preservation of the poem is poor: the earliest fragment is a single sheet of c.1460–70 (BL Harley 78, f.3; see Doyle 1959); the first complete manuscript is BL Royal 18 B.xvii, a volume that contains a copy of the C text of *Piers Plowman* to which strangely the *Crede* there forms an introduction; the third copy is Trinity College Cambridge R.3.15. An edition of the poem was printed three years after Crowley's editions of *Piers Plowman* (STC 19904), and the two were included together in the text put out in 1560–1561 (STC 19908). There are numerous parallels between the *Crede* and Langland's poem (see the notes to the edition of the former; and Turville-Petre 111–14; Lampe; Szittya 199–230; Kendall 73–80) which, even allowing for the traditional expressions of satirical attacks and the common alliterative technique, make clear that the author knew the earlier and greater poem well. In the *Crede* the figure of Piers is much more than the symbol that he became in later works: not least reminiscent of Langland is the way in which Piers is reserved to a relatively late stage in the dreamer's search, entering at line 421 (almost halfway through the poem), and the immediate authority the dreamer accords to his words. But the range of the *Crede*'s interests is tiny in comparison with Langland: the primary object of interest is the failure of the friars, who seem here to have taken on the dominant clerical role, to fulfil their pastoral duty of instructing the laity in the elements of religion. The dreamer engages members of each of the four orders in turn in conversation; the venality of each is castigated, their preoccupation with temporal wealth and especially with the adornment of their own church, their equation of shrift with the payment of money into their coffers. In disgust the dreamer turns away, despairing of finding anyone to teach him his creed. At this point, with suddenness to equal Langland's poem, Piers enters. Piers provides the necessary instruction, and likewise continues the condemnation of the contemporary clergy and preeminently of the friars. Langland's complex subject has been simplified to a single one, his ironic and allusive technique

to direct polemic. Perhaps more importantly, Langland's uncertain ideological outlook, an outlook which leaves him the freedom to criticize or praise
without preconceptions, has been shifted to a much less ambiguous one.
The sympathy for Brut is an expression of commitment only less clear than
the earlier praise of Wyclif:

> Wytness on Wycliff þat warned hem wiþ trewþe
> For he in goodnesse of gost grayþliche hem warned
> To wayuen her wikednesse and werkes of synne.
> Whou sone þis sori men seweden his soule,
> And oueral lollede him wiþ heretykes werkes! (528–32)

Both comments are from the mouth of Piers, the undoubted source of
authoritative truth in the poem. The *Crede* must therefore be accepted as
the work of a Lollard, even if a Lollard not on the extreme wing of the movement (Lawton 1981). Like Langland, but unlike Wyclif in his later writings
and almost all of his followers, the *Crede* author expresses some sympathy
for the founding ideals of the friars (464–65, but compare 460 where the
devil appears as their founder), though unstinted condemnation for the contemporary state of the orders. The opening of the poem appears to envisage
oral confession as reasonable (9–10), but this orthodoxy derives from the
dreamer, shown to be fallible. Piers's own account of the Eucharist at the
end (lines 822–30) is equivocal: the sixteenth-century printer substituted a
less ambiguous statement (see Skeat's note to 817–21), but comparable accounts can be found in the writings and trials of early Lollards. If there are
any echoes of Langland's poem in *Friar Daw's Reply* (Smart 42–53) or in the
sixteenth-century *God spede the Plough* (Skeat 1867, 69–74), these may well
come through the intermediary of the *Crede*.

Less overtly heterodox than the *Crede* are the two fragments that together
have come to be known as *Mum and the Sothsegger* (Embree; Wawn 1983,
282–87). Whether the two separately preserved sections belong together or
not does not matter in the present context. The first fragment, that in passus, seems to date from about 1399–1400, the second in continuous alliterative long lines from about 1403–06; the king of the first is Richard II, that
of the second Henry IV (Day and Steele xix–xxiv). It is clear that the author,
or authors, of both parts knew the A version of Langland's poem well, and
had some cognizance of B (xiv–xv). Skeat, in printing the first part as *Richard
the Redeless*, claimed Langland's authorship for it (1886 2:lxxxiv–lxxxv),
though few would now accept that view (Blamires). The purpose of the poem,
as the editorial title reveals, is to press the necessity for speaking truth openly,
however unpalatable to the hearers. The sphere with which the author is
concerned is not principally that of personal, moral behaviour but of public
action; the men he castigates are those in councils of the king and of promi-

nent persons, clerical and lay, who prefer to keep silent when self-interested schemers urge a course of action against the public good and who make no attempt to remedy the ills evident in the world. The abuses of the contemporary legal system, where nothing can be achieved without money, particularly excited the author's wrath. Both kings, Richard II and Henry IV, were, in this author's opinion, dominated by Mum. There is no obvious sign of Lollardy in either fragment, though, not surprisingly, there is some anticlericalism (lines M409–20, 669; see also Lawton 1981, 788–92). Here the understanding of *Piers Plowman* shown by the author is of a poem with an immediate social and political message, a tract for the times rather than the record of a spiritual quest.

Considerable obscurity surrounds the next two cases that must be considered, *The Praier and Complaynte of the Ploweman* (STC 20036, repr. 20036.5) and the work that traditionally goes under the name of *The Plowman's Tale* (STC 5099.5, 5100, 5101 and Thynne's and subsequent editions of Chaucer, STC 5068–81; Skeat 1897, 147–90). Neither survives in any medieval manuscript, but both were printed in the 1530s; the former claims to originate "not longe after" 1300, and the antiquity of the latter is asserted in its second appearance as part of Chaucer's *Canterbury Tales*; both appear to be of Wycliffite background, probably though at least in the former case not provably, of the early years of the fifteenth century (White 26–28; Hudson 1983, 172–73). But in addition to these opacities, it is unclear whether either shows knowledge of *Piers Plowman* and hence whether either properly belongs in this survey. Neither makes any direct allusion to Langland's poem, though there is an evident similarity of concern and some comparable phraseology. The author of the *Tale* (1066) lays claim to responsibility for *Pierce the Ploughman's Crede* also, a claim that, because of the wide discrepancy of poetic skill between the two works, is not altogether easy to accept (Wawn 1972, 28; Lawton 1981, 787; cf. Kendall 80–83). *The Plowman's Tale* has been much more fully examined by a recent critic: Wawn has shown from the language of the poem that the bulk of it must be accepted as of early origin, but that lines 1–52 and 205–28 were probably sixteenth-century additions (Wawn 1972, 1973). But without the first 52 lines, it is uncertain whether any connection with a ploughman, Langland's or another, can be made: the ploughman is introduced as the speaker in those opening lines, but later appears only in the dialogue with the Pelican towards the end of the poem (lines 1285, 1289, 1301) where his name is outside the metrical scheme of the stanzas and could have been introduced also by a later redactor, most probably the composer of the opening to reinforce his location of the poem.

In *The Praier and Complaynte of the Ploweman* the ploughman hardly exists outside the title. Even the figure in (sig. B.7) "And so lorde our hope is thou wylt as sone yhere a plowmans prayer and he kepe thyne hestes as thou wylt do a mannes of religyon though that the plowman ne may haue so muche syluer for his prayer as men of relygion," with its possible echo of B.10.468 (and Matthew 1902, 274), is a proverbial type and not perceptibly the man of the title. The problem here with both works is to make a fair assessment of the extent to which the spokesman, particularly by the sixteenth century, had become a commonplace: were the authors, or the later revisers, of these two works consciously reviving a figure which they, and their audiences, would have associated with Langland's poem? Or had the ploughman become a proverbial model of the upright, honest labourer, and, at least in Lollard circles, of the plain man with somewhat radical notions about the church and its role in society? In the latter case, any reminiscence of *Piers Plowman* could be unintentional. Such may seem to be the answer from the early sixteenth-century poem *A Lytell Geste howe the Plowman lerned his Pater Noster* (STC 20034). Here the *plowman* is certainly the typical labourer, who can learn the clauses of the Latin *pater noster* only as the names of men he is forced by a ruse of the parish priest to feed. But here, in a strangely unedifying work, the priest is the approved figure, the *plowman*, a wealthy citizen, put down. The position is complicated especially with the *Tale* by the association with Chaucer. Arguably Chaucer in his portrait of the Ploughman in the *Prologue* (CT 1.477–528 and cf. II.1166–83, X.22–60) was already drawing on this proverbial model, but it is not certain that we should follow Skeat in claiming a deliberate reminiscence here of *Piers Plowman* (1885, 863). Whether the description also had Wycliffite overtones is irrelevant here; but the later reformer who put the *Tale* into print, and apparently fostered its heterodoxy on the original (Wawn 1973) was merely extending what Chaucer may have begun.

The relevance of these two works to the present concern arises because of the apparent popularity of the ploughman figure, with asserted closer links to Piers, in the mid-sixteenth century. After 1550 such popularity is easily explicable from the printing of Langland's poem by Robert Crowley (see below). But it appears to have begun before that date. The three printed texts with titles referring to Piers are not dated by their issuers, but are listed by the revised STC as about 1550. They are *I playne Piers which cannot flatter* (STC 19903a), *A godly dyalogue and dysputacyon betwene Pyers plowman and a popysh preest* (STC 19903), and *Pyers plowmans exhortation vnto the lordes, knightes and burgoysses of the parlyamenthouse* (STC 19905). The second and third of these are hard to date on internal evidence. But the first is crammed with allusions to various events in the reign of Henry VIII, about which the writer has sharply political observations to make (Wawn 1973; King 324); the last event to which reference is made is the recantation of Nicholas Shaxton and William Crome in June 1546 (sigs. E.2^v–3), and it seems reasonable to conclude that the work was composed soon after this. The question arises immediately as to why Piers should have been chosen in each as the voice of reason, the spokesman for the author. All three texts are reformist in outlook: the second, the least interesting of the three (White 32–34), deals with the Eucharist, with Piers putting forward a memorial doctrine of the sacrament and a *popysh preest*, arrogant and ill-informed, the traditional account of transsubstantiation; it, like the other two, is strongly critical of the clergy. The *Exhortation* (White 28–30) is more concerned with the temporal consequences of the Reformation: whilst congratulating the king on the reception of Christ's true religion into England, the author laments the problems posed by the dissolution of the monasteries. As well as the secular lords' selfish tendency to convert their farms into sheep-runs and thereby displace labourers, the author describes the difficulties of absorbing the monks, canons, friars and nuns, together with their offspring, into the secular economy. He puts forward a scheme for the reclamation of land hitherto thought too poor for agriculture, for conversion of sheep pastures into arable land, and for the imposition of taxes on imported goods. The subject matter of *I playne Piers* (White 31–32) is more varied, and hence difficult to summarise: it covers the continued worldliness of the clergy, the attempts of many of them to persuade the king to revert to old doctrines and customs, and particularly their reluctance to allow the laity to possess the Scriptures in the vernacular: "You allowe they saye, *legenda aurea*, Roben Hoode, Beuys and Gower and al bagage besyd, but Gods word ye may not abyde . . ." (sig. E.3ᵛ); "We must come to mattens masse and euensonge, and harken them bable I wot not how longe, we vnderstand neuer a word whether they vs curse, or do they worse" (sig. E.8). It seems clear that none of this material is entirely alien to the world of Langland's original poem: there is the same concern for the poor, oppressed by the temporal claims of clergy and nobility alike, defenceless in the face of economic forces over which they have no control, but hungry not only for material but also for spiritual nourishment. There are also literary parallels, in the sharply satirical tone ("at one perlyament we haue but thre sacramentes, and in an other we haue seuen; some tyme must the worde of God be good for al men, some time but for ryche men," *I playne Piers* sigs. C.1–1ᵛ), the mocking use of proverb or rhyming tag, and it is tempting to wonder whether the frequency of alliteration in these prose works may owe something to Langland's poem. In all three Piers is the endorsed spokesman of reason, of moderate reform and of enlightenment. But how much knowledge of *Piers Plowman* do any of them actually show? The answer seems that, apart from the name of the spokesman, *provably* almost none. This, however, in many ways makes the situation more, not less, puzzling. For none of the authors thought it worthwhile to explain their figure, or to start by establishing his authority. Even if a ploughman were proverbial, and his value had been enhanced by association with Chaucer's Ploughman, this does not explain the personal name. Even if Latimer's *Sermon of the Plow* (1548) shows any awareness of Langland (as claimed by Kelly), there is no appeal to that name.

Most of the references, real or apparent, in the two centuries after the composition of Langland's poem associate it with reforming views — most often with views that at the time of composition would have appeared radical or heterodox. But it would be erroneous to imply that this was always the case. The striking exception is a work found only in a single manuscript, now British Library MS Harley 207; at the beginning, but not in the main scribe's hand, is the date 1532, a date that may be too early for credibility. Its title is *The Banckett of Iohan the Reve vnto Peirs ploughman, Laurens laborer, Thomlyn tailyer and Hobb of the hille with other* (unpublished, extract only in Hales and Furnivall 2:lxi–lxii). The subject of the discussion is primarily the Eucharist, the spokesman of the reformed faith (that specified to be of Luther, Oecolampadius, Karlstadt, Melancthon, Bucer, Joye, Bale, Turner, and Frith ff. 2ᵛ, 11ᵛ) is one *Doctor Dawcock*. The Doctor gets the worst of the argument, and finds it impossible to maintain his position, even though he is supported by *Jacke Jolie* and *Nicholas Newfangill*; given their names, all this is predictable. Less expected are the defenders of transsubstantiation and the old faith: *Iohan the reve, Peirs ploughman, Laurens laborer and Thomlyn tailyer*. Here Piers is entirely orthodox and conventional; perhaps more significantly, he is not the most important spokesman even of that viewpoint, as the main spokesman for the defence of the old religion is John the reve.

Perhaps the crucial event in *Piers Plowman* studies in the sixteenth century was the publication in 1550 of Robert Crowley's three editions (pp. 175–77 above) — crucial because it made the poem available to a wider audience in a form which, albeit marked by Crowley's radical Protestant leanings, nonetheless is a relatively accurate account of Langland's B version. The three impressions all bear the date 1550, but from collation of copies it seems that, whilst the first impression was taken from a lost manuscript, the second reflected a comparison of that first impression with another manuscript from which many readings were incorporated, and the third may add further "corrections" from yet another manuscript (Skeat 1869, xxxi–xxxv; Kane and Donaldson 6–7; King 1976, 346–47). Kane and Donaldson also indicated, but were not in a position to demonstrate fully, that there are further variations between individual copies of a single impression, reflecting modifications made during printing. There is also reason to think that Crowley was aware of the A and C versions of the poem, and may eclectically have incorporated some readings from those versions into his B text. Despite all this activity, Crowley was not a critical editor in the modern sense: his text is fairly clearly a conflated one, though the loss of his exemplar manuscripts makes this impossible finally to prove (cf. Kane 1965, 41), and he set about modernizing the orthography to make the poem more accessible to his contemporaries. His text is not, however, consistently altered to suit a mid-sixteenth-century puritan audience: though a little minor re-working and a very few omissions may be discerned, the majority of the text remains unaltered, even when updating would have presented little difficulty (King 1976, 347–49). The editor's own bias emerges rather from the preface he inserts, and from the marginal notes: from the former it is clear that Crowley saw the text as prophetical of the concerns of his own age, and its author as a contemporary and implicitly a follower of John Wyclif.

Crowley probably gained this last view, and perhaps his first knowledge of the poem, from John Bale. In his *Illustrium maioris Britannie Scriptorum . . . Summarium* Bale did not include Langland, but the poem seems to appear under the title *Petrum Agricolam* in the long list of works by Wyclif (f. 157). In his *Scriptorum Illustrium maioris Brytannie . . . Catalogus*, published in 1557–59 (1:474–75) is found the name of Robert Langland and the poem *Visionem Petri Aratoris*. Skeat (1885, xxiii) considered that, although this is subsequent to Crowley's edition, Bale was the source of Crowley's comments on the author of *Piers Plowman* (cf. Kane 1965, 40–46; King 1976, 334–45). The attribution to Robert Langland appears also in Bale's notebook (Lane Poole and Bateson 383, 509–10), and was entered by him into the copy of the B text Bale owned, now Huntington HM 128 (Kane 1965, 37–42). Bale in the *Catalogus* saw the author of *Piers Plowman* as "ex primis Ioannis Vuicleui discipulis unum" (1:474), and quoted in an appendix a passage from Wyclif as a parallel. Crowley states in his preface, "I did . . . consult such men as I knew to be more exercised in the studie of antiquities, then I my selfe haue ben. And by some of them I haue learned that the Autour was named Roberte langelande" (sig. *.2), and in the same paragraph mentions Wyclif. His sidenotes, together with the preface, convey Crowley's sense of the poem as prophetic of his own times, as well as suitably critical of the fourteenth-century corruption of the church (King 1976, 348–51; 1982, 320–36). The edition of 1561, to which the *Crede* was appended, was put out by Owen Rogers; it was not a new edition, but a rather inaccurate reprint of Crowley's third edition (Skeat 1869, xxxvi).

Crowley's efforts, part of a concerted plan to produce suitable reading matter of a reforming cast, were made at an opportune moment. The interest in native antiquities that might give authority to the new ecclesiastical dispensations, exemplified by the printing of Lollard texts in the 1530s and 1540s, fostered by the work of Leland, Bale and Foxe, makes it hardly surprising that Langland's poem, now readily accessible in the four editions, was frequently mentioned after Elizabeth's accession in 1559. Typical of the later incorporation of Langland's hero is the tract put together by one

T. F. (thought by White [30–31] to be Francis Thynne, an attribution rejected by revised STC), entitled *Newes from the North. Otherwise called the Conference between Simon Certain, and Pierce Plowman* (STC 24062). The main topic
of the work is the defects of legal processes and especially the venality and
pride of legal practitioners. The characterization of *Pierce* is hardly consistent: introduced as "a Countrie man a Neighbour, a iolly olde fatherly man,
bringing vnder his arme a fardel of Bookes, as many as he might well holde
vndernethe one of his armes" (sig. B.2ᵛ), *Pierce* nonetheless claims, "I am
no Schoole man" (sig. C.3ᵛ), whilst at the same time showing considerable
familiarity with the law. *Pierce* is a northerner; though in general his opinions are endorsed, he is not the dominant hero of the work. But despite the
name, *T. F.* shows no certain knowledge of Langland's poem, and his tract
concerns subjects only incidentally introduced in the earlier work.

Newes from the North seems to partake of the earlier adoption of the name
Piers Plowman as a typical and admirable mouthpiece for the author's viewpoint. In this it might be more correct to regard it as evidence of implicit
literary criticism rather than of demonstrable derivation. Though such
material is more frequent after the publication of Crowley's edition, it can
be found much earlier. John Audelay's references to *Mede þe maydyn* (Whiting 1931, xvii, poems 2/705, 12/11) may indicate that he knew the poem,
unless the name had become proverbial; Gavin Douglas's allusion to "Peirs
plewman that maid his workmen fow" (*Palice of Honour* 1714) is perhaps a
more certain instance, coming as it does immediately after a reference to
Rauf Coilyear. Claims for Skelton's knowledge of the poem (see Skeat 1885,
864–65) are stylistically more credible, even though he does not name it.
After the publication of the text, the author of *A Myrroure for Magistrates* (STC
1247, 1559) summarises the fable of the belling of the cat, a fable which
his open acknowledgement shows to come from Langland (sig.C.3ᵛ):

> Reade well the sentence of the Rat of renoune,
> Which Pierce the plowman discribes in his dreame.

Later similar allusions are too numerous to list. Perhaps one of the fullest
is the virtual paraphrase of the scene of *friar flatterere* and Contrition
(B.20.294–379) in Michael Drayton's *The historie of the life and death of the lord
Cromwell* (1609, STC 7201, pp. 34–37). In both of these it seems certain
that the authors had read at least a part of Langland's poem. Sadly this seems
rarely to be provable. Even the comments of critics such as William Webbe
in *A discourse of English poetrie* (1586, STC 25172, Smith 1:242) or George
Puttenham in *The arte of English poesie* (1589, STC 20519, Smith 2:62, 64–65,
150) who dutifully include *Piers Plowman* in their review show little familiarity with it. It is not simply that, for comprehensible reasons, sixteenth-century
interest in the poem is not ours—that men of that period valued it for its

social, moral and ecclesiastical commentary rather than for its allegory, its structure or its literary skill. Regretfully one must conclude that, at least after the immediate and usually Lollard imitations, *Piers Plowman* in the two and a half centuries after its composition was more honoured in the name than in the reading.

REFERENCES

Arnold, Thomas, ed. *Select English Works of John Wyclif.* 3 vols. Oxford: Clarendon Press, 1869–71.

Bale, John. *Illustrium maioris Britanniae Scriptorum . . . Summarium.* Ipswich, 1548 (STC 1295).

———. *Scriptorum Illustrium maioris Brytannie . . . Catalogus.* Basel: Oporinum, 1557–59.

Bawcutt, P. J., ed. *The Shorter Poems of Gavin Douglas.* Scottish Text Society. Edinburgh: Blackwood, 1967.

Bennett, J. A. W. "Chaucer's Contemporary." In Hussey 1969, 310–24, 352–53.

Blamires, A. G. "*Mum and the Sothsegger* and Langlandian Idiom." *NM* 76 (1975): 583–604.

Burrow, J. A. "The Audience of *Piers Plowman.*" *Anglia* 75 (1957): 373–84; rpt. with a postscript in *Essays on Medieval Literature.* Oxford: Clarendon Press, 1984. 102–16.

Clarke, M. V., and V. H. Galbraith. "The Deposition of Richard II." *BJRL* 14 (1930): 125–81. (Includes an edition of the Chronicle of Dieulacres Abbey, 1381–1403.)

Colaianne, A. J. "*Piers Plowman*": *An Annotated Bibliography of Editions and Criticism, 1550–1977.* New York and London: Garland, 1978.

Coleman, Janet. *Medieval Readers and Writers.* London: Hutchinson, 1981.

Cooper, Helen. "Langland's and Chaucer's Prologues." *YLS* 1(1987): 71–81.

Coulton, G. G. "*Piers Plowman*: One or Five?" *MLR* 7 (1912): 372–73.

Crowley, Robert, ed. *The Vision of Pierce Plowman.* London: Robert Crowley, 1550 (STC 19906); London: Robert Crowley, 1550 (STC 19907); London: Robert Crowley, 1550 (STC 19907a). A facsimile edition of the first of these appeared with an endnote by J. A. W. Bennett. London: Paradine Press, 1976.

Day, Mabel and R. Steele, eds. *Mum and the Sothsegger.* EETS 199. London: Oxford University Press, 1936.

DiMarco, Vincent. "*Piers Plowman*": *A Reference Guide.* Boston: G. K. Hall, 1982.

Dobson, R. B., ed. *The Peasants' Revolt of 1381.* 2nd ed. London: Macmillan, 1983.

Donaldson, E. Talbot. *Piers Plowman: The C-Text and Its Poet.* Yale Studies in English 113. New Haven: Yale University Press, 1949.

Doyle, A. I. "An Unrecognized Piece of *Piers the Ploughman's Creed* and Other Work by Its Scribe." *Speculum* 34 (1959): 428–36.

———. "The Manuscripts." In Lawton 1982, 88–100.

———. "Remarks on Surviving Manuscripts of *Piers Plowman.*" *Medieval English Religious and Ethical Literature: Essays in Honour of George Russell.* Ed. G. Kratzmann and J. Simpson. Cambridge: D. S. Brewer, 1986. 35–48.

Drayton, Michael. *The historie of the life and death of the lord Cromwell.* London: F. Kyngston for W. Welby, 1609 (STC 7201).

Embree, D. "Richard the Redeless and Mum and the Sothsegger: A Case of Mistaken Identity." *N&Q* 220 (1975): 4-12.

A godly dyalogue and dysputacyon betwene Pyers plowman, and a popysh preest, concernyng the supper of the lorde. London: W. Copland, c.1550 (STC 19903); London: W. Copland (STC 19903.5).

Gollancz, I., ed. *The Parlement of the Thre Ages.* London: Oxford University Press, 1915.

————, and Mabel Day, eds. *Death and Liffe.* London: Oxford University Press, 1930.

Gradon, Pamela. "Langland and the Ideology of Dissent." *PBA* 66 (1982 [for 1980]): 179-205.

Hales, J. W., and F. J. Furnivall, eds. *Bishop Percy's Folio Manuscript.* London: Trübner, 1867-68.

Hanford, J. H., and J. M. Steadman. *"Death and Liffe*: An Alliterative Poem." *SP* 15 (1918): 221-94.

Hazlitt, W. C., ed. *Remains of the Early Popular Poetry of England*, Vol. 1. London: John Russell Smith, 1864.

Hilton, R. H., and T. R. Aston, eds. *The English Rising of 1381.* Cambridge: Cambridge University Press, 1984.

Hudson, Anne. "A Lollard Sect Vocabulary?" *So meny people longages and tonges. . . . Essays presented to Angus McIntosh.* Ed. M. Benskin and M. L. Samuels. Edinburgh: The Editors, 1981. 15-30.

————. " 'No newe thyng': The Printing of Medieval Texts in the early Reformation Period." *Middle English Studies presented to Norman Davis.* Ed. Douglas Gray and E. G. Stanley. Oxford: Clarendon Press, 1983. 153-74.

————. "A New Look at the Lay Folks' Catechism." *Viator* 16 (1985): 243-58.

Hulbert, J. R. "The Problems of Authorship and Date of Wynnere and Wastoure." *MP* 18 (1920): 31-40.

Hussey, S. S. "Langland's Reading of Alliterative Poetry." *MLR* 60 (1965): 163-70.

I playne Piers which cannot flatter. London: N. Hill (?), 1546 (?) (STC 19903a); London (?), 1589 (?) (STC 19903a.5).

Kane, George, ed. *Piers Plowman: The A Version.* London: Athlone, 1960.

————. *Piers Plowman: The Evidence for Authorship.* London: Athlone, 1965.

————, and E. Talbot Donaldson, eds. *Piers Plowman: The B Version.* London: Athlone, 1975.

Kelly, R. L. "Hugh Latimer as Piers Plowman." *SEL* 17 (1977): 13-26.

Kendall, R. D. *The Drama of Dissent: The Radical Poetics of Nonconformity, 1380-1590.* Chapel Hill: University of North Carolina Press, 1986.

King, J. N. " Robert Crowley's Editions of *Piers Plowman*: A Tudor Apocalypse." *MP* 73 (1976): 342-52.

————. *English Reformation Literature: The Tudor Origins of the Protestant Tradition.* Princeton: Princeton University Press, 1982.

Knighton, Henry. *Chronicon.* Ed. J. R. Lumby. Rolls Series 92. London: Eyre and Spottiswoode, 1889-95.

Lampe, David. "The Satiric Strategy of *Peres the Ploughmans Crede.*" *The Alliterative Tradition in the Fourteenth Century.* Ed. B. S. Levy and P. E. Szarmach. Kent, OH: Kent State University Press, 1981. 69-80.

Lane Poole, R., and M. Bateson, eds. *John Bale's "Index Britanniae Scriptorum".* Oxford: Clarendon Press, 1902.

[Langland, William.] *The Vision of Pierce Plowman . . . whereunto is also annexed the Crede of Pierce Plowman.* London: Rogers, 1561 (STC 19908).

Lawton, David. *"Scottish Field*: Alliterative Verse and Stanley Encomium in the Percy Folio." *LSE* ns 10 (1978): 42–57.

―――. "Lollardy and the *Piers Plowman* Tradition." *MLR* 76 (1981): 780–93. —

―――. *Middle English Alliterative Poetry and Its Literary Background.* Cambridge: D. S. Brewer, 1982.

―――. "The Unity of Middle English Alliterative Poetry." *Speculum* 58(1983): 72–94.

A lytell geste how the plowman lerned his pater noster. [London: Wynkyn de Worde, 1510] (STC 20034). See Hazlitt 1864, 1:209–16, for a modern edition.

McGinnis, M. E. *"Piers the Plowman* in England, 1362–1625: A Study in Popularity and Influence." Unpublished Yale Ph.D. dissertation, 1932. Contains a full survey of the influence of and references to *Piers Plowman* as the topic was understood in 1932; also texts of *I playne Piers*, *Pyers plowmans exhortation*, and *A godly dyalogue . . . betwene Pyers Plowman and a popysh preest* (the original editions were here used, not McGinnis's transcripts) and extracts from other material difficult of access.

Manly, J. M. *"Piers the Plowman* and Its Sequence." *Cambridge History of English Literature* 2:1–42. Cambridge: Cambridge University Press, 1908.

Mann, Jill. *Chaucer and Medieval Estates Satire.* Cambridge: Cambridge University Press, 1973.

Matthew, F. D., ed. *The English Works of Wyclif hitherto unprinted.* 2nd rev. ed. EETS 74. London: Kegan Paul, Trench, Trübner, 1902.

Middleton, Anne. "The Audience and Public of *Piers Plowman.*" In Lawton 1982, 101–23.

A Myrroure for Magistrates. London: T. Marshe, 1559 (STC 1247).

Newes from the north. Otherwise called the conference betwene Simon Certain, and Pierce Plowman, faithfully collected by T. F. Student. London: J. Allde, 1579 (STC 24062).

Oakden, J. P., ed. *"Scotish Ffeilde."* Chetham Society ns 94 (1935).

Offord, M. Y., ed. *The Parlement of the Thre Ages.* EETS 246. London: Oxford University Press, 1959.

Pearsall, Derek, ed. *Piers Plowman by William Langland. An Edition of the C-Text.* London: Arnold, 1978.

Pierce the Ploughmans Crede. London: R. Wolfe, 1553 (STC 19904).

The plowmans tale. London: T. Godfrey, 1535 (?) (STC 5099.5); another edition London: W. Hill, 1548 (?) (STC 5100); edition with commentary London: G. E. for S. Macham and M. Cooke, 1606 (STC 5101).

The Praier and Complaynte of the Ploweman. Antwerp(?), 1531 (?) (STC 20036); London, c. 1532 (?) (STC 20036.5). The earlier version was reprinted in *Harleian Miscellany* 6:84–106 (London, 1744–46).

Puttenham, George. *The arte of English poesie.* London: R. Field, 1589 (STC 20519).

Pyers plowmans exhortation, vnto the lordes, knightes and burgoysses of the parlyamenthouse. London: A. Scoloker, 1550 (?) (STC 19905).

Robbins, Rossell Hope. *Historical Poems of the XIVth and XVth Centuries.* New York: Columbia University Press, 1959. (Edition of *The Crowned King* is no.95.)

―――, and J. L. Cutler. *Supplement to the Index of Middle English Verse.* Lexington: University of Kentucky Press, 1965.

Samuels, M. L. "Some Applications of Middle English Dialectology." *ES* 44 (1963): 81–94.

―――. "Langland's Dialect." *MÆ* 54 (1985): 232–47.

Simmons, T. F., and H. E. Nolloth, eds. *The Lay Folks' Catechism.* EETS 118. London: Kegan Paul, Trench, Trübner, 1901.

Skeat, W. W., ed. *Pierce the Ploughmans Crede*. EETS 30. London: Trübner, 1867.
———. *The Visions of William concerning Piers the Plowman . . . Text B*. EETS 38. London: Trübner, 1869.
———. *The Vision of William concerning Piers Plowman . . . General Preface, Notes and Index*. EETS 81. London: Trübner, 1885. (A list of references to the poem is given on pp. 863–74.)
———. *The Vision of William concerning Piers the Plowman in three parallel texts, with Richard the Redeless*. 2 vols. London: Oxford University Press. 1886.
———. *The Testament of Love* and *The Plowman's Tale*. In Vol. 7 (*Chaucerian and Other Pieces*), *Complete Works of Geoffrey Chaucer*. Oxford: Clarendon Press, 1897. 1–145, 147–90.
Smart, W. K. "*The Castle of Perseverance*: Place, Date and a Source." *Manly Anniversary Studies in Language and Literature*, Chicago: University of Chicago Press, 1923. 42–53.
Smith, G. Gregory, ed. *Elizabethan Critical Essays*. Oxford: Clarendon Press, 1904.
Steadman, J. M. "The Date of *Winnere and Wastoure*." *MP* 19 (1921): 211–19.
Szittya, Penn R. *The Antifraternal Tradition in Medieval Literature*. Princeton: Princeton University Press, 1986.
Turville-Petre, T. *The Alliterative Revival*. Cambridge: D. S. Brewer, 1977.
Walsingham, Thomas. *Historia Anglicana*. Ed. H. T. Riley. Rolls Series 28. London: Longman, Green et al., 1863–64.
Wawn, A. N. "The Genesis of *The Plowman's Tale*." *YES* 2 (1972): 21–40.
———. "Chaucer, *The Plowman's Tale* and Reformation Propaganda: the Testimonies of Thomas Godfray and *I playne Piers*." *BJRL* 56 (1973): 174–92.
———. "Truth-telling and the Tradition of *Mum and the Sothsegger*." *YES* 13 (1983): 270–87.
Webbe, W. *A discourse of English poetrie*. London: J. Charlewood for R. Walley, 1586 (STC 25172).
White, H. C. *Social Criticism in Popular Religious Literature of the Sixteenth Century*. New York: Macmillan, 1944.
Whiting, E. K., ed. *The Poems of John Audelay*. EETS 184. London: Oxford University Press, 1931.

Index

The index is meant to provide easy access to topics of discussion, authors (or their works), and the relevant scholarship. It does not record merely incidental references to Langland and *Piers Plowman*, since these occur on virtually every page; and it does not include the expanded bibliographical references at the end of each chapter. Alphabetization is letter by letter (e.g., Acts of Thomas, *a culpa et a poena*, Adam). The principal discussion in a series is indicated by italicized page numbers.

Abelard, Peter, 105
Abraham, as Faith, 53, 93, 124; as fruit of tree of charity, 53
accent. *See* meter
active life: as Dowel, 46; as Haukyn, 50–51, Langland's view of. *See also* Three Lives
Acts of Thomas, as early tour of hell, 122
a culpa et a poena. See indulgence
Adam: as bondsman, 69–70; forgiveness of, 56; as fruit of tree of charity, 53
Adam Davy's Five Dreams, 129
Adams, Robert, 11, 12, 13, 30, 32, 36, 38, 42, 43, 47, 58, 60, 61, *87–114*, 94, 95, 96, 97, 103, 108
ad pristinum statum, 75
Aelfric, prose of, 229
Aeneid, 123
Aers, David, 12, 13, 14, 17, 19, 40, 41, 52, 55, 56, 68, 95, 103, 104, 118, 127, 158n
Alain de Lille, *Anticlaudianus* and *Complaint of Nature*, influence of Bernard Sylvestris, 125
allegory: categories of, 118; Christian, 14; as "continued metaphor," 123; critical approaches to, 14; English tradition of, 128–30; four levels, *16*, 88, 118; French tradition of, 119,

126–28, 136; and *PP*, 8, 14, 53, *117–33*; vertical vs. horizontal, 95

Themes

arbor caritatis, 52; banquet, 49, 127, 136; castle, 122, 127, 157; debates, 129, 138; Four Daughters of God, 56–57; landscape, 127; marriage, 37, 125, 127, 128, 137; pilgrimage, 40, 125, *126–28*; Redemption, 53; sacraments, 128; seven deadly sins, 40, 101, 127, 156, 181, 191; ten commandments, 40; "tours of hell," 121–22, 126; virtues and vices, 124; *voies*, 126–27.
See also dreams, allegorical; imagery; metaphor; personification; tree of charity
Alford, John A., 17, 18, 19, 20, *29–65*, 38, 39, 50, 75, 159–160, 161
Allen, Judson B., 7, 17, 20, 42, 95, 96, 109
alliteration: after 1400, 2; "alliterative revival," 244, 253; "alliterative survival," 244; in *Beowulf*, 229; and caesura, 236; collocations, 239, 242, 243, 254; distinction between Old and Middle English practice, 227; as evidence of Langland's dialect, 208–10; formal (classical) vs. informal

alliteration *(continued)*
(non-classical), 234; ictus, 230, 231;
need for synonyms, 237–38; primary
vs. secondary, 225; in sermons, 158n;
staves, *225*, 231, 238, 243; and style
of *PP*, *223–49*; word choice influenced by, 169, *239–41*
*A Lytell Geste how the Plowman lerned his
Pater Noster*, 258
Amassian, Margaret, and James
Sadowsky, 38
Ambrose, St., 18
Ames, Ruth, 12, 14, 44, 54
anacrusis. *See* meter
anagogical level, 16. *See also* allegory:
four levels
anagram, as Langland's "signature," 7
Ancrene Wisse, and Langland's method of
argument, 168
Anderson, Judith, 130
Anima: on baptism, 100; on charity, 55;
on clerks' ignorance of French, 128;
dialogue with Will, 52, 106; on temporal possessions of Church, 75
Annunciation, and tree of charity, 53
Anselm of Havelberg, historicism of, 106
Antichrist: attack on Unity, 60, 104,
127; expected coming in 1360's, 11;
and "fools," 107; influence of Huon
de Meri's *Antecrist* on *PP*, 127, 136;
pope as, 111; as twelfth-century
theme, 95
anti-intellectualism, 105–06, 254
antimendicant writings. *See* friars: criticism of
Antoine de la Salle, use of authorial "signature," 7
apocalypse, *PP* as, 4, 10–12, 58, 103,
117
apocalypticism: of biblical prophets, 119;
of early Christians, 94; elements in
PP, 58–61, 68, 103–04; as "horizontal" approach to ultimate reality, 88,
93; and Joachim of Flora, 105; and
Langland's imagery, 58; and Lollards,
111; and monasticism, 106. *See also*
prophecy
Apocalypse of Golias, 119, 136
Apocalypse (Visio) of Paul, 122, 129
Apocalypse of Peter, 122
Apocalypse of Zephaniah, 122
Apocrypha, and visionary tours, 121–22
Aquinas. *See* Thomas Aquinas, St.
arbor caritatis. *See* tree of charity
Aristotle, in hell, 46

Aristotelianism, biblicism as reaction
against, 106, 107
Armitage-Smith, Sydney, 79
Arn, Mary-Jo, 88
Arnold, Thomas, 161n, 255
Arnould, E. J., 138, 141n, 142
Artes praedicandi: *antethema*, 160; concordance *(concordancia verbalis* and *realis)*,
20, 159; confirming authorities, 36,
165; on digression, 159; division *(divisio, partitio)*, 159, 160; influence on
making of *PP*, *155–72*; and Lang-
land's rhetoric, 237; *thema* 159, 160,
166, 167. *See also* preaching; rhetoric;
sermon
Aston, M., 73
Athanasian Creed: and pardon, 41, 42,
46, 152; and *redde quod debes*, 149; and
semi-Pelagianism, 96
Attridge, Derek, 226
attritionism, of Duns Scotus, 101
Audelay, John, 262
Auerbach, Erich, 14, 118
Augustine, St.: apocalypticism of, 94;
and exegesis, 18, 98; and Myth of
Er, 123; quoted, 41, 156
Augustinianism, 100, 103, 110; and
Langland's thought, 89, 96, 97; vs.
Pelagianism of *moderni*, 109
Ault, W. O., 70
authorship controversy. See *Piers Plow-
man*: authorship
avarice: chief sin in *PP*, 34, 145, 151;
personifications of, 137, 138. *See also*
Sins, Seven Deadly
Avery, M. E., 82
Ayenbite of Inwyt. See Dan Michel

Baildon, W. P., 82
Baker, Denise, 87, 96
Baker, Thomas, 251–52
Baldwin, Anna P., 6, 19, 38, 39, *67–81*,
67, 68, 75, 78, 79, 82, 83
Baldwin, J. F. (and J. S. Leadam), 82
Bale, John: attribution of *PP* to Robert
Langland, 261; and early interest in
PP, 6, 175; emendation of *PP*, 176;
source of Crowley's comments on
Langland, 261; theory of Wycliffite
influence on Langland, 109
Ball, John: letter of (use of *PP* as rallying
cry), 4, 5, 72, 251, 253; pseudonyms,
251, 252, 253
Banckett of Iohan the Reve unto Peirs plough-

man, *Laurens laborer, Thomlyn tailyer and Hobb of the hille with other*, 260

banquet scene (B.13.25-214), *49-50*, 90, 136; French analogues, 126,127. *See also* doctor

baptism: *in extremis*, 99; as "sacrament of the dead," 92; and salvation, *98-100*

Barney, Stephen A., 39, 40, *117-33*, 118, 124, 137

Barnie, J., 74, 77, 78

Barthélemy, Renclus de Molliens, *Li Romans de Carité*, 126, 137

Bateson, M., 261

Baum, Paul F., 228

Bayley, C. C., 77

Beguines, and spread of "perfectionism," 93

Bellamy, J., 82

belling the cat, fable of, 15, 33, *78-79*, 157, 262

Bennett, H. S., 69, 70

Bennett, J. A. W., 3, 67, 78, 79, 80, 164, 184, 185, 186, 253

Benskin, M., 202; and Margaret Laing, 202, 204

Benson, C. David, 34, 135

Benzie, William, 5

Beowulf: precedent for multiple authorship theory, 8; alliteration in, 229

Bernard of Clairvaux, St.: and scale of religious obligation, 91; quoted in Holy Church's speech, 166. *See also* Pseudo-Bernard

Bernard Sylvestris, *Cosmographia*, and platonic tradition of allegory, 125

Bestul, Thomas, 9, 125, 127, 129, 130

Bethurum, Dorothy, 17

Bible: as influence on allegory, 118-21; influence on Langland's pronoun use, 213-14; Langland's use of quotations from, 17, 20, 96, 159-60; *lectio divina*, 106; parables, 59, 100, 121, 149, 167; vernacular translation of, 259; Wycliffite Bible, 202
   Gen. 1:26, 55; *28, 37, 40-41*, 120
   Exod. 32, 44
   Levit. 19:3, 38
   Num. 12:6-8, 120
   Judges 9, 120
   Job 33:15, 120
   Ps. 14:15, 146; *19:8*, 105; *84:11*, 56; *143*, 156
   Prov. 24:16, 149
   Cant. 1:6, 165
   Ecclus. 48 49, 119

Isa. 5:7, 121, *14:14*, 35; *56:10*, 120
Jer. 3:23, 119; *23:27-28*, 120
Ezek., 120; *40-48*, 121
Dan. 7, 10, 120; *9:2*, 119
Zach. 4:1, 120
2 Mac. 15:11-16, 120
Matt. 4:4, 51; *5:17*, 44; *6:19-21*, 35; *13:38-43*, 58; *13:18-43*, 34; *16:19*, 59; *18*, 152; *18:35*, 59; *19:12*, 90; *19:16*, 159; *19:16-24*, 90; *23:37*, 90; *25*, 166n; *26:39*, 56
Luke 7:42, 40; *8:11*, 121; *10:7*, 38; *10:34*, 143; *14:8*, 49
John 1:14, 121; *4:34*, 121; *8:44*, 34, 35
Rom. 2:14-15, 35, 37, 38; *3:7*, 151; *8:38-39*, 50; *13:7*, 40
1 Cor. 12, 59
2 Cor. 12:2-4, 122
Gal. 4:24, 121
Ephes. 4:1-3, 59; *6:16*, 121
Phil. 2:7-8, 56
1 Tim. 6:10, 145
2 Tim. 3:6, 59
2 Thess., 111
James 1:3-4, 50; *2:26*, 36
1 John, 111; *4:8*, 36
2 John, 111
1 Peter [4:18], 98
Apoc., 120; *19:11-13*, 121
Apocrypha, 121-22

biblical exegesis: and allegory, 14, 94; drift toward tropological allegory, 94; four-fold method, *16*, 88, 118; friars' abuse of, 145, 146; *id est* tradition, 55; Langland's use of, 17, 18, 20, 117, 118; after Lateran IV, 18, 143; and the *moderni*, 107-06; of Moses's breaking of the tablets, 44; of I Pet. 4:18 ("vix salvabitur"), 98; relation to preaching, 155-56, 158n. See also *Piers Plowman*: critical approaches

biblicism: and eschatological rhetoric, 111; and Langland, 106, 110; and Wycliffites, 73

Biel, Gabriel: Donatist tendencies, 102; and perfectionism, 92

Birnes, William J., 19

Bischoff, Guntrum G., 88, 94, 95, 106

Black Death: references in *PP*, 67, 184; effects, 70-72

Black Prince, 186

Blamires, A. G., 129, 256

Bliss, A. J., 229, 231

Bloch, Howard, 3

Bloch, Marc, 69
Bloomfield, Morton, 10, 11, 12, 14, 17,
    18, 30, 32, 33, 36, 37, 41, 45, 47,
    48, 50, 55, 57, 58, 68, 87, 88, 91,
    92, 94, 95, 103, 104, 106, 117, 120,
    124, 125, 129, 135, 138, 141n, 149,
    150, 158
Boccaccio: *Il Teseida*, and visionary
    flights, 124; source of historical illus-
    trations, 3
Boethius: *Consolation of Philosophy*, 124;
    and Myth of Er, 123; influence on
    Bernard Sylvestris, 125
Bolton, J. L., 70
Book, figure of, 118
Book of Vices and Virtues, 46, 156
Boroff, Marie, 231, 238
Bourquin, Guy, 119, 126, 128, 137, 138
Bowers, John, 31, 33, 40, 45, 48, 57
Boyle, Leonard E., 161n
Bozon, Nicole, 128, 139, 163n
Bradwardine, Thomas, 110, 161n
Brandeis, Arthur, 161n
Braswell, Mary Flowers, 17, 138, 141n,
    142, 147
Bretheren of the Common Life, perfec-
    tionism of, 92
Brewer, Charlotte (and A. G. Rigg),
    181, 182, 188, 219n
Brigham, Nicholas, 16th-cen. writer on
    Langland, 6
Brink, August, 238
Brinton, Thomas, 161, 167; sermon on
    "belling the cat," 79, 157; as "Aungel
    of heuene" (B.Prol.128), 157
Bromyard, John: *Distincciones*, 162; and
    PP scholars, 157, 161, 167; on *redditio*
    principle, 150; and satire, 137, 139;
    Summa praedicantium, 140
Brooke, Rupert, 196
Brown, Carleton, 33
Brunner, K., 202, 216, 217
Brut, Walter: sympathy for, 256; trial
    mentioned in *Pierce the Ploughman's
    Crede*, 255
Bruyart, Jean, *Le Chemin de Povreté and de
    Richesse*, 128
Bunyan, John, 124
Burdach, Konrad, 13, 73
Burnley, J. D., 209, 213
Burrow, John, 2, 31, 41, 42, 43, 44, 45,
    48, 49, 102, 141n, 147, 148, 203,
    237, 240, 245, 252
But, John (A-version continuator), 182,
    188, 192

Cargill, Oscar, 67, 80
Carruthers, Mary, 12, 18, 38, 42, 44,
    50, 61, 95, 118, 130
castle. *See* imagery
Chadwick, Dorothy, 3, 67
Chalcidius, commentary on Plato's
    Timaeus, 123, 125
Chambers, R. W., 7, 13, 51, 97, 212,
    244-45
chansons de geste, as precedents for multi-
    ple authorship theory, 8
charity: vs. cupidity, 52; *Deus caritas*, 35,
    36; and Dowel, 52, 56; exemplified in
    Good Samaritan, 53, 124, 143; neces-
    sity of, 99; object of Christian in-
    terpretation, 16; and patience, 49;
    search for, *48-53*; and truth, 36;
    works of, 36. *See also* love; tree of
    charity
Charity, A. C., 121
Charland, Th.-M., 160, 167
Charles, R. H., 122
Chatman, Seymour, 229
Chaucer, Geoffrey: authorial "signature,"
    7; concern for text, 196; debt to tra-
    dition, 19; and Deguileville, 127,
    128; dream visions, 130; knowledge
    of Langland, 253; Langland's spell-
    ing, of equal status with, 219; lan-
    guage, 201, 204, 210-12, 213,
    216-17, 219, 235; life records, 19;
    and Macrobius, 123; metrical prac-
    tice, 196, 215, 217-18; phonology
    compared with Langland's, 210-12;
    Plowman's Tale attributed to, 258; as
    rhetorical poet, 2; and satire, 9, 33,
    135, 138, 139, 142, 143; and scribes,
    193, 194, 217; and *Summa virtutum de
    remediis anime*, 169; and *voies*, 127;
    works widely copied, 1
    ABC, 128
    trans. of Boethius, *Consolation of
        Philosophy*, 129
    Cant. Tales, 3, 29, 140, 176, 194,
        252, 257; *Frankl. Tale*, 33; *Gen.
        Prol.* 68, 258; *Pars. Tale*, 168;
        Summoner's Tale, 144
    "Lack of Stedfastnesse," 33
    trans. of *Roman de la Rose*, 129
    Troilus and Criseyde, 124, 193, 194,
        196, 253
    "Truth," 33
Cheney, C. R., 142
Chrétien de Troyes, 117
Christ: debate with the devil, 56-57;

hero of *PP*, 148; as "king" in Langland's prophecies, 104; as knight, 54; ministry, 58; as mother, 162; passion and crucifixion of, 53, 54, 56; as physician, 143; as Piers, 55–56; triumphal entry, 54

Chrysostom, John, 166

church. *See* Holy Church; Unity

Cistercian thought. *See* monasticism

Cicero, *Somnium Scipionis*, 123, 124

Clarke, M. V. (and V. H. Galbraith), 252

classes: censure of, 9; obligations of, 33, 39; relations between, 37. *See also* estates; satire

Cleanness. See *Gawain*-group

clergy, criticism of, 73, 110, 254, 259; as an estate, *72–76*

Clergy (personification): allegorical limitations of, 95; on Dowel, 49, 90; as "learning," 46; prophecy of, 75, 105; rivalry with Patience, 50

Cloud of Unknowing, 91

Coghill, Nevill, 13, 30, 42, 44, 46, 55, 56

Coleman, Janet, 19, 38, 43, 68, 77, 78, 80, 96, 97, 100, 107, 108, 109, 158n, 254

colophons, 30, 51, 189

commentary, influence of genre on *PP*, 20, 117, 155–56. *See also* biblical exegesis

complaint: distinguished from satire, 9, 135; and *PP*, 117, 162; in fourteenth century, 140. *See also* genre; satire

confession, 102, *141–43*; of allegorical sins, 40, 101, 145, 156, 181, 191; of Haukyn, 50–51; as healing, 143; and inner disposition, 99; after Lateran IV, 141–43; *Pierce the Ploughman's Crede* on, 256; prerequisite of pardon, 42. *See also* contrition; penance

conscience: "court of," 82; fallibility of, 38, 148; function of, 38; and patience, 49–52; and reason, as legal concepts, 38, 39; vulnerability of, 39

Conscience: as accuser, 37; adviser to king, 75, 78, 81, 83; allegorical limits of, 94; attack on, 60, 61; in banquet scene, 49–50; debate with Meed, *37–39*, 76–78, 79; and Hundred Years' War, 77; marriage to Meed, 37–38, 80; prophecy of, 94, 104

Constantine, Donation of, 110

contemplative life: and active life, 51;

Dobet as, 46; and Holy Ghost, 52

contrition: in confession, 99; distinguished from attrition, 101; tears as sign of, 51. *See also* confession

Contrition: and Friar Flatterer, paraphrased in Drayton, 262; sickness of, 60, 144

contritionism: Langland's, 98; Ockham's as influence on Langland, 101

Cooper, Helen, 33, 176

Cornelius, salvation of, 98

Cornelius, Roberta, 126 128, 136

coronation scene (Prologue). *See* king: coronation of

Coulton, G. G., 3, 254

counsel. *See* king: counsel

Courtenay, William, 106

Crome, William: recantation as clue to dating of *I playne Piers*, 258

Crowley, Robert: attracted to *PP* as prophecy of his own age, 11, 261; as editor of *PP* (1550), 5, 6, 175, 177, 255, 258, 260, 262; knowledge of Middle English, 175; radical Protestant leanings, 260; Spenser's use of edition, 6

Crowned King: influence on *PP*, 254

cupidity, 34; vs. charity, 52

Curtius, E. R., 14

Daniel, prophetic dreams of, 120

Daniélou, Jean, 121

Dan Michel of Northgate, *Ayenbite of Inwit*, 137

Dante, *Divine Comedy*, 122, 124, 127, 135

Daunt, Marjorie, 229

Davenport, F. G., 71

Day, Mabel, 235; and R. Steele, 256

Death and Liffe: influence of *PP* on, 254

debate: and English allegory, 56–57; Four Daughters of God, 56–57; as genre in *PP*, 117, 146. *See also* genre; *Piers Plowman*: critical approaches

Deguileville, Guillaume de, and Chaucer, 127, 128; tree allegory in *Le Pélerinage de l'Ame*, 127

de la Mare, Peter, as "Goliardeis" (B.Prol.139), 157

de la Pole, Michael, chancellor under Richard II, 81

de Rokayle, Stacy (Eustace): reputed father of Langland, 6

Deschamps, Eustace, 7

devil: debate with Christ, 56–57; medi-

devil *(continued)*
   cine against, 56; theory of "the devil's
      rights," 57; and tree of charity, 53,
      56; as Wrong, 34
"Devil's Charter," and charter of Fals
   (B.2.73-114), 138
Devlin, Mary A., 67, 161n, 184, 185
Devotio moderna, and Langland's perfectionism, 92
dialect: Chaucer's, 204; Gower's, 203-04;
   Langland's, 204-10; Middle English,
   201-02; of *PP* mss., 203, 204-10, 207
   (map); stratification in mss., 202,
   210. *See also* "relict" forms; scribal
   copying: translation
diction, 223-49. See also *Piers Plowman*:
   vocabulary
Dieulacres Chronicle: record of Peasants'
   Revolt, 252
Digby lyrics, on "truth," 33
Dillon, Janette, 238
Dionysius the Areopagite, 106
"dip." *See* meter
disendowment: of alien priories (1363),
   74; Langland's views on, 75, 110;
   Wyclif's arguments for, 75
distinctiones: as aid to verbal concordance,
   159; Bromyard's *Distincciones*, 161n,
   162; Langland's familiarity with, 17
divisio. See rhetoric: division
Dobest. *See* Dowel; Three Lives
Dobet. *See* Dowel; Three Lives
Dobson, R. B., 251
"doctor" (learned friar of B.13.25-214):
   on Dowel, 49; as "dyvynour" (pun),
   238; modeled after scribes and
   pharisees, 49; identified as William
   Jordan, 136
dominion, concept of: B.Prol.100-11,
   185; Fitzralph, 75; Wyclif, 73
Donaldson, E. Talbot, 6, 13, 29, 30, 33,
   41, 46, 48, 50, 51, 52, 55, 67, 68,
   72, 78, 79, 87, 91, 104, 135, 141,
   145, 148, 157, 164, 180, 185, 204,
   245, 253
Donatism: latent in *PP*, 102, 110
donum Dei, knowledge as, 146; as positive
   basis of Langland's satire, 149-50;
   poverty as, 149-50; unsalability of,
   146, 150
Douglas, Gavin, *Palice of Honour*: allusion
   to *PP*, 262
Dowel: alternative to indulgences, 43;
   definitions, 49, 52, 55, 90-91; inadequacy of desire alone, 61; origin in

pardon scene, 41-42; and Peasants'
   Revolt, 252; perfection of, *53-58*;
   Prologue to Life of, 45; as rubric, 30;
   search for, 51, 61; and "three lives,"
   45-46, 58, 90-91, 159, 167. *See also*
   Three Lives
Doyle, A. I., 253, 255; and M. B.
   Parkes, 194, 204
drama, as source of satire, 140
Drayton, Michael, *The historie of the life
   and death of the lord Cromwell*:
   paraphrase of *PP* (B.20-294-379),
   262
dreamer: as alter ego of Haukyn, 50; as
   Menippean hero, 138-39, 147; as
   participant in Passion of Christ, 54;
   progress of, 46, 47, 49, *54*, 55, *58*,
   99-100; relation to Piers, 55; self-
   recognition of, 48; as spectator, 41,
   44; waking moments of, *31*, 42, 57,
   60; as Will, 6, 45, 147
dreams: allegorical, 58, *117-33*; biblical,
   120-21; character of, 58; inner
   dreams, 31, 46-47, 52, 53; psychology of, 48; as structural units (table),
   31; types of, 120, 123; validity of, 42
Dronke, Peter, 52
Dufeil, M. M., 95
Dunning, T. P., 13, 29, 34, 36, 40-41,
   42, 46, 51, 87, 98
Duns Scotus, theory of attrition, 101

Edward II, misuse of patronage, 80
Edward III: allusions to in *PP*, 76, 80,
   186; bequest violated under Richard
   II, 81; peace agreement, 77; William
   of Wyckham and Alice Perrers as
   confidants, 80
Elde, 147, 148
Elliot, R. W. V., 205
Embree, D., 256
Emmerson, Richard K., 12, 103, 104
Empson, William, 196
end of the world, 11, 58. *See also*
   apocalypticism; eschatology
end-stopping: in Old English, 235; in
   PP, 235, 242; relation to scribal
   paragraphing, 236
enjambement: in *Mum and the Sothsegger*,
   235; in *PP*, 235, 242
epistemology: and *moderni*, 107; as theme
   in *PP*, 18
equity: as element of justice, 60; "good
   faith," 57, 60; king or chancellor as

source of, 82; as principle in Christ's debate with the devil, 57

Erbe, Theodore, 161n

eschatology: Langland's, 11, 94, 103–04; *PP* as eschatological plot, 61

eschaton (the Four Last Things), 124

estates: discussion of, *68–83* (peasantry, 68–72; clergy, 72–76; nobility, 76–83); failings of, 89; "truth" tied to theory of, 33, 39. *See also* classes; satire

etymology: Hebrew names, 121; *hepen* (B.15.459), 100; *hypocrisis* (B.15.111), 169; moral analogy with, 11

Eucharist: in *The Banckett of Iohan the Reve*, etc., 260; in *A godly dyalogue and dysputacyon betwene Pyers plowman and a popysh preest*, 259; Langland's view of, 98, 111; source of additional grace, 92; transsubstantiation, 259, 260. *See also* sacraments

exegetical criticism. *See* biblical exegesis; *Piers Plowman*, critical approaches

Ezekial: tour of New Temple, 121; visions of, 120

fable of the rats. *See* belling of the cat, fable of

facienti quod in se est, doctrine of, 91, 97

faith, in god, 51. *See also* Abraham

Fals: charter of, 138; marriage to Meed, 37, 137

Fasciculus morum, 156, 161n, 162, 164, 166n

Fasticulus, interpretation of "vix salvabitur" (I Pet. 4:18), 98

Favel: name derived from *Le Roman de Fauvel*, 128

Ferguson, A. B., 78

feudalism: breakup of, 33, 34, 70–71; description of, 69–70; vs. money economy, 70, 150; paradigm of man's relation to God, 32, 69; as social context of truth, 33, 69, 150; and Truth's pardon, 41

fiat voluntas. See will

figuralism, 14, 44, 95, 118, 144

First Enoch (Book of Watchers), 122

Fisher, John, 140, 141n

Fitzralph, William: *De Pauperis Salvator* as source of Wyclif's theory of dominion, 75; and Langland, 95, 100

Fletcher, Angus, 15

Flew, R. Newton, 107

Foliot, Gilbert: sermon technique compared to *PP*, 159

Folvilles (B.19.247), 82, 186

"Fool-hero," 138–39

fortitude, 60. *See also* virtues, cardinal

Foster, Frances A., 128

Four Daughters of God: in harrowing of hell scene, 56–57; Middle English versions preceding *PP*, 129

Fourth Ezra, 122

Fowler, D. C., 9, 72

Frank, R. W., Jr., 13, 29, 30, 31, 42, 43, 44, 45, 46, 50, 51, 53, 57, 59, 88, 91, 92, 103, 118, 135, 150, 156

Fraser, G. S., 233

free will. *See* Liberum-Arbitrium; will

French: influence of pronoun usage on Middle English, 213; knowledge of, 128; official status of, 201

Freud, Sigmund, 119

Friar Daw's Reply: echoes of *PP* in, 256

friars: abuse of biblical exegesis by, 145, 146; as agents of reform movement, 141, 142; conflict with secular clergy, 142; criticism of, 19, 95, 137, 140, 244, 255–56; on Dowel, 45; praise of by Grosseteste, 142–43; as preachers, 139; Robertson and Huppé's use of antimendicant texts, 18; as satrical objects, 140; Sire Penetrans Domos, 60; as undermining penitential system, 60–61, 102, 143–44

Froissart, Jean: on Edward III's desire for peace, 77; *Paradys d'Amours*, Chaucer's knowledge of, 127; writings as historical record, 4

Furnivall, F. J., 5

Fussell, Paul, 229, 233, 236

future contingents: Langland on doctrine of, 108. *See also* theology

Gaffney, Wilbur, 54

Galbraith, F., 75

Galbraith, V. H., and M. V. Clarke, 252

Gallemore, Melvin A., 167

Gasquet, Francis (Cardinal), 157

Gast of Gy, 129

Guwain-group: regional spelling in, 219; similarities with *PP*, 227

    Cleanness: word play in, 238

    Pearl, 127, 129, 238

    Sir Gawain and the Green Knight, 1, 29; alliterative pattern of, 216; synonyms for "man" in, 238; and truth, 33

genre, 10, 117; allegory, *117–33*;
apocalypse and prophecy, 4, 10–12,
103; commentary, 20, 117, 155–56;
complaint and satire, 4, 8–12, 117,
135–54; *consolatio*-debate, 117; mirror
for princes, 78, 81–82; quest, 117;
sermon, 15, 117, *155–72*. *See also* un-
der individual entries (allegory,
apocalypse, etc.)
Gilbert, Felix, 3
Gilbert, A. H., 78
Giraldus Cambrensis, 140
Giocarnis, Kimon, 146
Given-Wilson, C., 81
Glossa ordinaria, on I Pet. 4:18 ("vix sal-
vabitur"), 98
"Gobelyne," explanation of, 163
Godden, Malcolm, 45, 50, 51
*A godly dyalogue and dysputacyon betwene
Pyers Plowman and a popysh preest*, 258
God Spede the Plough, 256
Goldsmith, Margaret, 18, 55
Goliards, 137, 140, 141
"Goliardeis" (B.Prol.139), 78; as Peter de
la Mare, 157
Gollancz, Israel, 240, 253, 254
good faith. *See* equity
Goodridge, J. F., 35
Good Samaritan, 53, 54, 94, 95, 124,
143. *See also* charity
Gospel of Nicodemus: Middle English
version, 129; as source of harrowing
of hell, 122
Gower, John: *Confessio Amantis*, 194; and
date of *PP* C, 80; dialect of, 203–04;
Mirour de l'omme, 137; and satire,
139–40, 142, 143; "signature" of, 7;
Vox Clamantis, criticism of papal wars,
73
grace, 36, 59, *95–98*, 100, 108; age of,
58; and charity, 36; gifts of, 59–60;
and sacraments, 92; sanctifying, 43;
and works, 42, 43
grades of perfection. *See* perfectionism
Gradon, Pamela, 5, 73, 75, 87, 95,
97–98, 102, 106, 110, 111, 238, 240,
254
grammar: basis of Langland's rhetoric,
237; "infinites" (B.13.128), 90; as
metaphor, 11, 18, 38, 90, 94; and
moderni, 107–09. *See also* Langland,
William, language of; Middle English
Grant, Robert M., 121
Gray, Nicholas, 101, 102
Green, Richard H., 17

Gregory the Great, as exegetical source,
18
Gregory IX: Grosseteste's letter to (on
friars), 142
Gregory XI: English resentment of, 74
Gregory of Rimini, vs. Ockham's ethics,
108
Griffiths, Lavinia, 37, 38, 40, 52, 118,
128
Grisdale, D. M., 161n
Grosseteste, Robert: *Chasteau d'Amour*,
127; letter to Gregory IX in praise of
friars, 141–43; and *Visio Philiberti*,
129
guide-figure, 45. *See also potentia*
Guillaume de Lorris: *Le Roman de la
Rose*, inspiration for later allegories,
127; reference to Macrobius, 123. See
also *Roman de la Rose*
Gwynn, Aubrey, 67, 75, 185

Hall, H., 80
Halle, M., and S. J. Keyser, 229
Handlynge Synne, 156
Harding, Alan, 81
Hanford, J. H., and J. M. Steadman,
254
harrowing of hell: and "Gobelyne," 163,
164; Langland's dramatization of,
56–57; parallels in *PP* and *Death and
Liffe*, 254
Harrowing of Hell (Middle English ver-
sion), 129
Harwood, B. J., 48, 87, 96, 108
Hatcher, J., 71
Haukyn, *50–51*, 88, 90, 145, 147, 151,
181, 182, 191. *See also* active life
Hearne, Thomas, 176
Heiserman, A. R., 135
Hennecke, Edgar, 122
Henry IV: king in *Mum and the Sothsegger*,
156, 257
Henry VIII: allusions to reign of, in *I
playne Piers*, 258
heresy: and Langland's view of confes-
sion, 101; and papal rights, 76; use
of the term, 96; of Wyclif, 74. *See
Donatism; Pelagianism*
hermit: dreamer as, 45; Haukyn as, 50
"heteromorphic." *See* meter
Heusler, Andreas, 228, 231
Hewitt, H. J., 76, 77
Hieatt, Constance B., 119, 125, 231
Hill, Thomas, 155

Hilton, Rodney H., 68, 71, 72; and T. R. Aston, 252

Hilton, Walter, scale of religious obligations in, 91

Himmelfarb, Martha, 122

historians, and *PP*, 3–4, 67–68

historical allusions in *PP*, *67–86, 184–86*; Alice Perrers, 80; Black Death, 67, 70–72, 184; Black Prince, 186; drought, 67; Edward III, reign of, 76, 80, 186; Folvilles, 82, 186; forestalling incident, 186; Hundred Years' War, 76, 77; Normandy campaign, 67, 186; papal election, 185; papal schism, 74, 184; Peasants' Revolt, 72, 185; plenary indulgence (1375–76), 184; Richard II, coronation of, 78, 184; Richard II, councils, 80–81; Rome runners, 74, 184; Statutes of Laborers, 71; storm of 1362, 67, 186; Treaty of Bretigny, 76, 186; Wycliffite movement, 73

historical criticism. *See* Piers Plowman: critical approaches

history: God's action in, 57; of ideas, 12–15; and literary sources, 3–4; millennial schematizations of, 11–12; sacred, 88, 94; salvation, 93, 106; theories of 10–12

Hoccleve, Thomas, 7

Holcot, Robert, 100, 109, 156, 165

Holdsworth, William, 71

Holmes, George, 74, 77, 79, 80

Holy Church, 35, 55, 59, 89, 94; allegorical predecessors, 121, 122; speech of, *34–36*, 45, 55, *165–67*, 168, 214. *See also* Unity

Holy Ghost, 52

Homans, G. C., 67

"homomorphic." *See* meter

Hope. *See* Moses

Horace, 9, 137

Hort, Greta, 13, 29, 32, 98, 101

Housman, A. E., 195, 196

Hudson, Anne, 5, 19, 73, 95, 111, 161n, *252–66*, 252, 254, 257

Hulbert, J. R., 253

Hundred Years' War: Langland's criticism of, 76, 77; opposing views of Conscience and Meed, 76; and pope, 74

hunger, as recurring theme in *PP*, 41

Hunger (personification), 41, 71, 89, 95

Huon de Meri, *Li Tornoiemenz Antecrist*, 127, 136

Huppé, Bernard F., 67, 79, 80, 234, 238. *See also* Robertson, D. W., Jr., and Bernard F. Huppé

Hussey, S. S., 13, 31, 46, 91, 105, 136, 245, 253

"ictus." *See* alliteration

imagery: Langland's "conceptual and thematic" imagery, 237; in sermon tradition, 156, 161–67; simple figures, 237; early interest in, 5, 9; *vis imaginativa* as source of, 48

EXAMPLES

barn, 60, 118; battle of Crucifixion, 54; Book, 118; castle, 5, 32, 40; Christ in Piers's arms, 56; cross on coin, 137; food, 49, 51, 126; feudal imagery, 36, 69–70; field, 58; fruit, 53, 56, 91; "fullyng," 9; groping, 144; harrows, 60; hermit, 45; joust, 54; kalketrappes, 162–63; lamp without light, 36, 166; mealtime of saints, 164–65; money as goddess, 137; peacock, 5; pelican, 162; physician, 56, 60–61, 143–44; pilgrimage, 40–41; plowing, 40, 41, 42, 44, 70; plowman, 40, 257–60; props, 53; seeds, 58, 60, 121, 124; shepherd, 165; spark in sea, 156; *stella comata*, 157; triacle, 156, 166, 167; weapons of Grace, 60

See also allegory, themes; Christ; figuralism; Four Daughters of God; medical imagery; metaphor; Sins, Seven Deadly; tree of charity

Imaginatif, 46, *47–48*, 99, 100, 239

imago Dei, doctrine of, 55. *See also* truth

imitatio Christi, 110

Imitation of Christ, democratic perfectionism in, 92

individual, 45, 83, 88–90, 107, 151, 253

indulgence: *a culpa et a poena*, 42; A-text allusion to plenary indulgence of 1375–76, 184; and forgiveness of sin, 42; Langland's view of, 44; normal object of pilgrimage, 42; Truth's pardon, *42–44*; Wycliffite view of, 73, 254

"infinites." *See* grammar

I Pleyne Piers which cannot flatter, 258, 259

Isaiah, scorn for dreams and visions, 120

isochronous. *See* meter

Jacob's Well, 161

James, M. R., 122

Jauss, Hans Robert, 126, 138

Jean de Meun: joining of satire and allegory, 138. See also *Roman de la Rose*

Jehan de la Mote, *La Voie d'Enfer et de Paradis*, 127

Jennings, Margaret, 55

Jeremiah, distrust of dreams, 120

Jerome, St., 18, 98

Jesus. *See* Christ

Jews: salvation of, 100; as targets of criticism, 140

Joachim of Flora (Fiore): and English monasticism, 11, 105; influence on Langland's thought, 103

Joachites: prophecies rejected by Wyclif, 111

Job, 98, 120

John de Burgo, *Pupilla Oculi*, 101

John of Altavilla (Hanville), *Architrenius*, 125

John of Gaunt, as cat in belling of the cat fable, 79

John of Grimestone, 156, 246

John of Salisbury, *Policraticus*, 140

John the Baptist, as fruit of tree of charity, 53

Jordan, William. *See* doctor

Judas Maccabee, dream of Jeremiah, 120

Julian of Norwich, *Revelations*, 91

Jung, Marc-René, 126

Jusserand, J. J., 1, 3, 4, 67, 68, 77, 126, 157

justice: Christian, 150; and mercy, 56–57; as responsibility of king, 81; and penitential system, 40; personified as one of four daughters of God, 56–57; and reason, 39; seed of *spiritus justiciae*, 60, 75; undermined by Meed, 76. *See also* equity; law

Juvenal, 9, 137

Kail, J., 33, 37, 81

"kalketrappes," 162–63

Kaluza, Max, 228

Kane, George, 6, 7, 8, 19, 34, 61, 67, 135, 160, 180, 181, 182, 183, 187, 188, 189, 193, 197, 204, 205, 208, 209, 227, 230, 231, 232, 246, 252, 253, 261; and E. T. Donaldson, 175, 176, 178, 181, 182, 183, 187, 188, 189, 190, 191, 192, 193, 194, 208, 209, 211, 231, 232, 260

Kaske, R. E., 17, 18, 30, 36, 50, 237

Kaulbach, Ernest, 48, 98

Kay, Richard, 146

Kean, P. M., 33, 103, 240

Kellogg, Eleanor H., 79

Kelly, R. L., 260

Kempe, Margery, 236

Kendall, R. D., 255, 257

Ker, W. P., 157

Keyser, S. J., and M. Halle, 229

King, J. N., 11, 258, 260, 261

king: Christ as, 104; coronation of, 33, 78–79; and counsel, *78–81*; the ideal king, 33; as military leader, 76–78; right of appropriation, 60; as ruler, 33, 74, 78–81; as source of justice, 35, 60, 81–83; at trial of Meed, 39

Kirk, Elizabeth, 29, 31, 32, 41, 46, 49, 58, 108, 130, 137

Kittner, H., 205

Knight, Ione Kemp, 161n

Knight, S. T., 135

knighthood, 33, 35, 68, 168

Knighton, Henry, account of Peasants' Revolt, 251, 252

Knott, Thomas, 8

knowledge: converted into deeds, 52; *scientia* vs. *sapientia*, 105; two forms of (*affectus, intellectus*), 47, 48, 50

Knowles, David, 74, 99, 107

Kristensson, G., 202

kynde knowing, 35, 36, 45, 46, 48, 239

kynde wit, 39, 68, 78

Kyng Alisaunder: bound in mss. with *PP*, 253

labor, as way to salvation, 51

Laing, Margaret, and M. Benskin, 202, 204

Lamentationes of Matheolus: parallels with *PP*, 137

Lampe, David, 255

Landgraf, Arthur M., 97

Lane Poole, R., 261

Langland, William: attitude toward poetry, 6, 19–20, 48, 61; "autobiographical" passage in C text, 181; birth, 204; birthplace, 187, 204; brought up in Malvern, 204; cleric, 10; concern for text, 196; death, 185; identity concealed, 9

language of, *204–19* (conservatism of forms, 218; contrast with Chaucer's language, 205, 210, 218; dialect, 204–10; final -e, 215–16; grammar, 212–18; phonology, 210–12; regionalisms, 205; sociolinguistic status, 219; spelling, 210, 211; syntax, 234–37, 242); life records, 19; malcontent, 10; name, source of, 6; return to Malvern, 208; "Robert" Langland, 6, 261; son of Stacy de Rokayle, 6; spokesman for reform, 2, 5. See also *Piers Plowman*

Lateran Council of 1215 (Lateran IV), 17, 138, *141–45*, 147, 148, 149

Latimer, Hugh, "Sermon of the Plow," 260

Latin: influence on polite usage of Middle English pronouns, 213; official status of, 201; teaching of, 215

latria, 34

law: canon (on "meed"), 38; corruption of (by Meed), 81–83, 257; English, 39, 57, 74, 82; fulfillment in Christ, 44; Langland's knowledge of, 19; legal elements in *PP*, 19; moral law, 43, 99; natural law, 35–36, 38, 150; the New Law, 44, 60, 89; the Old Law, 44, 50, 60, 90; obligations rooted in, 150; positive, 38; and salvation, 57, 59. See also equity; justice; Statutes of the Realm

Lawlor, John, 13, 32, 61, 87, 135, 139, 229, 243

Lawton, David, 73, *223–49*, 228, 231, 235, 245, 253, 256, 257

lawyers: chastisement by king, 83; Christ and the devil as, 57; and *donum Dei* principle, 146, 149; target in Peasants' Revolt, 72; and Truth's pardon, 146; venality of, 146–47, 149–50, 157, 262

Lay Folks' Catechism: debt to A version, 254

Layamon's *Brut*, and alliterative meter, 245

Leadam, I. S., and J. F. Baldwin, 82

learning: as inward journey, *45–48*; necessity of, 50; relation to Dowel, 47, 49; and salvation, 46

Leclercq, Jean, 106, 107

Left, Gordon, 73, 110, 161

Lehmann, Paul, 138

Leonard, W. E., 228

Lewis, C. S., 13, 14, 118, 124, 230, 246

lexis. See *Piers Plowman*: vocabulary

Liberum-Arbitrium: in alliterative collocation, 239; in place of Haukyn, 191; and tree of charity, 52–53, 54

life. See active life; contemplative life; Dowel; Three Lives

"lift." See meter

liturgy: Langland's quotations from, 58, 102; and pattern in *PP*, 54, 93, 106–07, 127; Rutebeuf's *La Voie de Paradis* based on Lenten calendar, 127

Livre de seyntz medicines, 156

Lollards: Brut's trial, 255; criticism of oral confession, 102; and Langland's thought, 6, *109–111*, "lollares," 73; and *Pierce the Ploughman's Crede*, 256; and *Piers Plowman*, 73, 252, 263; as "poor priests," 6, 73; study of, 19; "true men," 252; use of plowman as model, 258

"lollares," 73

Lomas, R. A., 71

love: debt of, 59, 150; of enemies, 49; as fulfillment of law, 90–91; of God and neighbor, 35, 49, 89, 150, 152; Holy Church on, 36, 165–66; "love, law, and leaute," 240; Patience on, 49–50; and pardon, 59; and *redde quod debes*, 59, 151; relation to truth, 36, 165–66; as talisman, 50; as triacle, 166; and Trinity, 53

loyalty: as feudal virtue, 32, 33; "love, law, and leaute," 240

Lucan, *Pharsalia*, 123

Lucifer, 35, 165

Lucilius, 9

Luria, Maxwell, 127

Lydgate, John, translation of Deguileville's *Pèlerinage de la vie humaine*, 128

Maas, Paul, 196, 197, 198

Machaut, Guillaume de, *Dit dou Vergier*, 127

MacQueen, John, 123

Macrobius, commentary on *Somnium Scipionis*, 123, 125

Maddicott, J. R., 72, 82

Mäder, Eduard Johann, 129

Magdalen, as type of redeemed sinner, 46

Maguire, Stella, 50, 51

Maisack, Helmut, 105

Maitland, F. W., 71; and Frederick Pollock, 69

Maldon, Battle of, 148

Mandeville's *Travels*: bound in mss. with *PP*, 253

Manly, J. M., 7, 9, 157, 254

Mann, Jill, 10, 41, 49, 138, 253

manuscripts. *See* Piers Plowman: manuscripts; scribal copying

Map, Walter, *De nugis curialium*, 140

Marcett, Mildred, 136

marriage: allegorical, 124, 125, 157; as king's gift, 79; of Meed, 37, 79–80; metaphor of, 91; and tree of charity, 52

Martianus Capella, *Marriage of Philology and Mercury*, 124, 125

Martin, Jay, 138

Martin, Priscilla, 18, 29, 30, 32, 38, 58, 65

Matthew, F. D., 255, 258

Matthew of Janov, and perfectionism, 92

Matonis, A. T. E., 228, 231, 232, 245

McFarlane, K. B., 19, 73, 82

McGinn, Bernard, 94

McIntosh, Angus, 201, 202, 228, 229, 230, 232, 234, 245

McKisack, May, 76, 80, 81, 185

McLeod, Susan, 43, 44

McNamara, John F., 108

McNeill, John T., 143

medical imagery, 60–61, 143–44, 166. *See also* imagery

meed: in C text, 31–32; definition of, 37–38; as fourteenth-century literary theme, 33, 34, 36; of salvation, 38, *97*, 152

Meed, Lady, 109, 118, 135; avarice as source of her power, 145; and Conscience, 71, 76–78, 95; marriage to Conscience, 79–80; marriage to Fals, 37, 137; as personification of *tresor*, 37; significance of name, 37–38; trial of, *36–39*, *79–83*

Memoriale credencium, 169

Memoriale Presbiterorum, 101

Menippean satire. *See* satire

Mensendieck, Otto, 91

meritum de condigno (and *congruo*), 97. *See also* theology

Meroney, Howard, 13, 44, 46

mercede, as "measurable meed," 37, 38, 71

mercy: vs. justice, 57; personified as one of the four daughters of God, 56; as root of tree of charity, 52; truth as prerequisite, 39. *See also* grace

"mesure," 34, 37–39, 97. *See also* moderation

metaphor: allegory as "continued metaphor," 123; feudal metaphor, 70; and limits of language, 94; of marriage, 52, 91. *See also* allegory; grammar: as metaphor; imagery

meter, 215, 218, *223–49*; accent, 229, 230; anacrusis, 215, 231; dip, 11, 224; heteromorphic, 228, 233; homomorphic, 228, 233; hypermetric syllables, 217; isochronous, 229; lift, 224; prominence, 230; relation to rhythm, 223, 241; stress, 229–31. *See also* end-stopping; enjambement; modulation; rhythm

metrical system, 228, 232–34

Micha, A., 126

Middle English: dialects, 201–02; final -e, 215–16, 224; grammar, 212–18; influence of Chancery as standard, 201; spelling, 201, 202, 204, 211, 219. *See also* dialect; Langland, William, language of

Middleton, Anne, *1–25*, 2, 7, 18, 46, 48, 61, 87, 90, 91, 94, 253

Miller, Paul Scott, 10

Mills, David, 55, 56

Milton, John: Bentley's improvement of, 195–96; *Paradise Lost*, modulation in, 227

Minnis, A. J., 7, 17, 18, 48

Mirk, John, *Festial*, 161

mirror for princes (genre), and *PP*, 78, 81–82

Mitchell, A. G., 37, 38, 135

moderation, 37, 97; as Moderantia, 125

moderni: as influence on Langland, 107–09; nominalist philosophers, 19

"modulation": as counterpoint of meter and rhythm, 226; in *Paradise Lost*, 227; in *PP*, 227, *232–33*, 236, 241, 242. *See also* meter; rhythm

Mohl, Ruth, 138

monasticism: and anti-intellectualism, 105; Cistercian influence on Langland, 105, 107; and Joachism, 11, 105; as source of Langland's theology, *104–07*, 108; *scientia* vs. monastic *sapientia*, 105; and social meliorism, 105; Uthred of Boldon's defense of, 93

Morgan, Margery, 245

Morris, Richard, 137

Moses: archprophet, 120; and breaking of the tablets, 44; as theological virtue of Hope, 53, 94, 124

Mum and the Sothsegger: alliterative style, 234, 235; on king's counsel, 78; debt to *PP*, 256, 257

Murphy, J. J., 160

Murtaugh, Daniel, 32, 36, 38, 39, 44, 49, 55, 56, 58, 108

Muscatine, Charles, 118

The Muses Library, 176

Mustanoja, Tauno, 213

Myers, A. R., 77

Myrroure for Magistrates: summary of belling of cat fable, 262

mysticism, and *PP*, 46, 88, 91, 93–95, 240

Myth of Er. *See* Plato

Nature, as personification, 125

necessity: all things in common during, 74–75; as mother of Fates, 123

Need (personification), 60

Neilson, N., 69

Neo-Platonism, 106, 124; and allegory, 94, 123

Ne soliciti sitis, doctrine of, 42, 44, 50, 51

Newes from the North: figure of Piers in, 262

Newman, Francis X., 119, 125

Nigel de Longchamps, *Speculum stultorum*, 140

Noah, as type of "curatours," 9

Nolan, Barbara, 119

nominalist philosophers. *See* moderni

"Non dimittitur peccatum," etc., 40, 59. *See also* penance; restitution

Normandy Campaign (1359–60): allusion in A text, 67; allusion replaced in C text, 77

Norton-Smith, John, 135, 136, 148, 229, 233, 240, 246

"Nullum malum inpunitum," etc., 39

Oakden, J. P., 208, 224, 230, 231, 254

Oakley, Francis, 109

Oberman, Heiko, 92, 97, 102, 106, 107

Ockham, William of: influence of contritionism on *PP*, 101, 109

Ockhamists, as former name for *moderni*, 107

Oculus sacerdotis, 156

Odyssey, 123

Offord, M. Y., 254

Old English, influence on Middle English: alliteration, 232; meter, 227–30;

245; "not," 218; verbs, 216–17

oral-formulaic theory: as explanation for Middle English alliterative practice, 236

Origen of Alexandria: apocalypticism of, 94; and Myth of Er, 123

Orsten, Elizabeth, 50

Ovid: influence on medieval love allegories, 127

Owen, D. D. R., 122, 127

Owen, Dorothy, 14, 119, 126, 136

Owst, Gerald R., 3, 13, 79, 127, 129, 139, 150, 156–57, 158, 161

palmer, 40, 49

Palmer, J. N., and A. P. Wells, 74

Pantin, W. A., 93, 138, 141n, 142

papacy: dues of, 75; rights over English property, 76; schism, 74; wars of, 73

parables. *See* Bible

pardon: as indulgence, 42, 92; and justice, 40, 56–57; love as enabling mechanism of, 36, 59; and lawyers, 146; pardon episode, 20, *41–44*, 51, 56, 57, 68, 95, 96, 103, 109; Piers's pardon (end of *Vita*), *58–61*, 68, 149; satisfaction required for, 40; tearing of, 42, 43–44, 53, 96; theology of, 40, 57, 96–97, 109, 149. *See also* grace; indulgence

Parlement of the Thre Ages: as "formal" alliterative verse, 237; and *PP*, 129, 130, 253

Parliament: and the king, 78–81; parliaments of 1371, 74; 1376 (the "good"), 79, 157; 1377 (the "bad"), 79; 1386, 81

"passus," meaning of, 30

patience: as ground of charity, 49, 52; as name of tree of charity, 52

Patience: as collectivity of virtues, 50; as guide, *49–51*, 149

patient poverty, 51, 149

Patterson, Lee, 8, 17

Peace: complaint against Wrong, 39, *81–83*; and corruption of Unity, 61; one of four daughters of God, 56

Pearl. See Gawain-group

Pearsall, Derek, 118, 136, 158, 162, 164, 168, 182, 212, 234, 244, 245, 254

peasant: in England, *68–72*; as satiric spokesman, 138

Peasants' Revolt (1381): accounts of, 4,

Peasants' Revolt *(continued)*
  72, 251, 252; and use of the name
  Dowel, 252; Langland's reaction to,
  6, 73, 185; as misnomer, 252
Peifer, Claude J., 107
Pelagianism: and Langland's thought, 97,
  98, 100; *moderni* accused of, 108, 109.
  See also semi-Pelagianism
Pelikan, Jaroslav, 110
penance: confession as "tribunal" of, 40;
  and justice, 40; perversion of by friars, 60–61, 102, 143–44; poverty as
  form of, 72; as theme in *PP*, 42–43,
  59–61, 101–02. See also confession;
  redde quod debes; restitution
penitential literature: Langland's debt to,
  17, 101, 102, 138, 246; and Lateran
  IV, 141; relation to sermons, 155–56;
  as source of characterization, 142
penitential theory: deficiencies of, 101
Pépin, Jean, 118, 121, 123
Percy, Thomas: citations of *PP* from
  Crowley edition, 176
perfectionism, 88, *90–93*
Perrers, Alice, as model for Lady Meed,
  80
Persius, 9
personification, 14, 118; and philosophical realism, 94; and platonic tradition, *123–26*; types of, 125. *See also*
  allegory; *potentia*
pestilence. *See* Black Death
Peter, J. D., 9, 135
Peter, St.: as founder of Church, 68;
  Piers as namesake, 58; *petrus id est
  Christus*, 55–56, 59
Pfander, Homer, 155
Piehler, Paul, 121, 125
Pierce the Ploughman's Crede: authorship of,
  257; and *PP*, 176, 255, 261
Piers Plowman: audience, 10, 19, 205;
  authorship, 6–8, 177, 261; composition of, 20, 158–60; as exhortation,
  4–10; as historical illustration, 3–4;
  plot sequence, 32; reader responses,
  181; reception of, 1, 2, 16, 19, 72, 251
  ff.; revision of, 6, 7, 8, 184, 190, 191;
  unity of, 13, 16, 61, 158; vocabulary,
  32, 161, 205, *237–39*, 242–43 (examples: *dongeon*, 32; *ferme*, 52; *Gobelyne*,
  163; *hepen*, 100; *kalketrappes*, 162–63;
  mercede, 37, 38, 71; *tour*, 32; *vix*, 98).
  See also allegory: themes; historical allusions in *PP*; imagery; Langland,
  William: language of

CRITICAL APPROACHES
  biographical, 6–8; early study,
  175–77; exegetical, 16–18, 88; formal
  criticism, 12–20, *29–65*, 165–68;
  general trends, *1–25*; generic, 10,
  117; historical, *2 ff.*, *67–86, 251–66*;
  linguistic, *201–21*; metrical, *223–33*
  passim; rhetorical, 4–6; stylistic,
  233–49; textual criticism, 8, *194–98*.
  See also genre

MANUSCRIPTS
  copying, 1, 181, 182, *183–91*,
  191–94, 197, 253; classification, 183;
  dating, 67, *184–86*; dialects, 191,
  205–08; list of, *178–80*, 205–06; and
  literary executors, 183, 191; "lost leaf"
  theory, 8; marginal commentary,
  182; physical character, 19, 187, 235,
  242; provenance and circulation, 1,
  2, 19, 175, 187, 252; rubrics, 13,
  30–31, 40, 51; scribal translation in,
  192, 203; traditions of, 183, *188–91*;
  in wills, 2, 252; works bound with,
  252–53. *See also* Langland, William:
  language of

VERSIONS
  A text, 188–89; B text, 189–90; C
  text, 190–91; conjoint versions,
  179–80, 181; correspondences between, 30, 31; differentiation of, 7,
  29, *180–82*; dissemination, 186; sequence of, 7, 29, *177–80*; "Z text,"
  181–82, 189, 219n

Piers the Plowman: appearances (table
  of), 54–55; as author of poem, 5; in
  banquet scene, 49; and charity, 56;
  and Christ, 55–56, 59; Conscience's
  search for, 61; critical interpretations
  of, 5, 13, 55–56, 148, 252, 253;
  growth of, 44, *54–56*, 93–94, 96; as
  guide to Truth (on half acre), 40–41,
  71; and historical plowmen, 68; later
  use of name, 2, 4, 5, 72, 252, 255,
  258–60, 262; as maligned virtue, 96;
  and pardon, *41–44*, 51, *58–61*, 68,
  103, 149; *petrus id est christus*, 55–56,
  59; and pope, 59; symbolism of, 13;
  in tree of charity scene, 52–53; in
  "Visio Revisited," 58–61; as way of
  life, 56. *See also* pardon
pilgrimage: indulgence as goal of, 42; of
  the individual soul, 45 ff.; to Truth,
  39–44, 60. *See also* allegory: themes,
  pilgrimage

Plato, 125; Myth of Er (*Republic*),
123–24; as "poet," 169; source of
cardinal virtues, 124. *See also* Neo-
Platonism
Platonism, influence on medieval allegory, *123–26*; transmission by early
Christian writers, 123. *See also* Neo-
Platonism
Plotinus, 94
plowing. *See* imagery
plowman: Langland's focus on, 68, 72;
as satiric spokesman, 138; symbolism
of, 40, 257–60
Plowman's Tale: debt to *PP*, 257
political thought, and *PP*, 3, 7, 19, 33,
68
Pollock, Frederick, and F. W. Maitland,
69
Poole. *See* Lane Poole
"poor preachers," 6, 73
pope: as caretaker of "truth," 59; election
of, 185; Gregory the Great, 18;
Gregory IX, 142; Gregory XI, 74;
hostility toward, 74, 140; Piers as
figure of, 59; "popysh preest" in *A
godly dyalogue*, 259; Urban V, 74; and
war, 73, 184. *See also* papacy
Pope, J. C., 229
Post, Gaines, 146
potentia: as guide-figure, 121, 123, 125,
129. *See also* personification
potentia absoluta (and *ordinata*), doctrine of,
97, 109. *See also* theology
Potts, Timothy C., 38
poverty, as ideal, 110, 146, 149. *See also*
patient poverty
Praier and Complaynte of the Ploweman, 257
preaching, *155–72*; evidence of, 155;
handbooks, 155, 159; influence on
pronoun usage in *PP*, 214. See also
artes praedicandi; sermon
predestination, 46, 97, 99–100, 108, 110,
111
Price, Richard: proposal of three versions
of *PP*, 176
Prick of Conscience: manuscripts, 252
priest: in pardon scene, 41, 49, 110; as
detractor, 96
Proclys, 94
prominence. *See* meter
prophecy: biblical, 118–21, 124; of Clergy, 75, 105; of Conscience, 94, 104;
gift of, 60; inner dreams as, 53; of
Langland, 124; and *PP*, 10–12,
118–19, 120–21; political, 129. *See also*

apocalypse; apocalypticism
prudence: iconography of, 48; Imaginatif
as faculty of, 48; as seed, 60; in
twelfth century, 106. *See also* virtues,
cardinal
Prudentius, *Psychomachia*, 124
Pseudo-Bernard, and psychology of conversion, 105
Pseudo-Dionysius, and "vertical" eschatology, 94
psychomachia, 124, 127, 136. *See also*
Prudentius; virtues and vices
punctuation, editorial, 235
puns. *See* word play
Putnam, Bertha, 71
Puttenham, George: on *PP* as satire, 9,
135, 262
*Pyers plowmans exhortation unto the lordes,
knightes, and burgoysses of the parlyamenthouse*, 258, 259

Quilligan, Maureen, 118
quotations. *See* rhetoric, and use of quotations

Raoul de Houdenc, *Songe d'Enfer*, 126,
127, 136
rat parliament. *See* belling the cat, fable
of
ratio: Latin meaning implicit in Langland's Reason, 39
Raw, Barbara, 55, 56
reason, natural, 39
Reason: as adviser to king, 81, 83; and
Conscience, 38–39; puns on *ratio*, 39;
rebuke of Will, 105; sermon of,
39–40, 74, 102, 159, 162
"recklessness," 50
Redde quod debes: doctrine of, 40, 57,
59–60, 97, 144, 148, *149–52*;
Wimbledon's Sermon, 161. *See also*
penance; restitution, penitential doctrine of
Reeves, Marjorie, 95, 106, 129
Regalado, Nancy Freeman, 127
"relict" forms: as ms. readings preserved
from exemplar, 202, 203, 211, 212;
methods for isolating, 210. *See also*
dialect
restitution, penitential doctrine of, 40,
59, 149. *See also* penance; redde
quoddebes
Revard, Carter, 194
Reynolds, L. D., and N. G. Wilson, 206

rhetoric: and allegory, 14, 123; as basis of Three Lives, 13, 46; and critical approaches to *PP*, 4–10; invention, 17, 159; and preaching, 10, 158, 166; and satire, 10; and textual criticism, 197; and use of quotations, 17, 20, 158, 159 ff. *See also* etymology; grammar; meter; style

TERMS

adnominatio, 158; *amplificatio*, 46, 167, 237; *anacrusis*, 215, 231; *antethema*, 160, 167; *commutatio*, 158; confirmation, 160, 165, 166; *contentio*, 158; concordance, 20, 159–60; *concordancia realis*, 159; *concordancia verbalis*, 159; *dispositio*, 159; division (*divisio*), 37, 45, 159, 167; metaphor, 237 (*see also* imagery; metaphor); *partitio*, 160; personification, 169 (*See also* personification); repetition, 159, 237, 240; *similiter cadens*, 158; *thema* 159, 160, 166, 167; *traductio*, 158; variation, 237, 240
rhyme, 202, 209, 235, 332
rhythm: vs. meter, 223–27, 233, 241; "clashing," 224; "falling," 224; "rising," 224; "rhythmical system," 228, 230–31, 232–34. *See also* meter
Richard II: Langland's allusions to, 4, 33, 78, 79, 80, 81, 184; as king of *Mum and the Sothsegger*, 256, 257
Richard of Wetheringsette, *Summa*, 161
Richard the Redeless, 81, 256. See also *Mum and the Sothsegger*
Richardson, M. E., 186
Riehle, Wolfgang, 91
Rigg, A. G., and Charlotte Brewer, 181, 182, 188, 219n
Ritson, Joseph, 176, 177
Robbins, Rossell Hope, 9, 129, 252, 254
Robert of Flamborough, *Liber poenitentialis*, 147
Robert of Gloucester, *Chronicle*, 176
Robertson, D. W., Jr., 147; and Bernard Huppé, 15, 16, 17, 18, 20, 29, 30, 36, 42, 50, 87, 88, 95, 118
Robert the Robber, 40, 149, 252
Robinson, Ian, 215
Rogers, Owen, edition of *PP* (1561), 176, 261
Roland, Chanson de, 148
Rolle, Richard: compared with Langland, 240; regional spelling in, 219
Roman de Fauvel: parallels with *PP*, 137; as source of Langland's Favel, 128

Roman de la Rose, 129, 137. *See also* Guillaume de Lorris; Jean de Meun
"Rome runners" (B.4.128), 74, 184
Ross, W. O., 157, 160, 161, 164, 166
Rowland, Christopher, 88, 94
rubrics. See *Piers Plowman*: manuscripts
Rupert of Deutz, and revival of prophecy, 106
Russell, G. H., 6, 61, 98, 99, 180, 182, 191; and Venetia Nathan, 181, 192
Rutebeuf, 3, 7; *voies*, 126
Ryan, William, 158n
Rypon, Robert, 157

sacraments, *98–102*; allegorized, 128; of the dead, 92. *See also* baptism; confession; Eucharist; marriage
Sadowsky, James, and Margaret Amassian, 38
St. Jacques, Raymond, 94, 143, 155
St. Patrick's Purgatory, 122, 129
Salter, Elizabeth, 12, 14, 36, 52, 93, 94, 118, 135, 158, 160, 212, 228, 240, 245, 246; and Derek Pearsall, 158
salvation: and baptism, 99; of the heathen, 46, 47, *97–98*; Langland's view of, *90–93*, 96; individual vs. social, *88–90*; as theme in *PP*, 4, 35, 51, 92; and works, 38, 42, 43, *96–98*. *See also* grace
Samaritan. *See* Good Samaritan
Samuels, M. L., 187, 189, 190, 192, *201–221*, 201, 204, 205, 209, 210, 212, 213, 215, 217, 219, 253; and J. J. Smith, 204
Sapora, William, 231
Satan. *See* devil
satire, 4, 8–10, 37, *135–54*, 156; commonplaces of, 37, 137; vs. complaint, 9; estates satire, 10, 33, 126, 127, 138, 193–94; Menippean (encyclopedic), 117, 138, 147–48; penitential literature as source of, 156
satisfaction, 40. *See also* penance; *redde quod debes*
Schep (Sheep), John: pseudonym for John Ball, 251
Schmidt, A. V. C., 45, 52, 57, 61, 91, 97, 209, 232, 233, 237, 238
scholasticism: biblicism as reaction to, 106; elements in *PP*, 37, 45, 47, 145–46; and monasticism, 93, 105; and sermon structure, 159–60; and *vis imaginativa*, 47

Schumacher, Karl, 208, 227
Scogan, Henry: on Chaucer's "curious" language, 196
Scottish Feilde: influence of *PP* on, 254
scribal copying, 175, *193–94*; correction, 187–88; error, 196–97; in London, 211; method of, 192, 193, 202; paragraphing, 235–36, 238, 242; "relict" forms, 202, 204, 210; and rubrics of *PP*, 30–31; scribal responses to text, 193, 194, 197; translation, 175, 192, *202*, 203, 205, 211, 212; variation, 192–193, 194, 197. See also *Piers Plowman*: manuscripts
Scripture (personification), 46, 95, 99, 100, 105, 155
Secreta Secretorum: on counsel of kings, 78
Sege or Batayle of Troy: bound in mss. with *PP*, 253
semantic system of *PP*: linked to alliteration, 239–41
semi-Pelagianism: and Langland, 43, 96; and Robert Holcot, 100
sermon: composition of, 17; generic influence on *PP*, 117, 129, 139, *155–72*; of Holy Church, 36, 165–67; of Reason, 40, 162; scholastic or university style sermon, 159, *160*; *sermo ad status*, 39, 162; as source of allegory, 129. See also *artes praedicandi*; preaching
Seznec, Jean, 123
Shakespeare, William, *Hamlet*, 47
shame, power of, 47
Shaxton, Nicholas: recantation as clue to dating of *I playne Piers*, 258
Shepherd of Hermas, 122
Siege of Jerusalem: bound in mss. with *PP*, 253
Sievers, Eduard, 228, 229, 231
"signatures," use of authorial, 7
Simonie, The, as influence on *PP*, 136
simony, 149; of lawyers, 146
Simpson, James, 35, 106
sin, original, 91–92
Sins, Seven Deadly: confession of, 40, 101, 145, 147, 149; and Haukyn, 50, 145, 147; in penitential writings, 138; in sermons, 169; in Rutebeuf, 127. *See also* virtues and vices
Sir Gawain and the Green Knight. See *Gawain*-group
Sisam, Kenneth, 196
Skeat, W. W., 3, 5, 18, 29, 55, 126,

136, 157, *177*, 178, 180, 184, 186, 188, 190, 208, 230, 232, 233, 254, 256, 257, 258, 260, 261
Skelton, John, 138; knowledge of *PP*, 262
Sloth: place in Langland's hierarchy of sins, 151; model for, 156; study of, 138. *See also* Sins, Seven Deadly
Smalley, Beryl, 20
Smart, W. K., 256
Smith, Ben H., 118, 156
Smith, G. Gregory, 262
Smith, J. J., and M. L. Samuels, 204
Smithers, G. V., 209, 217
social gospel, 151
social orientation of *PP*, 58, *88–90*, 149; emphasized by early readers, 5, 253; and historians, 3–4; relation to truth, 33, 39, 40, 83, 151. *See also* individual
solicitude. See *ne soliciti sitis*
sociolinguistics: and language of *PP*, 214, *219*
Solomon, in hell, 46
Somer Soneday: compared with *PP*, 129, 130
"Song of the Husbandman," as influence on *PP*, 136
soul: progress of, 151; quest for Dowel; salvation of, 35. *See also* Anima
Southern, Richard W., 92, 93
Southworth, J. G., 215
Spearing, A. C., 41, 49, 50, 158, 159, 160, 168, 237, 239
Spenser, Edmund, 6, 208
Statutes of the Realm, 3; on export of sterling, 74; of Laborers, 71, 72; of Praemunire, 74; of Provisors, 74
Steadman, J. M., 253; and J. H. Hanford, 254
Steele, Richard, 81; and Mabel Day, 256
"stichic." See verse form
Stobie, M. M. R., 229
Stokes, Myra, 19, 33, 135, 146
Stone, R. K., 232, 236
Stones, E. L. G., 186
storm of 1362: allusion to, 67, 186
Strang, Barbara, 202
Straw, Jack: in Knighton's account of Peasants' Revolt, 252
stress. *See* meter
Strohm, Paul, 2
"strophic." See verse form
Strubel, Armand, 126
Study, Dame, 46, 147
style: formulaic, 193; Neo-Platonistic ten-

style *(continued)*
    dencies in, 94; and textual criticism,
    197. *See also* alliteration; imagery;
    meter; rhetoric
Summa virtutum de remediis anime, 169
supererogation, doctrine of, 91
Swieczkowski, Walerian, 158n
symbolism, 14; of Christ in Piers's arms,
    56; combined with allegory, 53. *See
    also* allegory; figuralism; imagery;
    metaphor
synderesis, 39
synonyms, and alliterative verse tradi-
    tion, *237-39*
syntax. *See* Langland, William: language
    of
Szittya, Penn, 60, 95, 111, 142, 255

Tavormina, Teresa, 52, 91
temperance, 60. *See also* virtues, cardinal
Ten Commandments: on honoring par-
    ents, 164; Langland's treatment of,
    contrasted with sermons, 169; as way
    to Truth, 40, 44
textual criticism, of classics and Bible,
    176, 198; Old French, 195; and *PP*,
    194-98
T. F., author of *Newes from the North*, 262
thema, as technical term, 160
theology: and definition of "meed," 38;
    Langland's, *87-114*
Theology (personification), 37
Thomas Aquinas, St., 55, 93, 98, 107,
    108
Thompson, Claud A., 240
Thoreau, Henry David, 107
Thorpe, James, 194-95
Thought (personification), 45, 46
Three Lives (Dowel, Dobet, Dobest):
    "doctor" on Dowel, 49; as formal divi-
    sions of *PP*, 13, 30; grammatical ba-
    sis of, 90; Langland's rejection of, 91;
    later historical connection with the
    name Piers, 252; and mysticism, 46;
    occurrences (list of), 45; as recurring
    motif, 45; as rhetorical amplification,
    13, 46, 159, 167; as rubrics, 13, 30;
    unity of, 90-91
Thynne, Francis: editor of Chaucer, 257;
    identified as T. F., author of *Newes
    from the North*, 262
Tomas of Ersseldoune, 127, 129; influence
    on *PP*, 136
tours, visionary, *121-122*, 126-27

Tout, T. F., 74, 79, 80, 81
Trajan, 43, 95, *97-98*, 100, 108, 109
translation. *See* scribal copying
Traver, Hope, 129
treasury of merit, 91
Treaty of Bretigny (1360): allusions in
    PP to, 76-77, 186
tree of charity, 52-53, 55, 56, 91, 253;
    analogue in Deguileville, 127; echoes
    in Usk's *Testament of Love*, 253; tradi-
    tion of diagrammatic allegory, 118
Trevelyan, G. M., 5, 67
Trevisa, John, 203, 219
triads: and aa/ax alliterative line, 240; in
    PP, 49, 150. *See also* estates; Three
    Lives
Trial of Satan: as genre, 57
Trinity: doctrine of, 52-53, 108; as
    model of truth, 35
Tristram, Hildegard L. C., 158n, 238
tropological level, 16, 94. *See also* al-
    legory: four levels
Troyer, Howard William, 13
truth: definition of, 11, *32-36*, 39, 40,
    55, 69, 165; as duty of king, 81; and
    feudal order, 33, 69, 70, 71; as
    fourteenth-century literary theme,
    33-34; and *imago Dei*, 55; knowledge
    of, 35, 36; and love, 36, 165-66;
    prerequisite for mercy, 39; and
    Will/the will, 35, 45, 54, 59. *See also*
    estates; loyalty
Truth: as God, 165; as lord of castle, 34,
    40; one of four daughters of God,
    56-57; pardon of, *41-44*; pilgrimage
    to, *39-41*, 45, 61, 103; sisters of,
    124. *See also* truth
"Truth is Best," 33
Tuck, J. A., 78, 79, 81
Tucker, Samuel M., 9
Turville-Petre, Thorlac, 130, 205, 244,
    253, 254, 255
Tuve, Rosemond, 128
typology. *See* figuralism
Tyrwhitt, Thomas, on corruption of *PP*
    texts, 176

Unity (the church), 60-61, 89, 95, 118,
    144, 148, 149, 150, 244
universities: and language study, 18; and
    religious revival, 141, 142, 145-46;
    Wycliffites driven from Oxford, 73
untruth: degrees of, 46; devil as source
    of, 35

Urban V, English dues withheld from, 74

Usk, Thomas, 7; allusions to *PP*, 253; execution as *terminus ante quem* of *PP* C, 253

usury, vs. permutation, 38

Uthred of Boldon, 93, 99

Utley, Francis, 129

Van Dyke, Carolynn, 124

Vasta, Edward, 88, 89, 92, 94, 104

"verse," as alliterative half-line, 224, 228

verse form: *PP* as stichic, 235; strophic, 235. *See also* alliteration; meter; rhythm

vices. *See* Sins, Seven Deadly; virtues and vices

Villon, Francois, 7

virginity, 52, 91

Virgin Mary, chamber of, 53

virtues and vices, 128; allegory of, 124, 127. *See also* Book of Vices and Virtues; psychomachia; Sins, Seven Deadly

virtues, cardinal, 60, 124, 169; as seeds, 58; as *spiritus*, 169

virtues, theological, 124

vis imaginativa, 47, 98. *See also* Imaginatif

Visio: as extension of Holy Church's speech, 36; focus of, 51; as scribal rubric, 30; the "Visio Revisited," *58–61*, 151

Vision of Fursey, 129

Vision of Tundale, 122, 129

visions. *See* dreams, allegorical

Visio Philiberti, 129

Vita: as extension of Holy Church's speech, 36, 45; as scribal rubric, 30; and truth, 59

"vix salvabitur" (I Pet. 4:18), exegesis of, 98

vocabulary. See *Piers Plowman*: vocabulary

Von Nolcken, Christina, 155, 167

Voyage of St. Brendan, 122

Waldron, R. A., 54, 236

Walsh, Katherine, 75, 95

Walsingham, Thomas: account of Peasants' Revolt, 251, 252

wanderer: combined in *PP* with fool-hero, 139

Wars of Alexander: bound in mss. with *PP*, 253

Warton, Thomas, 135; emendation of *PP* by, 176

wasters (A.7.139 ff.): as allusion to *Wynnere and Wastoure*, 130; Piers's call for vengeance on, 41

Wawn, A. N., 256, 257, 258

Webbe, William, *A Discourse Of English Poesie*, 262

Wells, A. P., and J. N. Palmer, 74

Wells, H. W., 13, 46

Wenzel, Siegfried, 138, 139, 141n, *155–72*, 156, 160, 169

Wesling, Donald, 135

Wetherbee, Winthrop, 125

Weye to Paradys: earliest *voie* in English, 127

Whatley, Gordon, 47, 87, 95, 97–98, 100, 102

Whitaker, Thomas: early editor of *PP*, 176, 177

White, H. C., 257, 259, 262

widowhood, 52

Wilks, M., 74, 76

will: in conflict with intellect, 47–48; in conformity with God's will, 55–56, 92, 165; *fiat voluntas*, 51, 56, 121; free will, 52, 108, 110; as literary theme, 33, 36; proper disposition of, 51; and shame, 47; and truth, 51, 58, 59

Will (personification), 6, 44, 45, 47–48, 49, 61, 88, 99–100, 104, 139, 147. *See also* dreamer

William of Palerne, and alliterative style of *PP*, 230, 245

William of St. Amour, and apocalypticism, 95

William of St. Thierry, 105

William of Wyckham, courtier of Edward III, 80

Williams, Arnold, 142, 145

Wilson, N. G., and L. D. Reynolds, 206

Wimbledon, Thomas, 157, 161

Windeatt, B. A., 192, 194–95, 197

Winfield, P. H., 81

Wit, 46

Wittig, Joseph S., 45, 46, 47, 48, 50, 87, 95, 98, 104, 105, 151

Wolffe, B. P., 79

Woolf, Rosemary, 29, 42, 96

word play, 7, 39, 119, 160, 234, 238, 239, 243

"words, works, and will," 49, 50, 52, 55, 240

Wright, Joseph, 212, 216, 217
Wright, Thomas, 7, 136, 140, 141, 176, 177
Wrong (personification), 34, 37, 39, *81–83*
Wyclif, John: on dominion, 73–74, 75, 185; *De Ecclesia*, 77; *De Potestate Papae*, and papal election, 185; as influence on Langland's thought, 73–74, *109–11*, 254, 261; recent study of, 19; Wycliffite movement, *72–76*
Wycliffites: driven from Oxford, 73; and lay piety, 93; literary influence of, 257; relation to *PP*, 72–76, 102, 254; sermons, 161; "two churches" doctrine, 111; Wycliffite Bible, 202. *See also* Lollards
Wynnere and Wastoure: correspondences with *PP*, 128, 130, 136, 253; author's condemnation of clumsy alliteration, 240

Yunck, John A., 9, 10, 34, 37, 61, *135–54*, 135, 136, 137, 141n, 146, 155
Yvain (Middle English), and truth, 33

Compositor:	Medieval & Renaissance Texts & Studies
Text:	10/12 Baskerville
Display:	Baskerville
Printer:	Maple-Vail Book Mfg. Group
Binder:	Maple-Vail Book Mfg. Group